THE ROBIN HOOD HANDBOOK

THE ROBIN HOOD HANDBOOK

THE OUTLAW IN HISTORY, MYTH AND LEGEND

MIKE DIXON-KENNEDY

SUTTON PUBLISHING

First published in the United Kingdom in 2006 by
Sutton Publishing Limited · Phoenix Mill
Thrupp · Stroud · Gloucestershire · GL5 2BU

British Library Cataloguing in Publication Data
A catalogue record for this book is available from the British Library.

ISBN 0-7509-3977-X

Maps by Bow Watkinson.
Typeset in 11/14pt Times.
Typesetting and origination by
Sutton Publishing Limited.
Printed and bound in England by
J.H. Haynes & Co. Ltd, Sparkford.

For all my friends
who have supported and encouraged me

'Nay,' quoth Robin. 'Fear nothing, For I will do thee
no harm.' Illustration from *Bold Robin Hood and his
Outlaw Band* by Louis Read.

CONTENTS

Robin Hood takes aim with his longbow. Anonymous engraving, *c.* 1860.
(*Mary Evans Picture Library*)

PREFACE

I suppose, like a great many other people of my age group, my first introduction to the legends of Robin Hood was Richard Greene swinging through the greenwood in the 1960s television series *Robin Hood*. Later my interest in this very British hero was rekindled through another television series, *Robin of Sherwood*, which not only re-awakened my fascination but also induced me to do my own research into the subject. This book is a result of that somewhat lengthy research, though it must be said that Robin Hood has not been my only avenue of research over the ensuing years.

Unlike many other writers and researchers on the subject I have not simply tried to determine the historicity of Robin Hood. That is not to say that I do not firmly believe that Robin Hood was a real man who has a definite place in our history rather than solely in our folklore, but it is rather an affirmation of my belief that to discover the historicity of a legendary character will ultimately destroy the magic and mystique of that character. Like King Arthur, whom I also firmly believe once walked on British soil, Robin Hood is essentially a legendary figure, and it is thus the legends of the character that I have concentrated on, before examining the history behind those legends.

My research has investigated the period during which the legends are believed to have first developed, but that historical background simply illustrates the necessity for the character rather than his actual life and times, and indeed whether or not he really lived at all. Robin Hood is an essential part of our heritage, and yet very little is ever written about the legends themselves. Hundreds of thousands of words have been written about the character in an attempt to discover the truth behind the legends, but all appear to bypass the legends themselves and concentrate on the daunting task of uncovering the history of the character and just why the legends developed, each resulting book turning out to be little more than the author's own personal conclusions. Rather than drawing my own immediate conclusions, of which I have many, I have simply retold the legends in chronological order, and will leave the majority of the conclusion-drawing, at this stage, to you, the reader.

This book is written in four main parts, each of which, I hope, can be enjoyed in its own right. Part One retells the legends of Robin Hood and his band of outlaws, the Merry Men, though whether or not they actually had much to be merry about is doubtful. Here you will not find the popular conception of the outlaw and his men swinging through the trees to right wrong (a mode of transport that there is no evidence Robin Hood or his men ever made use of), but rather an accurate retelling of the legends as they first appeared. Part Two is a concise A to Z of all the major players and places mentioned within the

Illustration from *Bold Robin Hood and his Outlaw Band* by Louis Read.

legends. It is here that you will find the historical influence on the legends, as well as gaining easier access to the relevant parts of the legends, in an easy-to-use ready-reference work in a form that has never before been presented.

Part Three concerns itself with a select number of the core source texts that any student of Robin Hood should study in order to glean a better understanding not only of the character, but also of the means by which the legends were propagated and advanced. Finally, the conclusions I have personally drawn have been included as Part Four and I sincerely hope this part will give you much food for thought. It should be noted that this final section simply relates my own personal conclusions and feelings on the subject, and is by no means a definitive statement of fact. Readers can make up their own minds.

I trust I have chosen the best format for the presentation of this book, as it offers easy access to the legends, characters and places that many know in essence, but few know in detail. I also hope that by writing this book I will help to stimulate interest in a very important part of our heritage, a heritage that is all too often overlooked despite its great relevance to modern society. If I have indeed succeeded in this last aim then I shall be only too pleased to hear from readers, especially from those with any comments or suggestions to pass on. Letters should be addressed to the publishers, who will ensure that they reach me.

Mike Dixon-Kennedy
Lincolnshire, 2006

ACKNOWLEDGEMENTS

As with the writing of any book there are a number of people I have to thank. First and foremost are the countless librarians, whose names I have never known, who have sought out and obtained unusual and rare volumes for me to study, along with unpublished manuscripts and documents, and who have thus increased my knowledge of the subject. To all of them, and to all others who have selflessly given their time and expertise to me without thought of reward, I say a great big thank you. Several other people more than deserve a mention, for without them this book would not exist. They are Christopher Feeney of Sutton Publishing for getting this volume accepted for publication, Sarah Cook for her excellent copy-editing, and Alison Miles for pulling the whole process together smoothly and relatively painlessly. Finally I have to thank my long-suffering son Christopher for enduring endless periods when my door has been firmly closed to him as I worked on the manuscript.

Robin Hood and two of his companions. Woodcut taken from the *Roxburghe Ballads*, *c*. 1630. (*Mary Evans Picture Library*)

Robin shoots one last arrow to show his companions where he wishes to be buried. (*Mary Evans Picture Library*)

PART ONE

Robin Hood and Sir Guy of Gisborne. Illustration
from *A Book of Old English Ballads* by George
Wharton Edwards.

Robin and his companions lend aid to Will o' the Green in an ambush. From *Robin Hood* by N.C. Wyeth (1917), p. 156. (*Mary Evans Picture Library*)

THE LEGENDS OF ROBIN HOOD AND HIS MERRY MEN

The legends of Robin Hood and his Merry Men, as presented here, are drawn from six major sources, as well as from a plethora of other literature, both ancient and modern. The six main sources are *A Gest of Robyn Hode*, *Robin Hood and Guy of Gisborne*, *Robin Hood and the Curtal Friar*, *Robin and the Monk*, *Robin Hood and the Potter* and *The Death of Robin Hood*. Though all of these works were written well after the traditional period ascribed to the hero of the tales, they contain the best-known elements of the legend. By taking the main themes that run through these works, and adding to them certain historical or legendary detail from other sources, the narrative that follows is, perhaps, the most complete version of the legendary life of Robin Hood.

The narrative is split into eleven sections, each covering a main area of the life and legends of Robin Hood, arranged in chronological order covering a time period that runs from the last years of the reign of King Henry II (say from *c.* 1185), through the reigns of Kings Richard I and John, and ends during the reign of King Henry III sometime after 1235. Popular legend makes the date of Robin's death 1247, which is not inconceivable. These are, of course, the traditional periods ascribed to Robin Hood, though some sources place different events in widely differing time periods. By arranging the material in chronological order and basing the text that follows on numerous sources, the confusion has been largely removed, and the legends run from the time when a young Robin Hood, aged around 25, was forced to become an outlaw, to his death, again as an outlaw, some fifty to sixty or more years later, aged about 85.

Obscure words have been left in situ as they better serve to give a flavour of the legends than would their modern counterparts. Explanations of these words may be found in Part Two of this book. At no point is dialogue included in the legends as this would detract from the legends themselves and, after all, how do we know what might have been said? These are legends that are woven around a quasi-historical background, and as such dialogue has no place in them.

The most obscure period of the life of Robin Hood follows the death of his beloved Marian when, having attained a royal pardon and adopted the life of a freeman of substance, Robin Hood once more returns to the forests to live out the remainder of his life beyond the law. During this period, which makes up the last section of the following narrative, many local legends sprang up about Robin Hood, but the majority of these stem from at least two hundred years after the core of the legends had been recorded and thus must be regarded as somewhat suspect. They can best be regarded as local endeavours to gain some connection to the famous outlaw whose name had already passed into our folklore by that time. As this is the case, only three events in the last fifteen years or so of Robin Hood's life have found their way into the following narrative; all three appear to have been current when the main core was being recorded.

The paragraph numbers added to the text are intended for use with Part Two, the cross-referenced guide to all the players and places within these legends.

1. THE OUTLAWING OF ROBIN HOOD

1   Having been absent from home for longer than he would have liked, Robert of Locksley returned to Barnisdale Forest en route for his home at Outwoods, which lay

Illustration from *Bold Robin Hood and his Outlaw Band* by Louis Read.

just beyond the fringes of the forest. As he walked through the broad-leafed trees of the dense forest at noon in the height of summer, dragonflies hovering lazily above the infrequent damp areas, Robert became aware that there were very few animals to be seen in the vicinity. Quietly he took up a position behind a great oak tree and looked out across a small clearing, expecting to see some of the hated foresters who kept watch over the king's deer that roamed the forest.

2   Robert of Locksley was a young man of about 25, his face bronzed by long periods spent in his beloved greenwood. His eyes shone brightly in a face that was full of compassion, and yet had a steely quality that had and would put many in their place. His head was covered with a mass of brown curls that were partially hidden under a green velvet cap into which he had idly stuck a plover's feather. He was dressed in a tunic of rough green cloth which was open at the neck and gathered around his waist by a broad leather belt, which held a dagger on his right-hand side and three arrows on his left. His thighs were covered with breeches of supple leather while his lower legs were protected by green woollen hose. On his feet he wore shoes of stout pig's leather.*

3   As he watched he caught a movement out of the corner of his eye. Slowly turning his head he saw the undergrowth move as three deer entered the glade on the opposite side. As he turned his head to watch the buck and two does an arrow flew across the glade out of the undergrowth and struck the first doe clean in the heart. The other two deer fled as the stricken doe fell to the ground. All remained quiet. Nothing stirred. The doe lay exactly where she had fallen, her killer waiting an appropriate time to make himself known for fear that the foresters might come running at any moment.

4   For a full five minutes Robert watched across the glade, every now and then looking to where he had seen the movement a little while before. His patience was rewarded when he saw a man creep out of the bushes, his knife drawn and held before him as he moved slowly, keeping low, across the open space to where his quarry lay. He was dressed in the rough garb of a villein, a rope around his waist holding together his homespun brown tunic, and his legs covered with tatty trousers of the same rough material. His feet were bare.

5   As he reached the doe he crouched down and deftly began to cut away the most tender portions of the carcass. Still watching, Robert made no effort to show himself, but instead wondered what had driven this man, a man he knew, to risk life and limb in such a reckless manner. Having cut away the meat he required the man wrapped his meal in a piece of rough sacking which he secreted beneath his tunic before making his way back across the glade, and from there on towards his home. Robert

---

* The description of Robert of Locksley's clothing is based on contemporary accounts of the clothes of a typical squire of the late twelfth and early thirteenth centuries. His cap was most likely to have been a velvet mop-cap rather than the pointed cap traditionally portrayed in the popularised versions of the legends.

followed him at a discreet distance until he managed to pass him, and then stepped out in front of him, blocking the pathway.

6 As the man saw that his route was barred his hand went for his knife, but suddenly he recognised Robert and strode swiftly towards him to greet him warmly, though some of the warmth left his voice as Robert questioned his motives. The man, whom Robert had recognised as Will Scarlet, carefully explained that in 'Master Robin's' absence, for that was how he and many others referred to Robert of Locksley, his brother-in-law John a'Green had been taken ill and died, and his sister and her three children evicted by Sir Guy of Gisborne to fend for themselves.

7 The very mention of Guy of Gisborne reminded Robert of his own position. He and his ancestors held a house and 160 acres of land on a legal rent from the lords of the manor of Birkencar, and had done so since the time when the manor had first been given to the lords by King William. However, the last lord of the manor, Sir Guy of Wrothsley, had bequeathed the manor and all its lands to the White Monks of St Mary's Abbey, and they coveted the land that Robert held as it was the most fertile and productive of all their lands. Yet as long as Robert paid his dues on time, there was no way they could ever legally take possession. However, Robert knew of the evil Sir Guy of Gisborne, and was aware that, with the connivance of the monks, he had long sought a way to dispossess Robert, even if that meant having him accused of some false crime and thus proclaimed an outlaw – upon which all his possessions and lands would be forfeit. This was the reason for Robert's return to his home, for while he was away he had heard that Sir Guy of Gisborne and the abbot were plotting to seize his lands.

8 Robert was snapped back out of his own thoughts as Will Scarlet continued to describe all that had befallen his family. His sister had come to him with her three children, but she had died of starvation a short time afterwards, whereupon two of the children had been taken in by kindly neighbours, Will Scarlet keeping young Gilbert as his own charge. It was to feed the child that he had taken to stealing the king's meat from the forest, an undertaking he would continue while there were still deer to be had.

9 Robert listened despondently to the story, not interrupting once. However, when Will Scarlet fell silent Robert turned to him and softly told him that he should have gone to Outwoods, for there his steward Scadlock would have provided for him. Will Scarlet replied that he was well aware of that, but he had not wished to make Robert any further enemies – enemies that, he added, were at that very moment scheming against him. Will Scarlet was astonished to learn that the news of those plans were the very reason for Robert's return to Outwoods, for while he was in residence he was confident that the monks and the foul Sir Guy of Gisborne would not dare move against him.

10 As Will Scarlet wondered how Robert had heard about the plans while he was away, Robert took him by the shoulder and told him, in a quiet but commanding voice, to

place the meat he had cut from the deer on the ground next to Robert's own bow and arrows. Will Scarlet immediately complied, though he was reluctant to put down the meat he had risked his life to obtain. However, just as he was about to question Robert, he heard the voices of two foresters coming down the path in the opposite direction.

11   A few moments later, with the meat and the bow and arrows safely hidden, Robert of Locksley and Will Scarlet were confronted by two burly foresters who barred their way, though one, less offensive than the other, moved aside when he recognised Robert. The other, who went by the name of Black Hugo, continued to bar the way, only moving aside as he saw the steely look in Robert's eyes, a look that chilled him to the bone. Robert and Will Scarlet passed the two foresters and continued on their way out of the forest. As they climbed a hill they saw Outwoods in the distance, and the village in the valley between them and Robert's home. As they walked down the incline towards the village Will Scarlet was amazed to see his meat, along with Robert's bow and arrows, lying in the grass. He rushed forward and picked them up before turning in amazement to his companion.

12   Robert of Locksley laughed as Will Scarlet questioned him as to the magic he had used to carry the items unseen out of the forest, even blaming the event on brownies or evil spirits. Robert chided him for his foolishness and bade him on his way. As Will Scarlet hurried down the hill Robert turned back into the forest and made for the

Robin espies a group of foresters and two captives. Illustration from *Bold Robin Hood and his Outlaw Band* by Louis Read.

road that wound its way through the forest from Barnisdale into Nottinghamshire. In his mind was the true reason for his return to the forest – his promise to protect the woman he loved as she travelled through the forest.

13   As Robert hurried through the dense undergrowth, his senses remained alert to danger at all times and he was aware that he was being accompanied by his forest friends, but soon his thoughts turned to the woman he had loved since they had played together in Locksley Chase. She was Maid Marian, the fair daughter of Sir Richard FitzWalter at Malaset. Though they came from differing stations, for she was the daughter of an earl and he was but a yeoman, they loved each other and had sworn that they would marry no other. That day Robert was to protect his love as she journeyed from her father's castle at Malaset to stay awhile with her uncle Sir Richard at Lee at Linden Lea, a short distance from Nottingham itself.

14   Having travelled quickly through the forest for upwards of 5 miles, Robert came to a road which led him down to a crossroads. Immediately he re-entered the thick undergrowth and quickly made his way to a small glade where the soil was sandy. There on the ground was a group of sticks. To the untrained eye they looked as if they had simply fallen from a tree, but Robert sank to his knees and inspected the twigs carefully, for they had been left there as a message to him by one of his woodland friends.

15   The twigs told him that one knight on horseback and eight knaves on foot were stationed not far from where he was, though he could not determine why. Thus he carefully made his way towards their position, his approach being made on hands and knees. As he carefully parted the bushes he scanned the knight and his meinie in an attempt to discover from their heraldry which lord they served, but this was useless as the men on foot were dressed in plain jerkins and the knight carried a simple, kite-shaped shield. As he mused over the identity of the knight and his men the horse shied and the knight commanded it to be still. Immediately Robert recognised the voice of Sir Roger de Longchamp; he had long coveted the Maid Marian, and had now obviously come to take her by foul means, as fair had failed, Sir Richard FitzWalter repeatedly refusing to give her hand to that treacherous knight, the brother of the proud Bishop of Fécamp, and the favourite of Duke Richard.

16   As Robert watched the knight astride his horse his thoughts turned to his own lineage, the one obstacle that prevented him from marrying his beloved Marian. He thought about the stories he had heard from Stephen of Gamwell, and wondered whether those stories were indeed true and that his family had once been the lords of Huntingdon. He knew that the earldom and lands of Huntingdon had been given to David, son of the Scottish king, and pondered on how his situation might have been different had not his forebears, according to Stephen of Gamwell, risen against the Normans, only to be driven from their home, lands and title.

Illustration from *Bold Robin Hood and his Outlaw Band* by Louis Read.

17   His reverie was brought to an abrupt halt as a man raced into the clearing and told Sir Roger de Longchamp that Marian was approaching with one other on horseback and the remainder of her party on foot. Immediately Sir Roger barked out a series of orders, and as he listened Robert slipped an arrow out of his belt and moistened the flight so that it would fly straight and true. As he did so, Maid Marian rode into view, with Walter, her father's steward at Malaset, riding beside her. As Robert watched he saw the knight charge into the clearing accompanied by his men.

18   Immediately Walter rode in front of his mistress to protect her and fought off the first blow from Sir Roger de Longchamp's sword with his stout staff, the sword carving a great splinter of wood out of it. Sir Roger again raised his sword to strike at Walter, but Walter was too quick for him and with a swift swipe of his staff knocked the weapon from Sir Roger's hand so that it dangled from the piece of cord looped around the knight's wrist. As Sir Roger struggled to regain his sword, his hand caught hold of the reins of Marian's horse. He raised his sword once more to strike at Walter, a blow that would doubtless have killed him, but as he did so Walter was tumbled from his horse by one of Sir Roger's men and the sword swept aimlessly through the air. As Walter lay unconscious on the ground Sir Roger de Longchamp

began to drag Marian's horse towards him – but suddenly he fell headlong to the ground, the shaft of an arrow jutting out of his right eye through the narrow slit in his helmet.

19   As Sir Roger de Longchamp fell heavily to the forest floor the fighting stopped. One of his men went over to the body of the knight and drew the crudely tipped arrow out of his eye, at the same time keeping a wary eye out for the archer who had moments before killed his master. Quickly he signalled that there was but one attacker and sent his men to the left to see if they could find him, but as they set off a small black arrow streaked through the air and struck him in the heart. As this arrow had come from the opposite side of the track the men quickly assumed that there was more than one archer and they turned and fled, a second small black arrow striking one of the fleeing men in the shoulder. This time it simply wounded the man who plucked out the shaft and carried on his way.

20   As the last of the men disappeared Robert came out of the woods and made himself known to Marian, who offered him her hand and thanked her 'Sweet Robin', for that was always how she referred to him, for saving her from the clutches of Sir Roger de Longchamp, though she feared that the knight's death would not fare her beloved well as Sir Roger's powerful and evil friends would seek to avenge him. Robert assured her that had he been King Henry himself he would have protected Marian in the same way.

21   Quickly, for fear that Sir Roger de Longchamp had friends close at hand, Robert helped Walter back into his saddle, and then bade the rest of the party to dust themselves down and follow him, as he would lead them to safety. As the party prepared to move, Robert dragged the fallen knight off the track and laid him out with his sword on his chest and his arms folded, before saying a short prayer over him for the forgiveness of his sins. He then did likewise for the knight's fallen comrade, before slashing Sir Roger's horse across its flank with an arrowhead to make it bolt; he hoped it would be found far away from where its master had fallen, thus throwing any pursuers off the trail.

22   Quickly Robert made his way back to where Marian, Walter and the others were waiting for him, and without saying anything took hold of Marian's reins and led the party off the road and along paths that were known only to him and his woodland friends. As they penetrated deep into the heart of the forest only Marian and Walter remained unafraid, for they had complete and absolute faith in Robert. The others, however, grew increasingly anxious as they became more and more convinced that they would be attacked by the spirits believed to live in the heart of the forest. Before long they formed into a huddle around Walter's horse, which led Walter to chide them for their childish superstitions and beliefs.

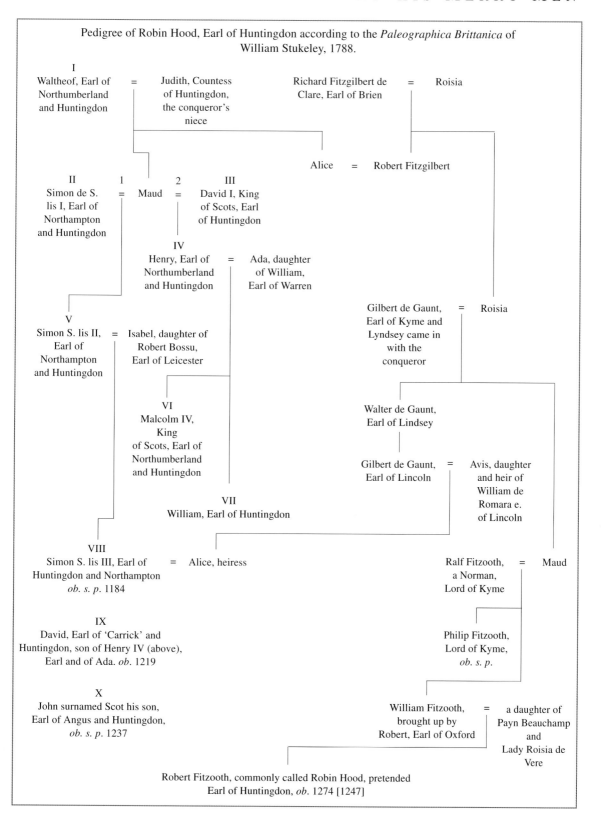

Pedigree of Robin Hood, Earl of Huntingdon according to the *Paleographica Brittanica* of William Stukeley, 1788.

I
Waltheof, Earl of Northumberland and Huntingdon
=
Judith, Countess of Huntingdon, the conqueror's niece

Richard Fitzgilbert de Clare, Earl of Brien
=
Roisia

Alice
=
Robert Fitzgilbert

II
Simon de S. lis I, Earl of Northampton and Huntingdon
1
=
Maud
2
=
III
David I, King of Scots, Earl of Huntingdon

IV
Henry, Earl of Northumberland and Huntingdon
=
Ada, daughter of William, Earl of Warren

V
Simon S. lis II, Earl of Northampton and Huntingdon
=
Isabel, daughter of Robert Bossu, Earl of Leicester

Gilbert de Gaunt, Earl of Kyme and Lyndsey came in with the conqueror
=
Roisia

VI
Malcolm IV, King of Scots, Earl of Northumberland and Huntingdon

Walter de Gaunt, Earl of Lindsey

Gilbert de Gaunt, Earl of Lincoln
=
Avis, daughter and heir of William de Romara e. of Lincoln

VII
William, Earl of Huntingdon

VIII
Simon S. lis III, Earl of Huntingdon and Northampton
ob. s. p. 1184
=
Alice, heiress

Ralf Fitzooth, a Norman, Lord of Kyme
=
Maud

IX
David, Earl of 'Carrick' and Huntingdon, son of Henry IV (above), Earl and of Ada. *ob.* 1219

Philip Fitzooth, Lord of Kyme, *ob. s. p.*

X
John surnamed Scot his son, Earl of Angus and Huntingdon, *ob. s. p.* 1237

William Fitzooth, brought up by Robert, Earl of Oxford
=
a daughter of Payn Beauchamp and Lady Roisia de Vere

Robert Fitzooth, commonly called Robin Hood, pretended Earl of Huntingdon, *ob.* 1274 [1247]

23   After a long while Marian began to discuss what might befall Robert for his timely intervention which had led to the death of the evil Sir Roger de Longchamp. As they talked Robert realised that he may have led them through the forest at too swift a pace and asked Marian if he had over-tired her in his haste to get away from the spot where Sir Roger de Longchamp had ambushed her party, and thus to put some distance between her and that evil knight's companions, whom he named as Sir Isenbart de Belame, Sir Niger le Grym, Sir Hamo de Mortain and Sir Ivo de Raby, among others.

24   All signs of exhaustion abruptly left Marian as she heard those dreaded names, and she quickly told Robert that she was not at all tired and that they should hurry on, though with enemies of that order she was now sorely afraid for her love. After several more miles ploughing through the thick undergrowth they came to the edge of the forest and there saw two knights riding at full pelt. Immediately Robert took a horn from around his shoulders and put it to his lips, the resulting blast causing the knights to gallop up to where Marian, Walter, Robert and the others stood on the fringes of the forest, with the castle at Linden Lea standing not a mile away on the crest of a hill.

25   The two knights were Sir Richard at Lee, Marian's uncle, and his companion Sir Huon de Bulwell, both of whom heartily thanked Robert for his timely intervention. At the same time they voiced their concerns, though Sir Richard at Lee thanked Robert warmly for ridding their land of one vile knight; he only hoped that Robert would live long enough to rid them of the rest of the wicked horde who resided at the castle of Wrangby – also known as Evil Hold. The castle was well named as most thought of it as nothing more than a crucet-house.

Illustration from *Bold Robin Hood and his Outlaw Band* by Louis Read.

26   For three days and three nights Robert stayed at Linden Lea with Sir Richard at Lee and his wife Lady Alice. During the day they hunted with hawks or went after wild boar in the forest, while at night they were entertained by minstrels or played games such as hoodman blind and chess. On the fourth morning Robert went into the woods to shoot small birds but had not gone far into the forest when he saw the face of a small man looking down at him. Robert immediately recognised his friend Ket the Trow, whom he called down to him to tell him his news, for Ket the Trow only showed himself if he had news to impart.

27   Ket the Trow, though a full-grown man, was no taller than a medium-sized youth of 13 or 14, but he had strong arms and legs from which the muscles stood proud, a full head of curly black hair, and a broad chest and shoulders. The only garments he wore were a stout leather jacket laced at the front and breeches of doeskin that reached no lower than his knees. His feet were bare, and his entire countenance showed that he lived a wild existence.

28   Quickly questioning Ket the Trow, Robert discovered that Ket had followed the men who had fled after Sir Roger de Longchamp's death; he described the route they followed as going through the forest to the north-west until they forded the brook at The Stakes. From there they crossed the moor to the Ridgeway, and thence through Hag's Wood and Thicket Hollow, by the Hoar Tree and the Cwelm Stone, over Gallow's Hill, and by the Mark Oak until they came to Dead Man's Hill, and from there by the lane of the Red Stones to the Evil Hold. Ket the Trow had hidden in the Mark Oak and had seen two knights riding out of the Evil Hold the following morning. They rode to the east and Ket followed them through Barnisdale Wood until he left them on the road to Doncaster.

29   Having left the two knights, Ket the Trow travelled to Outwoods and met Scadlock in Old Nick's Piece before going into the village. There he overheard many of the villagers in the alehouse talking of their plans to overthrow the evil Sir Guy of Gisborne after several of their number had been beaten that day. When Robert heard this he knew that trouble lay ahead. He thanked Ket the Trow and asked him to fetch his brother Hob, and, after saying goodbye to Marian, Sir Richard at Lee and Lady Alice, Robert returned to the forest and quickly made his way back to Barnisdale Forest. Soon after that he reached the open land that led through Will Scarlet's village, and thence travelled on to his home, Outwoods.

30   As he came out of the forest a feeling of unease spread over him. It was too quiet. No children played in the dust of the village street, and in the fields he could see no men working. As he pondered the reason he walked carefully on towards his house, and as he approached a woman appeared in the doorway of one of the village houses. She was far too distant for him to see who it was, but he could see her clearly enough to make out that she was shooing him away.

And soon they, Robin and Marian, were forced to part. Illustration from *Tales and Plays of Robin Hood* by Eleanor L. Skinner.

31   His suspicions aroused, Robert continued carefully on his way. Just as he was about to come into full sight of his home he ducked back behind a tree, for there under the spreading boughs of the very next tree stood a man-at-arms apparently watching something in the distance that amused him. Cautiously Robert sneaked up behind him and had almost reached him when his foot snapped a twig, but he still had the element of surprise and seconds later he laid the now unconscious man on the ground. As he stood up again, he saw the source of the man's amusement. It was a sight that made him groan audibly.

32   There, tied to posts in front of his home, were Scadlock and three of the villagers, and before each of them stood a man-at-arms with a vicious whip with knotted ends. A short distance away stood their master, the vile Sir Hubert of Lynn, who commanded that each man should be given a hundred lashes before being put to death. As Robert watched, the torture began. He sank to his knees and carefully removed the six arrows he carried in his belt and set them out on the ground before him. Then, in the fading light, he prayed to the Virgin Mary to guide his shafts.

33   Deliberately Robert took aim at Sir Hubert of Lynn. No sooner had he let the arrow fly than he was notching another to his bowstring so that it might be on its deadly way

before the first struck home. In rapid succession Robert fired off five of his six arrows, each of which found its allotted target. Sir Hubert of Lynn was the first to fall, as Robert had intended, and before his men could react the other four arrows had also struck home. Seeing so many men die in such rapid succession, the remainder of Sir Hubert of Lynn's men took to their heels and fled, one coming to a halt just yards from where Robert still knelt, his last arrow notched to the bowstring and ready to fly.

34   When the man caught sight of Robert he fell to the ground and yielded to him, insisting that until two days previously he had been a simple villein, and had been pressed into service by Sir Hubert of Lynn. Robert looked kindly on him and asked him his name, at which the newcomer replied that he was Dudda, or Dodd, son of Alstan, a villein at Blythe. Robert told Dudda to follow him and the two went down to Outwoods. They cut down Scadlock and the other men, and took them into the safety of the house where they dressed their wounds before Robert asked Scadlock what had happened.

35   Scadlock replied that on the previous day Robert had been declared an outlaw from the steps of the cross at Pontefract. That morning Sir Hubert of Lynn had come to take possession of the house and lands for the abbot of St Mary's Abbey, and there was nothing that he could do to prevent it, despite the efforts of four villagers, named Ward, Godard, Dunn and John, who had been at Outwoods when Sir Hubert of Lynn

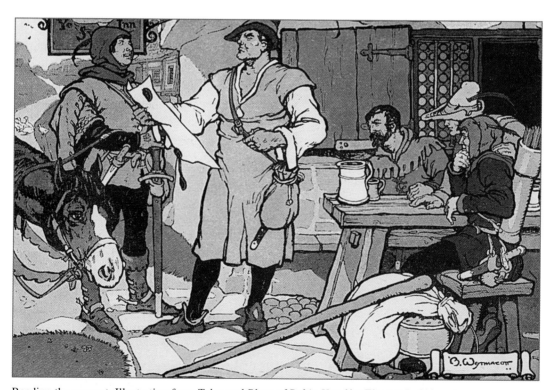

Reading the warrant. Illustration from *Tales and Plays of Robin Hood* by Eleanor L. Skinner.

arrived. Robert thanked them all for their valiant efforts, and they sat in the single great hall that formed his manor house and discussed their future as outlaws living in the forest. As they talked Scadlock heard people approaching and grew afraid that it might be Sir Guy of Gisborne and his men, but Robert assured him that even Sir Guy would not try anything during the hours of darkness.

36   Going outside, Robert greeted the villagers, thirty of them, who had come to the house to offer their services and pledge their allegiance to Robert of Locksley, whom they had always known as a fair and honest master, and with whom not one of them had ever had cause or reason to quarrel. As the throng came up to Robert one of the eldest among them, a man by the name of Will of the Stuteley but commonly called Will the Bowman, spoke for all the others when he said that they would all follow Robert if he would agree to lead them.

37   At first Robert tried to put them off by telling them that if they left then the work of the manor would fall onto the shoulders of their wives and their children. A few were indeed discouraged by these words and crept silently back to the village and to their sleeping wives and children, but many more had suffered more than they could bear, and they were determined to endure it no longer. As they debated the various merits of living as outlaws in the woods, or remaining to suffer at the hands of Sir Guy of Gisborne (who would next day become their master), a new face broke through and spoke to the assembled throng.

38   This was Much the miller's son, a young man who was far better educated than his fellow villagers. He had been told that the following day ten of the villeins were to be sold by Sir Guy of Gisborne to Lord Arnald of Shotley Hawe, a name that filled the gathering with much dread. Robert asked Much where he had come across such dire news. He replied that he had been in the alehouse in Blythe when he met Rafe, man to Lord Arnald's steward, who had told him that the ten to be sold were those who had given Sir Guy of Gisborne the most trouble. He did not know their names.

39   At once all those gathered, now reduced in number from thirty to just fourteen, realised they would be better off leading the lives of outlaws in the greenwood than suffering the continuing degradation and ill-treatment at the hands of Sir Guy of Gisborne or Lord Arnald of Shotley Hawe. As Robert looked around the eager faces he noticed that Will Scarlet was not among them; asking why, he was told that Will Scarlet had been caught killing a deer in the forest and was at that time awaiting transport from his prison to the courts at Doncaster where he would lose his right hand for his crime. As he heard this, all the final doubts vanished from Robert's mind, and he immediately agreed to lead the men. Their first task was to be the release of Will Scarlet.

40 As one, the villeins voiced their approval, and that approval was further enhanced when Robert told them of the demise of Sir Hubert of Lynn. Had Robert himself not brought about Sir Hubert's death, it would have soon followed at the hands of Will the Bowman, who told Robert that he had had an arrow blessed by a hermit for the evil knight, in repayment of the ill he had caused Will the Bowman's only son Christopher. Will the Bowman then turned to the thirteen others there present and made them all swear their allegiance to Robert of Locksley.

41 As they spoke Robert held up his hand for silence and told them that from that day, until they once again became freemen, he would no longer be known as Robert of Locksley. Instead, he said, he would be called Robin Hood, for he had always been known as Robin by those who knew and trusted him, and Hood because, until they once again walked as freemen without a price on their heads, he would hide as if under a hooded garment.

42 Quickly Robin Hood and the men who had sworn to follow him stole away into the night, leaving Outwoods behind them. They made their way through Fangthief Wood until they came to the wold upon which lay the village of Birkencar and the manor house that was the home of the evil Sir Guy of Gisborne. The manor was dark as Robin led his small force up to the very walls before making his way to the small underground cell where Will Scarlet was being held. As he approached, Robin heard the voice of a youth talking to the prisoner, a voice he quickly recognised as belonging to Gilbert, Will Scarlet's young nephew, who was commonly known as Gilbert of the White Hand.

Illustration from *Bold Robin Hood and his Outlaw Band* by Louis Read.

43 Quietly Robin approached the prison until he could just make out the huddled form of Will Scarlet behind the stout wooden poles of the door. Making himself known to Gilbert, Robin soon hacked the door open and Scadlock and two other men pulled out the badly wounded Will Scarlet. They laid him on the damp grass and tended his wounds. As he looked around, Robin could see the other men stacking great bundles of dried wood and kindling against the walls of the manor house, their intention being to burn Sir Guy of Gisborne alive.

44 As Robin came up to them he was stopped by Much the miller's son, Will the Bowman, and Kit the Smith, who told him that they intended to burn down the manor house, and thus rid themselves once and for all of Sir Guy of Gisborne. As they spoke the first flames were put to the wood that had been piled up, and soon the wall timbers were alight. But Robin reminded them that there were women in the house, and as they had no quarrel with the women they should be given free passage out.

45 Will the Bowman threw a stone at a window behind which the face of Sir Guy of Gisborne could be seen quickly darting back into the shadows. After shouting that the women should be sent out, Robin, Will the Bowman and Kit the Smith made their way round to the front door where another of their company raked away the burning brushwood to allow the screaming women to escape. Once the women were free, the man started to reposition the burning wood, but as he did so a spear cast from the shadows within struck him fatally in the throat.

46 As Robin and Will the Bowman restrained the others from rushing at the burning manor to avenge the death of their comrade, an arrow struck a tree near Will the Bowman. He called over Makin, the housekeeper of the burning manor, and asked who remained in the house. She replied that only the steward remained, and then added that he was not destined to die by the fire. Just then a cry went up from the rear of the manor, which sent Robin and Will the Bowman running to see what all the commotion was about. As they reached the back of the manor they saw a storehouse with its doors wide open, even though the frames were burning fiercely, and found their comrades frightened almost out of their wits.

47 When questioned, they said that the Spectre Beast had burst from the store and made away up the hill. Immediately Will the Bowman gave chase, though those who had seen the creature called at him to come back, fearing greatly for his life. Questioned again by Robin, they said that the Spectre Mare had burst forth and run straight at Bat the Coalman, also called Bat the Charcoal-burner, until at the last moment it turned and made off. Robin knew that Sir Guy of Gisborne had given them the slip, and returned to where he had left Makin. From her he learnt that Sir Guy of Gisborne had flayed a brown mare two days earlier and had hung the skin to dry in the store house. It was obvious to Robin that Sir Guy had simply wrapped himself in the hide

to make good his escape, a theory that was confirmed when Will the Bowman returned to say that he had seen Sir Guy of Gisborne throw off the hide and mount a horse standing in the pasture before making off, taking the hide with him.

48   With nothing more to be done at the manor, and with Sir Guy of Gisborne far away, no doubt already rousing his comrades against Robin and his group of villeins, Robin led his weary, half-angry, half-happy group of peasants into the forest that was to be their home and their sanctuary until the evil that was infecting the land could be put to flight, and once more they could walk free among their fellow men.

2. ALAN-A-DALE AND LITTLE JOHN

49   For many weeks after the burning of the manor at Birkencar, and the flight of Sir Guy of Gisborne, Robin Hood and his men remained safe in the depths of the Barnisdale Forest, their camp being located at a spot known to them as the Stane Lea, or Stanley. Here a small rivulet provided them with clear, clean water. The site obviously had far older religious connections, for at one end there stood a massive moss-covered stone where in ages gone by skin-clad warriors would undoubtedly have come to praise their gods, or beneath which some ancient tribal chieftain had been buried.

50   Every day Robin instructed his new followers in the use of the sword, quarterstaff and longbow, implements with which they were unaccustomed, their hands having been hardened over the years at the plough. Slowly at first they became used to these new weapons, as they needed to do if they were to stay alive for very long, and gradually

Illustration from *Bold Robin Hood and his Outlaw Band* by Louis Read.

Robin began to feel more at ease with those who had chosen him as their leader. Among their number were many whose skills could be put to great use. Will the Bowman, already skilled in the use of the longbow, instructed many of his comrades in archery, while Dickon the Carpenter showed others how to make longbows and arrow shafts. Even though they had been thrown together in a moment of great drama, they now pooled their knowledge and slowly became an organised body.

51   After several weeks of instruction Robin was pressed to know what they were going to do to show the strength of the oppressed to those in positions of influence who used their power corruptly. Robin gathered all his followers around him and told them that they should never hurt any woman, nor should they harm any person who was good, honest and hardworking, whether they be serf, villein, yeoman or knight. However, Robin was less reserved when it came to the Church, for those who held high office – abbots, bishops, priors, canons and monks – could expect no mercy from them, unless the cleric was known to them to be good and kindly, in which case he was to be spared. All those who passed through the forest would pay them a toll – or they would pay with their lives.

52   Speaking of the Church made Robin remember his own faith, and at that moment he told his men that they would that very day travel to Campsall and there celebrate mass and make their confessions. Quickly he led his men through the forest, down paths that few of them knew existed, across streams that none of them had seen before, and deeper and deeper into the forest. Yet none of them was afraid, for they all had complete faith in their chosen leader; they would follow him to the edge of a cliff, and over, if that was what he required. After quite some time Much the miller's son took an arrow from his belt and notched it to his bowstring, telling the others that he had sighted an elf or brownie, and that his arrow would prove it to his comrades who laughed at him. However, as Much loosed the arrow Robin struck his arm so that the arrow ploughed harmlessly into the earth only a few yards ahead of them.

53   Seeing the expression on his followers' faces, Robin explained that those who lived in the forest were his friends, and that they would also become their friends in time. He then instructed them that they should shoot nothing in the forest that did not seek to do them harm (unless, of course, it was for food). Throughout the rest of their journey to Campsall Much the miller's son endured the good-humoured ribbing of his friends, but no matter how much they teased him, he remained convinced that he had seen some supernatural dweller of the forest, even commenting that it had been Puck himself, or else Puck's brother.

54   Finally Robin Hood and his men came to the church at the little forest village of Campsall. One by one each of the men made his confession, Robin being the last to make his amends with God, and then mass was said at Robin's request. Robin and his men were not the only ones in the church that day, for sitting quietly at the back

was a young man dressed in the garb of a squire, his sword by his side and his steel cap in his hand. He was tall and strongly built, and Robin immediately decided that he was the squire to a noble family, and that he posed them no threat.

55   Halfway through the service a small man entered the church and made his way past the astonished outlaws to where Robin knelt. There he whispered in Robin's ear that they had been followed to Campsall by two of the knights of the Evil Hold, their whereabouts having been reported to the knights by a spy who had been camping near the Stane Lea for a few days. As quickly and as quietly as he had entered, the small man made his way back to the door of the church where Robin had asked him to keep watch until the mass was completed. Every one of the outlaws now knew that Much the miller's son had not been seeing things in the forest – a fact that brought a great smile of satisfaction to his lips.

56   As the mass drew to a close, an arrow sped through one of the narrow slit-like church windows and struck the opposite wall, whereupon the priest fled to his vestry at the rear of the building and Robin commanded his men to take up position by the windows. As they scattered, the young squire came up to Robin and asked what the problem was. When he heard that it was the knights of the Evil Hold who sought to kill them that day, the squire's face darkened at the mention of men like Sir Niger le Grym and Sir Hamo de Mortain, the evil consorts of Sir Isenbart de Belame, whom the squire referred to as the grandson of the fiend of Tickhill, and then he asked if he might be permitted to help Robin and his men.

57   Robin immediately agreed and asked the young man his name. He replied that he was Alan de Tranmire, son and squire of Sir Herbrand de Tranmire, and known to those he counted as his friends as Alan-a-Dale. Quickly Robin had Kit the Smith

Robin Hood and Alan-a-Dale. Illustration from *A Book of Old English Ballads* by George Wharton Edwards.

Illustration from *The Merry Adventures of Robin Hood* by Howard Pyle.

give Alan-a-Dale a longbow and a clutch of arrows, and they all took up their positions so that they could see what was going on outside.

58 Two knights sat proudly on their horses while around them their men-at-arms made ready a young oak they had felled and lopped clean of its branches to use as a battering-ram. Twelve of the twenty men-at-arms took up the burden of the young tree and made ready to charge at the door to the church. Inside two outlaws braced themselves at each of the narrow window slits, the one to the front kneeling, and the one behind standing, their arrows ready notched, and many with the bowstrings already drawn. Each man carefully took aim at the men-at-arms and then waited for Robin to give the command to shoot, a command that came only seconds before the men-at-arms launched their attack.

59 From the church a total of twenty-one arrows flew across the open space towards the men-at-arms, now running forwards at a slow trot. Eight of the twelve men carrying the battering-ram fell at once. Of the four who remained, two escaped unwounded while the other two pulled arrows from their arms before they too fled into the forest. One of the two knights tumbled to the ground as an arrow struck his horse straight in the heart. Dazed and bewildered for a moment, he quickly picked himself up and fled into the protection of the trees, hot on the heels of his comrade who had turned and fled as soon as the first volley of arrows had erupted from the church. Seeing them flee, the outlaws unbarred the door to the church and ran after them, their enemy's trail being easy to follow as they had careered carelessly through the undergrowth.

60 As his men chased after the knights and their men-at-arms, the hunters having become the hunted, Robin and Alan-a-Dale followed on at a more leisurely pace, and Alan-a-Dale told Robin that he too had a dispute with the knights of the Evil Hold. He loved Alice de Beauforest, whose father held lands on the edge of Sherwood Forest, but Sir Isenbart de Belame had threatened her father that, unless Alice was married within the year to an old and equally evil knight of his own choosing, then Sir Isenbart and his company would seize the Beauforest lands and burn down his

manor. As they walked and talked they came to the edge of a clearing, wherein they saw a knight on foot talking to a churl dressed in the simple rough apparel of a villein.

61   As they entered the glade the churl spoke to the knight, who challenged Robin and Alan-a-Dale. They had recognised the knight as the one they had unhorsed at Campsall church. As Alan-a-Dale unfastened his sword and shield and made ready to fight, the churl hurried away into the depths of the forest. Advancing on the knight, Alan-a-Dale addressed him as Sir Ivo le Ravener, one of the knights of the Evil Hold, for he had recognised him as one of the knights Sir Isenbart de Belame often sent to intimidate the manor of Beauforest. As they fought, Robin stood to one side, an arrow notched ready to his bowstring in case Alan-a-Dale should need his assistance, though ultimately that proved not necessary, for though the pair fought long and hard it was Sir Ivo le Ravener who eventually dropped his guard, allowing Alan-a-Dale to thrust his sword into the evil knight's throat.

62   As the knight fell, Robin heard a sound like the hissing of a snake and deftly leapt to one side just in time to see the blade of a knife slice through the air where he had been standing moments before. The man holding the knife fell to the ground with the force of the intended blow, but quickly recovered his footing and started to make off into the forest. As he fled, a small dark figure tripped him and leapt upon him, the two rolling on the ground for several minutes. When the churl lay dead, the little man got up and wiped the blood from the blade of his knife on a tussock of grass. The little man, who had earlier given Robin the warning in the church, was Hob o'the Hill, the brother of Ket the Trow. The dead man Hob identified as Grull, a churl of the Evil Hold, saying he was the one who had spied on Robin and his men at the Stane Lea.

63   Returning to the scene of the battle, Robin found Alan-a-Dale nursing a shoulder wound which he quickly dressed. Having regained his breath, Alan-a-Dale told Robin that he would return to his home at Werrisdale, even though at that time he was staying at Forest Hold, the house of his foster-brother Piers the Lucky; he would not go back there lest the knights of the Evil Hold sought revenge against an innocent party. When he felt strong enough, Robin helped Alan-a-Dale to his feet and the pair set off through the forest once more, this time heading for the forester's hut about a mile away where Alan-a-Dale had left his horse.

64   As all this had been happening, about a mile and a half away a giant of a man was making his way through the forest on the path that led to the very forester's hut Alan-a-Dale had mentioned. His dress was that of a common peasant, though few would dare to argue with him owing to his enormous and extremely strong frame. As he walked he whistled quietly to himself, seeming to enjoy the open air and his own

company, and every now and then carelessly swiping at a leaf on a tree with the huge quarterstaff he carried.

65   As he walked along he smelt the aroma of cooking meat, a smell that reminded him just how hungry he really was. Quietly, so as not to announce his approach, the man stole through the undergrowth towards the mouth-watering smell, and before long was peering out from the bushes on one side of a small glade, in the middle of which stood a horse tethered to a tree, in front of a crudely constructed hut. By the hut was a blazing fire over which several cutlets of meat had been hung on skewers, and it was these that had drawn him to the hut like a magnet.

66   As he watched a man came out of the hut and gently turned the skewers so that the meat might cook evenly. The large man's heart sank as he saw that the man was dressed in a tunic of green with brown hose, the silver badge of a hunting horn on his cap betraying the fact that he was a forester. In addition, his face was so surly that the watcher felt certain that he would rather see a man starve than share his meal with a stranger. Backing away to a safe distance, the man thought for a moment and then marched headlong into the clearing, dropping his quarterstaff as he approached. His appearance caused the forester, whose name was Black Hugo, to rise quickly to his full height – which was markedly shorter than that of the newcomer.

67   The initial shock at seeing the huge man lumber his way into the glade quickly evaporated and the forester venomously told the man to be on his way. Obediently the man tugged on his forelock and crashed away through the undergrowth, recovering his quarterstaff as he went. The forester went back into the hut and returned a few seconds later with a loaf. He cut a thick slice of bread before taking one of the skewers and sliding the meat onto the bread with his knife. He did the same with the second piece of meat, and was about to repeat the process with the third piece when the end of the quarterstaff struck him on the temple and rendered him senseless.

68   With a speed that belied his large frame, the peasant caught the skewer which had flown up into the air and carefully put the meat on the third thick slice of bread. Then he turned his attention to the forester, whom he lifted with consummate ease and bound to one of the posts of the wooden hut with some rope he found inside. Then, sitting on the ground in full view of the stunned forester, who had by this time begun to recover his senses, the peasant started to eat his meal. When Black Hugo saw that his food was being eaten he struggled vainly to free himself, and began to shout abuse at the peasant, who simply laughed at him and ate every last crumb that Black Hugo had originally intended for himself.

69   His stomach now full, the peasant crossed to where Black Hugo sat tied to the hut and offered to take him on in a contest with the quarterstaff, a challenge that Black

Hugo readily accepted, adding that he would soon have his revenge on the thief who had just denied him his meal. However, as the large man bent down to unfasten the ropes he heard voices coming towards them from the forest. Quickly, for fear that the voices belonged to other foresters, the man recovered his quarterstaff and hurried away just as Robin Hood and Alan-a-Dale entered the glade.

70   Seeing Black Hugo tied to the post of the hut, they quickly crossed over to him. They could not help but laugh at his sorry situation, and their amusement served only to increase the forester's already foul temper. Before long, seeing that his situation was hopeless, Black Hugo fell into a sullen silence. Robin told him that he would be left tied to the post until later that night, when, upon hearing the cry of the owl, he would find himself free. Then Alan-a-Dale collected his horse from where it stood patiently tethered, and he and Robin Hood left Black Hugo alone in the glade.

71   All afternoon Black Hugo remained tied to the hut post. As night fell he felt as if he were no longer alone, but no matter how far he craned his neck, he could see no one. Then, as he heard the sound of an owl crying in the distance, he pulled on his bonds – and to his amazement he found that they came free. Upon inspection he found that the rope had been cut with a sharp knife, but he had neither seen nor heard anyone, a fact that filled him with dread and made him hurry away from that spot which he felt was haunted.

72   Robin and Alan-a-Dale had walked together for a while through the forest before Alan-a-Dale mounted his horse and bade farewell to his new friend as he started on the short-cut that Robin had shown him to his home at Werrisdale. Having watched his new-found ally ride off, Robin turned his steps towards the Stane Lea, where he knew that his men would be waiting for him. Almost at the end of his journey he had to cross the brook that ran by their camp, but at the spot where he had chosen to cross it was deeper and wider, and the only way across was over a fallen log.

73   No sooner had Robin started to cross the log than a huge man appeared out of the undergrowth on the opposite side and also started to make his way across. Robin immediately recognised him by his sheer size as the man he had briefly caught sight of when he and Alan-a-Dale had come across the trussed-up Black Hugo. Robin was about to greet him warmly when the man told him to get out of his way.

74   Robin replied that as he had been the first on the bridge it was not his place to give way. The man refused to back down, so Robin told him that unless he yielded he would teach the impudent oaf a lesson he would never forget, and so saying he notched an arrow to his bowstring. The man stood his ground and said that he considered the odds to be unfair, for all he had was his quarterstaff, but that he would still give Robin a sound thrashing even if he did loose off his arrow.

Robin Hood fights Little John. Illustration from *Bold Robin Hood and his Outlaw Band* by Louis Read.

Robin Hood meeteth the tall stranger on the bridge. Illustration from *The Merry Adventures of Robin Hood* by Howard Pyle.

75 Robin, though annoyed at the attitude of the peasant who stood before him, could not help but admire his spirit, and suggested that, to equal the odds, he would cut himself a quarterstaff if the other remained where he was. He agreed, so Robin retreated from the bridge and cut himself a stout oak branch which he trimmed with consummate ease before returning to the bridge to face his opponent. The winner would be the one who could topple the other into the water below.

76 For a long while the two men went at each other, their staffs slashing through the air, each landing more than one blow on their opponent, but neither able to make a decisive move. However, just as it seemed that Robin was getting the better of his opponent, the huge man parried one of Robin's blows and, with a speed that he should not have been capable of, caught Robin in the side and sent him tumbling headlong into the waters below, just as sweat trickled into his eyes and temporarily blinded him.

77 Wiping the sweat away he was amazed to find that his opponent was no longer on the bridge, and quickly looking around saw Robin a short way down the stream sitting on the opposite bank, having crossed the stream without the aid of the bridge.

Robin Hood and his Merry Men by Edmund George Warren, 1858. (© *Christie's Images/Corbis*)

However, instead of continuing on his journey the large man made his way over to where Robin sat and splashed water over his face to refresh himself after his combat. When Robin asked him why he had been in so much of a hurry that he had refused to yield, the man told him that he had run away from his master, and was wanting to find somewhere to rest for the night. Taking him by the hand, Robin heartily congratulated him for his skill with the quarterstaff and invited him to join him and his men, whereupon he drew his horn and blew hard.

78   A few moments later the woods were filled with the outlaws. The first to arrive was Will the Bowman, who questioned Robin's bedraggled appearance. As Robin explained all that had passed the others appeared; without hesitation they sprang on the man and held him aloft, fully intending to throw him into the river. However, Robin told them that he had invited the man to join them, if he would. The man readily agreed and told them that his name was John o'the Stubbs, but most men called him John the Little.

79   Each man shook John the Little by the hand, and soon all returned to the Stane Lea where they ate their fill and drank brown ale. At the end of the meal, their hunger

satisfied and their thirst quenched, Will the Bowman toasted John the Little, saying that thenceforth he should be known as Little John. Then, sitting in a circle around the fire, Little John told them all how he had deprived Black Hugo of his lunch. Robin then added that he had left Black Hugo tied to the hut until the first cry of the owl, whereupon he would be loose.

80   When asked how he had managed to achieve such a feat, Robin replied that he had friends within the greenwood, and then told Hob o'the Hill to show himself. From a place in the shadows near Robin Hood a small figure arose, his black eyes shining in the light of the fire. All those there, with the exception of Robin, crossed themselves, while Much the miller's son took off his tunic and turned it inside out. One of them cried out that he was in the company of a boggart, a troll or a lubberfiend, and Rafe the Carter said that evil spirits such as this used to plait his horses' manes in the night and drive them mad. Still another said that evil folk such as this made green rings in the meadow which would poison any beast who ate them.

81   Robin severely scolded them all, saying that these were but the stories and beliefs of old women. He then told them all that Hob o'the Hill had a brother, Ket the Trow, and that they were both his dear friends, who had helped him many times, ever since he had rescued them from a clash with five knights. Hob and Ket had killed two of them, but the others set upon the small men and had all but killed them when Robin arrived just as one of the knights said that he would burn them alive in the same way as he had burnt their father on Hagthorn Waste. As the three knights dragged the almost lifeless bodies of Hob and Ket towards the fire, Robin saw a small door open in the side of a small hill; three women rushed out and prostrated themselves at the feet of the knights. One woman was old, but the other two were much younger and of incredible beauty. However, the knights were not moved by their pleas and said that they too should burn, along with Hob o'the Hill and Ket the Trow. At that Robin could bear it no longer, and killed the three knights with well-aimed arrows, and from that day on the two hill folk and all their kin had been his friends.

82   The first to rise from the circle around the fire was Little John, who bent down and offered his hand to Hob o'the Hill as a mark of friendship. One by one all the men gathered there shook the little man by the hand and offered him their allegiance. Hob o'the Hill thanked them all. He then told them that his father had been killed by Sir Ranulf of the Waste, the master of Hagthorn Waste. He welcomed the aid of Robin Hood and his comrades in ridding the countryside of such evil knights as Sir Ranulf, but he insisted that he and his brother, and the other creatures and people of the Underworld, would one day take their own revenge. Then Hob o'the Hill pledged his friendship and allegiance to each man gathered around the fire, and added that he, the kin of those who were once Lords of the Underworld and the

Overworld, of the Mound Folk, the Stone Folk and the Tree Folk, gave them an equal share in the earth, the wood, the water and the air of the greenwood and the surrounding moorland. Having spoken thus he moved out of the firelight and immediately vanished from sight.

3. THE SPY AND THE SHERIFF

83 All through the winter Robin and his men sheltered within the confines of the forest, and as signs of renewed life among the trees and the undergrowth welcomed the arrival of spring, Robin sent word to Alfred of Gamwell, telling him how he might travel in safety through the forest and come to the place where Robin and his men had spent the long, cold winter months. Following these instructions, Alfred of Gamwell came to the forest in the company of Simon his clerk and six men-at-arms; having called at Outwoods for final directions, he headed towards the scar of Clumber cliffs where he had been told to wait until Robin found him. He would not find Robin.

84 Having travelled less than a mile into the forest the travellers were startled when a loud voice commanded them to stand, and as they looked around to see who had spoken they saw that they were surrounded by at least twenty men dressed in dark-brown tunics, hose and hood, each having an arrow notched to his drawn bowstring. Careful to obey the large man who was obviously the leader of these outlaws, Alfred of Gamwell commanded his men-at-arms to drop their weapons. Then, having been disarmed, all eight were led away deeper into the forest.

85 After a short while a tall man dressed all in green, with his hood pulled far over his head so as to hide his face, came towards the party. With measured strides the man in green walked up to Alfred of Gamwell's horse and then threw back his hood to reveal his face, at the same time offering his hand in friendship to his cousin Alfred of Gamwell. In amazement Alfred stared into the face of Robin Hood, the man he had come to thank, as well as to warn.

86 Two years previously Robin Hood had heard of the fate of his cousin Alice of Havelond, whose husband Bennett, a well-to-do yeoman, had been imprisoned and held to ransom by a Scottish knight. In his absence their neighbours Robert of Prestbury and Thomas of Patherley had seized the manor of Havelond and thrown Alice out. For a year Alice had laboured to regain her rightful property and to release her husband, which she finally succeeded in doing when she had raised the required ransom. Bennett returned to his manor only to be set upon by Thomas of Patherley and Robert of Prestbury, who beat him almost to death. Alice had then travelled to the royal court and begged for help, only to be told that Bennett would have to make the appeal in person if the king were to hear it, but Alice knew that this would be impossible as the attack had maimed him.

87 Instead she travelled to Alfred of Gamwell, who told her that he would personally take her case to the king's court, but Alice knew that this would be of little use, so instead she came to the greenwood and sought out her cousin Robert of Locksley, who comforted her and told her that he would personally see to the return of her rightful property. A few days later the men of Scaurdale saw two houses burning in the distance and immediately knew that somehow vengeance had been rightly wreaked on the two robbers. It soon became known that 'Robin o'the Hood' had come out of the greenwood on that night and had killed both Thomas of Patherley and Robert of Prestbury, and had thus restored the manor to its rightful owner, the now crippled Bennett of Havelond.

88 Having described the killing of Thomas of Patherley and Robert of Prestbury, Robin turned to his cousin and asked him the true reason for his visit. Alfred of Gamwell replied that he had come to warn him about the evil schemes of Sir Guy of Gisborne, which he had learnt from Cripps, an old retainer at Outwoods. According to the information Cripps had given him, Sir Guy of Gisborne was now in league with Ralph Murdach, the Sheriff of Nottinghamshire and Derbyshire, and the pair of them were bribing men to dress as beggars to wander through the forest in an attempt to uncover the secret lairs of Robin Hood and his men – so that Ralph Murdach might curry favour by killing the outlaw and Sir Guy of Gisborne might gain the vengeance he lusted after.

89 When Robin and his men heard mention of Sir Guy of Gisborne their hearts were filled with hatred, and they enquired of Alfred of Gamwell how he now treated those unfortunates who had decided to remain at the manor. To their surprise Alfred of Gamwell told them that since the burning of the manor at Birkencar, Abbot Robert of St Mary's had threatened to take the manor from Sir Guy of Gisborne, blaming him for the revolt and saying that it was surely down to the fact that he mistreated the villeins of the village. From that day forth, though still a hard master, Sir Guy of Gisborne had treated the villeins more humanely, though in his heart the hatred now burnt deeper than before.

90 A short while later Alfred of Gamwell took his leave of his cousin, who provided him with an escort to the edge of the forest, where they showed him the road to Locksley village which lay to the south-west beyond the small town of Sheffield.

91 Three days after his cousin's visit, Robin was walking along the Pontefract to Ollerton and Nottingham road through the forest when he came upon a beggar shuffling along the road with heavy, weary footsteps. Robin quickly hid among the trees as Alfred's warning rang in his ears, and from his hiding place he watched the beggar approach. Although his attire was undoubtedly dishevelled, and he appeared to all intents and purposes to be a poor beggar, something about him made Robin

The Sheriff of Nottingham plotting against Robin sends a messenger to Lincoln. Illustration from *The Merry Adventures of Robin Hood* by Howard Pyle.

highly suspicious. He decided that the man had been dressed to play the part, and so he stepped into the road and called upon the beggar to stop.

92   Rather than obey the beggar speeded up, so that Robin had to run after him and physically bring him to a halt – whereupon the man turned and flourished his staff at Robin, who deftly ducked out of the way. Robin took a couple of steps back and told the beggar that as he was undoubtedly a rich beggar, or else a rich man in the guise of a poor one, he would have to pay a toll to pass through the forest. As the man flinched at the mention of a disguise, Robin continued, saying that he knew the man was no true beggar, and that unless he handed over his purse he would be run through by an arrow.

93   However, as Robin took an arrow from his belt and briefly glanced down to notch it to his bowstring, the beggar saw his chance and struck the bow from Robin's hand with his staff. Quickly Robin leapt back and drew his sword, but the beggar was too fast for him; catching Robin on the side of the head, he knocked him unconscious. The beggar then crouched over the fallen figure and reached for the dagger hidden in his cloak, but at that very moment three of Robin's men came out of the undergrowth and the beggar quickly made off.

94   One of these three men was Dodd, the man-at-arms who had yielded to Robin after the killing of Sir Hubert of Lynn. The other two were new recruits. Dodd immediately recognised the bow lying in the road as Robin's, and a few moments later they came across the stunned Robin who was just beginning to stir. As his wits returned, Robin told them all that had befallen him. He ordered the two new members of his outlaw band to go after the beggar, but to beware as the man was extremely cunning and could move with a speed that was unnatural for a man of his stature. Eagerly the two young men ran off down the road after the beggar while Dodd remained to care for Robin and to help him back to their camp.

95   The two men, Michael and Bat, also called Bart, quickly caught up with the beggar who was still following the road through the forest. Turning off the road the two

young outlaws ran through the undergrowth until they came to a spot where the road narrowed, and took up position behind two stout trees that would adequately hide them from anyone on the road. They did not have to wait long. As the beggar came between the two trees they leapt on him, one snatching away the staff while the other seized the dagger from the beggar's belt and held it to his throat.

96   Seeing that his life would be forfeit if he struggled, the beggar pleaded with the two outlaws to spare his life, saying that if they did he would handsomely reward them from his purse which he had hidden beneath his cloak. The two young men stood back and told the beggar to pay for his life, whereupon the man began to divest himself of the cloak and the heavy bags he was carrying. As he lifted the rope of one sack over his head Bat saw a small purse hidden under one arm; guessing that this was surely where the beggar kept his richest belongings, he leapt forward and cut the leather strap that held it in place. The beggar attempted to snatch it back but Bat had already moved out of his reach, and the beggar was encumbered by the bag he had been lifting over his head.

97   Knowing that he would now have to resort to trickery if he was to escape, the beggar told them that they could have everything else he owned. So saying, he bent down and started to undo another of the bags, which the two outlaws felt certain held the beggar's food. As they bent down to see what their prisoner was up to, the beggar threw great handfuls of flour into their faces and blinded them. Bat and Michael stumbled backwards away from the beggar rubbing in vain at their eyes. As they retreated, the beggar retrieved his staff and set about them, both of the outlaws being soundly beaten before their vision returned sufficiently for them to make good their escape.

98   That evening Bat and Michael returned to the camp and told Robin of their foolishness, and all that had happened with the beggar. Robin listened impassively and then asked if Bat still had the purse he had cut from under the beggar's arm. Bat reached inside his tunic and passed the pouch to Robin, who opened it and tipped out the contents. There were three rose nobles wrapped in a piece of rag, a ring with a design engraved into it, and lastly a piece of parchment which turned out to be a letter written in Latin. Patiently Robin worked out that the letter was addressed to Ralph Murdach, Sheriff of Nottinghamshire and Derbyshire. It was a letter of introduction for its bearer, one Richard Malbête, who had been recommended to the author of the letter by Sir Niger le Grym; Malbête was now being sent to Nottingham explicitly to help capture Robin Hood.

99   The letter was not signed, but instead, as was customary in those times, it carried the seal of the writer on a piece of blue wax. This seal – a wild man's head above a sword – belonged to Sir Guy of Gisborne. Robin then turned back to Bat and Michael and severely scolded them for their actions that day, but ended by saying

that he put it down to the enthusiasm of youth and their inexperience, and thus he would overlook the entire episode. As Bat and Michael were unused to hearing words of kindness, especially since their previous master at Warsop had been an evil man, they pleaded with Robin to give them a task so that they might prove their worth. Robin told them that he would no doubt shortly have a task to set them.

100 After talking with Little John for some time about the contents of the letter, Robin called Bat and Michael to him and told them that he had a task for them to carry out, a task that would not be easy, but they must not fail. Eagerly they both agreed as Robin told them to travel to Mansfield and there seek out the potter of Wentbridge and obtain the loan of the potter's cart, horse, pots and clothes as Robin intended to travel to Nottingham in disguise. As Bat and Michael turned to leave, Robin told them that he would meet them one hour after dawn the following day at the Forest Herne beyond Mansfield.

101 Bat and Michael were true to their word, and the following morning Robin disguised himself as the potter of Wentbridge and drove the potter's cart, drawn by a well-fed pony, into the market-place at Nottingham. He set up his stall and began to sell his

Ye Olde Trip to Jerusalem, Nottingham, reputedly the oldest pub in England. (*Mick Sharp Photography*)

Robin turns butcher and sells his meat in Nottingham.
Illustration from *The Merry Adventures of Robin Hood* by
Howard Pyle.

pots at such low prices that news of his wares quickly spread throughout the market. Word even reached Dame Margaret, the wife of Ralph Murdach, who came to the market to see what all the fuss was about. When Robin saw that Dame Margaret had come to his stall he offered to give her his remaining pots. Delighted with such a handsome gift, Dame Margaret responded that the potter should come with her so that he might dine with her and the sheriff at the market table.

102 As Robin accompanied Dame Margaret into the market hall they were met by Ralph Murdach the sheriff, a rich cordwainer who had bought his office from the grasping Bishop of Ely. Robin had only seen him once before. Dame Margaret explained to her husband that the potter had just given her the best of his wares. The sheriff also thanked him for the gift and invited him to eat with them and the other rich merchants of the market.

103 Within the market hall there were two tables arranged in a 'T', the upper one being occupied by Ralph Murdach, his wife Dame Margaret, and the richest merchants and highest-ranking officers of the sheriff's men. The lower table, at which Robin was seated, housed those who did not hold such privileged positions, but were still in favour enough to be invited to eat with the sheriff and his wife. At the doors to the hall poor folk and beggars crowded around and cried out for alms. During the course of the meal a large beggar broke through the crowd and boldly marched towards the tables. His progress was halted only a few feet away by one of the servitors, who caught hold of him and vainly tried to manhandle him back towards the doors. Robin looked up at the commotion and recognised the beggar as Richard Malbête, the beggar who had soundly beaten him in the forest.

Illustration from *The Merry Adventures of Robin Hood* by Howard Pyle.

104 As the servitor began to gain the upper hand, the beggar cried out that he had a message for the sheriff from Sir Guy of Gisborne, at which Ralph Murdach told the servitor to let the man speak. But the beggar refused to repeat his message in public, and told the sheriff that his purse had been stolen from him en route through the forest; losing patience, the sheriff commanded his men to eject the beggar and have him beaten from the town. Immediately a number of servitors fell on Richard Malbête and threw him from the hall. His cloak and bags were stripped from him and he was cruelly beaten out of the town and down the road towards the forest.

105 Inside the hall the diners joked and laughed at the beggar's expense before retiring to engage in a friendly shooting contest. Each of the sheriff's men took turns to shoot at a target, though not one of them could hit the bull's-eye. Seeing this, Robin remarked that he had once been a good bowman before becoming a potter, and asked the sheriff if he might be allowed to take part in the contest. The sheriff agreed and had one of his men give Robin a bow and a clutch of arrows. His first shot was nearer to the centre of the target than any of the arrows fired by the sheriff's men, who now stepped forward again to try to better their previous efforts, but not one of them could get nearer to the bull's-eye than Robin had. As he stepped up to fire his last arrow, Robin behaved with cool nonchalance, casually aiming at the target some two hundred yards away and turning his back before the arrow struck.

106 In the distance a man shouted that the last arrow had struck the peg* and split it into three pieces. A great cheer went up from all the bystanders watching the contest.

* The peg was a round piece of wood that marked the very centre of the bull's-eye, and stood slightly proud of the target.

Seeing the black looks of his own men, the sheriff came up to Robin and congratulated him, and gave him the freedom to carry a bow wherever he pleased. Robin replied that he had loved the bow all his life, and had with him, in his cart, a bow that had been given to him by Robin Hood himself, with whom he had shot.

107   The very mention of the name made the sheriff scowl. Hurriedly Robin explained that he had been stopped the previous year in the forest by Robin Hood, who demanded a toll of him. He had replied that he did not pay toll to anyone other than the king for the right to travel the king's highway, and would fight him with staff or shoot a round of arrows with him to see who was the truest of them. Robin Hood, so Robin continued, had accepted the challenge, and through that contest Robin Hood had said that for his courtesy the potter should be free to travel the forest for as long as he might live. Robin was, of course, relating how he had himself become the friend of the potter of Wentbridge, but so good was his disguise that the sheriff could not see through it.

108   The sheriff, hearing the story, asked the potter if he knew where Robin Hood might be hiding. In all innocence Robin replied that he thought his camp was at Witch Wood, and said that for a suitable reward he would lead the sheriff and his men to where he had heard that Robin Hood and his band of outlaws had spent the winter. The sheriff readily agreed to the asking price of 100 pounds, and then offered Robin a prize of 40 shillings for winning the shooting contest, but Robin refused to take it, saying that he was sure his last bolt had hit the peg only through a chance gust of wind, and that the prize should go to the best of the sheriff's own men. By so doing he won the respect and admiration of those men.

109   The following morning, in the company of the sheriff and ten of his men-at-arms, Robin Hood drove the potter's cart out of Nottingham and led them deeper and deeper into the forest into parts which neither the sheriff nor any of his men had travelled before. As they continued on their way Robin told the sheriff that he would take them to within half a mile of Witch Wood, but from there the sheriff would have to make his own plans on how to seize Robin Hood and his men. The sheriff agreed and asked the potter what kind of place the Witch Wood was. Robin answered that it was an evil place, the haunt of a vile witch. Beyond it was a fresh forest, but within, where the cliffs rose, there were many caves wherein dwelt the witch and her evil spirits. He said he had heard Robin Hood himself was one of her kin, and that while he was in the greenwood he was under her protection, adding for good measure that the witch was the spirit of the forest, and could use her powers to kill any man or imprison him for all eternity under her spell.

110   By now the sheriff and his men were becoming increasingly uneasy. Robin continued to pile on the torment as they came into a clearing where three stones stood beneath a

An encounter between Robin Hood and the Sheriff of Nottingham. Illustration by W. Otway Cannell in *The Book of the Epic* (1916). (*Mary Evans Picture Library*)

large oak tree. These, he told his audience, were called Three Stane Rigg. According to legend, he said, during the daytime they were just stones, but at night they became three hags who did the bidding of the evil witch who lived within the Witch Wood. Just then, as the sheriff commented nervously that they ought perhaps to have brought a priest along with them, the woods were filled with shrieks of unnatural laughter. Immediately four of the ten men-at-arms turned their horses and rode away while the others looked anxiously this way and that to see if they could discover the source of the eerie laughter.

111 Again the shrieks rang around the forest, whereupon the final six men-at-arms turned and fled. As they did so Robin stood up in the cart and cracked his whip. In reply the clear sounds of a horn could be heard and twenty men dressed in brown tunics appeared from the trees. Immediately Sheriff Murdach realised that he had been tricked and captured. Though angry, he resigned himself to his fate as Little John took hold of his reins and led him through the undergrowth to the outlaws' temporary camp. There he was fed while the outlaws took their toll of him – his armour, his weapons and his horse. Then, as the sheriff was released to make his way back to Nottingham on foot, Robin brought out a palfrey which he told the sheriff was a gift from Robin Hood to the Dame Margaret.

112 The sheriff waited until it was quite dark before he came to the gates of Nottingham and demanded to be let in. However, his plan to avoid being seen did not work as the sorry tale had already been circulated by the men-at-arms who had fled back to Nottingham, and thus the sheriff had to endure the ignominy of riding through streets full of curious people. As he reached his house and dismounted, the crowd began to laugh, and continued to laugh even after the sheriff had angrily slammed the door of his house behind him.

4. FRIAR TUCK

113 Throughout the year that Robin Hood and his men had lived in the safety of the greenwood, many men had come to join them, raising their numbers from just twenty to fifty-five. Among these newcomers were Sim of Wakefield, Arthur-a-Bland from Nottingham, a cousin of Little John's, Peter the Doctor and a pilgrim by the name of Nicholas, whom Gilbert of the White Hand had found injured in the forest and brought back to their camp.

114 Nicholas had been a cotter and smith to the abbot of Newstead Abbey, whose harsh treatment had finally led him to flee into the forest. Helped by Gilbert of the White Hand, he had been brought to Elfwood Scar, the site of many caves within Barnisdale Forest, where Robin and his men took shelter whenever the weather turned bad, the caves providing them with warmth and comfort when the forest was wet. There he gladly accepted the fellowship of the other outlaws and swapped stories with them, and from that day forth was known simply as Nick the Smith. Peter the Doctor related that he had once been bettered by a curtal monk who had been cast out of Fountains Abbey, though to be reminded of the occasion caused him great embarrassment.

115 Once, so Peter the Doctor reported, he had been accosted by a huge monk, Tuck by name, whom he wished he could bury in the deepest, darkest hole in Windleswisp Marsh. During their chance meeting the doctor had been taken in by the apparent innocence of the huge man, who enquired about the potions and medicines the doctor carried, and then asked if he could cure his ailments. Then, as Peter reached into his bag for a potion to cure stiffness in the joints, the monk had seized and bound him, and then forced him to swallow each and every potion, pill and powder he had been carrying.

116 Robin listened intently and then asked where the monk might be found. Peter, however, replied in a round-about manner that the monk was not one to be taken lightly, for he considered no man to be his better, and would no doubt outdo Robin himself if he were given the chance. Furthermore, the monk had a number of huge dogs, which Peter supposed were demons in disguise, to protect him should he ever be beaten.

The north aisle of the monastic church at Fountains Abbey, North Yorkshire. (*English Heritage © 2003, Foto Scala Firenze/HIP*)

117 However, Nick the Smith knew of the monk and came to his defence, saying that Friar Tuck was not an evil man, and that he came to comfort the poor and tend to the sick without any thought of reward. Though many, knight and robber alike, had attempted to oust him from his dwellings, not one had succeeded, and many had been beaten almost to death in their attempts. Peter the Doctor, on the other hand, would hear no good of the monk, and added that Friar Tuck had been thrown out of Fountains Abbey for his evil ways, remarking that he had sought sanctuary in the greenwood solely because there he could be left alone to his evil devices and designs.

118 Little more was said about the monk as by that time the rain had ceased and the forest was once more bathed in rich, strong sunlight. The outlaws each went about his allotted tasks, while the main group kept a watch on a rich convoy from the Bishop of York which was on the road from Kirkstall to Ollerton. The convoy was duly waylaid and the outlaws were able to replenish their stocks, as well as lightening the bishop's coffers into the bargain.

119 It was thus a few days before Robin could set out through the forest in search of the curtal monk spoken of by Peter the Doctor and Nick the Smith. Having first instructed Little John to follow on with a dozen men, Robin set out on horseback towards the region of the forest that bounded the lands of Newstead Abbey. After several hours' travelling he reached Lindhurst Wood, where he began to feel as if he were being watched. Several times he halted his horse as he passed through the Eldritch Oaks, and sat quite still listening, but all he could hear each time was the faint rustling of leaves. Finally he dismounted in a small glade and made a sound like that of a small bird. A few moments later he was joined by Ket the Trow. Robin asked the little man if he were quite alone in the forest.

120 Ket the Trow answered that there were none on his path who would wish Robin harm, an answer that did not quite satisfy Robin, though he knew that Ket the Trow spoke the truth. Robin tethered his horse to a tree and set off on foot towards the stream by which Friar Tuck had his home. Sure enough, on the opposite bank was a sturdily built low house surrounded by a wide moat on three sides, the stream forming the fourth. Across the stream lay a plank for access, which could be raised by two ropes that came from the house to its furthest end. From the house a path led away to a place where the stream was shallow enough to be forded, and thence on into the trees.

121 Robin followed the path alongside the stream until he came across Friar Tuck sitting in quiet contemplation beneath a tree. Robin notched an arrow to his bowstring and then commanded the monk to ferry him across the stream on his back lest he should have to get his feet wet. Friar Tuck did not move at first, so Robin repeated his order, adding that if he did not he would be shot where he sat. The monk rose and bent his

The merry friar carrieth Robin across the water. Illustration from *The Merry Adventures of Robin Hood* by Howard Pyle.

The friar took Robin on his back. Illustration from *Bold Robin Hood and his Outlaw Band* by Louis Read.

back, so that Robin could climb on. Then, slowly and carefully, Friar Tuck carried Robin across the stream until they reached the far bank.

122 As Robin began to dismount, Friar Tuck threw him to the ground and then told him that, unless he returned the favour and ferried him back to the far bank, he would do Robin serious harm. Furious to have had his own trick turned against him, Robin reached for his dagger, but the monk seized him by the wrist in a hold so powerful that it could have easily shattered Robin's wrist. Seeing that he was beaten, and wondering why the monk had not soundly beaten him, as he certainly had the power to do, he bent his back and quietly ferried the corpulent friar back across the stream.

123 As Robin reached the opposite bank the monk climbed down, laughing at the way in which Robin had so easily been duped. His laughter caused Robin a moment of madness. Rushing at the monk, he caught him around his broad midriff, the pair of them rolling on the ground until they slid down the bank into the stream. Immediately Robin sprang to his feet and dashed to the spot where he had dropped his bow and arrows. Quickly picking them up he notched an arrow to his bowstring and turned to face the monk, but he had vanished. A few seconds later the monk reappeared from behind a broad oak tree, wearing a helmet and carrying a shield and staff.

124 Immediately Robin fired an arrow at him, but the monk simply knocked it away with his shield. Three more times Robin fired, but each time to no effect. Seeing that his arrows were of little use, Robin reached for his horn and told the monk that he only had to blow to have the monk taken by his men – but Friar Tuck jovially replied that

he simply had to whistle and Robin and any who might care to join the mêlée would be torn to pieces by his dogs.

125 As Friar Tuck spoke, Robin heard the noise of someone crashing through the undergrowth. He turned to see a youth running towards him with a hood pulled far over the head to hide the face. As he watched he became aware that other people were running towards him in pursuit of the youth, and he was about to bring him down with an arrow when he caught a glimpse of the face beneath the cowl. Immediately he threw down his bow and arrow and ran to the youth, throwing back the cowl to reveal none other than Maid Marian.

126 Hurriedly she told Robin to blow his horn as those who followed her meant him harm. As she spoke, Robin heard a screech as if some bird had fallen prey to a hawk, and immediately recognised the sound as the warning signal of Ket the Trow. As Robin raised his horn to his lips, Maid Marian spoke to Friar Tuck. Seconds later the monk raised two fingers to his mouth and whistled at a pitch too high for men to hear.

127 Already the first of Marian's pursuers were breaking from the undergrowth, and at once Robin recognised them as the men-at-arms of St Mary's Abbey, their leader being none other than Black Hugo himself. Robin Hood, Friar Tuck and Maid Marian backed towards the stream as Robin let arrow after arrow fly at the advancing men, each arrow he let fly increasing the odds steadily in their favour.

128 Just as the three reached the edge of the stream, ten huge hounds bounded into the clearing and set about the men-at-arms, who slashed wildly at the huge beasts with their daggers and swords. After a while, when five of the ten dogs had been killed, Friar Tuck called them off. As they backed off Black Hugo looked across the fields in the distance and saw Robin's men hurrying towards their position. He immediately ordered his men to retreat, and as they disappeared back into the forest the first of Robin Hood's band reached the clearing, followed a few seconds later by the rest of the outlaws. All of them went crashing into the undergrowth in pursuit of the fleeing men-at-arms.

129 Robin turned to Maid Marian as if to scold her, but Marian sensed his mood and begged him not to be angry with her for she had longed to be with him again, and had only come to the greenwood to see how he was. All three solemnly crossed the ford in the stream and were soon approaching Friar Tuck's home across the plank that acted as the drawbridge. As they walked Robin asked Marian how she had come to know Friar Tuck, whom Robin still considered a rascal. Marian told him that Friar Tuck was a good friend of Sir Richard at Lee, and it was with his help, and that of Ket the Trow, that Marian had known just where to find Robin that day.

130 As they entered the monk's home a lady rose from her seat. Maid Marian ran to her and embraced her warmly before introducing her to Robin. Her name was Alice de Beauforest, the love of Alan-a-Dale. Alice took Robin's proffered hand, remarking that she had often heard of him – and that Sir Ranulf de Greasby swore every night that he would one day hang Robin Hood from the walls of Hagthorn Castle.

131 Just then Friar Tuck entered and Robin Hood turned his attentions to the monk, who had greatly risen in his estimation, beyond almost any other he had ever known. He shook the monk warmly by the hand and from that moment they became firm friends, though Friar Tuck commented that he had considered Robin Hood his friend ever since he had heard how he and his followers had set fire to Birkencar manor, and then how Robin had managed to trick the sheriff.

132 During their conversation it transpired that Maid Marian had spent a great deal of time in the company of Friar Tuck, who had taught her woodcraft and introduced her to Hob o'the Hill, Ket the Trow and their mother and sisters, and it was through them that she had been kept informed about all that had befallen her love. The sound of a horn outside interrupted their conversation as Little John and the other outlaws returned to the monk's home. They had chased the men-at-arms all the way to the highway beyond Harlow Wood, where they met up with two knights, one of whom wore a shield with a red tower on it, while the other carried a blank white shield.

133 Immediately Robin knew that these two knights were Sir Niger le Grym and the evil Sir Isenbart de Belame himself. Little John and the others had watched until the knights and their men had departed, and had then made their way back to Robin.

Robin Hood, Maid Marian and their companions eat, drink and make merry in Sherwood Forest. Illustration by F.P. Stephanoff in G.A. Hansard's *The Book of Archery* (1845). (*Mary Evans Picture Library*)

A short while later, having eaten the meal prepared for them by Friar Tuck, Robin Hood, Maid Marian and Alice de Beauforest mounted their horses, which had been tended by a waiting-woman, and left Friar Tuck to return to the castle of Sir Richard at Lee where both were staying. As they rode along Robin noted that Alice de Beauforest seemed sad, and remarked on it.

134 Marian told Robin that Alice was sad because her true love Alan-a-Dale had been outlawed, and that she and her father had been forced to agree to Alice's marriage to the evil old knight Sir Ranulf de Greasby. At the mention of the outlawing of Alan-a-Dale, Robin asked how this had been accomplished, whereupon Alice told him that Sir Isenbart de Belame had had him proclaimed outlaw for the killing of Sir Ivo le Ravener. At the same time he had imposed such a heavy fine on Sir Herbrand de Tranmire that it seemed likely Sir Herbrand would be ruined.

135 Robin replied that he had been present when Alan-a-Dale had slain Sir Ivo le Ravener in a fair fight, but he failed to see how the news had reached Sir Isenbart de Belame as the churl who had spied on them had been killed by Ket the Trow. Maid Marian replied that a forester had taken the news to the lord of the Evil Hold, after seeing Alan-a-Dale, his shoulder badly wounded, collect his horse from the glade in which it had been tethered.

136 Robin immediately guessed that the carrier of the false news was none other than Black Hugo, and after he was told that the forester had said no more than that, Robin related the tale of how Little John had robbed him of his meal, and how Robin and Alan-a-Dale had left him trussed to the post of the house. The story caused both Maid Marian and Alice de Beauforest to laugh aloud. Calling to Little John to show himself, Robin introduced him to the Maid Marian and then took Alice to one side and spoke to her about Alan-a-Dale.

137 She told him that Alan-a-Dale had written to her about Robin Hood, and that she feared for his safety now that her marriage to Sir Ranulf de Greasby had been fixed for three days hence on the feast of St James at the church at Cromwell. Robin considered for a moment and then asked Alice de Beauforest if there was anyone she trusted enough to take a message to Alan-a-Dale. She replied that there was one, John (or Jack), the son of Wilkin who lived by the Hoar Thorn at Cromwell. Quickly Robin asked Alice if she had something on her that would identify the bearer immediately as a friend, and Alice slipped a ring from her finger and gave it to Robin. As she did so the waiting-woman, who had been riding a few paces behind, came up to Robin and held out a thick silver ring, asking him to have his man also take this to Jack with the message that if he did not do the Lady Alice's bidding, then he might have his own ring back, for if that were the case then Jack was no match for the likes of Netta o'the Meering.

138 Having devised a plan, Robin called Will the Bowman to his side and quickly told him to ride to Cromwell with the two rings and there find Jack, son of Wilkin. Moments later, Will the Bowman rode away to the east towards the River Trent, while Robin and the remainder of his men escorted Maid Marian and Lady Alice de Beauforest back to the safety and comfort of the castle of Sir Richard at Lee.

5. THE MARRIAGE OF LADY ALICE AND ALAN-A-DALE

139 Jack, son of Wilkin, was a villein at the manor of Sir Walter de Beauforest at Cromwell, where John the Thinne, Sir Walter's steward (also called John the Steward), regarded the lad as one of the most willing of the younger workers on the manor. Jack had come to the notice of Lady Alice de Beauforest many years before, and before the death of his father he had been made one of her falconers. However, after Wilkin's death Jack had had to give up his prized position so that he might work the land in order to keep a roof over his mother's head.

140 As was common practice at that time, Jack had no surname, but was instead simply known as the son of Wilkin, though Wilkin was not his father's true name. His real name was Will, but as he was such a small man, he was commonly called by the diminutive meaning 'Little Will'. Jack himself had various names. He was Jack, son of Wilkin, or Jack Will's son, or Jack Alice's son (after his mother), or Jack-a-Thorn from the old hawthorn that grew next to his home. Today Jack Will's son and Jack Alice's son would be Jack Wilson and Jack Alison.

141 Jack's one burning ambition was to one day become a freeman, just as Nicholas o'the Cliffe and Simon the Fletcher from his very own village had done. He knew from his mother that four generations before, during the reign of Edward the Confessor, his family had indeed been freemen, but their status had been stripped from them by the Norman invaders.

142 Jack had never travelled very far from his home, though the land within a 3-mile radius of Cromwell was as well known to him as the back of his own hand. However, three times during the preceding twelve months Jack had been asked to travel far away from the village, through forests where he knew all manner of evil spirits dwelt, each time taking a message from Lady Alice de Beauforest to her love Alan-a-Dale in his hiding place in the wasteland between Sherwood and Werrisdale. Jack also knew that not all the spirits who dwelt in the forest were evil. Indeed he had heard tell of Sturt of Norwell, a serf who had gone to the aid of a fairy in the forest, and had ended up marrying the fairy's daughter; his descendants were still living as freemen in Norwell, where they were among the village's most respected inhabitants.

143 One of Jack's regular chores was to collect firewood from the edge of the forest. As he tied down the last bundle of wood onto his cart, he was approached by a man who

asked him if he was Jack, son of Wilkin. Cautiously Jack studied the newcomer for a few moments before asking what business it was of the stranger's. With a laugh the man reached into his tunic and placed two rings on the end of his dagger; holding them up, he asked Jack if he recognised them.

144 Jack's hand flew for the handle of his dagger as he saw the rings of Lady Alice de Beauforest and her maid Netta o'the Meering. Angrily he challenged the man to tell him how he had come by the rings, and said that if he had harmed their rightful owners he would kill the man before he could reach for his own weapons. Immediately the man told Jack that he had been given the rings by his own master, who had been given the rings by their owners, and then he repeated the message from Alice de Beauforest. Jack flushed as he listened to Lady Alice's kind words and asked what his task was to be. When the newcomer told him that all he had to do was take him to where Alan-a-Dale was hiding, Jack replied that he would do so willingly, and then asked who his new travelling companion was.

145 The man told Jack that he was Will the Bowman, the comrade of Robin Hood. Upon hearing that his companion was an outlaw Jack was troubled for a moment, but then, as he realised that Will the Bowman could quite easily have killed him if he had wanted to, Jack offered him his hand and they shook on a solemn pledge of friendship.

146 Immediately they set off down the forest path. A short distance from his house Jack fixed a sprig of greenery to the horse's halter and then slapped it on the rump to send it cantering back home, the sprig being a message to his mother that he had once more been sent to run an errand for Lady Alice de Beauforest. A mile further down the road Will the Bowman asked Jack why he had not asked what message came with the silver ring. Jack simply replied that as he was sure it would not be a soft message, he did not want to hear it. When Will the Bowman repeated Netta's words Jack reacted angrily, saying that he did not need the scolding of a maid to undertake any mission for his lady. Stormily he strode off with Will the Bowman following on behind. Neither raised the subject again throughout their journey.

147 On the morning of the wedding, just two days later, all the villeins of the village of Cromwell gathered to watch their young mistress marry the old tyrant Sir Ranulf de Greasby, who came from the fenlands to the east. As they gathered around the church ten men-at-arms rode into the village wearing Sir Ranulf's livery. They rode proudly through the village and took up position at the church porch, five on each side. They smirked at how long it had taken their lord to persuade Lady Alice de Beauforest to marry him, and mused on what had befallen his previous wife. A vibrant and beautiful maiden when she first arrived at Hagthorn Waste, she had run away after two years and was found dead the next morning in Grimley Mere, face down and frozen stiff.

148 As they talked a tall minstrel dressed in a gaudy doublet and patched hose strolled up to the gates of the churchyard and started to make small talk with the villagers gathered there. Seeing him, the men-at-arms called him over and ordered him to play some music suitable for a wedding day. The minstrel duly complied, and before long all the men-at-arms and the villagers were participating in the music. As the third song came to a close, four horsemen rode up to the church, with Sir Ranulf de Greasby at their head.

149 He was an old, grey knight with a red, ugly face and cruel lips. His clothes were the best that money could buy, under a cloak of fine silk. His belt was encrusted with diamonds, and his sword-hilt embellished with many fine gems. The three men who rode with him were younger knights from his castle by Hagthorn Waste. One of them was his nephew Sir Ector of the Harelip, also called Sir Ector de Malstane, whose reputation for cruelty was matched only by that of his uncle.

150 When his men reported that the Lady Alice had yet to arrive at the church, Sir Ranulf de Greasby was all for riding up to the manor and bringing her to the church by force, but he found his way barred by the minstrel, whose name, he said, was Jocelyn. He suggested that he might entertain them while they waited for the maiden to arrive. Gruffly Sir Ranulf de Greasby agreed, adding that if the song were not to his liking then the minstrel would suffer at his hands.

151 Jocelyn the minstrel tuned his lute and then sang a lilting air with a short chorus, which the villagers joined in with. As the first chorus reached an end an eerie, scornful laugh echoed around the churchyard. Everybody, including the minstrel, looked all around to see where the laugh had come from, but as nothing or no one could be seen, Jocelyn continued his song.

152 At the end of the second verse the laugh reverberated around the churchyard once again, this time seeming to be nearer at hand, and more mocking. Sir Ranulf de Greasby turned to the minstrel and asked him for an explanation. Jocelyn could offer none, so Sir Ranulf ordered his men to search the churchyard and the vicinity, but they could find nothing. Hearing this, Sir Ranulf de Greasby turned to Jocelyn and told him that he would know that it was the minstrel himself who was causing the laugh if the same thing were to happen for a third time, and then he ordered Jocelyn to play a third verse of the song.

153 This Jocelyn did, after first protesting his innocence. As the last words of the chorus rang out the laugh returned, loud and fierce, and this time it seemed to come from directly over the heads of Sir Ranulf de Greasby and his men. All looked upwards, but there was nothing to be seen except clouds scurrying across the blue sky. The laugh died down for a moment, and then a croaking laugh came from over the road.

As it approached the church, all the time growing in volume, all those at the church distinctly heard a voice within the laugh cry out 'Colman Grey! Colman Grey!'

154 As he heard this, Sir Ranulf de Greasby shouted that an evil spirit had come to possess him, and jerked his horse's reins so hard that it took fright and galloped around the churchyard with Sir Ranulf still on its back, his whip in his hand. As the horse careered around the churchyard, Sir Ranulf slashed this way and that with the whip as if trying to protect himself from the unseen spirit he thought had come to take him. It was only when Sir Ector of the Harelip saw Lady Alice de Beauforest, her father and their party approaching from the manor house in the distance that he caught hold of his uncle and told him to cease his wild rampage.

155 Seeing his bride approaching in the company of Sir Walter de Beauforest, a friend of the family, Lady Alice's maid and a house villein, Sir Ranulf de Greasby called over Sir Philip de Scrooby, one of the young knights who had accompanied him, and asked him to seek out the minstrel. Sir Philip agreed to find the minstrel if Sir Ranulf de Greasby would pay him with the hound Alisaundre and two merlin hawks named Grip and Fang, all three animals being the old knight's favourite hunting animals. Grudgingly Sir Ranulf agreed to the price, and Sir Philip de Scrooby and two of the men-at-arms rode off just as Lady Alice and her entourage arrived at the gates to the churchyard. In silence they made their way to the entrance to the church, where Lady Alice's maid, Netta o'the Meering, arranged her lady's dress before Sir Walter de Beauforest took his daughter's arm and led her into the church, where the priest was waiting to perform the ceremony.

156 As Sir Ranulf de Greasby took Lady Alice de Beauforest's hand and led her towards the priest, who opened his book in readiness, a movement was seen along one wall

Robin Hood steps betwixt the groom and his bride. Illustration from *The Merry Adventures of Robin Hood* by Howard Pyle.

Robin Hood stops a wedding. Illustration from *A Book of Old English Ballads* by George Wharton Edwards.

and a man stepped into the light of the altar candles. It was the minstrel, but now he held a longbow instead of his lute. The lute was now being carried by a second person, Gilbert of the White Hand, his gaudy doublet replaced by a jerkin of green. Staring hard at Sir Ranulf de Greasby, the minstrel told everyone in the church that the marriage of the Lady Alice de Beauforest to the evil knight was not as God had intended.

157 Sir Ranulf de Greasby was furious that a mere woodsman had the audacity to stand in the way of his marriage and immediately drew his sword, thinking that the man in front of him was Alan-a-Dale, the outlaw whom the Lady Alice de Beauforest loved. As Sir Ranulf stepped forward a croaking voice from the rafters above his head said 'Colman Grey! Colman Grey!' Hearing the words, Sir Ranulf looked upwards, and as he did so a short black arrow pierced him through the throat and he fell dead at the foot of the altar.

158 Even before Sir Ranulf de Greasby's body had hit the ground, the minstrel had raised a horn to his lips and sounded a resounding blast. When the knights and men-at-arms heard the note they realised that the minstrel was none other than Robin Hood. Sir Ector of the Harelip was the first to react. Drawing his sword, he rushed at Robin Hood. As the two engaged in a battle to the death, their swords clashing loudly in the quiet church, the doors burst open and ten of Robin's men poured into the confined space. Immediately they began to do battle with the men-at-arms and the knights.

159 As they fought, a scream echoed around the church and Sir Walter de Beauforest saw that his daughter was being carried off by one of the knights, Sir Bertran le Noir, who had come from Hagthorn Waste that day. Netta o'the Meering was desperately tearing at the knight's clothes in a futile attempt to rescue her lady. The knight struck Netta an almighty blow which rendered her senseless, and made off towards the door just as Robin Hood managed to slay Sir Ector of the Harelip.

160 The knight who had taken hold of Lady Alice de Beauforest had intended to make for the horses and escape before he could be stopped, but as he came out of the church he found his way barred by two men engaged in mortal combat. One was Sir Philip de Scrooby, the knight who had gone in pursuit of the minstrel. The other was unknown to the knight, but Lady Alice immediately recognised him as her love Alan-a-Dale, and she called out to him to save her.

161 Seeing his opponent momentarily distracted by Lady Alice's call, the knight sought to strike Alan-a-Dale a mortal blow, but as he raised his arm Jack, son of Wilkin, struck the knight with his staff. This caused the knight to miss Alan-a-Dale and embed his sword in the ground, whereupon Alan-a-Dale regained his senses and the fight resumed. The lull in the fighting had, however, allowed the knight time to carry Lady Alice de Beauforest to the horses. Knocking her senseless, he threw her across a saddle before mounting and making off, cutting down as he went two villagers who tried to bar his way.

162 Outside the confines of the churchyard Sir Bertran le Noir thought that he had made good his escape, but no sooner had that thought entered his mind than he felt someone leap onto the horse behind him, and before he could do anything about it he saw the glint of a knife in the sun moments before it struck him full in the heart. It was the faithful Jack who had come to the aid of his lady, and as Sir Bertran fell dead Jack took hold of the horse's reins and tumbled the lifeless body of the knight to the ground. Carefully Jack then climbed down and lifted the unconscious body of Lady Alice de Beauforest from the horse.

163 Meanwhile, Alan-a-Dale had managed by a stroke of good luck to duck under Sir Philip de Scrooby's guard and strike him a blow straight to the heart. As Sir Philip fell dead to the ground, Alan-a-Dale set off down the road to where Jack was tending his mistress. She was just reviving as Alan-a-Dale arrived. Lady Alice took Jack by the hand and there and then promised him that from that day forth he would be a freeman, and that her father would give him some land free of all tithe and title.

164 Inside the church the battle had come to an end. Two of Robin Hood's men had met their deaths, but all the knights and men-at-arms had been killed except one. The sole survivor was a man-at-arms who had slipped out of a side door and made off into the

forest like a frightened rabbit. Robin Hood and Sir Walter de Beauforest came out of the church to see Alan-a-Dale leading Lady Alice back towards them, Jack following behind deep in conversation with Netta o'the Meering, who had recovered from the blow she had received and gone to tend to her mistress.

165 Looking around, Robin Hood explained to Sir Walter de Beauforest what had happened that day, and how he now feared that his meddling would place Sir Walter, his lands and his manor under even greater threat from Sir Isenbart de Belame and the knights of the Evil Hold. Sir Walter knew that naught but good could come from the events of the day, and thanked Robin and his men for what they had done. He offered to help them in any way he could, no matter how high the risk, although he acknowledged that he was only a weak man compared to the knights of the Evil Hold, and that at a time when even the king's own sons were fighting among themselves and plunging the whole country into a civil war, there was little he could do on his own to fight tyranny and oppression. Yet, he added, with friends like Robin Hood and his brave band, honest men could sleep at peace in their homes, and villains like the knights of the Evil Hold would forever have to watch their backs.

166 Sir Walter's main concern, however, was for his daughter, the Lady Alice, and what would become of her once Sir Isenbart de Belame learnt of the battle that day. It was agreed that Alice de Beauforest and Alan-a-Dale would go with Robin Hood and his men into the greenwood, where Friar Tuck would marry them after legally publishing the banns of marriage at a church near his cell, after which they would remain with the outlaws until such time as they might be allowed to return freely to their rightful home.

Robin helps Alan-a-Dale to stop the marriage of Alan's sweetheart Alice de Beauforest to Sir Ranulf de Greasby. Illustration by Walter Crane in *Stories of Robin Hood and His Merry Men* by Henry Gilbert. (*Mary Evans Picture Library/Edwin Wallace*)

167 That very night in the great hall of the castle at Wrangby, so rightly called the Evil Hold by all just men, Sir Isenbart de Belame sat at the high table in the company of many others as evil as himself, among them Sir Niger le Grym, Sir Hamo de Mortain, Sir Baldwin the Killer and Sir Roger of Doncaster. All were impatiently waiting for Sir Ranulf de Greasby and his new bride to join them. Suddenly a small black arrow flew over their heads and struck the table just in front of Sir Isenbart de Belame. Sir Niger le Grym was the first to react. Drawing the arrow out of the table, he untied the piece of parchment wrapped around the shaft.

168 On the parchment, written in blood, was a list of names: Sir Roger de Longchamp, Sir Ivo le Ravener, Sir Ranulf de Greasby, Sir Ector de Malstane, Sir Philip de Scrooby and Sir Bertran le Noir. Beneath these were listed all the other knights of the Evil Hold, their names written in black, but each one underlined in blood.

169 Shortly after the death of Sir Ranulf de Greasby and his comrades, and the delivery of the ominous list to the knights of the Evil Hold, King Henry died and his son Richard, popularly known as Coeur de Lion (the Lionheart), came to the throne. Shortly afterwards he set off on his crusade, and some of the knights of the Evil Hold decided to travel east with the king. Sir Isenbart de Belame, however, remained at home, biding his time until he could have his revenge on Robin Hood and all those who had dared stand in his path.

6. SIR HERBRAND DE TRANMIRE

170 Life in Barnisdale Forest was generally kind to Robin Hood and his men, though on occasion, when no travellers had been stopped and charged their toll for some time, Robin would become restless and yearn for the company of someone other than his faithful followers. On one such occasion, Robin sent Little John, Much and Will the Bowman to the Sayles by Ermine Street to see if they could not find some wayfarer to bring back to their camp to share their meal with them.

171 The three men rode off through the greenwood, passing on their way some ruined houses that had once been occupied by Woolgar and Thurstan, two freemen of Danish lineage, whose lands had been unjustly seized by Sir Isenbart de Belame. Woolgar was killed as his family were dragged from their home, and his wife and children had become serfs at the Evil Hold, while Thurstan had fled to the forest vowing that one day he would return and have his vengeance.

172 Finally the three riders came to the place Robin had sent them to, where five roads met. Four of the roads were empty, but on the fifth, that running north to Barnisdale, was a solitary rider, who had come from Pontefract some 7 miles away. Upon closer inspection the three outlaws could see that the rider was a knight dressed in chainmail, a lance in his right hand, his head bent as if in deep thought. As he rode

along he did not at first see Little John, who dismounted and knelt on one knee to greet the knight, telling him that they welcomed him to the greenwood and that their master craved the knight's acceptance of an invitation to dine.

173 The knight stopped in surprise and looked down at the kneeling figure of Little John for some time before asking him who his master was. Little John replied that it was Robin Hood, whereupon the knight answered that as he had heard only good things of this man, he would be honoured to accompany his men and dine with them.

174 Some time later the four riders returned to Robin Hood's camp, where the knight was made welcome and sat down to eat with Robin and his men. After the meal Robin spoke to his guest and asked him, as a knight of obvious honour, to make some payment as a toll for being given free passage through the forest. Rather than take umbrage at such a request, the knight replied that he had very little that he could give Robin Hood, adding that he had no more than half a pound left in all the world.

175 Robin, somewhat disbelieving, told Little John to search the knight's saddle-bags. If the knight was telling the truth, then no levy would be made against him, and if he had need of more then Robin would gladly lend it to him. Moments later Little John returned with a single silver coin in his hand, proof that the knight was indeed true to his word, for that coin was worth just 10 shillings. Accepting that the knight was a man whose word was his bond, Robin took him by the hand and asked how he had fallen on such hard times, for even his armour and his horse showed signs of decay and neglect.

176 The knight told Robin that he had been set upon by the men of the Evil Hold after his son had killed a knight in a fair fight. The dead man had been one of Sir Isenbart de Belame's evil band, and following his death the men of the Evil Hold had descended on the knight and demanded huge payments as compensation; they sought to break him so that they could seize the lands that the knight's family had held for more than a hundred years. Already he had paid them 400 pounds, and when they demanded yet more he had been forced to go to the abbot of St Mary's Abbey to borrow a further 400 pounds. That was where he was heading when he had encountered Little John and the others, who had brought him into the company of Robin and his honourable band of outlaws. If the debt were not repaid to the abbey by the following day then the knight's lands would be forfeit.

177 Robin and his men listened with sad faces to the knight's story. It was a story they had heard from a number of other people during their time in the greenwood. As the knight rose to take his leave, Robin Hood asked him if he knew anyone who would stand surety against a loan. The knight simply laughed and told them that when he had been a man of substance he had had friends a-plenty, but after the plague of the

The unfortunate knight. Illustration from *Tales and Plays of Robin Hood* by Eleanor L. Skinner.

Evil Hold had descended on him, none wanted to know him. Now he only had the Virgin Mary to pledge as surety.

178 At this, Robin took the knight by the hand and told him that he needed no other to hold surety in his eyes, and then, turning to Little John, he told him to go to his treasury and count out 400 pounds, and to make sure that none of the coins was cut so the abbot would not be able to throw out a single coin as bad and thus seize the knight's lands.

179 A short time later Little John returned with a cloth inside which he had carefully placed 400 pounds in gold. He handed the cloth to Robin, who in turn passed it on to the knight, saying that, on the surety of the Virgin Mary, he was lending the money to the knight on the single condition that it be repaid a year and a day from then. As the knight took the money he wept as he thanked Robin for his help, and said he had often heard from his son that Robin Hood was perhaps the most honourable man in all of England.

180 Robin, his curiosity pricked by the mention of the knight's son, asked who it was that spoke so highly of him. The knight replied that his son was Alan-a-Dale, whereupon Robin hugged him as he realised that his guest that day had been none other than Sir Herbrand de Tranmire. Their new friendship was further cemented when Sir Herbrand promised to do all he could to help Robin and his men destroy the wickedness that lay within the confines of the Evil Hold. Then Robin sent Little John

back to the storehouse. He returned a few moments later carrying a fine suit of armour and leading a sturdy horse, both of which Robin presented to Sir Herbrand de Tranmire.

181 When Sir Herbrand was dressed and mounted, he made to leave, but Robin took hold of his reins and remarked that a fine knight such as him could not possibly go to the abbey without a suitable squire in attendance, and who better to serve that task than Little John. So it was agreed, and minutes later Sir Herbrand and Little John rode away from Robin Hood's camp in the heart of Barnisdale Forest and made for St Mary's Abbey. For quite some time the roads they followed were quite empty, as the two rode along discussing the tyranny of the Evil Hold. However, as they turned a corner they came across a group of six men in the road.

182 Five of the men were holding their swords in their hands, while the sixth walked in front wearing only a shirt and holding a cross to his chest. Little John recognised the group as the kin of a wronged person escorting the villain, who had sworn to leave the country, to his ship to make sure that he upheld his oath of exile. As Little John and Sir Herbrand de Tranmire rode up to them, the party stopped and Sir Herbrand asked what the felon had done.

183 The eldest of the five carrying their swords answered that the criminal, whose name was Richard Malbête, had come to their shop in Mercers Row, Pontefract, and there befriended their father John le Marchant, who revelled in hearing the stories Richard Malbête told. One night Richard Malbête had killed their father and made off with a great deal of gold, but little good it did him as they chased him down so ruthlessly that he was forced to seek sanctuary in St Michael's Church, and then abjure before the coroner and leave the country. He added that they were taking the murderer to Grimsby, whence he would leave England never to return.

184 Seeing that the five men were within their rights and only upholding the law, Little John and Sir Herbrand de Tranmire took their leave of them and rode on, finally reaching the gates of York as the very last rays of daylight were fading from the sky and the city gates were about to be closed. Once inside the city they went to an inn that the knight knew, and there they spent the night.

185 The following morning the chapter house of St Mary's Abbey was thronging with people. Abbot Robert took his seat next to the prior, in the company of all the chief officers of the abbey, for this was the regular day on which tenants came to pay their dues. Others in the chapter house that morning included the Sheriff of York, several knights, a king's justice, who was in the area trying cases for the crown, and a number of monks who acted as clerks. They sat at a table crowded with parchments detailing their business that day.

186 Throughout the morning the villeins and tenants came and went, some paying their dues in money, others in goods, and a great many of them complaining about some wrong that had been handed down to them. Every complaint was summarily dismissed by the abbot. About halfway through the morning a tall knight entered the chapter house dressed in half-armour, a hauberk covering his body, his sword slung from a belt around his waist. He was followed by a squire carrying his mace and his helmet. As he approached the table the abbot rose to greet him, for this was Sir Niger le Grym, the abbot's friend and ally, who had come to York that day to see the downfall of Sir Herbrand de Tranmire and to take possession of the lands of Werrisdale in person.

187 At midday the entire party, save the lower members of the order, left the chapter house and went to the great hall, where they seated themselves at a long table on

The abbot receives a plea. Illustration from *The Merry Adventures of Robin Hood* by Howard Pyle.

which a feast had been prepared. Halfway through their meal they were interrupted as Sir Herbrand de Tranmire and his squire Little John made their way over to the table. Sir Herbrand was no longer wearing the clothes that Robin Hood had given him, but rather the old armour that was his own.

188 Sir Herbrand knelt reverently before the abbot, and told him that he had come to him that day to ask for tolerance in the matter of the repayment of the debt of 400 pounds. He asked for a further four months to repay the money. The abbot refused point-blank, whereupon Sir Herbrand turned to the king's justice and implored him to intercede on his behalf. The justice would have none of it, for his position in life was to uphold the law, and as the law stated that Sir Herbrand de Tranmire had to repay his debt on that day, then he would forfeit his lands that very day if the debt were not repaid. The justice would personally see to it that the law was upheld.

189 Next Sir Herbrand turned to the Sheriff of York and implored him to beseech the abbot to allow him more time, but the sheriff refused, so the knight once more turned to the abbot and asked him if, rather than taking his lands from him, he would simply hold them until such time as the debt was repaid, but the abbot would not hear of it. Sir Herbrand de Tranmire then reminded the abbot of their former friendship, and remarked that this must surely test that friendship to the very limits. Being reminded that he had indeed once sworn friendship with him drove the abbot into a frenzy of anger, and he called Sir Herbrand de Tranmire a false and traitorous knight, whereupon Sir Herbrand reacted angrily, saying that the abbot lied. He had never been a false knight, and had fought overseas for his country, as well as in jousts and tournaments before King Henry and the King of Germany.

190 Hearing of the knight's exploits, the justice was moved to speak on Sir Herbrand's behalf. He asked if, rather than accepting the 400 pounds that day, the abbot would accept more money if repayment was delayed. The abbot thought for a moment and then said that he would wait four months and accept a further 200 pounds – 600 pounds in all.

191 Sir Herbrand could hold up the pretence no longer and lashed out in an angry tirade against all those seated around the table, before taking the cloth out of his tunic and emptying the 400 gold pounds onto the table in front of the abbot, who was too surprised to do anything other than sit and gape at the money. The prior rose from his place and quickly counted the money; finding that it was the right amount, he made out a receipt for Sir Herbrand de Tranmire which freed him of any debt to the abbot.

192 Clutching his receipt, Sir Herbrand walked laughing out of the hall followed by Little John. They rode back to the inn, changed their clothes and dined, and then left the city, riding to the west as Sir Herbrand wished to return quickly to Werrisdale to

PRIOR VINCENT

Illustration from *Bold Robin Hood and his Outlaw Band* by Louis Read.

tell his wife all that had befallen him. Little John said that he would continue to ride with him as he feared that Sir Niger le Grym, having been outwitted that day, would seek revenge as they travelled along the road.

193   As they rode they both kept a sharp lookout among the thick trees, but they saw only a few villeins. However, as they climbed the steep ascent towards what was known as Cold Kitchen Rigg a small arrow glanced off Little John's shield and fell to the ground. Sir Herbrand de Tranmire immediately drew his sword. Little John looked down and saw that the bolt was short and had a black shaft – it was a signal that trouble lay ahead. As he looked down two knights charged out of the trees ahead of them, riding headlong down the steep incline. The first knight engaged in battle with Sir Herbrand, while the other bore down on Little John, who only just had time to unsheathe his sword to fend off the first blows. Sir Herbrand ably fought off the first knight's attack and struck him a such crashing blow on his helmet that the knight fell from his horse; his foot caught in his stirrup, and he was dragged away down the hill, the descent surely killing him if the blow hadn't already done so. No sooner had the first knight been dispatched than a third joined the fray, engaging Sir Herbrand even more ferociously than the first.

194 Little John was having a much harder time of it, and it was all he could do to fend off the blows raining down on him. The two men were matched in strength and ability, and just as Little John began to think he might lose the struggle, the knight, his arm raised to deliver a killing blow, suddenly sat bolt upright and then tumbled from his saddle onto the ground. The feathers of a black bolt were all that was visible of the arrow that had entered his body just below the armpit and struck him through the heart.

195 Seeing the second knight fall, the man attacking Sir Herbrand de Tranmire broke off and quickly rode away in the direction of Wrangby and the Evil Hold. Sir Herbrand was all for pursuing him, but he had been wounded, and neither he nor Little John had strength enough left to fight further. Just then a small figure darted across the road ahead of them, startling Sir Herbrand de Tranmire who thought that it might be another attacker.

196 Little John quickly explained that the little figure was a friend of his. Had it not been for his timely warning they would have been caught unaware by the ambush, and Little John himself would be dead now if his little friend's bolt had not killed his opponent. Dismounting, Sir Herbrand de Tranmire went over to the knight on the ground, lifting the visor to reveal the face of Sir Niger le Grym. It was a sight that filled both Little John and Sir Herbrand with delight, for that was one less knight in the Evil Hold to deal with. Little John then retraced his journey down the hill until he came to the horse of the first knight to attack them. He found the dead knight a short distance away.

197 Stripping him of his armour, Little John threw the knight's body over the saddle, and then led the horse back to where Sir Herbrand de Tranmire was waiting on the hillside. He had already stripped the armour from Sir Niger le Grym. The two then set off again, leading the two captured horses, laden with the dead knights, along the road until they came to a deserted chapel. Here they laid the dead knights before the altar and said a prayer for their deliverance. Then they went on again, still with the two horses and the armour of the dead knights, for these were theirs now by rights, through the forest, lodging at an inn overnight before reaching Werrisdale the following day. They were warmly welcomed by Sir Herbrand's wife, Dame Judith.

198 Two days later Little John made ready to leave to return to Robin Hood. Dame Judith gave him provisions for his journey and a gold ring, and Sir Herbrand de Tranmire gave him a strong horse and gold to the value of Sir Niger le Grym's armour and horse (which were Little John's by rights), and bade him farewell, adding that should ever the need arise, especially due to the actions of the evil Duke John in the absence of King Richard, he would gladly join Robin Hood and his comrades, and could arm and bring a hundred men with him.

199 After escaping from Little John and Sir Herbrand de Tranmire, the third knight, whose name was Sir Bernard of the Brake, rode long and hard until he reached the Evil Hold. On the verge of exhaustion, he rode straight into the hall where Sir Isenbart de Belame and his horde were eating. There he told the assembled company about the deaths of Sir Niger le Grym and his comrade. As he described how they had ambushed Sir Herbrand de Tranmire and his squire, a man-at-arms hurried into the hall carrying a short black arrow into which seven notches had been cut, each one stained with blood. The arrow had been shot through the castle's portcullis.

200 Immediately Sir Isenbart de Belame ordered his men to search the area around the castle, but despite their efforts they could find no trace of the person who had shot the arrow into the castle. They searched in vain until darkness fell, forcing them to call off the hunt. As the last man clattered back over the drawbridge and the portcullis was lowered, a small figure emerged from the moat and looked up at the castle. It was Ket the Trow, whom Robin Hood had asked to keep watch on the comings and goings of the evil horde of Wrangby. For an hour or more Ket stayed quite still watching the castle, an arrow notched to his bowstring in the hope that he might yet be able to kill another of the evil men who lived within. But no chance offered itself and so Ket the Trow made his way silently back to the forest. Climbing to the top of the tallest tree, from where he could watch the Evil Hold, he settled down to rest, sleep coming to him as the very last light went out in the castle.

7. REUBEN OF STAMFORD

201 It was winter in the Black Wood, and many of Robin's men had sought winter lodgings with families in the villages surrounding the forest. Some, however, had decided to remain under the protection of the greenwood, and had moved their camp from the open into one of the many caves in an area that contained numerous standing stones and earth barrows. Robin Hood and the twelve men closest to him had spent some time in the company of Sir Walter de Beauforest, but they too had returned to the confines of the forest a few miles to the east of Mansfield in a place known as Barrow Down. Here Robin and his men occupied one of the numerous barrows, which kept them dry and warm, and hid them from the eyes of those who, even through the worst weather, continued to hunt for them.

202 Every day the outlaws would fan out around their camp to look for signs that someone had approached their camp during the night. It was on one of these sorties that Will the Bowman came across the signs of a youth's passage through the forest. He carefully followed the trail until he heard a low sobbing sound in the trees ahead. Silently he crept up to a small clearing where he saw a girl picking blackberries from a bramble-bush and placing them in a worn basket.

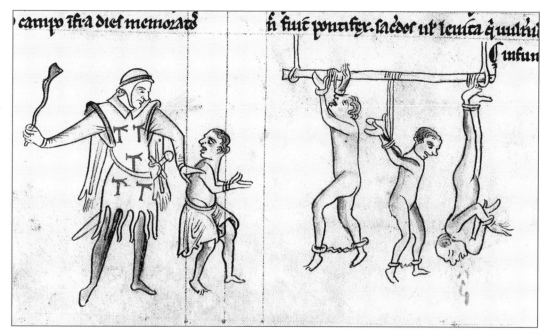

Tortures depicted by Matthew Paris in his *Chronica Majora*, Corpus Christi College, Cambridge, Ms 16 f.44v. *(The Master and Fellows of Corpus Christi College, Cambridge)*

203   As the girl worked, the tears flowed freely down her face, but her sobs were strangely muted as if she were afraid of being overheard. Her hands were torn and bleeding from the thorns on the bush, and her feet, which were bare, were blue from the frost. Will the Bowman watched her for a few moments and then strode purposefully into the clearing. The girl started and clutched her basket to her as she turned and stared in terror at the newcomer. Then she threw herself at Will the Bowman's feet and beseeched him to kill her there and then, and no longer to search for her father, who was near death.

204   Looking down, Will the Bowman recognised the girl as a Jewess, and he immediately understood her fear of discovery, since the Jews in York had been mercilessly slaughtered by Richard Malbête. He spoke gently to the girl, telling her that she had nothing to fear, for he was not like those she sought to escape from; helping her to her feet, he asked her to take him to where her father was hidden.

205   The girl led the way through the thick undergrowth until they came to a chalky cliff. There, in a large cave, screened from view by some dense bushes, lay the girl's father on a bed of bracken, his face drawn and white. For a moment both Will the Bowman and the girl thought that he was dead, but as they entered the cave the old man woke up and the girl ran to his side and took his hand. For a few moments they spoke together until the old man became aware of Will's presence. Immediately his eyes widened in fear and he began to tremble.

206 Will the Bowman quickly crossed to the old man and knelt down beside him, assuring him that neither he nor his daughter had anything to fear from him. Seeing that both were near the point of starvation, Will reached into his pouch and pulled out some bread and slices of venison which he gave to the girl. She fed her father before taking anything herself, and once the food had been devoured Will was pleased to note that both had a far better colour than before. He knew, though, that without warmth and attention they would both die. He told them that he would go back to his master and bring help for them.

207 The old man thanked Will, and asked him who his beneficent master was. When Will replied that it was Robin Hood, the old man told Will to take his master greetings from Reuben of Stamford and his daughter Ruth, and said that if Robin Hood would help him and his daughter to reach their kin in Nottingham, then he and his men would earn the gratitude not only of Reuben and Ruth, but also of all the other Jews in that city.

208 Will the Bowman thanked Reuben for his kind words, and said that the only gratitude and thanks Robin Hood required was the knowledge that he was helping the oppressed. With that, Will left the cave and quickly made his way back to Barrow Down, where he told Robin and the others about the old Jew and his daughter, their flight from the terrors of York, and their hopes of reaching their kin in Nottingham.

209 Robin thought for a moment and then told Will the Bowman to take two horses and transport Reuben of Stamford and his daughter Ruth to the Lynchet Lodge on Wearyall Hill. Will did as he was bidden, and soon the old man and his daughter were safely ensconced in the lodge on the side of the hill, where they were gradually nursed back to health by Robin Hood and his men.

210 At last, when Reuben had almost recovered his strength, Robin Hood felt able to ask him about the events in York. Reuben related how the trouble had started when good King Richard had been crowned at Westminster and then immediately announced that he was to leave on the crusade. Many of the knights who chose to accompany the king owed great sums of money to the Jews, and so before they left they incited the crowd to turn upon the Jews and burn them out, by so doing destroying all records of outstanding debts.

211 Before the king departed, he rounded up the ringleaders of the riot and either hanged them or had them branded with hot irons. Yet not one month after the king had left, the trouble began again in towns and cities across the land. Many lords and knights had decided to join their king in the Holy Land, and before they went they once again roused the rabble against the Jews, the worst troubles being in Stamford, Lynn and Lincoln. Reuben had been living in Lincoln at that time, but had got word of the coming trouble and quickly left for York before the riots broke out.

A multangular tower in York. (*Mick Sharp Photography*)

212 In York a baron by the name of Alberic de Wisgar had borrowed a great sum of money from Rabbi Eliezer, the leading member of the Jewry in York at that time, and being an evil man Alberic sought to find a way out of repaying his debt. When he heard what had been happening in the other towns and cities, he incited the people of York to revolt against the Jews, in which task he was helped by one Richard Malbête, a man whom Robin Hood and many of his men had already encountered. All the Jews fled for safety to the castle, and there they were besieged by the local population, knights and peasants alike. For three days the Jews, armed with nothing more than lumps of rock torn from the castle walls, managed to fight off the crowds, but eventually they could hold out no more and the castle was overrun.

213 Many of the Jews killed their loved ones and then took their own lives to save themselves from Richard Malbête's butchery, but Reuben had not been able to do likewise, and so had found a place where he and his daughter Ruth might hide in the hope that they would remain undiscovered. From their hiding place they had watched the dreadful massacre. When one Jew, by the name of Ephraim ben Abel, had pleaded with Richard Malbête to spare his life, that vile man had simply beheaded him where he knelt. When all the Jews in the castle were dead, the rabble ran to the cathedral, where they took out and burnt all the records of the money that had been lent. Thus they were freed from their obligations.

214 Reuben of Stamford then told them how he and Ruth had been discovered some time later by a compassionate man-at-arms, who smuggled them out of the castle and disguised them as soldiers so that they might leave the city. He then guided them through the forest and put them on the road to Nottingham, telling them as he

departed that he had wanted no part in the massacre, and that even now the king's justices were descending on York to punish the perpetrators. The knights had already left for the crusade, and those who knew they could definitely be recognised had fled northwards towards Scotland. Of Richard Malbête he had heard nothing, though rumour said that he was heading for Nottingham, to be taken into the employ of the sheriff there.

215 Robin listened to all that was said with a great sadness, and when Reuben of Stamford had finished speaking he asked how he might be of assistance. Reuben replied that he had been on his way to Nottingham where he had another daughter and a son, who would surely be grieving for him as dead. If Robin could take a message to them then he would be forever in his debt.

216 Robin immediately sent Will the Bowman to Nottingham with a message that Reuben had given him, a small part of it being in Hebrew so that Will would be recognised as a friend rather than a persecutor. Dressed in the lowly attire of a pilgrim, lest he be identified by anyone he had stopped for tolls in the forest, Will entered the city of Nottingham through the Bridlesmith Gate an hour before sunset and made his way slowly through the streets of the city towards the house of Silas ben Reuben, Reuben's son, who was one of the chief men of the Jewry of Nottingham.

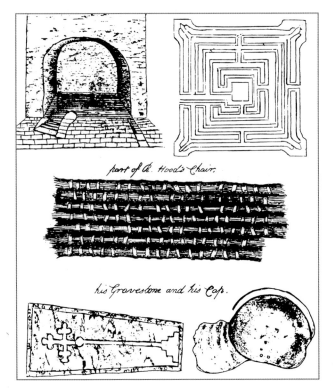

The Robin Hood relics at St Anne's Well, Nottingham. After drawings by John Throsby, *c.* 1797. From R. Thoroton, *Antiquities of Nottinghamshire*, edited by Throsby, 1797.

217 Before long Will the Bowman came to the street he was seeking and knocked on the ninth door he came to, as he had been instructed. When a wicket in the door opened and he was asked to give some sign of recognition, Will repeated the Hebrew words that Reuben of Stamford had taught him. Immediately the bolts on the door were drawn back and Will the Bowman was pulled into the house, the door being quickly rebolted behind him. The man he faced was Silas ben Reuben himself. Upon hearing the good news of his father and sister, Silas gave thanks to God in Hebrew, and then offered a reward to both Robin Hood and Will the Bowman. For the former there was a green leather baldric emblazoned with pearls and precious stones, while Will accepted a knife of the finest Spanish steel.

218 Silas ben Reuben offered Will the Bowman accommodation for the night, but Will answered that he would rather go to a tavern he knew near the gate so that he might slip out of the city at first light when the gates were opened for the day. Silas thanked him once again for the news of his father and sister, and told him that he would meet with Robin Hood and his kin at the prearranged place a few days hence.

219 After bidding him farewell, Will the Bowman slipped out of the house and started to make his way towards the tavern, but as he went he became aware of two men some paces ahead of him who seemed to change their pace as Will did, and constantly looked behind them to make sure that Will was still there. As Will grew suspicious, and grasped the handle of the knife given to him by Silas ben Reuben, a hand took hold of his shoulder and pulled him into an alleyway, where he was greeted as a friend of Silas ben Reuben's and shown a short cut to the tavern that would take him well away from the spies who wished to persecute not only the Jews, but also all those who associated with them.

220 Will the Bowman thanked the stranger and quickly made his way to the tavern by the city gate without further trouble. There he ate and drank his fill, and as night fell he made his way upstairs to the communal sleeping room where he found himself a spot in the corner and lay down to sleep.

221 Will the Bowman stirred early the following morning, even before the first light of dawn, and picked his way carefully across the room, stepping over the sleeping forms of the other people in the room. But as he made his way to the head of the stairs he caught a sleeping man with the heel of his foot, causing the man to wake and ask why he was awake so early in the morning. Will replied that he was a poor pilgrim travelling to the holy shrine at Walsingham, a long journey that demanded an early start, but the man chose not to trust him and followed him down the stairs to where three other men were waiting.

222 As they reached the foot of the stairs the three other men approached Will the Bowman, two holding him firmly while the third inspected his left hand, holding it out to show the corn on his forefinger that indicated frequent use of the bow. Immediately the fourth man, who was obviously the leader, commanded the men to seize Will the Bowman, exclaiming that at last they had managed to trap one of Robin Hood's men. Will was far quicker than the three slow-witted men who held him, and shaking off his pilgrim's cloak he sprinted for the door, where he started to lift the heavy bar from across the door.

223 The four men soon regained their thoughts and leapt on Will, who turned to fight. He fended off one man with the bar from the door, but was soon outnumbered and the other three managed to hold him. When the innkeeper entered the room to see what all the noise was about, the leader told him to fetch some rope, which he did, and a few minutes later Will the Bowman was secured. The door was flung open and Will the Bowman was led away to the prison, though as he was taken away the innkeeper signalled to him that word of his capture would be taken to Robin Hood.

224 Good to his word, the innkeeper sent a man into the forest minutes after the city gates had been opened for the day. All through the day the man travelled through the forest until he was met by Kit the Smith, who, upon hearing of Will's misfortune, took the man to meet Robin Hood. He told his story again to Robin, and said that even as he was leaving the city he had seen the timbers and the rope being brought to build a gallows – gallows that the Sheriff of Nottingham felt certain would see the end not only of Will the Bowman, but also a great many others of Robin Hood's men. His confidence was boosted by the fact that he had just taken into his employ a crafty thief-taker by the name of Captain Bush, or Beat the Bush, though most people simply referred to him as the Butcher.

225 As soon as Robin Hood's men heard that Will the Bowman was to be hanged before the gates of the city the following morning, they immediately roused themselves to go to the rescue of their kinsman, even if that meant they had to tear down the whole city.

226 Meanwhile, back in Nottingham Will the Bowman had been interrogated by the sheriff and his new aide, but they had gathered nothing from him and so had thrown him into the prison to await his death the following morning. As Will was led away, the sheriff began to pace uneasily up and down the hall, at which Captain Bush proposed a plan that would lead the sheriff straight to Robin Hood and the rest of his men. However, though initially interested, the sheriff would have nothing to do with the plan once he heard that it meant freeing Will the Bowman and following him back into the greenwood.

227 Seeing that it was fruitless to pursue the idea any further, Captain Bush instead suggested that it might be better to stir up the people of Nottingham against the Jews, with whom Robin Hood and his men were so obviously involved. This plan was not well received either, as the sheriff had no desire to have his lands confiscated by the king's justice – the fate of the ringleaders in Lincoln and York – and even went so far as to accuse his new aide of plotting against him.

228 Captain Bush knew that it would be pointless to pursue the matter any further and left to check on the construction of the gallows from which Will the Bowman would swing the following morning. However, rather than going straight to the Northgate, where the gallows were being constructed, Captain Bush went to the market-place and told one of his men, Cogg the Earless, to keep a close watch on Silas ben Reuben. Bush felt certain that the Jew would leave the city soon to meet Robin Hood, and he wanted to be able to arrange an ambush. In truth, his intention was not to capture Robin Hood, but rather to capture Reuben of Stamford and extract from him the secret of where Rabbi Eliezer had buried his vast treasure.

229 From the market-place Captain Bush went to the Northgate, which he passed through before climbing the small hill, appropriately called Gallow's Hill, on the top of which the gallows were nearing completion. Satisfied with what he saw, Captain Bush returned to the city and to his lodgings.

230 The following morning was cold and overcast. Outside the city walls the gallows stood ready for their grisly task, while by the gate stood an old palmer who occasionally glanced up at the gallows with tears in his eyes. Ten years previously this man had left Birkencar after killing a man and had gone to Rome to expiate his crime, and then travelled on into the Holy Land. Just three days earlier he had returned to Birkencar, and from there had hurried to Nottingham via Ollerton, in the hope that he would be able to speak with Will the Bowman again, for this man was none other than Will's elder brother.

231 As the old man stood and waited, the gates to the city were opened and twelve men-at-arms came through, their swords drawn. Between them strode Will the Bowman, bound in strong rope, his head held defiantly high. Behind these men walked the Sheriff of Nottingham in his robes of office, and beside him was Captain Bush, with a cruel smile of triumph across his face. A short distance behind them followed a man with a ladder, and a small group of townsfolk who came to see the gallant Will of the Stuteley hanged that cold and cheerless morning.

232 The party climbed the hill and Will of the Stuteley was placed beneath the arm of the gallows. The ladder was put against the upright and a man hurried up it to throw the rope over the arm. As the preparations for his hanging were being made, Will the

Bowman scanned the countryside in the hope of seeing the green-clad forms of his comrades-at-arms erupting from the forest, but instead all he saw was the old palmer hurrying up the hill towards him. Sensing that all was lost, Will turned to the Sheriff of Nottingham and asked a boon of him, that he be allowed to die fighting with a sword in his hand rather than by the rope. The sheriff laughed coldly and refused.

233   As the preparations to hang Will the Bowman were completed, the palmer forced his way through the cordon of sheriff's men and pressed on until he was able to place his hands on Will's shoulders. As he looked him straight in the eye, the two brothers greeted each other warmly, only for Captain Bush to roughly push the palmer to the ground and kick him savagely.

234   Worried that at any time Robin Hood might appear at the forest's edge, which lay but a short distance away, the Sheriff of Nottingham barked orders to Captain Bush to hurry up with the execution. From the arm above the coiled rope was lowered and the noose placed around Will the Bowman's neck. As the slack was taken up, the noose tightened ferociously and Will gasped. But just as he was about to be hauled into the air a stone flew out of some bushes near at hand and struck Captain Bush squarely on the temple, knocking him senseless. Even before Captain Bush had slumped to the ground, Little John and Ket the Trow, who had so accurately thrown the stone, were running past the Sheriff of Nottingham's men up to Will the Bowman. Quickly they cut his bindings.

235   Recovering their senses, the men-at-arms rushed towards Little John, but he deftly parried the first blow with his staff and ripped the sword out of the soldier's hand.

Little John hastily cut Will Stuteley's bonds. Illustration from *Bold Robin Hood and his Outlaw Band* by Louis Read.

He threw the sword to Will the Bowman and then took a second sword from another soldier whom Ket the Trow had laid low, and back to back the two outlaws fought off the sheriff's men. Sensing danger, the Sheriff of Nottingham started to back away, though as he did so he vigorously encouraged his men to kill the two outlaws. As the fight continued, with neither side giving ground, three arrows suddenly struck the men-at-arms. Two of them fell dead instantly, while the third was wounded so badly that he too would soon succumb. The other men-at-arms turned and saw Robin Hood and his men quickly advancing towards them out of the forest, and straight away they fled back through the gates of Nottingham. Meanwhile, Ket the Trow had recovered the rope used to bind Will the Bowman, and was now using it to secure the unconscious Captain Bush.

236 Robin and his men soon covered the distance from the forest edge to Gallow's Hill, and amid the great rejoicing that Will had been saved, it was discovered that the man Ket the Trow had bound was none other than Richard Malbête, who had been masquerading under the name of Bush. Now he would receive the justice he so rightly deserved.

237 Robin Hood was quick to order his men to return to the forest lest the Sheriff of Nottingham should return with reinforcements from the castle, and before long the outlaws and their prisoner were safe beneath the canopy of the greenwood. After a joyous reunion with his brother, Will the Bowman told Robin that he had arranged for Silas ben Reuben to go to the Hexgrove, also known as the Witchgrove, on the high road by Papplewick, at two o'clock that very afternoon. As time was therefore of the essence, Robin asked Ket the Trow to travel back to Barrow Down and lead Reuben of Stamford and his daughter Ruth to the appointed meeting place. Robin and his men would go there directly.

238 Robin Hood and his party moved off towards the Hexgrove. Richard Malbête had now regained consciousness and was berating Robin and his men as common criminals who would one day swing for their crimes. About half a mile from Hexgrove one of Robin's many scouts ran up to the outlaws with a message to Robin that Dick the Reid had spotted six archers in the company of a richly dressed man riding at great speed along the road towards the Hexgrove, adding that he thought they would reach the trees at about the same time as Robin and his men. Having relayed his message, the scout disappeared back into the depths of the forest. As it happened, Robin and his men were the first to arrive and secreted themselves among the trees of the grove.

239 It was only a matter of a few minutes before the seven horsemen entered the clearing. The leader was a man of obvious rank, wearing clothes that denoted his high position, and with a face that left no one in any doubt of his authority and

power. The six riders who accompanied him were archers, who wore jerkins and long boots that reached halfway up their thighs. Robin watched as they crossed the glade and then, when they were no more than a dozen paces from him, he stepped out into their path, pulling the bound Richard Malbête with him. The leading rider reined his horse to a rapid halt and looked down at Robin Hood and his prisoner, and then, pointing at the bound figure of Richard Malbête, he commanded his men to seize him.

240 Robin held up his hand and told the rider that the man was his prisoner, and none would take him from him. Somewhat taken aback, the rider glared down at Robin and told him that he was Sir Laurence of Raby, a marshal of the king's justice, and that the man Robin held was wanted to answer the most serious crimes, crimes for which he would forfeit his life. Robin simply laughed, whereupon Sir Laurence of Raby told his men again to seize the prisoner and, if he chose to stand in their way, to deal with the upstart as they saw fit.

241 All six of the archers dismounted and made their way towards Robin, who calmly put his fingers to his mouth and whistled shrilly. The six archers stopped abruptly as twenty of Robin's men appeared from their hiding places, each holding an arrow notched to his bowstring. At this, Sir Laurence of Raby lost his temper and accused Robin and his men of standing in the path of the king's justice, a crime for which he would see them pay dearly.

242 Robin simply replied that he did not stand in the path of *true* justice, but as he had been on the wrong end of the so-called king's justice himself, he thus placed little faith in it. He did, however, add that he could see Sir Laurence of Raby was a true man and suggested that he should bide a while with the outlaws, so he could oversee the justice they intended to hand out to Richard Malbête, and ensure it was true and legal.

243 Sir Laurence of Raby smiled warmly down at Robin, whom he had recognised as soon as he stepped into the road in front of him, and said that as he knew Robin Hood to be a fair and just man, he would rest with him and his stalwart men and sit in judgement with Robin over Richard Malbête. At these words the outlaws lowered their weapons and stood passing the time with the marshal's archers.

244 Minutes later they were joined in the clearing by Ket the Trow, leading four other outlaws and Reuben of Stamford with his daughter Ruth. As soon as the girl saw Richard Malbête she screamed that he was the man who had been responsible for the slaughter of her people in York. Robin turned to Reuben and asked him if this was the case. Reuben calmly and clearly replied that it was, he himself having witnessed Richard Malbête killing men, women and children with relish.

245 Satisfied with the reply, Robin turned to Sir Laurence of Raby and asked him for what crimes the king's justice sought Richard Malbête. The marshal replied that he had committed many crimes, but was especially wanted for the death of Ingelram, the king's messenger at Seaford, the death of John le Marchant in Pontefract, and the theft of a pair of spurs from the house where the king slept in Gisors, France, but worst of all was his leadership of the riots against the Jews of York and Lincoln. As he finished speaking he looked straight into the eyes of Richard Malbête and, in unison with Robin, condemned him to be hanged.

246 Five minutes later the marshal bade Robin farewell as he looked for the last time at the lifeless body of Richard Malbête swinging gently on the rope thrown over the lowest bough of a massive oak tree. No sooner had Sir Lawrence and his six archers departed than Robin and his men were joined in the clearing by Silas ben Reuben and his men. After greeting his father and his sister warmly, and thanking Robin for all he had done, the party set off along the road for Godmanchester in the company of twelve outlaws, who were to act as their guides and guards until they safely reached their destination.

247 News of the justice handed out by Robin Hood and the king's justice in the forest that day travelled far and wide throughout the counties of Nottinghamshire, Lincolnshire, Yorkshire and Derbyshire. Wherever the news spread, men who had never done a wrong thing revelled in the telling, and those with secrets they wished to keep hidden trembled in fear.

8. THE GOLDEN ARROW AND THE DEATH OF THE SHERIFF

248 On the day that Sir Herbrand de Tranmire was due to repay the debt of 400 pounds to Robin, the outlaws waited impatiently at their camp in the heart of Barnisdale Forest. Midday came and went, but there was no sign of the knight, and Robin was growing restless. He called Little John to him and told him to travel to Ermine Street, where he had encountered the poor knight the year before, and see what he could find. Little John immediately set off in the company of Arthur-a-Bland, Will the Bowman and Much the miller's son, and in their absence Robin sat impatiently in his camp making arrows.

249 At length a scout ran into the camp and told Robin that Little John and his party were returning in the company of four monks, six archers and seven sumpter horses. As they rode into the camp Robin took one look at the leading monk and laughed out loud, for it was none other than the wicked Abbot Robert of St Mary's Abbey. Quickly the four monks were taken into the midst of the camp while the six archers were held securely at the periphery. Little John went to one of the sumpter horses and shortly returned with a bag in which, he informed Robin, he had found exactly 800 pounds.

Robin stops the monks as they ride through Sherwood Forest. Illustration by Petherick in *Robin Hood's Ballads* (1867), p. 27. (*Mary Evans Picture Library*)

250 Robin exclaimed that the Virgin Mary had indeed held surety for the loan owed to him, and had even had the grace to repay him twice the sum owed. When the abbot asked what Robin meant by that he explained that he had lent the money to Sir Herbrand de Tranmire to repay the foul abbot. Seeing the horror on the abbot's face as he realised that he had been repaid by an outlaw, Robin remarked that not only had he helped in the repayment of the unjust debt, but he had also had a hand in killing two of the three knights of the Evil Hold who had attempted to ambush Sir Herbrand and his squire – at which point he introduced Little John to the abbot as that very squire.

251 The abbot remained silent as he listened, his mood turning blacker by the minute as he realised how he and the lords of Wrangby had been tricked out of the lands they sought to take possession of.

252 Robin and his men then entertained the abbot and his men to a sumptuous feast, after which Robin told the abbot that he must hear the outlaws' confessions. The abbot refused, so Robin had him tied to a tree like a common criminal, and told him that he would remain there, with neither food nor water, until he changed his mind. The abbot remained resolute at first, and only yielded when the other monks in his party beseeched him to do as asked so that they might be allowed to return to the safety of the abbey. The abbot celebrated mass with the outlaws and then reverently listened to their confessions.

253 As the last confession was being heard a scout entered the camp and told Robin that a knight and twenty men-at-arms were approaching the camp. Robin guessed who the knight was, and sure enough moments later Sir Herbrand de Tranmire rode into the camp and greeted Robin Hood and his men, and then, with some surprise, greeted Abbot Robert.

254 Robin told Sir Herbrand de Tranmire that the Virgin Mary had seen good her surety and had already doubly repaid the debt due that day. When Sir Herbrand asked what he meant, Robin explained how the abbot had arrived in the forest with 800 pounds upon his person, which he had yielded in full payment of the debt. The abbot could stand no more and begged to be allowed to return to the abbey, so Robin told his men to guide the fat monk and his party back to the road that would lead them to St Mary's Abbey.

255 In the camp Robin refused to take the 400 pounds the knight had brought to repay the outlaw, but gratefully accepted the gift of 100 longbows and 200 steel-tipped arrows. The knight and his men-at-arms spent the night in the greenwood with Robin and his men, and the following day departed to return to their manor, while Robin and his men went deeper into the forest. There was to be no trace left of the camp Abbot Robert had been taken to, as Robin knew the abbot would have no qualms about revealing his whereabouts to the evil knights of Wrangby.

256 However, Abbot Robert had been so shamed by the experience in the forest that he refused to speak of it to anyone, and within a month had fallen sick. He never recovered from the illness that plagued him, and the following spring he died and was buried by the monks of the abbey. They chose one of their own order to replace the abbot, and then sent him to London to be approved by the High Chancellor William de Longchamp, who was acting as regent while King Richard was away on the crusade.

257 William de Longchamp, however, did not accept the new abbot of St Mary's Abbey, and instead, urged on by his cousin Sir Isenbart de Belame, he appointed his nephew Robert de Longchamp to be the new abbot. Almost immediately, following the advice of his uncle, Robert de Longchamp began to plot against Robin Hood and

sought to ally himself with many of the knights who had encountered the outlaw and fared poorly. Soon his allies included the lords of the Evil Hold, Sir Guy of Gisborne and Ralph Murdach, the Sheriff of Nottingham.

258　Many ambushes were laid and many raids launched deep into the greenwood, but on every occasion the outlaws gained the upper hand. The knights lost numerous men but Robin did not lose a single one, and those who were injured recovered speedily, for their wounds were light. At length an uneasy peace seemed to cover the land, and Robin and his men lived at ease in the depths of the greenwood. On many occasions, in heavy disguise, they ventured into the towns and cities so that they might learn what was afoot.

259　On one such occasion, when Robin and Much the miller's son were in Doncaster, they heard a crier proclaim that the Sheriff of Nottingham was to hold an archery competition for all the archers of the land, and the prize for the best archer in England beyond the Trent was to be an arrow with a shaft of silver and feathers of red gold. Both Robin and Much immediately suspected that this was another of the sheriff's plots to lure them into a trap, but still Robin determined to go and win the prize. Quickly they hurried back to the Stane Lea (where the outlaws had their camp at that time), and over the course of the next few days they laid their plans.

260　Robin would disguise himself as a vagabond and take part in the competition along with six other outlaws who had proved themselves worthy, while the remainder of the outlaws would enter the city to be ready for any surprises the sheriff might try to spring. Each man would enter the city via a different gate at a different time so that no one would suspect that they were in fact together.

261　The relevant day came and the outlaws mingled unnoticed among the throngs of people who descended on Nottingham to witness the archery tournament. The roads from Ollerton and Mansfield were full of people coming to see the spectacle. All made their way to a level piece of ground to the north of the city, not far from the gallows where Will the Bowman had almost met his death.

262　A rough scaffold of seats had been erected near the arena's target area, and there sat the Sheriff of Nottingham with his wife Dame Margaret, the officers of the city, and numerous knights from Nottingham and further afield. Nearby stood the marshals, who would oversee the tournament and ensure that the rules were followed.

263　The first challenge was to shoot at a broad target placed at 220 yards distance.* One hundred archers were to take part, each man being allowed three shots; those who

---

* The distance would have been paced out, each pace approximating to 1 yard.

Left: Illustration from *Bold Robin Hood and his Outlaw Band* by Louis Read.

Right: Illustration from *Bold Robin Hood and his Outlaw Band* by Louis Read.

did not get two of their three arrows within a certain ring on the target were not allowed to shoot again. After each round the target was moved 10 yards further away, and by the time it had been placed at 300 yards there were just twenty archers left in the contest. They included Robin Hood, Little John, Scadlock, Much the miller's son, Gilbert of the White Hand and Reynold, the seventh outlaw having been eliminated in a previous round.

264 The target was now removed and a wand set up in its place, the aim being to strike the wand. By the end of the first round of shooting at the wand seven of the remaining twenty had been forced out, among them Scadlock and Reynold. The wand was moved progressively further away, and by the time it reached 400 yards there were only seven archers left in the competition: Robin Hood, Gilbert of the White Hand, three bowmen in the service of the Sheriff of Nottingham, a man-at-arms of Sir Gosbert de Lambley, and an old man who went by the name of Rafe of the Billhook.

265 These seven were next to fire at roavers, targets that were set up at various points so that the archer had to use all his skills to judge the distance and thus make the best

shot. Watkin, the bailiff of Nottingham, called the seven to their mark, the first three to shoot being the sheriff's men-at-arms.

266 The first two missed the wand and were eliminated, but the third hit the top of it and thus progressed to the next round. Of the others, all came close, but it was only Robin who managed to hit the mark, actually splitting the wand in two. The two remaining competitors, Robin Hood and the sheriff's man, whose name was Luke the Red, then continued to shoot, but they appeared equally matched as in each round both managed to hit the wand. At this, the sheriff asked the two archers to come up with a method for determining which was the better, for they could not share the prize.

267 Robin suggested that they should turn their backs as the wand was set up, and then, when they turned, a man should count to three whereupon they must fire or be eliminated. Luke the Red agreed to the contest, though he freely admitted that he had only seen such a feat achieved once before, and that was by Old Bat the Bandy, chief archer to Stephen of Gamwell.

268 Luke the Red elected to go first and turned his back as the wand was set up. Then Watkin told him to turn and slowly counted to three, whereupon Luke the Red fired his arrow. It fell short of the mark. Then it was Robin's turn. He turned his back as the wand was set up, and then Watkin told him to turn and quickly counted to three. Robin let his arrow fly as the word 'three' was spoken, and watched as it flew straight and true and split the wand in two. A huge cheer went up as the sheriff's horn was sounded to announce the awarding of the prize.

269 Robin calmly walked towards the Sheriff of Nottingham and there, on bended knee, received the silver arrow from Dame Margaret, who instantly recognised Robin but bit her lip so that she did not betray the archer's true identity. Something in her actions, however, made the sheriff suspicious. He called Watkin over to him and told him to confront the winning archer, who had by this time made his way through the crowd and was now in the midst of his own men.

270 As Watkin forced his way towards him, he called out that he was arresting Robin Hood in the name of the king. Even as he spoke the words Little John picked him up and threw him senseless to the ground. Realising they had been discovered, one of the outlaws blew a strong blast on his horn, and quickly all the outlaws came together, forming ranks against the sheriff's men gathered on the opposite side of the arena. Bystanders fled for safety as flight after flight of arrows raced across the field.

271 The first flight of arrows from the sheriff's men caused no injuries, though the return volley from the outlaws was so thick that the sheriff's men scattered in a vain attempt to escape the deadly arrows raining down on them. Slowly the outlaws,

Robin's golden prize. Illustration in *Robin Hood's Ballads* (1867), p. 191. (*Mary Evans Picture Library*)

keeping their ranks, backed towards the forest, but it was over a mile away. Flurry after flurry of arrows crossed between the two opposing factions, and as they retreated the outlaws saw a rider galloping towards the castle, a sure sign that the sheriff had sent for reinforcements.

272 As they retreated Little John fell to the ground with an arrow in his leg, but Robin would not leave him and Much lifted the huge man across his shoulders and carried him out of harm's way. Before long Robin saw a number of horsemen issue forth from the city gates, the Sheriff of Nottingham at their head. Their intention was clearly to keep them out of the forest and trap them in the open. Quickly Robin looked around and saw a small clump of trees that would provide them with some shelter; only a short distance further stood the castle of Sir Richard at Lee.

273 Rapidly now the outlaws retreated, and before long they reached the safety of the clump of trees, where they could better hold the sheriff's men at bay. Robin knew that they could easily make the distance to the castle of Sir Richard at Lee, but he was reluctant to draw his friend into a dispute with the Sheriff of Nottingham and the evil knights of Wrangby. Instead he concentrated on controlling the sheriff's men until nightfall, when he hoped the outlaws would be able to slip back into the safety of the forest.

274 The plan was a sound one, but the riders Robin had seen coming out of the city gates must have realised what was in Robin's mind, and they rode to the rear of the trees so as to cut off the outlaws' only possible escape route. As Robin pondered their predicament, he saw a solitary knight riding down the hill from Sir Richard at Lee's castle. The knight proved to be none other than Sir Richard himself, who implored Robin to seek sanctuary with him. At first Robin refused, saying that if he did so then the Sheriff of Nottingham and the knights of the Evil Hold would have a legitimate reason to dispossess him, but Sir Richard at Lee would not take no for an answer and at last Robin agreed.

275 The distance to the castle was not great, and it was lucky for the outlaws that it was close at hand, for they only just managed to reach the edge of the moat before the riders from Nottingham, under the leadership of Watkin, bore down on them. The outlaws stood their ground and killed a great many of the riders with a well-aimed flight of arrows, before hurrying to safety over the drawbridge, which was raised even as the very last of them, Robin Hood himself, was still crossing.

276 Outside the riders circled and shouted insults at the castle, but they quickly retreated when a flurry of arrows cut more of them down. They retreated to where the Sheriff of Nottingham and his party were watching the proceedings, and shortly thereafter the sheriff sent a herald under a flag of truce to demand that Sir Richard at Lee surrender the outlaws he was harbouring. Sir Richard replied that he would not, as

The young Knight of the Lea overcomes the Knight of Lancaster. Illustration from *The Merry Adventures of Robin Hood* by Howard Pyle.

the men who now shared his home were more law-abiding and true than the sheriff and his men. Knowing that he could do nothing against the knight without a warrant issued by the king or the High Chancellor, the sheriff was forced to return to Nottingham, where he plotted his revenge against Robin Hood and all those who had chosen to take his side.

277 Inside the castle Sir Richard at Lee took Robin to one side and told him that Sir Richard FitzWalter's steward Walter had come to him that very morning to say that his master had died and Maid Marian was in danger of being seized by the strongest lord in the region, who desired her lands. When Robin heard this he knew the time had come for him to take Marian into the forest to live in safety, and there he would have Friar Tuck marry them.

278 Arrangements were quickly made for Robin and twenty of his men to ride to Malaset in far-off Lancashire, while the remainder of his men were to return to the safety of their camps in the forest. The ride was long and hard, and on the second evening Robin and his party approached the castle at Malaset. It appeared dark and deserted, but a clear blast on Robin's horn brought Walter the steward to the ramparts. When he saw who had ridden up to the castle, he quickly ordered the drawbridge lowered and the portcullis raised to admit Robin and his men. He welcomed them warmly, though when questioned as to the whereabouts of Maid Marian he had to admit that he did not know where she was. She had slept in the castle but when Walter had gone to her chambers that very morning she was nowhere to be found. The entire castle had been searched, and Marian was nowhere within its walls.

279 Walter related that since the death of Sir Richard FitzWalter three days earlier, Marian had been approached by many knights who sought to make her and her lands their own. However, Marian had been able to rebuff them all. The previous morning the sacrist of St Mary's Abbey had come to the castle with a message from the Lord Bishop of Ely and High Chancellor of England William de Longchamp, which told Marian that she was to remain in the castle until Sir Scrivel of Catsty arrived to be her guardian.

280 The following day Robin and his men left the castle to begin their search for Maid Marian, but after a week's efforts they had found no sign of her. Robin's despair was exacerbated when he received word from Walter that Sir Scrivel of Catsty had taken possession of the castle of Malaset with a hundred knights; finding on his arrival that Maid Marian had disappeared, he was now also looking for her. Reluctantly Robin gave up his search in Lancashire and returned to his camp at the Stane Lea in the heart of Barnisdale Forest. Hardly had he arrived when he heard the sound of a single horse approaching. His heart leapt when he saw that the horse bore a maiden: he hoped it was Marian, but it was in fact the wife of Sir Richard at Lee.

The Sheriff of Nottingham orders his men to seize Robin Hood. Illustration by F.P. Stephanoff in G.A. Hansard's *The Book of Archery* (1845). (*Mary Evans Picture Library*)

281 Lady Alice quickly told Robin that her husband was in trouble. He had gone hawking at their lodge at Woodsett, but had been seized by the Sheriff of Nottingham, who had bound him to a horse and was now leading him back to judgment in Nottingham. It did not bode well. Robin immediately called together his men and told them that eighty of them were to go with him to rescue Sir Richard from the clutches of the sheriff, while the rest were to remain at the Stane Lea to protect the camp and the wife of the knight they sought to release.

282 Having seized Sir Richard in the hope of ingratiating himself with the Bishop of Ely, the Sheriff of Nottingham was keen to make good time back to his home. Thus, as they passed through Worksop he only allowed his men time to water their horses and eat a light repast before pushing them quickly onwards. They marched on relentlessly with their captive until they were deep within the heart of Clumber Forest, toiling up the steep incline known as Haggar Scar. There a voice boomed out of the shadows and they came to a rapid halt. Fearfully looking all around them, they saw the eighty outlaws with arrows notched to taut bowstrings.

283 Ten paces in front of the sheriff, Robin Hood stepped from the trees with his bowstring pulled taut and an arrow pointed straight at him. The sheriff was on the

point of commanding his men to attack when Robin released the bowstring. The arrow flew straight and true. It hit the Sheriff of Nottingham, passing through his heart and killing him instantly.

284 Seeing their master dead, the fifty men-at-arms dropped their weapons. Robin freed Sir Richard at Lee and helped him down off his horse. Quickly the outlaws marched the men-at-arms over the crest of the hill before sending them on their way back to Nottingham with the sheriff's body.

285 As quickly as they had appeared on the scene, the outlaws melted away into the depths of the forest, and shortly before the sun set Sir Richard at Lee was reunited with his wife in the camp at the Stane Lea. There the outlaws feasted in honour of the newest recruits to their number, and before long the entire camp fell into a contented sleep. The only person still awake as the first owl announced its presence was Robin Hood himself, who wondered what had happened to his love, Maid Marian.

286 Certain that his forest friends Ket the Trow and his brother Hob o'the Hill might have news for him, Robin Hood set out through the forest to the clearing in which stood the two low earthen barrows that were home to Ket and Hob, their sisters and their mother. As he came into the clearing he saw the shadow of a man creeping up one of the barrows, and knew at once that it was someone trying to creep up on the brothers unawares. However, just as Robin was about to race into the clearing and challenge the man, a small form rose from the top of the mound and leapt onto the creeping man. There was a brief struggle, and then the small figure stood up and wiped the blade of a knife on the grass.

287 Robin then hurried over to where Ket the Trow sat on the barrow nursing a wound in his shoulder. Looking down at the still body of the man Ket had just killed, he was surprised to see that he was dressed in the Lincoln green that the outlaws wore. Ket the Trow told Robin that three days before the man had killed Dring, one of Robin's men, by Brambury Burn, and had stripped him of his clothes so that he might spy on Ket the Trow, who was still searching for Maid Marian at Robin's behest.

288 Ket stood and beckoned Robin to follow him into his home, as he needed to attend to his injured shoulder. A short time later, having helped Ket the Trow dress the wound, Robin was led to the far end of the barrow, which was partitioned off from the rest by a rich curtain. There, peacefully sleeping in the company of Ket's sisters and his mother, was Maid Marian.

289 Quietly Ket led Robin back into the main chamber of the barrow. After Robin thanked him profusely, Ket the Trow explained how Maid Marian came to be lying in the barrow.

290   As he had been asked to do, Ket had travelled to Malaset to keep a watch over Maid
Marian, arriving at the castle the night before Robin and his men arrived. He entered
the castle and found the maiden, who told him that she had already decided to come
to the greenwood, for it was only there that she felt she would be safe after the death
of her father. Together Ket the Trow and Maid Marian had set out before first light
and travelled swiftly for many miles until they came to Catrail Rig. Here Maid
Marian was seized by twenty men under the leadership of Grame Gaptooth, a man-
at-arms to the lord of Thurlstan, one of the evil horde of Evil Hold.

291   Ket had followed Grame Gaptooth and his men to the Black Tower and watched
forlornly as they had taken Marian inside and raised the drawbridge. The Black
Tower was the most formidable fortress of any of the foul knights of the Evil Hold.
The following day two riders set forth, returning the next day in the company of
Sir Isenbart de Belame and Sir Baldwin the Killer, their undoubted intention being to
take Maid Marian to the castle at Wrangby.

292   That night Ket the Trow finally managed to slip into the Black Tower and freed Maid
Marian from the tower itself before he went on the rampage through the castle and
killed many of the men sleeping there. Once outside the walls, they travelled hard by
night and hid during the day, and on the third day they encountered Dring by
Brambury Burn. Dring said he would convey the good news of Marian's rescue to
Robin. However, they had been seen, and the man now lying dead on the barrow had
killed Dring, assumed his guise and then followed Ket to his home, which they
reached just three hours before Robin arrived.

293   That night Robin slept in the barrow on a bed of bracken with Ket the Trow beside
him, and in the morning he was reunited with Maid Marian. That very day, having
returned to the Stane Lea with Marian, and after revelling in the joy of his
comrades, Robin set out to see Friar Tuck to ask him to prepare for their
forthcoming marriage.

9. KING RICHARD RETURNS

294   When it became known that Robin Hood had married Marian FitzWalter, the
common man rejoiced, as did all those who lived their lives by the king's law.
However, those who saw this marriage as an affront to the king sought to destroy
Robin Hood once and for all. The loudest voice among all those calling for the death
of the insolent outlaw was that of William de Longchamp, the High Chancellor, who
vowed to send a great army into the forests of Clipstone, Sherwood and Barnisdale,
to stamp out for good the troublesome outlaws and their leader. Word quickly spread
that the army was to be dispatched to the castles of Nottingham in the south, Tickhill
and Lincoln in the east, the Peak in the west and York in the north, but it proved to
be little more than rumours, and nothing ever came of it.

Two scenes from the life of Richard I, taken from *Effigies regium Anglie*, Cott Vitt A XIII f.5. (*British Library, London/Bridgeman Art Library*)

295　William de Longchamp was forced to flee the country and the castles at Nottingham and Tickhill fell into the hands of Earl John, the king's brother, and for three years after that the earl was at such loggerheads with his barons that none bothered with the trifling insignificance of the outlaws of Sherwood and Barnsdale. During this time the news reached England that King Richard I had been taken prisoner and was being held for a huge ransom of 150,000 marks in a castle in Germany.

296　To secure the release of the king every man in the country was to be taxed, from the clergy to the layman, the yeoman to the villein, the knight to the squire. Each had to pay one quarter of his year's income. Many begrudged having to pay for the release of their absentee king, and as a result the ransom was collected extremely slowly.

297　Throughout all this time Robin and Marian enjoyed a happy and contented life in the greenwood. Marian had quickly adapted from her life of privilege and comfort, taking eagerly to the simple trappings of a woodsman's wife, living in a wooden hut and having nothing but homespun cloths or animal fleeces for clothing.

298　When the news of the king's ransom reached Robin Hood and his men, it was readily agreed that they should give half of all they had collected during their time as outlaws to speed the return of the king to his country. Thus Robin sent half of their store of gold and silver under strong guard to London, where it was delivered into the hands of the mayor with a note explaining who it was from and for what purpose it was to be used.

299　From that date forth Robin and his men set aside half of everything they took as toll to further their aim of seeing the king restored to his rightful throne. When Robin discovered that many wealthy merchants, knights, canons and abbots were being slow in paying their due tax, Robin and his men would pay them a visit and obtain from them that which was due. If the man readily gave up his taxes then Robin and his men would do nothing further, but anyone who resisted was stripped of his goods and left with little more than the clothes he wore.

300 Many ended up paying their taxes twice, once to Robin Hood and then to the legal tax collectors (who paid no heed to those who argued that they had already paid their due to the outlaw). Each time Robin and his men collected together a trunk full of silver and gold it would be dispatched to London. News of these payments soon reached the ears of the people, good and bad, and one man who was particularly impressed was Hamelin, Earl of Warenne, one of the king's treasurers, who made up his mind that when the time was right he would seek out Robin and his men and reward them for their loyalty to the crown – loyalty which far surpassed that of many of those who had sworn public oaths of allegiance.

301 At long last Richard I was released from his prison in Germany. When it was proclaimed throughout the land that the king was on his way back to England, most of his enemies who held castles in the name of his brother Earl John, who had plotted to take the crown for himself, fled the country in fear of the king's vengeance. Others were besieged by the king's friends and soon surrendered to the king's mercy, but those who held the castle at Nottingham steadfastly refused to relinquish the it.

302 When King Richard landed at Sandwich and heard that the castle at Nottingham refused to submit to his councillors, he immediately marched north at the head of a vast army and laid siege to the castle, quickly reducing the outer walls to ruins and capturing many of the defenders – whom he hanged in full sight of the castle. Two days later those left inside, among them Ralph Murdach (the brother of the Sheriff of Nottingham whom Robin Hood had slain), surrendered to the king and his men, and the castle was taken.

303 That night, as King Richard and his councillors sat in the great hall of Nottingham Castle, the topic of conversation changed to Robin Hood, the outlaw who ran amok in the forests of Clipstone, Sherwood and Barnisdale, according to William de Longchamp, who had returned to England with the king. William de Longchamp said that he did not think King Henry would have allowed the lawless behaviour of the outlaw and his men to continue, but this comment simply led to a rebuke by the king who said that since William de Longchamp had been left to rule in his absence, it was thus *his* position to have driven the outlaws from the forests long before. William de Longchamp sat and fumed in his seat, while those who hated him, and had previously forced him to flee the country, smiled at his discomfort.

The king, the bishop and the sheriff. Illustration from *Tales and Plays of Robin Hood* by Eleanor L. Skinner.

304 Hamelin, Earl of Warenne, had been listening to all that had been said, and quietly added that if the High Chancellor had been able to catch Robin Hood the king would probably still be rotting in his German prison. Asked to explain his remark, Hamelin related how Robin Hood had sent half of the wealth gathered as tolls from travellers through the forest to the Lord Mayor of London with explicit instructions that the booty was to be used to speed the king's release. Seeing the looks of amazement around the table, Hamelin continued that not only had Robin Hood given half of all he had collected, but that he had also taken it upon himself to gather the legal taxes from those subjects who did not freely give of their wealth to see the release of their beloved king from prison. All this money Robin Hood also sent to the Lord Mayor of London, while many of those who had been forced to give their taxes to Robin Hood had also been made to pay a second time when the king's own tax collectors came to their homes.

305 Hearing this the king and all his nobles, save William de Longchamp, laughed heartily. The king expressed his gratitude to a man he had never met, but one who seemed more just than any man in his direct service, and remarked that had it been left to Robin Hood alone he may not have had to spend so long in his prison in the castle of Hagenau. As his words sank in, King Richard scanned the faces of those seated in his presence, for he knew that many of them had been swayed, if only a little, by the promises of his traitorous brother Earl John of Mortaigne.

306 Rising from his seat, King Richard then toasted Robin Hood and made a promise to those in his company that he would meet with the outlaw and thank him personally. Sitting down again, he enquired how this just man had become an outlaw in the first place. William de Longchamp explained that Robin Hood had killed Sir Roger de Longchamp, his brother, along with five men-at-arms of the abbot of St Mary's.

307 However, before the king could react, Hamelin, Earl of Warenne, interrupted to say that Sir Roger de Longchamp had been killed as he sought to seize Marian FitzWalter – and would indeed have borne her off to his castle, the Evil Hold, had not Robin and his men intervened and killed Sir Roger de Longchamp with a well-aimed arrow that struck through the eye-slit of his visor.

308 King Richard nodded solemnly as he heard the account, and told William de Longchamp that he considered Robin Hood's action that day to have been just, for he knew of the machinations of Sir Roger de Longchamp, and he for one could not grieve for the death of such a foul and treacherous knight.

309 William de Longchamp, alarmed to see that the king's heart was set firmly in favour of Robin Hood, decided to put matters straight by telling Richard about Robin's subsequent actions. He said that not only had Robin Hood gathered around him a band of lawless cut-throats, he had also dishonoured the king by marrying the royal ward Marian FitzWalter, by killing the Sheriff of Nottingham, and by causing a knight of the realm to give up his lands and title and take to the forests as a common criminal.

310 This last statement changed the king's mood, for until he heard that one of his own knights had turned his back on the kingdom, King Richard was willing to forgive the actions of a man whom he considered was acting justly. However, at this the king banged his fists on the table and demanded to be told the name of the knight who had acted thus. William de Longchamp spoke up: it was Sir Richard at Lee, who held lands at Linden Lea by Nottingham.

311 King Richard stood up and proclaimed that not only would he take his lands, but that he would also have his head. The lands of Linden Lea would be given to the person who could bring the king the head of Sir Richard at Lee. However, as he spoke an old knight stepped forward from the gloom at the edge of the hall, and told the king that while Robin and his men roamed free in the forest none could ever hold the castle. The king asked the old knight's name and asked him to explain. The knight replied that he was Sir John de Birkin, a friend of Sir Richard at Lee. Since Sir Richard had been forced to flee his home, he elucidated, the new Sheriff of Nottingham had tried repeatedly to take the castle, but was forever held at bay by Robin Hood and his men, who would not see Sir Richard at Lee's lands fall into the hands of anyone other than their rightful owner.

312 King Richard sat and thought for a moment before turning to those assembled in the great hall. Slowly he declared that from all he had heard that night it would seem that the truly just men lived in the forests, and that those who broke the law sought the sanctuary and protection of the king's name. He then turned to Sir John de Birkin and told him that he would travel to the forests to meet Robin Hood.

313 The following morning King Richard and his party left Nottingham Castle and rode into the forests to hunt deer and, perchance, to meet Robin Hood. At Rufford Brakes they startled a hart, but it proved too fleet for them and, though they chased it for many miles, far to the north into Barnisdale Forest, they eventually lost the scent. The party repaired to the house of the Black Monks of Gildingcote for the night.

314 Every day for a week King Richard and his party hunted in the forests, but never once did they encounter Robin Hood, nor any of his men. At length, growing somewhat impatient, King Richard called to him Sir Ralph FitzStephen, the chief forester of Sherwood, and told him that if he wanted to keep his position he would have to find Robin Hood. For two days Sir Ralph and his foresters scoured the forests for signs of Robin Hood and his men, before reporting back to the king, who was staying at the castle of Drakenhole.

315 Sir Ralph FitzStephen learnt that Robin Hood and his men were haunting the roads by Ollerton, and thus had been travelling far out of the way of the king and his party. He suggested that the king and five others should disguise themselves in monks' robes, and Sir Ralph would guide them along the Ollerton road – and thus into contact with Robin Hood and his men.

316 The king immediately agreed, and chose Hamelin, Earl de Warenne, Ranulf, Earl of Chester, William, Earl of Ferrers, Sir Osbert de Scofton and Roger Bigot to go with him. Within the hour they were on their way. They looked like five rich monks. There were two horses carrying their baggage and three others piled high with provisions, all the horses being in the charge of two foresters dressed as monastic servants. The party travelled along the road without incident until nightfall, when they turned off the road and made their way to the house of the canons of Clumber. Here they were cordially greeted and shown into the guest chambers.

317 The hall into which the king and his party were shown was dimly lit by smoking torches fixed to the walls. Four other men were in the hall, three merchants and a minstrel, who plucked at his citole. Provisions were brought from the baggage horses, and as the king and his party ate their fill at one of the tables, an argument erupted between the merchants and the minstrel. The merchants were berating the minstrel for his lack of knowledge of all matters concerning money. It appeared he had been robbed that very day as he returned from the fair at Nottingham.

318 The king, still wearing his monk's cloak, asked who had robbed the minstrel. He replied that every penny in his possession had been taken from him by Robin Hood, and warned the monks that if they were to follow the same road they would likely suffer the same fate. With that the minstrel left his table and settled down in one corner of the hall. Wrapping himself in his cloak, he settled down as if to go to sleep.

319 As he settled down the door to the hall opened and an old couple entered. They were greeted with lavish gestures by the minstrel, who sprang to his feet and asked them how they came to be passing that way. The old man replied that they were on their way from Nottingham to Tickhill to retrieve their son from the castle prison there. Hearing this, the king asked how the boy had come to be in prison, whereupon the old woman told those in the hall that her son had worked long and hard for Peter Greatrex, the armourer at Nottingham, but had desired to travel abroad to see if he could not fare better. Some time later, so the old woman said, they were told that their son had been taken as a runaway to the prison at Tickhill, where he had been chained so soundly that one foot had perished.

320 The king spoke kindly to the woman, saying that he did not see how they were to take their son out of that place, but the woman, tears flowing down her face, simply replied that they were the boy's parents and were sure that their Dickon had done no wrong.

321 The old man put his arm around his wife and told her to dry her eyes, for had Robin Hood himself not promised them that very day that their son would be returned to them. The king once more spoke, asking the old man to explain. It happened that they were travelling down the road from Nottingham when they were stopped by a man dressed all in green, who told them that his master, Robin Hood, wished to speak with them. The old man and the old woman had gone with the man, who led them to where Robin Hood and his men waited. There they were feasted and only after they had eaten their fill were they asked their purpose in the forest. When the old man explained, Robin Hood told him he would see to it that their son was returned to them when they reached Tickhill, and then gave them a silver penny to aid them on their way, adding that if any other rogue should stop them in the forest they were to say they had been given free passage through the greenwood by Robin Hood and that the fate of Richard Malbête would be upon any who detained them.

322 At his table the king listened keenly to the story and, as the old couple sat down to eat their meagre provisions, he asked Hamelin, Earl of Warenne, what was meant by the fate of Richard Malbête. Hamelin and Sir Ralph FitzStephen then told the king all that had befallen that evil man – how he had murdered the Jews in Lincoln and York, and had finally met with due justice at the hands of Robin Hood in the forest in the presence of Sir Laurence de Raby, the marshal of the king's justice.

323 The following morning the king and his party set off once more along the Ollerton road. They had gone no more than 5 miles when they found their way blocked by a man dressed from head to foot in Lincoln green and carrying a longbow that was far taller than the man himself. As the party came to a halt the man, who was none other than Robin Hood himself, raised his fingers to his lips and blew a shrill whistle, whereupon the bushes parted and twenty of his men showed themselves.

324 Robin addressed the man he thought was the abbot, not aware that it was the king in disguise, and told him that he and his rich party must pay a toll to pass through the forest. The king replied that he had no more than 40 pounds with him, as he had been charged with the entertainment of the king at Blythe, but what he had he would willingly give. He then commanded that his purse be brought forth, and when Robin had counted out the 40 pounds he told the king that, as he was a man of his word, he would take only half of what he was offered. So saying he put 20 pounds back into the purse and handed it back to the king before stepping out of his way and gesturing to him to pass.

325 The king, however, did not spur his horse forwards, but instead took out from under his cloak a parchment scroll bearing the royal seal. He told the outlaw that this document brought him the greetings of King Richard I, who wished to meet with Robin Hood, under free passage, at Nottingham three days hence. Robin took the parchment and read it before handing it back. Then he invited the king to dine with him and his men in the greenwood, an invitation Richard was quick to accept.

326 Some time later the king and his party were led into the clearing where Robin Hood and his men had their camp at that time. After a fine feast, Robin told his guests that they would stage a shooting contest so that the 'abbot' might tell the king what kind of men they were. After shooting at normal targets, Robin set up a wand on top of which he placed a garland of flowers. The aim was to shoot through the garland, those who failed being buffeted with the forearm and thus eliminated.

327 All the men shot well, but only two managed to pass their arrows straight through the garland. One was Gilbert of the White Hand, the other Robin Hood. They continued the contest, until finally Robin missed by no more than a hair's breadth just as Maid Marian, Sir Richard at Lee, Alan-a-Dale and Dame Alice his wife rode into the clearing.

328 Robin submitted himself to the buffet of the 'abbot', who at first was reluctant. However, when Robin urged him on he rolled up his sleeve and duly knocked Robin to the ground. As Robin fell, Sir Richard at Lee quickly dismounted from his horse and ran to Robin's side, shouting that the abbot was none other than the king, for Sir Richard at Lee had recognised him. As Sir Richard knelt before him, the king

Robin Hood's encounter with Richard I, who is travelling in disguise. Illustration in *Robin Hood's Ballads* (1867), p. 249. (*Mary Evans Picture Library*)

The king began to roll up his sleeve. Illustration from *Bold Robin Hood and his Outlaw Band* by Louis Read.

Robin and his Merry Men kneel before Richard I and swear their loyalty to him. Illustration by Walter Crane in *Stories of Robin Hood and His Merry Men* by Henry Gilbert. (*Mary Evans Picture Library/Edwin Wallace*)

threw back his cowl and doffed the robes concealing his surtout emblazoned with the leopards of Anjou and the fleur-de-lis of France.

329 At once all the outlaws fell to their knees while Maid Marian and Dame Alice curtsied to their king. King Richard reached down and bodily lifted Robin to his feet, saying that he had never met a man so honourable and that from that day forth he and all his men were pardoned for the crimes they had committed – provided that Robin abandoned life as an outlaw and lived once more as a lawful man. Robin willingly agreed, whereupon the king beckoned Marian to approach; joining her hand with that of her husband, he told them that he gave his full blessing to their union.

330 Then his face turned stern and he looked Robin straight in the eye. For a moment Robin feared the worst, but the king spoke in a gentle voice as he thanked Robin for all he had done in his absence, especially for helping to raise the king's ransom. However, the king added, he could not let his crimes go entirely unpunished, and he therefore 'sentenced' Robin to live a quiet and law-abiding life as lord of the lands of Malaset. He ordered Hamelin to ensure that FitzWalter's lands were duly and properly turned over to Robin and Marian.

331 Next the king called forward Sir Richard at Lee. Having listened to that knight's story, he pardoned him and restored to him his castle and lands at Linden Lea. Finally Alan-a-Dale and Dame Alice were presented to the king, who, having heard of the wrongs they had suffered, granted them full pardon and title to the lands of

Robin is pardoned by Queen Katherine. Illustration by Petherick in *Robin Hood's Ballads* (1867), p. 160. (*Mary Evans Picture Library*)

Beauforest that Alice's father had formerly held. Then the king turned to his party and told them that he would deal with the lords of the Evil Hold, who had plotted against the throne with Earl John, but first he must deal with the traitor King Philip of France and force him to flee from Normandy and Aquitaine. Then, so he continued, he would return to Nottingham and sweep the evil lords of Wrangby from the face of the earth.

332 Two days later, after King Richard I had left Nottingham to return to London, the king's messenger handed a parchment bearing the royal seal to the guard at the Evil Hold who took it immediately to his master Sir Isenbart de Belame. After reading the scroll, Sir Isenbart realised that the king had forsaken him in favour of the outlaws of Sherwood and Barnisdale. Furiously he threw the parchment onto the fire, his heart set even more firmly on revenge, and his hopes now resting on the death of King Richard and the accession of Earl John.

Richard I joins the hands of Robin Hood and Maid
Marian in marriage. Illustration by Walter Crane in
Stories of Robin Hood and His Merry Men by Henry
Gilbert. (*Mary Evans Picture Library*)

333 Meanwhile, Robin and Marian returned to Malaset, where they took back the castle
from the evil Sir Scrivel of Catsty. With them went Hob o'the Hill and Ket the Trow,
along with their two sisters; their mother had died a short time before and was now
buried in the barrow they had long called their home. Little John became Robin's
steward at Malaset, while Gilbert of the White Hand lived as a freeman in a cottage
on lands given to him by Robin, where he lived with Sibbie, one of the fairy sisters
of Hob o'the Hill and Ket the Trow. The other sister, Fenella, married Wat Graham
of Car Peel, a borderlands fighter of some repute.

334 The other outlaws of Sherwood and Barnisdale yielded and pledged their oath of
allegiance to King Richard, and shortly afterwards left with him for the shores of
Normandy. Many of them died on French soil, and after the king's death only some
twenty returned to England. They made their way to Malaset where Robin gladly
settled land on each and every one of them. Among those who returned were Will the
Bowman and Much the miller's son. Arthur-a-Bland had been killed during the siege
of the castle of Chaluz where Richard I had met his death, while the ageing Scadlock
had been drowned in a storm just off Rye.

335 For sixteen years thereafter Marian and Robin lived in peace and contentment at
Malaset, but within the confines of the castle at Wrangby, the so-called Evil Hold,
Sir Isenbart de Belame bided his time until he could take his revenge. He took the

Robin Hood and Little John: a relief by James Wood (1952) at Castle Green, Nottingham.

counsel of Sir Guy of Gisborne, Sir Baldwin the Killer, Sir Roger of Doncaster and Sir Scrivel of Catsty, and slowly they laid their plans against the upstart Robert of Locksley, for Robin had reverted to using his true and proper name in these times of relative peace. In 1215 Robin and his men, those former outlaws who had returned from Normandy and entered his service, marched south under the banner of the barons and met King John at Runnymede, where the king was forced to sign the Magna Carta, a document that was supposed to put an end to tyranny and oppression.

10. THE DESTRUCTION OF EVIL HOLD

336 Following the signing of the Magna Carta, Robert of Locksley and his men stayed on in London until the early part of the winter, when they once again hurried north upon receiving news that King John had reneged against the terms of the treaty and, with the aid of foreign mercenaries, was now plundering the lands of all those who had stood against him. Quickly Robert and his men hurried northwards through lands which had not known peace for long, and which now seemed ready to be plunged into the depths of a bloody civil war. Everywhere they went they came across the dead and the injured, who wandered aimlessly around the still smouldering ruins of their master's manor or castle. Robert worried in case the same fate might befall Malaset before he could return, and with such thoughts foremost in his mind he quickened the pace and hurried towards his home and his beloved wife.

337 As Robert crested the ridge above Malaset he gave a low and audible groan, for below him thin wisps of smoke drifted lazily into the sky, although the castle appeared otherwise untouched. Robert and his men raced down the hill and into the

courtyard of the castle, where all the wooden furniture had been burnt. Yet still the stone walls stood strong and proud, unbroken by the assault Robert knew they would have been subjected to.

338 Everything was quiet, too quiet, as Robert hurried up the twisting staircase that led to Marian's chamber. The door was closed. He opened it slowly and stepped inside. There on the bed lay the lifeless body of his beloved Marian, all the colour gone from her cheeks and lips. Beside her lay a short black arrow. Hiding behind a curtain was Sibbie, the wife of Gilbert of the White Hand. Venturing forth, she told Robert that Sir Isenbart de Belame himself had killed Marian as she spoke to him from the gatehouse, using the same arrow that Hob o'the Hill had fired into the hall of the Evil Hold.

339 Sibbie told them that all this had happened the day before. After Marian's death, Sir Isenbart de Belame and his horde had stormed the castle, but had been unable to take it and instead satisfied themselves with torching everything that would burn. They had gone back to his foul castle with Hob o'the Hill and ten others as captives to be tortured in his dungeons.

340 Robert then crossed over to the bed where he kissed the cold forehead of his beloved wife, and then knelt in silent and reverent prayer. That night, under the light of a hundred torches, Marian was laid to rest beside her father in the little church of Malaset, and afterwards all returned to the castle where they spent the night preparing themselves for the battle they knew lay ahead. At dawn Robert set out from the castle at Malaset, knowing full well that he would never return, and led his band of men across the hills and dales towards the foul stronghold of Sir Isenbart de Belame.

So the great reaper repeath among the flowers. Illustration from *The Merry Adventures of Robin Hood* by Howard Pyle.

341 Before he left he sent messengers to Sir Herbrand de Tranmire to request the help that had been promised him so many years before. Though Robert knew that Sir Herbrand himself would now be too old to take part in the fighting, he none the less asked that noble knight to send him men to help in the onslaught, even if he himself was unable to attend. Their allotted meeting place was the Mark Oak by Wrangby Mere. Messengers were also sent out to other knights, yeomen and villeins who had suffered at the hands of the knights of the Evil Hold, and en route they stopped at every manor and castle to enlist help – help that was always forthcoming. By the time Robert approached the castle at Wrangby he led a force of some three hundred men of all ranks, from knights to villeins.

342 As they approached the castle Robert rode a little distance ahead, but stopped just short of a measured bowshot from the castle. There he stood in his stirrups and bellowed that he wished to speak with Sir Isenbart de Belame. On the ramparts two helmeted heads appeared, one wearing the bronze helmet that was the special attribute of Sir Isenbart de Belame. Seeing him appear, Robert demanded that Sir Isenbart de Belame and his forces vacate the castle and give themselves up to true and proper justice for their many crimes, not least the murder of his wife Marian. If they refused then Robert's men would take the castle by force and slay all those they found within.

343 Sir Isenbart de Belame replied that he had no intention of surrendering to a common outlaw, and if they had not left his lands by morning he would ride forth from the castle and kill them all. As he turned to leave the ramparts Ket the Trow raced forward and, in the dwindling light, fired a single arrow at the two heads so far above them. The arrow struck Sir Isenbart's companion through the eye-slit of his visor, though at such an angle that it simply grazed the man's forehead. However, Sir Isenbart quickly retreated out of sight for fear that someone who could fire an arrow with such accuracy in the half-light could surely repeat the feat, and the next arrow would certainly be intended for him and would strike more deeply.

344 That night Robert gathered all the knights who had ridden to give him aid under the boughs of the Mark Oak, and there they discussed how they might take the castle. One, Sir Fulk of the Dykewall, could not see how they might succeed, but the young Squire Denvil of Toomlands had a suggestion. They could float across the moat on rafts under the protection of their upturned shields, and having crossed the moat could cut the chains to the drawbridge and then smash the portcullis. Thus they would gain free entry to the castle, and could once and for all rid the country of the plague of the Evil Hold.

345 So it was agreed, and Ket the Trow was sent into the village of Wrangby to enlist the help of the villeins there, but though some appeared willing, and were even urged to

come to Robert of Locksley's aid by Cole the Reeve, the villagers eventually refused to help, saying that the castle was held by men in league with the devil. It had been besieged six times before and never defeated, and they could not see how Robert and his men could succeed now. With that they refused to lend their weight to the forthcoming battle.

346 When Ket the Trow told Robert all that had passed, he simply continued with his preparations. He commanded his men to cut down the trees they needed to build the rafts and battering-rams for the following day's action. However, as the sun rose Robert saw the villagers coming towards their position under the leadership of a man he recognised from the tournament at Nottingham, one Rafe of the Billhook, who came to Robert and told him that he had persuaded the villagers that their only hope of salvation lay with Robert of Locksley, or Robin Hood as he was once called, and they were now ready to do his bidding. Rafe added that he had waited a long time for his revenge since he had been cast out of his cottage near Barnisdale Forest by the evil lords of Wrangby, who had killed his wife and baby. This statement led Robert to recognise Rafe of the Billhook as none other than Thurstan of Stone Cot, whom Sir Isenbart de Belame and his horde had displaced some thirty years before.

347 After eating a hearty breakfast and celebrating mass, Robert of Locksley urged his men forwards. Under the guidance of Will the Bowman and Will Scarlet, the archers held the bowmen of the Evil Hold at bay while the rafts were carried down to the moat. They were swiftly poled across. The attackers under the command of Little John and Gilbert of the White Hand, were protected from above by their shields, and

Robin's arrow whizzes through the sheriff's window. Illustration from *Bold Robin Hood and his Outlaw Band* by Louis Read.

from behind by the archers, and not one lost his life in the crossing of the moat. Soon the sounds of metal on metal indicated that work had commenced on the massive chains holding the drawbridge aloft. All around them flight after flight of arrows flew through the air, but not one came near the two smiths working on the chains, for the archers within the castle were being held at bay by the bowmen in the forest, and every time one was foolish enough to show himself on the ramparts or at an arrow slit, he was mercilessly cut down.

348 All seemed to be going in Robert's favour until the inner gates of the castle were thrown open and archers began to shoot at the smiths through the portcullis. Both smiths were cut down and fell into the water. Immediately two more took their place, this time protected by bowmen balancing on the very top of the drawbridge, who fired down through the portcullis. With a great clatter the first chain gave way, followed seconds later by the second, the bowmen on the drawbridge having to leap clear as it came crashing down onto the opposite bank with such force that it shed all its boards. All that remained of it were the two main beams running along on either side, while the rest of it was now floating in the moat beneath.

349 Quickly Robert's bowmen streamed across the drawbridge, picking off the defending archers who had positioned themselves within the inner gates of the castle (which were quickly closed). From under the trees forty men appeared bearing the huge trunk of an oak tree that had been felled during the night and shaped into a battering-ram. Carefully they advanced on the castle, crossing the moat on the two surviving beams of the drawbridge. Then they swung the trunk back and forth against the bars of the portcullis, each strike weakening its structure and making it groan.

350 Inside the castle the inner gates were once more thrown open and a deadly rain of arrows tore into the men with the battering-ram, but wherever a man fell another quickly took his place. The inner gates were closed once again after Robert and his archers let fly such a flurry of arrows that almost all those within the castle met with their end.

351 Steadily the portcullis was being weakened by the onslaught of the oak trunk, when suddenly a warning was shouted that fire was being poured down on them. In an instant Robin and almost all of the men on the remains of the drawbridge had dived into the moat as molten tar, lighted brands and red-hot stones rained down on them from the ramparts above. Those who were not quick enough died in the firestorm which quickly engulfed the drawbridge, devouring not only the battering-ram but also the castle gates and portcullis.

352 Robert knew that the knights of the Evil Hold had now sealed themselves into their castle, and had almost certainly burnt down their only defences. He ordered that

none should be allowed to leave the castle while he retired to the forest to order the cutting of more trees for rafts, and to rest awhile ahead of the renewed fighting later that afternoon. As he returned to the camp in the company of Sir Fulk of the Dykewall and another knight by the name of Sir Robert of Staithes, he saw a great number of men-at-arms approaching. They were led by two knights on horseback; each was carrying a shield, one emblazoned with three white swallows and the other with five green trees. Robert immediately recognised their bearers and rushed over to greet Sir Walter de Beauforest and Alan-a-Dale. Quickly Robert told them all that had passed that morning, and what he hoped would happen that afternoon.

353 During the lull in the fighting, while the great fire before the castle burnt itself out, Ket the Trow wandered around trying to find some way to gain entry to the castle and free his brother. As he walked he saw a sword glint twice in the sunlight on the ramparts, and an answering flash from some distance away among the trees. Ket knew this to be a signal and carefully crept up to where he had seen the flash in the trees. He immediately recognised the thirty horsemen he found in the cover of the forest as the men of Thurlstan from whom he had rescued Marian many years before, and their leader was none other than Grame Gaptooth, who was now himself the lord of Thurlstan. Ket quickly and quietly made his way back to Robert and gave him the intelligence he had gathered, and as he was doing so they were joined by 10 knights and 100 men-at-arms sent by Sir Herbrand de Tranmire, who was himself now too old to take part.

354 Quietly Robert gave his orders. The new rafts were laid across the charred remnants of the beams of the old drawbridge, and his men set back at strategic points, for Robert intended to let the men of the castle rush out at them – and then he would have them in his clutches. When all was prepared, Robert and his men waited patiently, knowing that the attack would come shortly before sunset.

355 Sure enough, in the dying rays of the sun the portcullis was slowly raised and from the castle Sir Isenbart de Belame issued forth at the head of his forces, while out of the forest rode Grame Gaptooth and his thirty men. Robert's forces held their positions and then, with a mighty roar, Sir Herbrand's 10 knights and 100 men-at-arms joined battle. Caught between Robert's equally divided forces, the hordes of Sir Isenbart de Belame and Grame Gaptooth had to check their progress, whereupon they were set upon from all sides. No quarter was asked for, and none given. Peasant fought knight on equal terms, and soon the ground was covered with the bodies of men from both sides.

356 Through the carnage strode Rafe of the Billhook, his great shining blade glowing red with the blood of those he had felled, his eyes searching this way and that for the distinctive bronze helmet of Sir Isenbart de Belame himself. Likewise Robert, in the

Robin Hood and Little John. Illustration from *Tales and Plays of Robin Hood* by Eleanor L. Skinner.

company of Little John, sought out the foul fiend of Wrangby Castle, Little John this time wielding a double-headed axe with the same consummate ease as he did his more usual staff.

357 For almost an hour the battle raged until most of the knights of the Evil Hold had been killed. Sir Isenbart de Belame himself was surrounded by the villeins of Wrangby, along with Rafe of the Billhook who sought to cleave that evil knight's head from his shoulders. Already his billhook had cut deep into the knight's shoulder, right down to the bone, and now he raised it again and would have surely decapitated the knight had not Robert thrown his shield into the path of the flashing blade.

358 Rafe of the Billhook looked around as Robert strode towards him telling him to desist, for to kill the knight in such a manner would do his rank justice, and Robert wanted him to swing from the gibbet like a common criminal. Sir Isenbart de Belame was furious that he should be denied an honourable death, but soon found himself bound hand and foot and carried unceremoniously into the castle of Wrangby, which had by now fallen to the forces of Robert of Locksley. Of all the knights of the Evil Hold only Sir Roger of Doncaster had managed to escape with his life, and he now rode hard away from the scene of the battle, his cowardice saving him from certain death that day.

359 The castle itself had fallen to a plan devised by Ket the Trow and Squire Denvil of Toomlands. They had hidden in the moat when Sir Isenbart de Belame and his men sallied forth from the castle to do battle, and then slipped in to the castle and quickly overpowered the forty men still within the walls.

360 A short while later Robert sat in the great hall of the castle at Wrangby in the very place that had been occupied for years by Sir Isenbart de Belame, and there he sat in judgement on the only two survivors of the battle that day – Sir Isenbart himself and Sir Baldwin the Killer. As they were brought into the hall they cast their eyes all around them, knowing full well that they were living through their last moments on earth.

361 As they were brought before him and the other knights, Robert appealed to those present to lay their charges against the two captives. One called out that Sir Isenbart de Belame had put out his father's eyes, while another cried out that when the harvest had failed and he had been unable to pay his dues, Sir Isenbart de Belame and Sir Baldwin the Killer had ridden his son into the ground and killed him. Ket the Trow then stepped forward holding aloft the arrow Hob o'the Hill had previously shot into this very hall, with which, so he told the assembled company, Sir Isenbart de Belame had killed the lady Marian. Hob o'the Hill, who had been freed from the dungeons by his brother, then hobbled forwards and told how Sir Isenbart de Belame and his knights had stood by and joked when Sir Ranulf of the Waste had burnt their father Colman Grey.

362 Robert stood and called for quiet. He had heard enough. He turned to the knights gathered there and asked them to pass sentence on the two prisoners. Each said that as Sir Isenbart de Belame and Sir Baldwin the Killer had acted as common criminals they should be stripped of their rank, and thus should also forfeit their right to die by the sword. Instead they should be taken from the hall and hanged from the gallows that had already been built for that very purpose.

363 And so it was done. The ground outside the castle was still covered with the bodies of those who had fallen in the battle, and even as the two evil knights breathed their last the chambers of the castle were filled with straw so that when they were torched they would burn so fiercely that even the stone walls would crumble. As Robert and his men rode away from the castle, Ket the Trow took up a single black arrow, the shaft of which had been dipped in tar. Setting the shaft on fire, he accurately shot the arrow through an arrow slit into the castle. Flames were soon licking from room to room, and then the whole building was ablaze, the glow from the fire visible many miles away.

364 All through the night Robert and his men watched the burning castle from the shelter of the Mark Oak, and in the morning they rode towards the blackened, smouldering ruin that had once been the most feared castle in all England. There Robert of Locksley turned to his men and told them that from that day until his last he would return to the greenwood, and would thenceforth once more be known as Robin Hood. His home within the forests would be open to any who cared to join him.

11. THE DEATH OF ROBIN HOOD

365 From that day forth Robin Hood once again took to living in the greenwood that he loved so much. The lands of Malaset passed into the hands of a distant cousin of the Earl FitzWalter, who ruled them well and treated all the villeins and yeomen with due regard. Many of those who had once before lived with Robin in the shade of the broad-leafed trees of the forest also forsook their homes and once again wore the Lincoln green that was the sign of their freedom, and their numbers quickly swelled by those who sought to escape the tyrannies of King John and to fight for justice and freedom.

366 With little to do in the forests of Sherwood, Clipstone and Barnisdale, Robin led his men to the north where they followed the marauding armies of mercenaries that were allied to the king and on many occasion righted the wrongs that that army did in the name of the king. In 1216 King John died at Newark Castle and his son Henry was proclaimed king and acknowledged by all the barons and lords of the realm, whereupon Robin and his men returned to their old haunts in Barnisdale Forest. The lands of Wrangby that had for so long been the centre of all things evil passed into the hands of a kinsman of the Earl of Warenne. He was a just and fair man, and soon the persecution of Sir Isenbart de Belame and the other knights of the Evil Hold became no more than a passing memory.

367 However, others further afield were not so lucky, and oppression and fear still gave Robin and his men plenty to do. Roving bands of robbers dressed in the livery of certain great lords infested the forests and fell upon the rich and the poor alike. Yet always at the back of Robin's mind was the fate of Sir Roger of Doncaster, who had fled the battle at Wrangby. His manor was now under constant surveillance by Ket the Trow and Hob o'the Hill, for it was widely known that Sir Roger waited for the time when he could ambush Robin Hood and kill him.

368 It came to pass one day, as Robin, Little John and Will Scarlet were on the boundaries of Barnisdale and Sherwood Forests, that Ket the Trow came to report that he had seen Sir Roger of Doncaster and a troop of his men leave the manor at Syke that very morning. They were heading towards the Stone House by Barnisdale Four Wents, where, so Ket thought, they would lie in wait for the bishop's convoy due to pass that way that day from Wakefield Abbey to Lincoln.

369 Immediately Robin sent Little John and Will Scarlet back to the Stane Lea to call together their men so that they might finally dispose of Sir Roger of Doncaster, while Ket the Trow he sent to find Will the Bowman. Left alone in the forest, Robin thought for a few minutes before heading south along secret paths until he came to a well-used but narrow path. Here he spotted a man dressed as a yeoman, carrying a longbow and a sheaf of arrows, who was looking furtively up and down the pathway.

Jews Court, Steep Hill, Lincoln. (*Mick Sharp Photography*)

370 Robin stepped out of the undergrowth onto the path and asked the yeoman if he was lost and where he was going. The yeoman replied that he was on his way to Roche Abbey but had become lost in the forest. Robin said that he could lead the yeoman to the road he required, adding that he was indeed far off the correct path. In reply, the man said that he had been told at Balby to follow the road that went through the hamlet of Scatby, but he had seen no other signs of life until Robin, though he did not know that was who he was addressing, had appeared. Robin laughed and said that Scatby was only a mile or two from where they stood.

371 Then Robin indicated the yeoman's longbow and arrows and challenged him to some sport with the bow. The yeoman accepted, boasting that he was as fine a bowman as any, and better than the thieves who roamed the forests. Robin took no notice of the jibe and went to a hazel bush where he cut down two straight wands and stripped them of their bark so that they might be more easily seen. One wand he placed in the ground with a rough garland of leaves on it, and then measured out a distance of fifty paces before sticking the other wand in the ground. The idea of the contest was to shoot through the garland of leaves.

372   Robin went first and his arrow flew straight through the garland. The yeoman grumbled that this was no fair contest, but nevertheless shot, missing the mark by a good distance. Robin clapped him on the back and congratulated him on his fine attempt before notching another arrow to his bowstring. This time his shot split the wand in two. At this the yeoman said the shot was a fluke, and that some breeze had altered the course of the arrow. Robin chided him for being so unsportsmanlike, and then went to cut a new wand to replace that which his arrow had rent in two.

373   As Robin bent over a hazel bush some twenty paces away from the yeoman he heard a shout and turned to see the yeoman fire an arrow at him, for he was one of the false robbers who sought to rob from both the rich and the poor, and who was in the service of an evil lord.

374   Robin fell headlong into the bushes, his feet sticking up out of the undergrowth. All was still as the yeoman laughed and strolled towards him. However, as he approached Robin suddenly leapt out of the bushes with the yeoman's own arrow notched to his bowstring, and as the yeoman fled down the path Robin took careful aim, even though the man was weaving from side to side to throw him off. Judging the moment to be just right, he released the bowstring.

375   The arrow struck the fleeing man squarely between the shoulders, its point travelling straight through the man to protrude from his breast, the force of the blow lifting him off his feet. Hardly had the yeoman hit the ground when Robin heard the breaking of branches behind him. Throwing down his bow and drawing his sword, Robin turned to face the strange man who came at him, his sword already drawn, from within the trees. The man looked like a small brown horse walking on its hind legs, its teeth bared and its great mane flowing behind.

376   Robin laughed as he recognised the man under the horse's skin as Sir Guy of Gisborne, and then the two were locked in a fierce battle, the heat of Sir Guy's attack being equally matched by the cool-headedness of Robin Hood's. For a long time both men parried the other's blows, but Robin soon began to learn his opponent's moves and then, when he judged the moment right, his blade swept over Sir Guy's guard and cut the evil knight in the shoulder. The wound hardly checked Sir Guy's fury, and moments later he managed to sweep his blade under Robin Hood's, catching the outlaw under the arm, though the wound was no more than a scratch. Before the knight could withdraw his sword arm, Robin replied with a lightning-fast stroke, embedding his sword almost to the hilt in Sir Guy of Gisborne's chest. The knight dropped to his knees as Robin withdrew the blade, before rolling forwards onto the ground.

377   As Robin Hood rested, panting, on his sword he was joined by Hob o'the Hill, who had watched the fight. He congratulated Robin on his sword play, but then reminded

Robin drove his blade through Sir Guy's body. Illustration from *Bold Robin Hood and his Outlaw Band* by Louis Read.

him that they still had to deal with Sir Roger of Doncaster. Hob told Robin that he had been following Sir Roger and his men as they travelled north towards Barnisdale Forest, but they had doubled back and now lay in ambush at Hunger Wood, where Will the Bowman and his party of outlaws were keeping watch over them.

378 Robin quickly told Hob o'the Hill to run to Barnisdale Forest, find Little John and instruct him to come to Hunger Wood. Once there, he was to force Sir Roger of Doncaster and his men-at-arms between the two flanks. Then, finally, they might be rid of him and his kind. Robin himself hurried to find Will the Bowman, who told him that he had been keeping watch on Sir Roger of Doncaster's men, who were under the leadership of a Brabanter by the name of Fulco the Red.

379 Robin, Will the Bowman and the other outlaws were waiting for news of Little John's progress when a scout ran up and told them that Sir Roger of Doncaster's men were approaching Beverley Glade. Robin and Will the Bowman quickly instructed their archers to hide themselves in the trees to await the arrival of the enemy. They did not have to wait long before the eighty mercenaries – sixty men-at-arms and twenty crossbowmen – were led into the clearing by Fulco the Red. He was clothed in mail from head to foot, and his face turned the hearts of those who saw him to stone, for his was the cruellest countenance that any of them had ever seen.

380 As the last of the mercenaries came into the clearing, Robin gave the signal and the first flight of arrows from his own archers cut into the enemy. That first flurry killed

twenty men, one to each arrow, and among those who fell were fifteen of the crossbowmen. Confusion reigned for a few seconds, just long enough for Robin and his men to fire a second volley of arrows, killing another twelve of the mercenaries.

381 Then the mercenaries recovered from their initial surprise and, at a great yell from their leader Fulco the Red, dashed into the trees around the clearing whence the arrows had cut them down. Robin and his men now stealthily retreated, stopping every now and then to shoot even more of the foreigners, though they still more than outnumbered Robin and his men. They themselves had lost three men during the first onslaught.

382 As they fought from tree to tree, Robin and his men continued to have the upper hand, but before long Robin was saddened to see that he had already lost eight of the twenty men with him, and for all that the mercenaries continued to press forward. Suddenly Fulco the Red caught sight of an outlaw hiding in a bush and rushed at him. The outlaw, Gilbert of the White Hand, took to his heels and fled to the very tree behind which Robin was standing, with Fulco the Red in hot pursuit.

383 As Fulco the Red reached the tree Robin leapt forward and the two engaged in a bitter sword fight. They were equally matched and neither could gain the upper hand. Seeing that his leader was engaged in a fight to the death, another of the mercenaries crept up behind Robin Hood, but he was thwarted by Will the Bowman, who ran to help his master only to be hacked down by another mercenary. With his dying breath Will the Bowman shouted a warning to Robin, but he had no need as an outlaw's arrow from behind one of the bushes put paid to the mercenary stealing up on Robin, while another dealt with the man who had killed Will the Bowman.

384 Still Robin and Fulco the Red fought hand to hand, neither giving any quarter. Suddenly Robin parried a blow and in a flash had sliced the point of his sword through the mercenary's mail and cut his breast open. Incited by the pain, Fulco the Red lunged at Robin, who simply struck the blow down and then brought the edge of his sword down on his opponent's neck with such force that he almost severed the head from the body. As Fulco the Red fell lifeless to the ground a great cheer went up from the outlaws, who pressed home the advantage they now had over their leaderless enemies.

385 Then, just when it seemed that the mercenaries had recovered from the shock of seeing their leader fall, the woods came alive with men in Lincoln green as Robin and his weary men were joined by Little John and some sixty other outlaws. The mercenaries were quickly put to flight, but Little John had had the foresight to position half of his men across their line of escape, and before long not one mercenary lived, and thus there was no one to carry the news of their utter defeat to the ears of Sir Roger of Doncaster, waiting at the edge of the forest with half a dozen men-at-arms.

386 Sir Roger and his men sat and waited for news from Sir Guy of Gisborne and Fulco the Red, but the only person they saw coming out of the forest was a charcoal burner. He told them that he had passed the bodies of seventy or more foreigners in Beverley Glade, whereupon Sir Roger of Doncaster and his men turned and rode swiftly away from the forest, never to return. For many years after that fateful day the glade in which Robin had wreaked his vengeance on the foreign mercenaries was known as Slaughter Lea instead of Beverley Glade, and from that day for many years Robin and his men were left undisturbed in the shelter of their beloved greenwood.

387 For fifteen years after the rout of the Brabant mercenaries under Fulco the Red, Robin Hood and his men lived in peace in the forests of Sherwood, Barnisdale and Clipstone, and through all that time they continued to right the wrongs of oppression and tyranny, whether in the locality of the forest or indeed much further afield.

388 On one occasion they travelled to Westmorland to fight on behalf of Sir Drogo of Dallas Tower, who had been forced to flee his lands by the border men after he had punished one of their clansmen. With the aid of Robin Hood and his outlaws, the young knight was able to force the border men from his lands, and the ferocity and tenacity with which Robin Hood and his men fought instilled such a feeling of fear and dread into the hearts of the border men of the clans Jordan, Armstrong, Douglas and Graham that they never again sought to venture south of the Scottish border – and especially not to do battle with any knight who was the friend of Robin Hood.

389 On another occasion Robin Hood travelled north to teach a young squire of Thurgoland to pay due kindness and respect to his mother Avis. This woman had been a neif on the lands of Sir Jocelyn of Thurgoland, whom she had married. They had a son named Stephen. This cruel and harsh boy became lord of the manor on the death of his father, at which point his mother, according to the laws of the day, was once more reduced to the role of serf, a role her son made sure she served by returning her to a hovel in the village where she was made to work as hard as any other villein. News of his mother's villeinage spread far and wide.

390 Then one night, while Squire Stephen and his men were feasting in their hall, thirty men in dark robes, their heads hooded, strode into the hall and took Squire Stephen away. For a time no one knew where he had gone, but the news soon began to circulate that Robin Hood had taken him away to teach him to have proper respect for his mother and for all those who worked for him. After many months Squire Stephen reappeared at the manor of Thurgoland dressed in villein's rags, and there he sought out his mother whose forgiveness he asked, and from that day forth he lived as a true noble and treated all those on his manor with due respect and attention.

Robin Hood's Bay,
North Yorkshire.
(*Mary Evans
Picture Library*)

391 On a third occasion Robin Hood and his men fought a long and hard sea-battle with
the pirate Damon the Monk, who had been harrying the Yorkshire coast, the pirate
ship being brought ashore after Robin had killed the pirate and hanged all his crew
from their own yard-arm. The bay in which the sea-battle took place has since that
day been known as Robin Hood's Bay.

392 After ten years of his second period as an outlaw, Robin and his men were resting at
their camp at the Stane Lea when a lady rode into their midst. For a moment Robin
was unsure who she was, but when she dismounted and kissed him on the cheek, he
recognised her as his cousin Alice of Havelond. She told him that her husband
Bennett had died three years before, and now that both she and Robin were old and
grey, perhaps it would be better if he gave up his life in the greenwood and came to
live with her at Havelond. Robin refused to give up the life he loved, so Alice told
him that she would travel to the abbey at Kirklees, where their aunt, Dame Ursula,
was the abbess. She asked Robin to visit her there whenever he might have the
chance. This he promised to do and then sent three of his men to escort his cousin to
the abbey at Kirklees.

Kirklees gatehouse in the nineteenth century. Etching from
Joseph Ritson, *Robin Hood*, 1887.

393 From that day forth Robin visited the abbey every six months, and while there had
his blood let as a remedy for the onslaught of old age, resting afterwards at Kirklees
for two or three days as he waited for the wound in his arm to heal. For many years
Robin made his twice-yearly visits to the abbey. One summer, feeling his age, he
decided to visit the abbey again to have his blood let. This time he took Little John
and a number of other outlaws with him, and when they reached the edge of the
abbey's lands, Robin told Little John to wait for him under the cover of the trees.
Should Robin have need of him, he would blow his horn.

394 At the abbey Robin was greeted by his aunt, who told him that Alice of Havelond
had died in the spring and been buried with due respect in the abbey churchyard.
Robin paid his respects to his cousin at her grave and then went back into the abbey
to have his blood let. The abbess led him upstairs into a chamber where she prepared
to let his blood, offering him a drink of wine as she went about her business. Soon
Robin fell into a deep sleep, for the wine had been drugged, and Dame Ursula
opened a vein and let Robin's life-blood flow steadily into the jar she had positioned
on the floor beside his bed. As the jar began to fill, the abbess moved to the door and
beckoned to the person waiting outside.

395 Into the room stole a haggard and bent old man. It was none other than Sir Roger of
Doncaster, who had paid Dame Ursula handsomely to betray his greatest enemy.
Now he smiled in triumph at the sight of Robin Hood lying on the bed, his life-blood
flowing slowly away into the jar beside the bed. Ursula urged him to end it all there
and then with his dagger, but Sir Roger would not, and instead hurried from the room
and out of the abbey.

396 That evening, as Little John sat in the shade of the trees of the forest, his ears pricked up as he heard three faint blows of the horn. Quickly he leapt to his feet and rushed towards the abbey with the rest of his men hot on his heels. They crashed into the great hall and demanded to know where the abbess was, but she was nowhere to be found. Then they asked where their master Robin Hood lay, but not one of the nuns gathered there even knew that he had come to the abbey. Just then Hob o'the Hill rushed into the great hall and told Little John that he had found Robin.

397 Quickly Little John followed the small man up the stairs and into the chamber where Robin lay almost dead on the bed. Seeing his friend lying there, Little John asked for leave to burn the abbey and all those within it who had been a party to this crime, but Robin would have none of it, for he knew that only one person had betrayed him, his aunt, and she would already be far away.

398 Quietly he asked Little John for his bow and an arrow and then, while Little John supported him, Robin Hood let fly his last arrow. It soared out over the abbey lands and fell next to a path within the forest. Little John lay his friend down even before the arrow fell and promised to do as he was asked when Robin Hood told his friend to lie him in the ground where his arrow had fallen. Robin Hood then breathed his last, and a great howl went up from the abbey as Little John and the other outlaws lamented the death of their friend and master.

Robin Hood shoots his last arrow. Illustration from *A Book of Old English Ballads* by George Wharton Edwards.

Robin shooteth his last shaft. Illustration from *The Merry Adventures of Robin Hood* by Howard Pyle.

399 That night Little John carried Robin Hood from the abbey and, with the other outlaws, stood in honour over his body. Then, as the morning sun rose, they dug a grave at the spot where Robin's arrow had fallen, and there laid him to rest, with a sod of turf under his head, and another under his feet. The ageing Friar Tuck spoke the required words as they said farewell to the man they had loved best in all the world.

400 Afterwards they learnt of the visit of Sir Roger of Doncaster to the abbey on that fateful day, and immediately Hob o'the Hill and his brother Ket the Trow made off after him, pursuing him with such venom that the knight only just managed to board a ship at Grimsby and leave the shore before they could catch up with him. Sir Roger sought refuge in France and died there a short while later.

401 Following the death of Robin Hood the outlaws of Sherwood, Clipstone and Barnisdale quickly broke up, some fleeing overseas and others taking on new guises in towns and villages where they could be sure of assistance from those Robin Hood had helped. Little John and Will Scarlet travelled to Cromwell, where they were given lands by Alan-a-Dale, now the lord of those lands, while Much the miller's son was made bailiff at Werrisdale, which Alan-a-Dale also owned after the death of his father Sir Herbrand de Tranmire.

Robin and Little John. Illustration in the *Roxburghe Ballads*, *c.* 1630. (*Getty Images*)

402 Gilbert of the White Hand travelled to the north where he sought fame with the sword, the stories of his deeds and exploits being told for generations to come. Of Ket the Trow and Hob o'the Hill nothing further was ever heard, and though Alan-a-Dale offered them lands at Cromwell, they preferred to remain in the greenwood, and there, though they were never again seen by man, they tended the grave of Robin Hood until their time also came to an end.

PART TWO

Young Robin shoots at squirrels. Illustration from
Bold Robin Hood and his Outlaw Band by Louis
Read.

Robin defeats Nat of Nottingham at quarterstaff. From *Robin Hood* by N.C. Wyeth (1917), p. 257. (*Mary Evans Picture Library*)

An A–Z of People and Places

This concise and easy-to-use reference guide explains all the players and places mentioned in the legends, as well as offering historical, geographical and bibliographical details from a great many other sources. Below are details of the various conventions used to make the dictionary entries easy to cross-reference both to other dictionary entries and to the legends themselves.

- The use of CAPITAL LETTERS indicates a separate entry for the word or words in question.
- Where a headword has alternative spellings these are shown in the form **Gam~mell**, **~well**, this example giving the valid spellings **Gammell** and **Gamwell**. If the variation is simply a difference of one or more letters, then the letters so affected are enclosed in brackets, e.g. **Barn(i)sdale Forest**.
- The use of *italics* indicates that the reference is to a text. *ITALICISED CAPITAL LETTERS* indicates that there is a separate entry for the relevant item.
- Where more than one entry appears under a headword, each entry is preceded by a number. Further references to these words within the dictionary are followed by the appropriate number in superscript, e.g. **Ralph Murdach**[2].
- Numbers in square brackets at the end of an entry indicate the relevant paragraph numbers in Part One, e.g. [34, 38, 324]. Where paragraph numbers are consecutive, the numbers are given in the form [328–9] or [247–56].
- Map references, where given, relate to the maps in Appendix One. Such references appear at the end of the relevant entries in the form {A4}, which would point to grid reference A4 on any of the relevant maps in Appendix One. Ordnance Survey grid references are also given in some cases, in the form (OS123 AA4578), where the first part indicates the Ordnance Survey 1:50,000 sheet number (Landranger series), and the second part gives the two letters of the 100,000-metre square in which the point lies, with the first two numbers being the easting and the final two numbers the northing.

ABBESS The female superior in spirituals and temporals of a community of twelve or more NUNs. With a few necessary exceptions, the position of an abbess in her convent corresponds generally with that of an ABBOT in his monastery. The title was originally the distinctive appellation of Benedictine superiors, but in the course of time it came to be applied also to the conventual superior in other orders, especially to those of the Second Order of St Francis (Poor Clares) and to those of certain colleges of canonesses. An abbess as a rule has a right to wear a ring and bears the crosier as a symbol of her rank, but lacks the jurisdiction belonging to abbots.

ABBEY A monastery canonically erected and autonomous, with a community of not fewer than twelve religious members, either MONKs under the government of an ABBOT or NUNs under that of an ABBESS.

Principal parts of an abbey are:

- almonry – the office of the almoner, responsible for the distribution of alms
- calefactory – (from the Latin *calefacere*, to warm) the heated room in an English monastery where the monks retired occasionally to warm themselves, especially after Matins
- cellars – for stores
- cells – the individual chamber or hut of a nun, monk or hermit. The word can also apply to a small monastery or nunnery dependent on a larger house
- chapter house – a building attached to a monastery or cathedral used for the meetings of the chapter (a body of clerics instituted for observing greater solemnity of divine worship and, in cathedral churches, for assisting the bishop according to Church law as his senate and council and governing the see during vacancy). In monasteries the chapter house was used daily after Prime for the reading of the *Martyrology* and *Necrology*, the correction of

faults, the assignment of daily tasks and the exhortation of the superior, and again later for evening collation. Secular canons used it for the formal transaction of public business of common interest to the body corporate. The shape of the chapter house varied. In England it was the object of careful design, culminating in the polygonal chapter house of which Lincoln Cathedral (1240–60) has perhaps the earliest example
- choir – the part of the church reserved for the stalls of canons, priests, monks and choristers, separated from the rest by low carved partitions of stone or wood
- cloister – (from the Latin *claudere*, to enclose) in ecclesiastical terms cloister means an enclosure for religious retirement; formally, it signifies the legal restrictions imposed on those who are enclosed. Present canon law requires every convent or monastery of regulars, on its completion, to be encloistered
- conference room
- dormitory
- guest house
- infirmary
- kitchen
- novitiate – the quarters occupied by a novice, a trainee who will spend a minimum of one year learning the roles of the order he or she has entered, and preparing for life as a monk or a nun. At the end of the training period the novice takes the vows and enters the order as a full member
- oratory – (from the Latin *oratorium*, from *orare*, to pray) as a general term an oratory signifies a place of prayer, but technically it means a structure other than a parish church that is set aside by ecclesiastical authority for prayer and the celebration of mass
- parlour or locutorium – (from the Latin *locutor*, one who speaks) as the name suggests, this was a place where the members of the order met and talked, and received their guests.
- refectory – the dining room for the members of the religious order
- workshops

The chief abbey buildings are constructed around a quadrangle; in the more usual English plan the church is on the northern side.

Friar Tuck and the abbot. Illustration from *Tales and Plays of Robin Hood* by Eleanor L. Skinner.

ABBOT A title given to the superior of a community of twelve or more MONKs who are all dedicated to a life of celibacy and religious seclusion. The name is derived from *abba*, the Syriac form of the Hebrew word *ab*, and means 'father'. In Syria, where it had its origin, and in Egypt it was employed as a title of honour and respect, and was given to any monk of venerable age or of eminent sanctity. It did not originally imply the exercise of any authority over a religious community. From the east the word passed over to the west, where it was soon received into general use to designate the superior of an ABBEY or a MONASTERY. The abbot was usually elected by his contemporaries by secret ballot, either for life or for a set number of years. The authority of an abbot is twofold: one, paternal, by which he administers the property of the abbey and maintains discipline and the observance of the rule and constitutions of the order; the other, quasi-episcopal.

ABBOT ROBERT The evil, scheming, money-grabbing abbot of ST MARY'S ABBEY in YORK, an ally of Sir ISENBART DE BELAME and the other knights of the EVIL HOLD. For many years Abbot Robert had plotted with the likes of Sir GUY OF GISBORNE to seize the lands held under rent by ROBERT OF LOCKSLEY, but their plans never came to fruition as Robert of Locksley was particularly careful to ensure that his dues were always paid on time.

Following the killing of Sir ROGER DE LONGCHAMP, after which Robert of Locksley was declared an outlaw, the abbot sent Sir HUBERT OF LYNN to take possession of the manor of LOCKSLEY known as OUTWOODS. Robert of Locksley killed Sir Hubert and then he and the oppressed villagers went after Sir Guy of Gisborne, but the latter escaped. Abbot Robert was furious with Sir Guy, whom he blamed for the villagers' revolt, and from that day Sir Guy had to temper his anger under threat of having his own manor at BIRKENCAR taken away from him.

In league with the knights of the Evil Hold, Abbot Robert had planned to take the lands of Sir HERBRAND DE TRANMIRE, but again the plans he so carefully laid came to nothing after ROBIN HOOD lent Sir Herbrand the 400 pounds he needed to pay his debt to the abbot, who had lent him that sum to pay the fine imposed on him after his son ALAN DE TRANMIRE had killed Sir IVO LE RAVENER.

Once a month Abbot Robert, his PRIOR and his clerks would gather in the chapter house of St Mary's Abbey to collect the dues and rents from their tenants, and it was on just such an occasion that Sir Herbrand de Tranmire came to him, accompanied by LITTLE JOHN acting as his squire, to repay the loan of 400 pounds. At first the knight pretended that he had not been able to collect the money, much to the delight of Abbot Robert and those gathered with him, who included the SHERIFF OF YORK and Sir NIGER LE GRYM, the latter being one of the knights of the Evil Hold.

Some time later the abbot was travelling through the forest in the company of four monks, six archers and seven SUMPTER horses, when he was brought into the camp of Robin Hood by Little John on the very day that Sir Herbrand de Tranmire was due to repay Robin Hood the 400 pounds he had lent that knight to pay off the debt to the abbot. The abbot had been carrying 800 pounds in his bags, which Robin took as repayment of the loan to Sir Herbrand, doubly repaid to him under the guidance and blessing of the Virgin Mary. Robin then had the abbot say mass for the outlaws and hear their confessions, though the abbot did not do this until

Robin had left him tied to a tree like a common criminal for some time.

Just as the last confession had been heard Sir Herbrand de Tranmire rode into the camp to repay Robin, but Robin would take none of the knight's 400 pounds as he had already been repaid twice that amount by the abbot. Seeing that the abbot's humiliation was complete, Robin sent him on his way. Soon afterwards the abbot fell ill, and he died in the following spring. His replacement was refused by Sir WILLIAM DE LONGCHAMP, the HIGH CHANCELLOR, who appointed his own nephew ROBERT DE LONGCHAMP as the new abbot.

[89, 185, 249–57]

ABEL, EPHRAIM BEN See EPHRAIM BEN ABEL.

ABJURE To renounce or retract a crime, especially under oath. When RICHARD MALBÊTE was forced to abjure before the coroner following the murder of JOHN LE MARCHANT in PONTEFRACT, he would have been forced to take an oath known as 'abjuration of the realm'. This oath was an alternative to being made an OUTLAW for a criminal who had claimed sanctuary. The abjuror was obliged to confess his crime and then renounce England in full knowledge that he would only legally be permitted to return following a royal pardon.

[183]

A'GREEN, JOHN See JOHN A'GREEN.

AIDS, FEUDAL Also known as auxilia, these were a source of royal revenue under FEUDALISM. Feudal aids were paid by all those who held land of the king. They were taken when a king's son was knighted, when his daughter was married and, in the event of the king's capture, to pay for his ransom. Thus it was feudal aids rather than a specific tax that ROBIN HOOD and his men helped to collect from those reluctant to pay.

AL(L)AN-A-DALE The name by which ALAN DE TRANMIRE, son and squire of Sir HERBRAND DE TRANMIRE, preferred to be known. Popular belief makes Alan-a-Dale one of the MERRY MEN, but the principal legends do not bear this out. Nor do they make him a minstrel. Instead his story is quite separate from that of ROBIN HOOD. Although their paths crossed on several occasions, Alan-a-Dale never was a mainstream member of the band of outlaws who chose to follow Robin Hood.

The first meeting between Alan-a-Dale and Robin Hood happened at the church at CAMPSALL shortly after Robin and his men had taken to a life in the greenwood. Having gone to the church to say mass and make their confessions, Robin and his men were told by KET THE TROW during the course of the service that they had been followed by two of the knights of the EVIL HOLD. Alan-a-Dale was already in the church when Robin and his men arrived, and only introduced himself to Robin after the service had come to an end and the church had come under attack. Hearing that Robin and his followers were up against the knights of the Evil Hold, with whom Alan-a-Dale also had a quarrel, he offered his services which were readily and gladly accepted.

After the knights attacking Campsall Church had been put to flight, Alan-a-Dale and Robin Hood talked about their quarrels with the knights of the Evil Hold. Alan-a-Dale told Robin that he loved ALICE DE BEAUFOREST, whose father held lands on the edge of SHERWOOD FOREST. However, Sir ISENBART DE BELAME, the lord of the Evil Hold, had threatened to force her father, Sir WALTER DE BEAUFOREST, from his lands unless Alice married a knight of his choosing.

As Robin and Alan-a-Dale walked they came across a CHURL talking to a knight. They recognised the latter as one of the two who had attacked Campsall Church, and Alan-a-Dale called him by name – Sir IVO LE RAVENER. Alan-a-Dale and the knight engaged in single combat, with Alan-a-Dale eventually emerging victorious when he slew the knight. At this the churl, whose name was GRULL, attempted to kill Robin Hood but was instead himself slain by HOB O'THE HILL.

Following the battle Alan-a-Dale told Robin that he would return to his home at WERRISDALE rather than to the home of his foster-brother PIERS THE LUCKY at FOREST HOLD, where he had been staying, lest Sir Isenbart de Belame sought retribution against one who was innocent, and the two quickly set off through the forest to collect Alan-a-Dale's horse from where he had left it tethered beside a forester's hut about a mile away. As they reached the hut they just caught sight of a huge man leaving the clearing, where they found the forester BLACK HUGO tied to one of the posts of the hut. Alan-a-Dale and Robin decided to leave the forester tied up, and soon continued on their way until Robin put Alan-a-Dale on the road to Werrisdale and the two took leave of each other. It was to be quite some time before their paths crossed again.

Robin Hood next heard of Alan-a-Dale when he went to meet the curtal monk FRIAR TUCK for the first time. After meeting the monk, he was joined by

Alan-a-Dale lieth beside the fountain. Illustration from *The Merry Adventures of Robin Hood* by Howard Pyle.

MAID MARIAN, who was being chased by the men of the Evil Hold under the leadership of Black Hugo; having fought them off with the aid of LITTLE JOHN and others of his band of outlaws, Robin Hood was led into Friar Tuck's home and introduced to Alice de Beauforest. She told him that Alan-a-Dale had been outlawed for the killing of Sir Ivo le Ravener, and she now feared that she would be lost to him for ever as she was to be married in three days' time to an evil old knight by the name of Sir RANULF DE GREASBY, the lord of HAGTHORN CASTLE, the marriage being forced upon her father by Sir Isenbart de Belame (who also sought to ruin Sir Herbrand de Tranmire for his son's crime).

Robin thought about the predicament for a moment and then asked Alice de Beauforest for a token that Alan-a-Dale would instantly recognise. She gave Robin a ring which he passed on to WILL THE BOWMAN, along with a ring from Alice's maid NETTA O'THE MEERING. Robin then told

Will the Bowman to hurry to CROMWELL and seek out one JACK, SON OF WILKIN, who would take him to Alan-a-Dale's hideout. Alice's ring, and that of Netta o'the Meering, would instantly identify Will the Bowman as a friend.

Will the Bowman duly found Jack, son of Wilkin, and together they travelled to the wastelands between SHERWOOD and Werrisdale where they found Alan-a-Dale and told him of Robin's plan to thwart the evil intentions of Sir Isenbart de Belame.

Two days after the meeting between Will the Bowman and Jack, son of Wilkin, the VILLEINs of the village of Cromwell assembled at the church to witness the ill-matched wedding of Alice de Beauforest and Sir Ranulf de Greasby. However, moments before the ceremony was to begin, Robin Hood interrupted the proceedings and Sir Ranulf was killed by a small black arrow fired down from the rafters above him. Fighting broke out in the church and one of Sir Ranulf's knights, Sir BERTRAN LE NOIR, sought to make off with

Alice de Beauforest, but as they came out of the church they found their path blocked by Sir PHILIP DE SCROOBY, another of Sir Ranulf's supporters, who was locked in battle with Alan-a-Dale.

Momentarily distracted by the sight of his beloved, Alan-a-Dale almost lost his life, but just in time Jack, son of Wilkin, struck Sir Philip de Scrooby with his STAFF, causing the knight's sword to miss Alan-a-Dale. Recovering from the shock of seeing his love being borne away, Alan-a-Dale resumed his sword fight and eventually killed Sir Philip de Scrooby, whereupon he went to look for Alice de Beauforest. He found her a short distance from the church being tended by Netta o'the Meering and Jack, son of Wilkin. The latter had rescued her when he leapt onto the back of Sir Bertran le Noir's horse and stabbed the knight in the heart.

Alan-a-Dale and Alice de Beauforest travelled into the forest with Robin Hood and his men and were subsequently married by Friar Tuck. What happened to Alan-a-Dale after his marriage is a little sketchy. Some sources say that he lived with Robin Hood in the forests, and thus joined the outlaw band, while others say that he lived with his father-in-law, both of them under the protection of Robin Hood, which rendered them safe from attack or retribution by Sir Isenbart de Belame.

It is therefore some time after Robin Hood had helped Alan-a-Dale to marry his beloved that he reappears in the main legend. Some years have passed and RICHARD I has returned to England, having been released from captivity in Germany after the huge ransom demanded had been paid with considerable help from Robin Hood and his men. Robin Hood has met the king, who is disguised as a monk, and has just received a buffet from him for failing in an archery contest, when Alan-a-Dale, his wife Dame Alice, Sir RICHARD AT LEE and Robin's wife, the Maid Marian, enter the camp. Sir Richard at Lee recognised the king, who revealed himself and then duly pardoned all those he found in Robin Hood's company of any crimes they had committed, and at the same time restored to Alan-a-Dale and his wife the lands of DE BEAUFOREST, to which they immediately returned. If the legends do in fact follow history, this would have been in 1194.

There is now a gap of some twenty-two years in the association between Alan-a-Dale and Robin Hood, during which time Alan-a-Dale and his wife presumably lived at peace with Sir Walter de Beauforest at Cromwell. It is only after King John has reneged on the terms of the MAGNA CARTA, and Robin and his men are besieging the Evil Hold,

that Alan-a-Dale and his father-in-law join the outlaws to help them in their task, his own father Sir Herbrand de Tranmire now being too old to participate in the fighting. However, the legends do not tell us how Alan-a-Dale fared in the fighting at the Evil Hold, though he must have survived for after the death of Robin Hood he gave lands at CROMWELL to both Little John and WILL SCARLET, while he also gave lands to MUCH THE MILLER'S SON at Werrisdale, which he had by that time inherited after the death of his father. Alan-a-Dale also offered lands to Ket the Trow and his brother Hob o'the Hill, but they refused as they preferred to live out the remainder of their lives in the forests.

What eventually became of Alan-a-Dale and his wife is not recorded, but it seems likely that they simply lived out the remainder of their lives in peace as lord and lady of the manors of Cromwell and Werrisdale. Whether or not Alan-a-Dale had any heirs is also unrecorded.

[57, 60–1, 63–4, 69–70, 72–3, 130, 134–7, 142, 144, 157, 160–1, 163–4, 166, 180, 327, 331, 352, 401–2]

ALAN DE TRANMIRE The real name of ALAN-A-DALE, son of Sir HERBRAND DE TRANMIRE and Dame JUDITH. The 'de Tranmire' element of his family name signifies 'of Tranmire' or 'of Tranmere', which, if taken literally, would indicate that Sir Herbrand and his son hailed from Merseyside, as Tranmere is today a part of Birkenhead.

[57]

ALBERIC DE WISGAR Powerful baron of YORK who, having borrowed a large sum of money from RABBI ELIEZER, sought to cancel out that debt by inciting the people of York to revolt against the Jews, in which task he was helped by the evil RICHARD MALBÊTE. The Jews took refuge in the castle, but when that was eventually overrun the people of York hurried to YORK CATHEDRAL, where they took out and burnt all the records of debts. Alberic de Wisgar seemed to have succeeded in his aim, but the king's justices descended on York shortly afterwards and punished all those who had taken part. Alberic de Wisgar's lands were confiscated.

Historically the name Wisgar appears to have connections with the small woollen town of Clare in Suffolk and Thaxted in Essex. An entry in the Domesday Book reads:

[At] CLARA [Clare] Aluric held as a manor 24 carucates of land in the time of King

Edward. Then 40 villeins, afterwards 3S, 310W 30. Thcts and afterwards so bordars, now 30. Then as now 20 serfs. Then 12 ploughs on the demesne, afterwards 6, 110W 7. Then 36 ploughs belonging to the men, afterwards 30, now 24. 37 acres of meadow. Woodland for 12 swine. Then as 11(1W 1 null. Now 5 arpents of vineyard. . . . Then as now a market. Now 43 burgesses. Aluric son of Wisgar gave this manor to St John in the time of King Edward. . . . However, after King William came he seized it into his own hand. . . .

It is quite conceivable, therefore, that the reference to Wisgar in the Robin Hood legends is not a reference to a particular place, but rather indicates a region of Suffolk and Essex that was, before the Norman invasion, under the control of either the Wisgar family or an individual of that name.

[212–13]

ALEXANDER II (1198–1249) The son of William (I) the Lion and Ermengarde de Beaumont, he was crowned on 5 December 1214. Taking advantage of King JOHN's problems, he intervened in the BARONS' WAR in 1215 in pursuance of Scottish claims to the three northern counties. John's northern barons swore fealty and homage to Alexander, though upon John's death in 1217 they switched their allegiance to the new English king, HENRY III. Alexander made an incursion as far

King Alexander II (1198–1249) of Scotland. (*Getty Images*)

south as Dover, but eventually, by the treaty of YORK (1237), abandoned these claims in return for lands in England. By the treaty of Newcastle (1244), he acknowledged Henry III of England as his liege lord. Alexander II's first wife was King John's daughter Joan, whom he married at York Minster on 19 June 1221 when she was just eleven years old. She died childless on 4 March 1238. His second wife was Marie de Coucy, the daughter of a French baron, whom he married on 15 May 1239. She bore him a son on 4 September 1241, who later succeeded to the Scottish throne as Alexander III following the death of Alexander II near Oban during a military expedition to the Western Isles in an attempt to wrest them from the Norwegian crown, a feat his son achieved in 1263. If ROBIN HOOD was indeed involved with the conflict of the barons that led to the signing of the MAGNA CARTA, it is quite possible that he came into contact with Alexander II, and may well have been at York in September 1237 when Alexander II and Henry III established their respective kingdoms along the River Tweed and the Cheviot Hills to the Solway Firth.

ALFRED OF GAM~MELL, ~WELL A cousin of ROBERT OF LOCKSLEY who, following the instructions supplied to him by his cousin, travelled to the greenwood and was greeted by his cousin. Alfred told him of the plans of Sir GUY OF GISBORNE, who was by that time in league with RALPH MURDACH,[1] the SHERIFF OF NOTTINGHAM. Alfred of Gamwell related how the pair were hiring men to disguise themselves as beggars and wander through the forests in order to gather intelligence that would lead to the capture of ROBIN HOOD and his men. (See also STEPHEN OF GAMWELL).

[83–5, 87–90]

ALICE, LADY The wife of Sir RICHARD AT LEE. Always friendly towards ROBIN HOOD, it was Lady Alice who brought him the news that her husband had been taken prisoner by the SHERIFF OF NOTTINGHAM. Following the rescue of her husband by Robin and his men, Lady Alice and Sir Richard at Lee lived with the outlaws until RICHARD I restored to them their lands at LINDEN LEA, though the legends refer to the king talking only with Sir Richard at Lee, and it may well be that Lady Alice had died in the intervening period.

[26, 29, 280–1]

ALICE DE BEAUFOREST The daughter of Sir WALTER DE BEAUFOREST and the beloved of ALAN DE TRANMIRE, better known as ALAN-A-

DALE. Alice de Beauforest's father had received an ultimatum from Sir ISENBART DE BELAME that, unless his daughter married Sir RANULF DE GREASBY, an evil old knight, he would be hounded off his property, his lands seized and his manor burnt. Though ROBIN HOOD knew of Alice's plight from his first meeting with Alan-a-Dale, it was to be quite some time before he actually met the lady in question.

This happened when Robin Hood travelled to acquaint himself with FRIAR TUCK. Having beaten off the attackers led by BLACK HUGO, who had followed MAID MARIAN to Friar Tuck's home, Robin was taken into the portly monk's home and introduced to Alice de Beauforest, who had travelled to the forest with Maid Marian. Alice told Robin that her marriage to Sir Ranulf de Greasby had been arranged for three days' time, and also that Alan-a-Dale had been falsely accused of killing Sir IVO LE RAVENER and had thus been proclaimed outlaw.

Robin devised a plan and sent WILL THE BOWMAN to seek out Alan-a-Dale. Three days later, during the wedding itself, Robin and his men killed Sir Ranulf de Greasby and his comrades, though Alice herself was almost abducted by Sir BERTRAN LE NOIR. He was killed as he made off with her by JACK, SON OF WILKIN. Afterwards Alice de Beauforest and Alan-a-Dale travelled into the heart of the forest with Robin and his men, and were subsequently married there by Friar Tuck.

The legends do not make it wholly clear what happened after that, for some sources say Alice and her husband remained with Robin in the forests, while others say they lived with her father Sir Walter de Beauforest. Whichever is the truth, virtually nothing more is heard of Alice and her husband until after RICHARD I's return to England. The king travelled to the forest disguised as an abbot to meet with Robin Hood, and just as Robin was receiving a buffet from the king for failing in an archery contest, Dame Alice, her husband Alan-a-Dale, Sir RICHARD AT LEE and MAID MARIAN rode into the camp. Sir Richard at Lee instantly revealed the identity of the king, who grants them all pardon and restores the DE BEAUFOREST lands to their rightful owner. Alan-a-Dale and his wife then return to their lands, and nothing further is heard of Alice de Beauforest. It can safely be assumed she lived out the rest of her life in peace at her father's manor.

[60, 130, 133–4, 136–9, 142, 144, 146–7, 150, 154–7, 159–64, 166, 327, 329, 331]

ALICE OF HAVELOND A cousin of ROBERT OF LOCKSLEY, Alice was the wife of a well-to-do YEOMAN by the name of BENNETT, who had been imprisoned and held to ransom by a Scottish knight. In his absence, ROBERT OF PRESTBURY and THOMAS OF PATHERLEY seized the manor of HAVELOND and evicted Alice. For a year she laboured to raise enough money to release her husband, but when Bennett returned to reclaim the manor of Havelond he was so severely beaten by Thomas of Patherley and Robert of Prestbury that he was lucky to escape with his life.

Alice of Havelond then petitioned the king on her husband's behalf, but was told that the king would only hear an appeal made by Bennett himself. This was impossible as the attack had left him a cripple. Alice then turned to ALFRED OF GAMMELL, another of Robert of Locksley's cousins, who offered to make the appeal on her behalf. Knowing that this would be useless, Alice of Havelond appealed to ROBIN HOOD, who assured her that her rightful property would be returned to her. Sure enough, a few days later the men of SCAURDALE saw two houses burning in the distance, fires that signified Robin Hood's rightful vengeance on the two robbers.

Many years later, following Bennett's death, Alice of Havelond came to the forests to ask Robin Hood to leave the life of an outlaw and live out the remainder of his days with her at Havelond. When Robin refused, she told him that she would spend the rest of her life at the abbey at KIRKLEES, where their aunt, Dame URSULA, was the abbess. Robin visited his aunt and his cousin once every six months at the abbey, until that fateful day when Dame Ursula betrayed him to Sir ROGER OF DONCASTER. Alice of Havelond had died in the previous spring and been buried in the abbey churchyard.

[86–7, 392, 394]

ALISAUNDRE A hunting hound owned by Sir RANULF DE GREASBY. Sir PHILIP DE SCROOBY demanded Alisaundre as payment for searching for the mysterious minstrel JOCELYN, along with the merlin hawks GRIP and FANG, payment to which Sir Ranulf grudgingly agreed.

[155]

ALSTAN A VILLEIN from BLYTHE, Alstan was the father of DUDDA or DODD, a man-at-arms who had been pressed into service by HUBERT OF LYNN. Dudda yielded to ROBERT OF LOCKSLEY after Hubert himself and four other men-at-arms had been killed.

[34]

AMERCEMENT A money penalty imposed on an offender in the lord's court during Anglo-Saxon and NORMAN times. The word comes from the French *à merci*, meaning at the mercy of (the lord or king). Originally the amount of an amercement was arbitrary and such fines were a fruitful source of income for a lord. It gradually came to be fixed in many cases, while the MAGNA CARTA stipulated that a freeman should be amerced according to his means. It was by the process of amercement that ABBOT ROBERT was able to deprive the newly outlawed ROBERT OF LOCKSLEY of his manor and lands, and how Sir ISENBART DE BELAME was able to fine Sir HERBRAND DE TRANMIRE for the death of his comrade at the hands of ALAN DE TRANMIRE, and then to impose a second fine after the first had been paid.

ANGEVIN Royal dynasty descended from the counts of ANJOU. The comital dynasty originated in the tenth century, and in 1128 Geoffrey Plantagenet, Count of Anjou, married Matilda, daughter of Henry I of England. In 1154, on the death of King Stephen, their son succeeded to the English throne as HENRY II. Although the dynasty survived until the death of Richard III in 1485, only Henry II and his sons RICHARD I and JOHN were styled Angevin kings, the remainder of the dynasty being more popularly known as Plantagenets. Under Henry II the Angevin empire stretched from Scotland to the Pyrenees, taking in England, much of Wales and Ireland, NORMANDY, Anjou and AQUITAINE. Most of the French possessions (including Anjou) were lost by King John.

The Angevins were noted for their ruthless exercise of royal power, which they greatly extended, arousing in the process considerable baronial and ecclesiastical hostility. This hostility culminated in the crisis of the MAGNA CARTA and later the BARONS' WARS.

ANGOULÊME Angoulême in western central France, the former capital of the historic province of Angoumois, is now the capital of the *département* of Charente. It is situated 275 miles south-west of Paris, 51 miles south-west of Limoges and 68 miles north-east of Bordeaux. The *ville-haute* (upper town) is on a plateau overlooking the juncture of the Anguienne and Charente rivers some 230 feet below.

In 507 the Franks under Clovis I took the town from the Visigoths. From the ninth century it was the capital of the counts of Angoulême. The town and the region became an English possession when Prince JOHN married ISABEL OF ANGOULÊME.

During the Hundred Years War, from 1337 to 1453, it was repeatedly fought over by the French and English. In the fifteenth century Angoulême began its industrial development, fostered by the town's seaport on the navigable Charente river. During the late sixteenth century the town was involved in the bitter religious wars between the Catholics and Protestants.

Angoulême's Byzantine Cathedral of St-Pierre was built in the twelfth century (1105–28). A domed Romanesque edifice, its façade boasts a richly ornate collection of seventy-five Romanesque sculptures, each in its own niche. In contrast, the interior is stark; it has four domes and is without aisles. It was considerably damaged by the Calvinists during the religious wars of the sixteenth century, and was repaired during the seventeenth. Between 1866 and 1875 the cathedral was extensively restored. Today, its west front's twelfth-century statuary, based on themes of the Ascension and the Last Judgement, is generally undamaged. Near the first doorway is a superb Christ in Majesty, surrounded by the Evangelists.

A town hall was built in the nineteenth century on the site of the château that was the birthplace of François I's sister, Margaret of Angoulême. Today, only the thirteenth-century Lusignan and the fifteenth-century Valois towers remain.

ANGOULÊME, ISABEL OF See ISABEL OF ANGOULÊME.

ANJOU Region and former province of west central France, Anjou corresponds roughly with Maine-et-Loire and parts of Indre-et-Loire, Mayenne and Sarthe *départements*. Angers, the historic capital, and Saumur are the chief towns. A fertile lowland, Anjou is traversed by the Loire, Mayenne, Sarthe, Loir and Maine rivers. It is chiefly an agricultural area with excellent vineyards producing the renowned Saumur sparkling wines. Originally occupied by the Andecavi, a Gallic people, the region was conquered by Caesar. Anjou fell to the Franks in the fifth century and became a countship under Charlemagne in the ninth. By the tenth century it was in the hands of the first line of the counts of Anjou (see ANGEVIN), who expanded their holdings vigorously. Fulk Nerra, who founded the Angevin dynasty, acquired Saumur from the counts of Blois. His successor, Geoffrey Martel, won Touraine from Blois (1044) and Maine from Normandy (1051). Fulk (d. 1143), the grandson of Fulk Nerra, after protracted wars with Henry I of England over the possession of Maine, married his son Geoffrey to Henry's daughter Matilda. Geoffrey ruled Anjou from 1129 to 1151, and conquered Normandy, of which he was crowned duke in 1144. His son, later HENRY II of England, married ELEANOR OF AQUITAINE and with her inheritance ruled most of western France. When Henry II's grandson, Arthur I, Duke of Brittany, rebelled against his uncle, JOHN of England, he won the support of PHILIP II of France, to whom he paid homage (1199) for Anjou, Maine and Touraine. After Arthur's death, Philip II seized all Anjou in 1204. In 1246, Louis IX of France gave Anjou in appanage to his brother Charles, Count of Provence, who later also became King of Sicily and Naples. Charles II of Naples gave Anjou as dowry to his daughter Margaret when she married Charles of Valois, son of Philip III of France. When their son became King Philip VI of France in 1328, Anjou was again reunited with the French crown. John II of France, however, made Anjou a duchy (1360) and gave it to his son Louis (later Louis I of Naples). Louis XI of France inherited Anjou after the deaths of René, grandson of Louis I, and of Charles of Maine, René's nephew and the last of the Angevin line in 1480 and 1481 respectively. Anjou was definitively annexed to France in 1487. In the sixteenth century Anjou was held in appanage at various times; the last duke was Francis of Alençon and Anjou. The region was devastated during the Wars of Religion (1562–98). During the French Revolution the rising of the Vendée, the royalist revolt against the revolution, occurred in Anjou.

[328]

AQUITAINE A province of south-west France extending from the Pyrenees to the River Loire and roughly corresponding to the south-western third of France. It was one of the three divisions of ancient Gaul. After 500 years of Roman rule, it fell to the Visigoths in the fifth century and then to the Franks who defeated the Visigoths in 507. The Franks rarely maintained strong control over Aquitaine, and in about 725 it was raided by the Muslim conquerors of Spain. The Frankish leader Charles Martel crushed these invaders in 733, and Aquitaine became part of the Carolingian empire.

In the ninth century the leading counts and other nobility gradually freed themselves of royal control. Bernard Plantevelue (r. 868–86) and his son William I (r. 886–918), whose power was based in Auvergne, called themselves dukes of Aquitaine, but their state disintegrated. William V (r. 995–1030) founded a new duchy of Aquitaine based in Poitou, which reached its zenith under William VIII (r. 1058–86). When William X died (1137), his daughter ELEANOR OF AQUITAINE married Louis VII of France, whom she divorced in 1152 to marry HENRY II of England, bringing the region to him as her dowry. The province formally became an English possession in 1154. Eleanor maintained an elegant chivalric court at Poitiers. Her sons RICHARD I and JOHN, and their successors as kings of England, were dukes of Aquitaine (later known as Guienne).

The French conquered Poitou in 1224 and other parts of Aquitaine in the next century. English victories during the Hundred Years War enabled Edward III to reconstruct the old duchy in the 1360s, but France finally conquered the remainder of it in 1453.

[331]

Illustration from *Bold Robin Hood and his Outlaw Band* by Louis Read.

ARMS, ASSIZE OF A legislative enactment made in 1181 that required all freemen (*tota communa liberorum hominum*) to supply themselves with weapons and military equipment according to their wealth. The 1181 Assize of Arms said:

1. Whoever possesses one knight's fee shall have a shirt of mail, a helmet, a shield and a lance; and every knight shall have as many shirts of mail, helmets, shields and lances as he possesses knight's fees in demesne.*

2. Moreover, every free layman who possesses chattels or rents to the value of 16 marks shall have a shirt of mail, a helmet, a shield and a lance; and every free layman possessing chattels or rents to the value of 10 marks shall have a hauberk, an iron cap and a lance.†

3. All burgesses and the whole community of freemen shall have [each] a gambeson,‡ an iron cap and a lance.

4. Besides, each of them shall swear to have these arms before the feast of St Hilary, to be faithful to the lord king Henry – namely, the son of the Empress Matilda – and to bear these arms in his service according to his command and in fealty to the lord king and his kingdom. And henceforth no one having these arms shall sell them or pledge them or lend them or alienate them in any other way; nor shall a lord in any way alienate them from his men, either through forfeiture or through gift or through pledge or in any other way.

5. If any one having these arms dies, his arms shall remain to his heir. If, however, the heir is not of age to use arms in time of need, that person who has wardship over him shall also have custody of the arms and shall find a man who can use the arms in the service of the lord king until the heir is of age to bear arms, and then he shall have them.

6. Any burgess who has more arms than he ought to have by this assize shall sell them, or give them away, or in some way alienate them to such a man as will keep them for the service of the lord king of England. And none of them shall keep more arms than he ought to have by this assize.

* That is to say, as many knights as remain charged against his demesne.
† Presumably less elaborate armour than that required of the other group.
‡ A padded surcoat.

7. No Jew shall keep in his possession a shirt of mail or a hauberk, but he shall sell it or give it away or alienate it in some other way, so that it shall remain in the king's service.

8. No one shall carry arms out of England except by the command of the lord king; no one is to sell arms to another to carry out of England; nor shall a merchant or any other man carry them out of England.

9. The justices shall have [a report] sworn by lawful knights, or by other free and lawful men of the hundreds and neighbourhoods and boroughs – as many as they see fit to employ – as to what persons possess chattels to the amount that they should have a shirt of mail, a helmet, a lance and a shield according to what has been provided; so that they shall separately name for those [justices] all men of their hundreds and neighbourhoods and boroughs who are worth 16 marks in either chattels or rents, and likewise those who are worth 10 marks. And then the justices shall have written down [the names of] all those jurors and other men, [recording] how much in chattels or rents they [each] have and what arms, according to the value of the chattels or rents, they should [each] have. Then, in their presence and in a common assembly of those men, they shall have read this assize regarding the possession of arms, and they shall have those men swear to have arms according to the value of the aforesaid chattels or rents, and to keep them for the service of the lord king according to this aforesaid assize, under the command of and in fealty to the lord king Henry and his kingdom. If, moreover, it should happen that any one of them, who ought to have these arms, is not in the county during the period when the justices are in that county, the justices shall set a time for him [to appear] before them in another county. And if he does not come to them in any county through which they are to go, and is not in that land [at all], they shall set him a time at Westminster toward the octave of St Michael; so that, as he loves his life and all that he has, he shall be there for swearing his oath. And they shall command him, before the aforesaid feast of St Hilary, to have arms according to the obligation resting on him.

10. The justices shall have proclamation made in the counties through which they are to go that, with respect to those who do not have

such arms as have been specified above, the lord king will take vengeance, not merely on their lands or chattels, but on their limbs.

11. No one who does not possess 16 marks or 10 marks in chattels is to swear concerning free and lawful men.

12. The justices shall command through all the counties that no one, as he loves his life and all that he has, shall buy or sell any ship to be taken away from England, and that no one shall carry any timber or cause it to be carried out of England. And the lord king commands that no one shall be received for the oath concerning arms unless he is a freeman.

In 1225 the scope of the legislation was increased to include VILLEINs as well. It remained in force until the Militia Act of 1662. The Assize of Arms was used to great effect by men of wealth to assemble what amounted to private armies, which they could use more or less as they pleased, so long as they assisted the monarch in times of need. This corruption of power is widely illustrated in the legends of ROBIN HOOD and his men, especially in the case of Sir ISENBART DE BELAME and the knights of the EVIL HOLD.

ARMSTRONG One of the four border clans routed by ROBIN HOOD when he came to the aid of Sir DROGO OF DALLAS TOWER. The other clans were DOUGLAS, GRAHAM and JORDAN.

[388]

ARNALD OF SHOTLEY HAWE, LORD The cruel lord to whom, as reported by MUCH THE MILLER'S SON, Sir GUY OF GISBORNE had arranged to sell the ten most troublesome VILLEINs of the manor of BIRKENCAR. It was this, among other things, including the outlawing of ROBERT OF LOCKSLEY, and their continued vicious treatment at the hands of Sir Guy of Gisborne, that persuaded the original fourteen to join Robert of Locksley as outlaws living in the forest.

[38–42]

ARTHUR-A-BLAND A resident of NOTTINGHAM and a cousin of LITTLE JOHN, Arthur-a-Bland joined ROBIN HOOD in the second or third year of his time as an outlaw. He is only mentioned directly in the legends when he and WILL THE BOWMAN went with Little John to bring ABBOT ROBERT and his entourage to the outlaw camp. Following the pardoning of Robin Hood and all his men by RICHARD I, Arthur-a-Bland joined the king in his

expedition against PHILIP II of France. He was killed at the castle of CHALUZ, where Richard I also met his death.

[113, 248, 334]

ARTHUR OF BRITTANY (1187–1203) Grandson of HENRY II and nephew of RICHARD I, Arthur was named as heir apparent by Richard in 1190, but the king subsequently recognised his own brother JOHN as heir. After John's accession, Arthur claimed English territories in France with the help of PHILIP II of France. In the ensuing conflict he was captured and soon afterwards died (13 April 1203), some sources suggesting that Arthur was perhaps murdered by John.

Illustration from *Bold Robin Hood and his Outlaw Band* by Louis Read.

The stout bout between Little John and Arthur-a-Bland. Illustration from *The Merry Adventures of Robin Hood* by Howard Pyle.

AUXILIA Alternative name for feudal AIDS.

AVICE OF GLOUCESTER Also known as Isabel, Avice married Prince JOHN in 1189 and was Queen Consort from 1199, but she remained childless. John was absolved from the marriage in 1200 in order to marry ISABEL OF ANGOULÊME. Avice retired to estates in Berkhamsted and married the justiciar Geoffrey fitzPeter; after his death in 1213 she married the justiciar HUBERT DE BURGH. She died in 1217. It seems quite likely that she would have travelled with her first husband to NOTTINGHAM during Richard I's absence, in which case ROBIN HOOD and his men would have known of her, and may even have had direct contact with her.

AVIS A NEIF who married Sir JOCELYN OF THURGOLAND and gave him a son, Squire STEPHEN. Following Sir Jocelyn's death, Stephen forced his mother back into villeinage, but he was abducted by ROBIN HOOD and made to realise the error of his ways. Upon his release he was reunited with his mother, whom he then brought back into the manor and treated with the respect due to her.

[389–90]

B

BALBY Village (OS111 SE5501) beside the River Don just to the south-west of DONCASTER, a town with which it is today joined.

[370] {K9}

BALDRIC A sash or belt worn over one shoulder, passing diagonally across the body and under the other arm, either as an ornament or a support for a sword or bugle. It was normally worn over the right shoulder, with the sword hanging vertically beside the left leg.

[217]

BALDWIN THE KILLER, SIR One of the evil companions of Sir ISENBART DE BELAME, and thus one of the knights of the EVIL HOLD. He accompanied Sir Isenbart to the BLACK TOWER after GRAME GAPTOOTH had captured MAID MARIAN, their intention being to take Marian to the Evil Hold. Their plan was thwarted when KET THE TROW managed to free Marian and escape with her during the night.

Sir Baldwin the Killer only receives a brief mention or two in the legends, which do not say how he gained his epithet, though it is not hard to guess. Along with Sir Isenbart de Belame himself, Sir Baldwin was taken captive after ROBIN HOOD and his forces had stormed the castle at WRANGBY. The two knights were brought before Robin and his men, and an unnamed villager from the village of Wrangby accused them of riding his son into the ground when his crops had failed and he had been unable to pay his dues. Sir Baldwin the Killer suffered the same fate as his lord, and was hanged from gallows like a common criminal outside the castle, where the ground was still littered with the bodies of those killed in the battle.

[167, 291, 335, 360–3]

BANDY, OLD BAT THE See OLD BAT THE BANDY.

BARG(H)AST This archaic name, commonly used in the Sheffield area, was applied to a demonic spirit that could take various forms. The most common form appears to be part man, part wolf with black fur. The word is applied in the legends to the SPECTRE BEAST, which was actually Sir GUY OF GISBORNE cloaked in the flayed hide of a horse.

[47]

BARN(I)SDALE The term Barnsdale originated in the medieval period and was used to denote the area of the old West Riding of YORKSHIRE between the River TRENT in the east and KIRKLEES in the west, and WORKSOP in the south and PONTE-FRACT in the north. At this time the area was known as BARNSDALE FOREST and was used as a hunting ground by the nobility. The term forest is perhaps a misnomer as although there was much woodland, there also existed areas of open common land as well as several villages including CAMP-SALL, Smeaton, WENTBRIDGE, Burghwallis and Askern.

Through the centre of Barnsdale Forest passed the old Roman road from Doncaster to the north of the country. This road forked at Barnsdale Bar, the highest point in the district. The western fork continued via Pontefract and Castleford to Hadrian's Wall, while the eastern fork, known as Watling Street, continued via Wentbridge and Ferrybridge to the city of YORK.

Following the departure of the Romans the roads continued to be used in medieval times, but Barnsdale Forest gained a reputation as the home of bandits and outlaws who preyed upon travellers using these roads. One such bandit was ROBIN HOOD, whom the ballad *Gest of Robyn Hode* placed firmly in Barnsdale Forest.

During the seventeenth and eighteenth centuries Watling Street and the Roman road through Barnsdale became part of the GREAT NORTH ROAD from London to Edinburgh. Stagecoaches passed this way, calling at the inns at Redhouse, Skelbrook and Wentbridge, and when the roads were turnpiked a toll-bar was placed in the fork at Barnsdale Bar.

[12, 172] {G7–M10}

BARN(I)SDALE ~FOREST, ~WOOD The name given to the forested area of BARNISDALE. It is within this forest that ROBIN HOOD appears to have been most active, though he was also associated with both SHERWOOD FOREST and CLIPSTONE FOREST. Today Robin Hood is almost always associated with Sherwood Forest just north of Nottingham, probably because his most famous exploits concern the SHERIFF OF NOTTINGHAM.
[1, 28–9, 49, 114, 170, 181, 248, 280, 294, 295, 303, 313, 332, 334, 346, 366, 368, 377–8, 387, 401]
{I7–K9}

BARNISDALE FOUR WENTS Location within BARNISDALE FOREST. It is mentioned in the legends as the place where KET THE TROW reported to ROBIN HOOD that Sir ROGER OF DONCASTER was travelling with a troop of men-at-arms. Though the precise location of Barnisdale Four Wents is unclear, it is most likely to be in the vicinity of WENTBRIDGE, just to the west of the GREAT NORTH ROAD. In the traditional time ascribed to Robin Hood, this was a clearly defined and well-used route through the area, though not necessarily following the exact route of the modern road.

[368] {J8}

BARON After the NORMAN conquest the term baron came to denote a man or vassal of a great noble, especially the monarch. Until the thirteenth century the term was applied to all tenants-in-chief who held land directly from the monarch. During the thirteenth century the distinction between the greater barons (those summoned to court by personal writ) and the lesser barons (those summoned by general writ) was well established thanks to the MAGNA CARTA.

BARONS' WARS There were two Barons' Wars, the first lasting from 1215 to 1217 and the second from 1264 to 1267. If the historical placing of the life of ROBIN HOOD is correct, then it is the former war that is of concern to students of the outlaw.

The first Barons' War broke out between King JOHN and his BARONs after the king had failed to honour the terms of the MAGNA CARTA. The barons offered the English crown to Louis, son of PHILIP II of France. Louis landed in Kent in May 1216 and quickly took most of south-east England before moving against King John who had been campaigning successfully in the Midlands and the north. John died at NEWARK in October 1216 (possibly from poison), and with the crowning of HENRY III and the reissue of the Magna Carta the tide turned in favour of the royalists. The defeat of the barons at LINCOLN and the capture of the French supply ships off Sandwich forced Louis to accept the treaty of Kingston upon Thames, signed on 12 September 1217; he was paid 10,000 marks and returned to France.

The second Barons' War came about after Henry III renounced in 1261 the Provisions of Oxford (1258) and the Provisions of Westminster (1259), which had vested considerable power in a council of barons, and reasserted his right to appoint councillors. The barons, led by Simon de Montfort,

Earl of Leicester, finally resorted to arms in 1263 and forced the king to reaffirm his adherence to the Provisions. In 1264 a decision in favour of the crown by Louis IX of France as arbitrator led to a renewal of war, but de Montfort's men defeated Henry's forces at the Battle of Lewes, and the king once again submitted to government by council. Early in 1265 de Montfort summoned his famous representative Parliament to strengthen his position, which was threatened by the possibility of an invasion by Henry's adherents abroad. The invasion did not take place, but an uprising against de Montfort by the Welsh 'Marchers' (Englishmen living along the Welsh border) led to his defeat by the king's son (later Edward I) at Evesham. De Montfort was killed in the battle, but some baronial resistance continued until 1267. The barons failed to establish control over the crown, but they helped prepare the way for the constitutional developments of the reign of Edward I.

BARROW DOWN Unspecified location a few miles to the east of MANSFIELD which derived its name from the large number of earthen barrows – ancient burial mounds – found there. Its location to the east of Mansfield would mean that Barrow Down was in CLIPSTONE FOREST. ROBIN HOOD and his men are said to have used one of the barrows as their winter quarters. Regrettably a study of modern maps cannot pinpoint Barrow Down, and the location given on map 7 can only be taken as a rough guess.

[201, 208, 237] {K13}

BA(R)T One of the younger members of ROBIN HOOD's band of men, though why he became an outlaw is not made clear. He features in the story of RICHARD MALBÊTE, along with MICHAEL. The two young outlaws, in the company of DODD, came across a senseless Robin in the forest. Dodd stayed with their master while the two younger men went after the beggar they saw leaving the scene along the forest path. They stopped and disarmed the beggar – Richard Malbête in disguise – who told them he had money in his bags. Thus distracting the inexperienced outlaws, Richard Malbête temporarily blinded them with a cloud of flour, and then beat them with his STAFF before they could clear their eyes sufficiently to make their escape.

Though beaten, they travelled back to Robin and told him all that had passed, and gave him the pouch they managed to take from the beggar. The pouch contained a letter from Sir GUY OF GISBORNE to the SHERIFF OF NOTTINGHAM. Telling the youthful outlaws that he will overlook the episode, Robin promised to set them a task to test their mettle. Soon he sent Bart and Michael to find the potter of WENTBRIDGE and obtain from him the loan of his cart, pony and pots so that Robin could travel into NOTTINGHAM in disguise to learn more about the sheriff's plans to capture Robin and his men. The task set was not a hard one, though Bart and Michael did not know that, for the potter and Robin were on good terms following a meeting in the forest some time earlier.

[94–101]

BAT THE ~CHARCOAL-BURNER, ~COALMAN
One of the villagers who went with the newly outlawed ROBIN HOOD and others from the village of LOCKSLEY to burn down the manor of BIRKENCAR in their failed attempt to kill Sir GUY OF GISBORNE. Bat the Charcoal-burner is specifically mentioned as having been frightened by the BARGAST that was Sir Guy of Gisborne dressed in the skin of a flayed horse, though after that one incident he does not feature again in the legends.

[47]

BEAT THE BUSH One of the various pseudonyms applied to RICHARD MALBÊTE, along with Captain BUSH and the BUTCHER, after he had travelled from YORK, following the massacre of the Jews there, and entered the service of the SHERIFF OF NOTTINGHAM.

[224]

BEAUFOREST The name of the manor occupied by Sir WALTER DE BEAUFOREST and later by ALAN-A-DALE and ALICE DE BEAUFOREST. The lands were said to lie on the edge of SHERWOOD FOREST, and must have been somewhere near the village of CROMWELL, for it is there that Alice de Beauforest was to be forced into marriage with Sir RANULF DE GREASBY. Modern maps show one feature in the vicinity of Cromwell that might well have been the location of Sir Walter de Beauforest's manor. This is a moat (OS120 SK7863) approximately 1.8 miles to the north-north-east of Cromwell Church. This location is further supported by the proximity of the village of NORWELL, from where STURT OF NORWELL hailed. The extent of the manor and its demesne, however, cannot today be accurately determined, and the location shown on map 7 must therefore be regarded only as a reasonable assumption.

[60–1, 331] {M13}

BEAUFOREST, ALICE DE See ALICE DE BEAUFOREST.

BEAUFOREST, SIR WALTER DE See WALTER DE BEAUFOREST, Sir.

BELAME There is no such place as Belame, but there is a Bellême in the Penche district of northern France. The bloodthirsty Robert de Bellême, Earl of Shrewsbury, held the castle at TICKHILL, and Alan-a-Dale describes Sir ISENBART DE BELAME as the grandson of the fiend of Tickhill.

[56]

BELAME, SIR ISENBART DE See ISENBART DE BELAME, Sir.

BENNETT The husband of ALICE OF HAVELOND. A well-to-do YEOMAN, he was taken captive and held to ransom by a Scottish knight, his absence allowing THOMAS OF PATHERLEY and ROBERT OF PRESTBURY to seize the lands of HAVELOND and evict Alice. She spent the next year raising the ransom, but when Bennett returned the two thieves set upon him and beat him to within an inch of his life, leaving him crippled.

Alice of Havelond sought the help of the king, but was told that the king would only hear the appeal if Bennett appeared in person. Alice knew that this was impossible, so took her case to her cousin ALFRED OF GAMMELL. He offered to take the appeal to the king but, knowing this to be pointless, Alice then appealed to her other cousin, ROBIN HOOD, who assured her that he would deal with the thieves. Sure enough, a few days later the houses of Thomas of Patherley and Robert of Prestbury were burnt to the ground with the thieves still inside, thus allowing Bennett and his wife to return to their rightful lands.

Nothing more is heard of Bennett in the legends until Alice of Havelond travelled to meet Robin Hood to ask him to give up his life as an outlaw. When he refused, she told him that she would spend the remainder of her life at KIRKLEES abbey, where their aunt Dame URSULA was the abbess, Bennett having died three years previously.

[86–7, 392]

BERNARD OF THE BRAKE, SIR One of the three knights who ambushed Sir HERBRAND DE TRANMIRE and LITTLE JOHN after Sir Herbrand had repaid the loan of 400 pounds to ABBOT ROBERT. His companions were Sir NIGER LE GRYM and an unnamed knight, all three being knights of the EVIL HOLD. Only Sir Bernard of the

Brake survived the battle, and he fled to the castle at WRANGBY to tell his lord, Sir ISENBART DE BELAME, what had happened. No more is heard of Sir Bernard of the Brake, and it can be assumed that he died, along with most of the other knights of the Evil Hold, when ROBIN HOOD and his men took the castle at Wrangby.

[193–5, 199]

BERTRAN LE NOIR, SIR 'Bertran the Black', one of the three knights who accompanied Sir RANULF DE GREASBY to CROMWELL for Sir Ranulf's marriage to ALICE DE BEAUFOREST, the other two knights being Sir ECTOR DE MALSTANE and Sir PHILIP DE SCROOBY. After ROBIN HOOD had brought the wedding to an abrupt halt and fighting had broken out in the church, Sir Bertran le Noir attempted to make off with the bride, and would have got clean away had not JACK, SON OF WILKIN leapt onto the horse he was escaping on and stabbed him in the heart.

[159, 162, 168]

BEVERLEY GLADE The clearing within SHERWOOD FOREST where ROBIN HOOD and his men fought the BRABANT mercenary FULCO THE RED and his men, who were acting under the orders of Sir ROGER OF DONCASTER. All the mercenaries were killed, though the fight resulted in the deaths of WILL THE BOWMAN and many more of the outlaws. For many years after the fight the clearing was known as SLAUGHTER LEA instead of Beverley Glade. Today there is no way of positively identifying the location of Beverley Glade.

[379–86]

BIGOT, ROGER See ROGER BIGOT.

BILLHOOK, RAFE OF THE See RAFE OF THE BILLHOOK.

BIRKENCAR Sir GUY OF GISBORNE's manor, which he held on rent from ST MARY'S ABBEY in YORK. The manor was burnt by ROBIN HOOD and the villagers of LOCKSLEY shortly after ROBERT OF LOCKSLEY had been declared an outlaw at PONTEFRACT, but Sir Guy of Gisborne managed to escape wearing the flayed skin of a young horse that made him appear as a BARGAST in the form of the SPECTRE MARE. Unfortunately the precise location of the manor of Birkencar cannot be determined.

[7, 42–9, 89, 131, 230]

Illustration from *Bold Robin Hood and his Outlaw Band* by Louis Read.

BIRKIN Village (OS105 SE5326) approximately 5 miles north-east of PONTEFRACT, that appears to have been the home of Sir JOHN DE BIRKIN.

{K7}

BIRKIN, SIR JOHN DE See JOHN DE BIRKIN, Sir.

BISHOP Clergyman consecrated as the ecclesiastical governor of a diocese, and thus having spiritual and administrative powers over that diocese, known as a bishopric. Originally bishops were chosen by their congregations, but in the Roman Catholic Church they are now appointed by the Pope, though some bishops have been political appointments. Bishops are seen as divinely instituted members of the ecclesiastical hierarchy, and successors of the Apostles. The Sacrament of Orders, i.e. consecration, confers on bishops their spiritual power in the church, and imprints on their souls an indelible spiritual character. In the hierarchy of orders they are superior to priests.

BLACK HUGO A forester in the employ of the knights of the EVIL HOLD. On one notable occasion he was bested by LITTLE JOHN, who tied him to the forester's hut and then ate the lunch Black Hugo had prepared for himself in full sight of his angry captive. However, just as he was about to release Black Hugo, having challenged him to a contest with QUARTERSTAFFS, ROBERT OF LOCKSLEY and ALAN-A-DALE entered the clearing and Little John hurried away. The newcomers left Black Hugo tied to the hut, Robert telling him that he would remain bound until he heard the cry of an owl, whereupon he would find himself free. Sure enough, when Black Hugo heard an owl and tested his bonds, they immediately came free, the rope having been cut by a sharp knife, but as Black Hugo had neither heard nor seen anything he hurried away for fear that the spirits might turn against him.

Later Black Hugo took the news of the killing of Sir IVO LE RAVENER to the Evil Hold, that news leading to the outlawing of Alan-a-Dale. ROBIN HOOD was told about this by ALICE DE BEAUFOREST on the occasion when he had travelled to meet FRIAR TUCK for the first time. While he was engaged in combat with the curtal monk a youth rushed out of the forest pursued by several others. The youth was none other than MAID MARIAN, and her pursuers led by Black Hugo, were from the Evil Hold. They broke off their attack when they saw Little John and the other outlaws hurrying to Robin's aid. What became of Black Hugo after that is not recorded, but it seems fairly safe to assume that he remained in the employ of Sir ISENBART DE BELAME, and was in all probability killed when Robin and his forces stormed and took the castle at WRANGBY.

[11, 66–71, 73, 79, 127–8, 136]

BLACK MONKS Monastic order at GILDINGCOTE, where RICHARD I lodged while travelling through SHERWOOD FOREST hoping to meet ROBIN HOOD. Black monks were so-called as they wore black habits, identifying them as Benedictine brothers. Some sources identify the Black Monks as Dominican Friars, but this is erroneous as the Dominicans were normally referred to as Black Friars and, anyway, their order was not

founded in England until 1221 – and thus outside the time-frame for the origin of the legends of Robin Hood.

[313]

BLACK TOWER The castle of GRAME GAPTOOTH, the Black Tower is described as the most formidable fortress of any of the knights of the EVIL HOLD. MAID MARIAN was taken there by Grame Gaptooth, and then rescued by KET THE TROW. There are no means available to us today to determine just where this fortress might have been, if indeed it actually existed.

[291–2]

BLACK WOOD An unidentified portion of BARNISDALE FOREST, though it is also thought that it may be a seasonal name given to the leafless forest in winter.

[201]

BLYTH(E) Village (OS111/120 SK6287) north-east of WORKSOP and south-east of TICKHILL, whose church stands on the site of an eleventh-century Benedictine monastery. The village was the original home of DODD, or DUDDA, the son of ALSTAN. It was also where MUCH THE MILLER'S SON encountered RAFE, man to the STEWARD of Lord ARNALD OF SHOTLEY HAWE, in the village alehouse, from whom he learnt that Sir GUY OF GISBORNE intended to sell ten VILLEINs to Lord Arnald. This piece of intelligence was the reason why the villagers of LOCKSLEY and the manor of BIRKENCAR decided to follow ROBERT OF LOCKSLEY into the forests to live as outlaws.

Blythe is interesting to students of medieval history, for it was between Blythe and Tickhill that RICHARD I licensed one of the five official tilting-grounds of England in 1194. The exact location of this site cannot now be accurately determined, but the most likely location is slightly to the west of the village of Harworth, and slightly north and west of Styrrup, in an area today known as Styrrup Carr (OS111 SK6090) {L10}. The siting of this tilting-ground near Tickhill would seem to suggest that the king held the area in great esteem, the ground possibly being located there as a gesture of thanks to the likes of Robin Hood and his men for their assistance in securing his release from imprisonment at HAGENAU.

[34, 38, 324] {L11}

BOGGART In their tattered and dusty clothing, boggarts are dark and hairy household spirits. They are more bothersome than bogies. They are usually recognised owing to the unusual number of mishaps that occur while a boggart is in the house. The only way to eliminate a boggart is to leave the house, although sometimes this doesn't work as boggarts can be transported with household items. Tradition in the north of England holds that hanging a horseshoe over the door will prevent a boggart from entering the house, but it cannot get rid of one once it has taken up residence.

The name boggart was sometimes applied to HOB O'THE HILL and KET THE TROW, as well as PUCK and just about every other supernatural being from fairies to TROLLs. As a surname, Boggart was, however, almost exclusively applied to Puck.

[80]

BORDAR Alternative name for a COTTER, the lowest order of VILLEIN. The term is Anglo-Saxon in origin and gradually came to be replaced by the NORMAN term cotter.

BOWMAN, WILL THE See WILL THE BOWMAN and WILL OF THE STUTELEY.

BRABANT A former duchy of western Europe lying between the rivers Schelde and Dijle, Brabant derived its name from the Carolingian pagus of the same name. It came under the rule of the counts of Louvain, who enlarged their domain considerably between the tenth and twelfth centuries, with the county of Ukkel-Brussel, the abbeys of Nijvel and Gembloers, and the domains of Antwerpen and Orthen. From about AD 1100 onwards they called themselves dukes of Brabant.

After the acquisition of Maastricht (1204), the County Daelhem (1244) and the Duchy of Limburg (1288), they controlled the important trade-route between Bruges and Cologne. Additionally their port of Antwerp also played an important role in world trade. The relationship between the dukes and their subjects was arranged by ducal charter established as early as 1312 and abolished in 1794 as a result of the French rule.

In 1406 Duchess Johanna of Brabant was succeeded by Antoon of Burgundy. The first university in the Netherlands was founded in Louvain in 1425 by the latter's son, Jan IV of Brabant. After his death (1427) and that of Antoon's other son, Fillips of St-Pol (1430), leaving the house of Brabant without heirs, the duchy was ruled by Fillips the Good of Burgundy. The same year he founded the Gulden Vlies (Golden Fleece) knighthood.

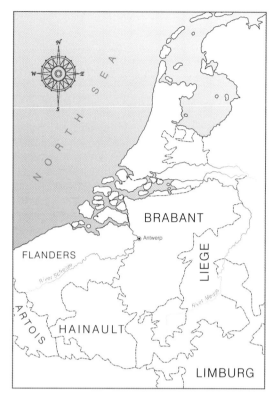

The Low Countries.

After the marriage between Fillips's granddaughter Maria of Burgundy and Maximilian of Austria (1477), Brabant came under Habsburg rule. During this period Brabant took the lead over Flanders, which had been the leading region for centuries.

During the sixteenth century the duchy shared the wealth derived from its main port Antwerp, but that was overshadowed by the outbreak of the Eighty Years War between the Netherlands and the Spanish Habsburgs. The duchy's wealth fostered a rise in arts and sciences, putting Brabant at the heart of the known world. Under the Westphalia Treaty, which concluded the war in 1648, the duchy lost most of its estates north of Antwerp to the Republic of the Netherlands. These estates now form the Dutch province of Noord-Brabant. The remainder of the duchy stayed under Habsburg rule. It played an important role during the revolts against the Austrian Emperor Joseph II in 1787–9 and against King Willem I of Orange Nassau in 1830.

During the rule of Napoleon I Bonaparte, from 1795 to 1814, the remaining southern estates of Brabant were split into the Département de la Dyle (later the Belgian province of Brabant) and the

Département des Deux-Nethes (now the Belgian province of Antwerpen). Following the decline of the French empire, the three parts were once more reunited in one state from 1814 to 1830, until the final separation of Belgium from the Netherlands in 1839.

Due to the recent administrative division of Belgium into Flanders, the Walloon provinces and the capital Brussels, the province of Brabant was split up once more into Flemish Brabant, Walloon Brabant and Brussels. Thus the historical Brabant now consists of no fewer than five parts, one of which lies in the Netherlands, the other four in Belgium.

[378, 387]

BRAKE Epithet of Sir BERNARD OF THE BRAKE that simply indicates that where Sir Bernard came from was heavily wooded, and cannot thus be identified today.

BRAKE, SIR BERNARD OF THE See BERNARD OF THE BRAKE, Sir.

BRAMBURY BURN Unidentified stream or brook, beside which KET THE TROW met DRING, who said that he would take news of MAID MARIAN's escape from the Black Tower to ROBIN HOOD. However, Dring had been spied on talking to Ket the Trow, and was killed before he could leave the side of the stream, his killer being a man in the employ, or wishing to be in the employ, of the EVIL HOLD. He hoped to ingratiate himself there by bringing news of Maid Marian's whereabouts.

[287, 292]

BRIDLESMITH GATE One of the many gates that led into the city of NOTTINGHAM, today it lies in the centre of the modern city. Though not originally called Bridlesmith Gate, it has certainly been known by that name, or something very close to it, since at least 1304, the name reflecting something of the importance of the smiths of Nottingham. At or near Bridlesmith Gate, on a site now lost, was a Saxon mint which remained in use until the fire of Nottingham in the terrible reign of King Stephen, at which time 'Sweyn the moneyer' was in charge.

[216]

BRITTANY The English name for Bretagne, a region of north-west France in the Breton peninsula between the Bay of Biscay and the English Channel.

The Breton peninsula was part of the major area of Celtic influence around 200 BC. After 49 BC, it became part of the Roman province of Gallia, and when this was divided into three was included in one of the imperial provinces, Lugdunensis. As Roman authority weakened, Gaul was overrun by the Huns but they withdrew after the battle of the Catalaunian fields in 451. During this time the area was settled by Britons from across the Channel, who gave it its modern name. Through their influence, part of Brittany or 'Less Britain' held to the Celtic Church while the rest became Roman Catholic like the remainder of France.

Brittany was never entirely part of the Frankish empire, although it lost land in the reorganisation of the Breton March in 811. From about 844 to 940 it was a centre of Viking activity. In 1171 the duchy of Brittany was inherited by GEOFFREY OF BRITTANY, son of HENRY II, and it remained in the possession of the ANGEVIN dynasty until 1203 when Geoffrey's son ARTHUR OF BRITTANY was murdered by King JOHN. It was claimed as part of the ANGEVIN empire of the Norman kings of England from 1326 and was known as the duchy of Brittany until it was annexed by the French in 1491.

The gatehouse of Nottingham Castle. Photo by Peter Chèze-Brown.

BROWNIE A benevolent, shaggy supernatural being, often referred to as an ELF and popular in folklore around England and Scotland. The brownie is the British counterpart of the Scandinavian *tomte* and the Russian *domovoi*. Customarily brownies are said to inhabit houses and aid in tasks around the house, but they do not like to be seen and will only work at night, perhaps in exchange for small gifts or food. They usually abandon the house if their gifts are called payments, or if they are offered gifts of clothes (no matter how shabby their own clothes are). In some stories brownies have no noses.

[12, 52]

BULWELL Today a suburb of NOTTINGHAM (OS129 SK5345), Bulwell was once a separate village and famous as the site from where the stone used to construct NOTTINGHAM CASTLE was quarried. In the legends of ROBIN HOOD, Bulwell was the home of Sir HUON DE BULWELL, the friend of Sir RICHARD AT LEE.

{K15}

BULWELL, SIR HUON DE See HUON DE BULWELL, Sir.

BURGH, HUBERT DE See HUBERT DE BURGH.

BUSH, CAPTAIN The alias used by RICHARD MALBÊTE after he had fled from YORK following the massacre of the Jews, and under which name he entered the service of the SHERIFF OF NOTTING-HAM in the role of thief-taker. During this time he was also known as BEAT THE BUSH, or simply as the BUTCHER. While in the employ of RALPH MURDACH,[1] Richard Malbête was instrumental in the capture of WILL THE BOWMAN, but was himself seized by ROBIN HOOD and his men when they came to rescue their comrade. He was subsequently summarily tried and hanged in the forest for his many crimes.

[224, 226–31, 233–6]

BUTCHER, THE Name given to Captain BUSH, or BEAT THE BUSH, by the people who knew of his reputation as a cold and ruthless murderer. Captain Bush was in fact an alias used by RICHARD MALBÊTE while he was employed as a thief-taker by the SHERIFF OF NOTTINGHAM.

[224]

CAMPSALL Village (OS111 SE5413) lying almost midway between DONCASTER and PONTEFRACT. It was to Campsall that ROBIN HOOD and his men travelled, shortly after taking to life in the forests, to celebrate mass and make their confessions. They were followed to the church by two knights of the EVIL HOLD, along with their men-at-arms, who attacked the church just as mass came to an end. Robin and his men, helped by ALAN-A-DALE, successfully fought off the attack. This meeting between Robin and Alan-a-Dale was the start of the long association between the two men. Local legend says that Robin married MAID MARIAN at Campsall Church.

[52–6, 59, 61] {K8}

CANON A priest who is a member of a cathedral chapter, though a canon was also a clerk who lived according to canon law with others in the clergy-house, or in a house within the precinct or close of a cathedral or collegiate church. Canons are governed by general and particular legislation. The principal development of canon chapters received its impetus from the Carolingian period, Charlemagne demanding that clerics live either in monasteries or in chapters. Louis the Pious enacted legislation to a similar effect. The thirteenth century brought this institution to its juridical maturity.

CAR PEEL, WAT GRAHAM OF See WAT GRAHAM OF CAR PEEL.

CATRAIL RIG Unidentified location between MALASET and BARNISDALE FOREST where MAID MARIAN, at that time travelling with KET THE TROW, was taken captive by GRAME GAPTOOTH. Though the location is uncertain, a rig is usually an ancient site with standing stones, so any site having one or more standing stones between LANCASHIRE and South YORKSHIRE might be considered as a contender. However, it should also be noted that the word catrail is normally associated with a dyke or ditch, so it would be sensible to only consider sites that have a series of standing stones contained within a boundary ditch.

[290]

CATSTY, SIR SCRIVEL OF See SCRIVEL OF CATSTY, Sir.

CEORL Anglo-Saxon word from which CHURL is derived. Ceorls were freemen, farmers and independent landed householders who ranked between SERF and noble and formed the mainstay of the Saxon kingdom, based as it was on a rural economy. The term free in an Anglo-Saxon context can be misleading, since there were many degrees of freedom. Ceorls were *'folcfry'* (folk-free), that is, free in the eyes of the community. They enjoyed *weregilds* and had the right to seek compensation for other free kinsmen and kinswomen. They were allowed to bear arms and could be considered 'fyrd worthy' and 'moot worthy'. This meant they were considered worthy to serve in the fyrd (a sort of local army) and take part in folk meetings. Ceorls were also liable for taxes, and in court were entitled to have three of their peers support their oath.

There were three main classes of ceorl, although the dividing lines between them were indistinct. First were the *geneatas*, the peasant aristocracy who paid rent to their overlords. The word *geneat* originally meant companion, implying that the class originated from the lord's household, often receiving land as a gift. Second were the *kotsetla*, who paid no rent but had to perform numerous duties for their overlords. Third were the *gebur*, who were totally dependent on their lord.

By the eleventh century wealthy ceorls could become thegns or nobles, although most ceorls lost their personal freedom after the NORMAN conquest. Churl, the Norman version of ceorl, thereafter came to mean an ill-bred person. See also GEBUR, GENEAT, KOTSETLA.

CHALUZ Also spelt Chalûs, Chaluz was the castle home of a French baron, a vassal of Richard's enemy, the Viscount of Limoges, whom RICHARD I besieged after a trivial dispute over treasure-trove. During the siege the king was riding around the walls of the castle looking for a weak point for his assault when he was struck in the shoulder by an arrow or crossbow bolt. Enraged that their king had been wounded, his men stormed the castle and all but one of the defenders were hanged. The sole survivor of the siege was the archer whose arrow had wounded the king. Richard pardoned this man from his sickbed, but after Richard's death on 6 April 1199 his pardon was instantly forgotten and the luckless archer was flayed alive. Legends record

that ARTHUR-A-BLAND also died during this siege.

[334]

CHANCELLOR See HIGH CHANCELLOR.

CHAPTER The name given to a body of clerics, presided over by a dean, instituted for observing greater solemnity of divine worship and for assisting the bishop at cathedral churches, acting according to Church Law as his senate and council and governing the see during vacancy. The name arose from the custom of reading a chapter of the rules at a prescribed daily gathering of the members. In dioceses that have no cathedral chapters the board of diocesan consulters functions as the bishop's senate. Chapters are of various kinds, such as cathedral, collegiate, secular and regular, and consist of dignities and canonicates. The principal offices include those of canon theologian and canon penitentiary. The institute known as the chapter is derived from the presbytery of the early centuries; it grew in importance during and after the eighth century and was thoroughly established in the thirteenth. By the eleventh century the chapter had also assumed responsibility for the election of a new bishop.

CHESTER, EARL OF RANULF, Earl of Chester, was one of the party who travelled with RICHARD I through the forests in search of ROBIN HOOD. He was also one of the five nobles the king chose to take with him, all disguised as monks, along the OLLERTON road where Sir RALPH FITZSTEPHEN said they would soon meet Robin Hood.

[316]

CHRISTOPHER The son of WILL THE BOWMAN, Christopher suffered harsh treatment at the hands of HUBERT OF LYNN, though what that treatment was remains unclear.

[40]

CHURL A surly, ill-bred person, as often as not a farm labourer. The word is NORMAN and is derived from the Anglo-Saxon CEORL.

CITOLE A medieval instrument, one of the ancestors of the guitar, which developed into the cittern. The citole was a plucked instrument, popular in the thirteenth and fourteenth centuries. Of no standard shape, the entire instrument was made from a single piece of wood, in contrast to instruments such as the lute. Its small size made it suitable for use by wandering minstrels.

[317]

CLIFFE Village (OS105 SE6632) some 2.5 miles east of Selby in YORKSHIRE that may have been the home of NICHOLAS O'THE CLIFFE.

{L6}

CLIFFE, NICHOLAS O'THE See NICHOLAS O'THE CLIFFE.

CLIPSTONE FOREST Though today a part of SHERWOOD FOREST, Clipstone Forest was once a completely separate area of forest centred around MANSFIELD and located to the north of Sherwood Forest, between Sherwood and BARNISDALE FOREST. There is still a sizeable forest remaining there today. In the middle of the twelfth century HENRY II built a hunting lodge in the heart of the forest near the village of Clipstone, this lodge later being renamed King John's Palace. It remained in use for over three hundred years and was extended several times. RICHARD I spent a few days relaxing at the lodge in 1194 after capturing NOTTINGHAM CASTLE from the supporters of his usurping brother John. Richard I entertained the King of Scotland at the lodge and records show how impressed he was with the forest.

[294, 303, 366, 387, 401] {K13–L14}

CLUMBER (FOREST) An area of forest within the northern reaches of SHERWOOD FOREST, and just to the south of the town of WORKSOP. Today very little remains of the forest, many of the trees having been felled to provide timber for the construction of the fleets required to defend the country against the French and the Spanish. At its approximate centre is Clumber Park, the former home of the dukes of Newcastle. The house itself was demolished in 1938, but many of the architectural features of the estate, which is now administered by the National Trust, still survive.

[83, 282, 316] {K11–M12}

COGG THE EARLESS Associate of Captain BUSH, who told him to keep a watch on the house of SILAS BEN REUBEN in NOTTINGHAM. Nothing more is said about this character, who undoubtedly owes his epithet to the fact that he had lost an ear, though which one is unclear.

[228]

COLD KITCHEN RIGG A steep ascent that Sir HERBRAND DE TRANMIRE and LITTLE JOHN had to climb on their way back to WERRISDALE after Sir Herbrand had paid off the debt of 400 pounds to ABBOT ROBERT. During their ascent of Cold Kitchen Rigg, the exact location

of which remains unclear, Sir Herbrand and Little John were attacked by Sir NIGER LE GRYM, Sir BERNARD OF THE BRAKE and one other unnamed knight of the EVIL HOLD.

[193]

COLE THE REEVE The manorial STEWARD of the village of WRANGBY, who supervised the daily affairs of the manor. Thus he was presumably the steward of the EVIL HOLD. However, Cole the Reeve is recorded as having advised the villagers of Wrangby to help ROBIN HOOD and his men take the castle, and it would appear that Cole the Reeve was as fed up with the knights of the Evil Hold as everyone else.

[345]

COLMAN GREY The father of KET THE TROW, HOB O'THE HILL, SIBBIE and FENELLA. His wife's name is not recorded. Colman Grey was caught and burnt to death by Sir RANULF DE GREASBY while Sir ISENBART DE BELAME and his evil horde watched and laughed.

[153, 157, 361]

CORDWAINER Archaic name for a shoemaker or leather worker, the word originating from *cordwain* or *cordovan*, the white leather produced from goatskin in Cordoba, Spain. The description of the SHERIFF OF NOTTINGHAM as a rich cordwainer would seem to suggest that anyone with money enough could buy any position they desired. It would also suggest that RALPH MURDACH[1] definitely had ideas well above his station.

[102]

CORONER Official of the justice system devised by HUBERT WALTER in 1194. Elected in the county courts, the coroners took over some of the duties of the SHERIFF who had, by the enactment of Hubert Walter, been prohibited from acting as justices within their own counties. The primary function of coroners was, as it is today, to hold inquests on those who died suddenly, accidentally or by foul play, but they also looked after the king's interests in a number of other respects. They took oaths and abjurements, valued the effects of a man accused of murder (for the levy of the murder fine), and generally administered the interests of the crown with respect to what would today be called death duties. The coroner appears in only one place in the legends of ROBIN HOOD, and that is when RICHARD MALBÊTE has to ABJURE to him after killing JOHN LE MARCHANT.

[183]

COTSET Alternative form of KOTSETLA. Derived from the Old English *cot-saeta* ('cottage-dweller'), the word cotset appears in the Domesday Book to denote the lowest rank of feudal bondsmen who were bound to work for their feudal lord.

COTT~ER, ~AR The NORMAN name for a VILLEIN who occupied a cottage and land, usually 5 acres, in return for labour on the demesne one or two days a week. A cotter is the same as a BORDAR, the Anglo-Saxon name for a villein in this position.

CRIPPS An old retainer at OUTWOODS, who told ALFRED OF GAMMELL of the plans of Sir GUY OF GISBORNE and the SHERIFF OF NOTTINGHAM to disguise men in their pay as beggars to wander through the forests and gather intelligence that might lead to the capture of ROBIN HOOD and his men.

[88]

CROMWELL Village (OS120 SK7961) to the north of NEWARK and just to the east of the River TRENT, lying beside the GREAT NORTH ROAD. The village seems to have been within the lands of the manor of BEAUFOREST, as it was to the church at Cromwell that Sir RANULF DE GREASBY travelled to marry ALICE DE BEAUFOREST.

[137–9, 142, 147, 401–2] {N13}

CRUCET-HOUSE A torture-house, as opposed to a single chamber within a building used for the torture of prisoners. However, the term was used for a particular form of torture, rather than the building itself. It was a short and narrow chest of no great depth into which the prisoner was placed along with a large quantity of sharp rocks. When the lid was forced closed, the occupant would be lacerated and crushed.

[25]

CRUSADE The name given to any of the holy military expeditions undertaken in the eleventh, twelfth and thirteenth centuries by the Christian powers of Europe to recapture the HOLY LAND from the Muslims. RICHARD I, PHILIP II of France and the Emperor Frederick I Barbarossa led the Third Crusade (1189–92). After the fall of Acre, Richard I took Jaffa and was within 12 miles of Jerusalem when his supplies ran out. He was forced

A battle between crusaders and Muslims. Fr 22495 f.43. (*Bibliothèque Nationale, Paris/Bridgeman Art Library*)

to make peace with Saladin, and on his way home to England was taken prisoner and held to ransom.

[169, 210, 214, 256]

CURTAL Originally a curtal was a horse that had its tail docked, but the term soon came to be applied to other things that were cut down or shortened. Thus when FRIAR TUCK is described as a curtal monk it indicates that he wore a short cloak that stopped either just above or just below the knees. In later times the term came to be used in a derisory or belittling manner, and it may be in this derogatory way that the term was sometimes used to refer to Friar Tuck, especially by those who opposed him and his way of life.

[114, 119]

CWELM STONE The standing stone that stood on the route followed by the men fleeing back to the EVIL HOLD after the killing of Sir ROGER DE LONGCHAMP. The exact location of the Cwelm Stone remains a mystery.

[28]

DALLAS TOWER, SIR DROGO OF See DROGO OF DALLAS TOWER, Sir.

DAMON THE MONK Legendary sea-pirate who had been harrying the Yorkshire coast. ROBIN HOOD killed the pirate, and had his entire crew hanged from their ship's yard-arm. He then brought the ship ashore, the location of the battle being known since that time as ROBIN HOOD'S BAY.

[391]

DAVID I, KING OF SCOTS (c. 1080–1153) The sixth son of Malcolm III Canmore and Queen (later St) Margaret, David was sent (together with his sister) to the Norman English court of William II at

Kings David I (c. 1054–1153) and Malcolm IV (1141–65) of Scotland. Taken from an illuminated initial in the charter of Kelso Abbey, c. 1153. (*Getty Images*)

the age of 9 and spent over thirty years there. In 1100 his sister Maud (known as Matilda in England) married William II's son Henry, who became king in the same year.

When David's brother Edgar died in 1107, David became king of southern Scotland (below the line of the Forth and Clyde). His brother Alexander I was unhappy at this arrangement but David had more knights than Alexander with which to defend his inheritance. After all, Henry I had given David the 'Honour of Huntingdon' (country manors in eleven counties), made him prince of Cumbria and married him to a widowed heiress of Northumberland.

When Alexander I died in 1124, David set off for Scotland, accompanied by many knights and courtiers from Norman England, many of whom became the future aristocrats and even kings of Scotland, including Bruce, Balliol and FitzAlan (who later became the Stewart kings).

David established a feudal system in Scotland and introduced many novel ideas such as silver coinage, promoting education and giving audiences to rich and poor alike. Stirling, Perth and Dunfermline were made royal burghs, which meant they could engage in foreign trade. David also founded fifteen religious houses, including the abbeys at Jedburgh, Kelso and Melrose.

His was a long and largely peaceful reign, though he did have to deal with rebellions by the Earl of Moray in 1130 and the Bishop of the Isles in 1140. He also decided to take advantage of Henry I's death to push the Scottish border further south. In 1138, at the Battle of the Standard near Northallerton, he did not follow up an attack by the Scottish knights and decided to leave the field of battle. While it was by no means a rout, the English army had clearly won the day. However, in 1139, under the Treaty of Durham, King Stephen of England not only recognised Scotland as an independent kingdom, but also ceded Northumbria.

David died peacefully in Carlisle on 24 May 1153 at the age of 69. He had ended his days gardening and tending orchards below Edinburgh Castle and in Haddington. His only son Henry had died in 1152, so he was succeeded by his 12-year-old grandson Malcolm IV.

His connection to the legends of ROBIN HOOD relies solely on his marriage in 1113 to Maud (or Matilda), daughter and heiress of the Earl of HUNTINGDON (see p. 11).

[16]

DEAD MAN'S HILL Unidentified hill that presumably had a gallows at its summit. It features as a highlight on the route taken by the fleeing men-at-arms after ROBERT OF LOCKSLEY had killed Sir ROGER DE LONGCHAMP.

[28]

DEMESNE That area of a MANOR that was retained by the lord and farmed for his own provisions and income. The word simply means 'domain'. The demesne was worked by the villeins purely to provide for the lord and his household, the amount of work the villeins did on the land relying on what they owed the lord, their feudal debt. As the serfs' labour services came to be commuted to money payments, the demesne lands were often cultivated by paid labourers. Eventually many of the demesne lands were leased out either on a perpetual (and therefore hereditary) or a temporary (and therefore renewable) basis so that many peasants functioned virtually as free proprietors after paying their fixed rents. In England the term ancient demesne referred to those lands that were held by the crown at the time of the Norman Conquest in 1066, as recorded in the Domesday Book. The term demesne also referred to the crown or royal demesne, which consisted of those lands reserved for the crown at the time of the original distribution of landed property. The royal demesne could be increased, for example, as a result of forfeiture. Such lands were managed by stewards of the crown and were not given out in fief.

Very few demesnes remain today, and even fewer are called by that name. However, the Huntroyde Demesne may be found at OS103 SD7834, approximately 15 miles south-west of GISBURN.

{C6}

DENVIL OF TOOMLANDS, SQUIRE A young squire who joined ROBIN HOOD and his men for the siege of the castle of WRANGBY. It was his plan to float across the moat on rafts under the cover of their shields so that two blacksmiths might cut the chains securing the drawbridge and thus allow Robin and his men access to the EVIL HOLD. The plan worked, though not entirely as Squire Denvil had planned, for the knights of the Evil Hold threw burning pitch, fire-brands and hot stones down onto those working on the fallen drawbridge, and thus set fire to their own portcullis.

Later, again at the suggestion of Squire Denvil, rafts were actually laid across the remains of the drawbridge, this time not to facilitate the entry of the besieging forces but rather to allow those inside the castle to ride out. When they had, Squire Denvil and KET THE TROW, who had hidden in the moat, led a small force into the castle and killed the few remaining men they found inside. Thus they secured the castle for Robin and his troops.

[344, 347–51, 359]

DERBYSHIRE County of northern central England that fell under the jurisdiction of the SHERIFF OF NOTTINGHAM, whose full title was the Sheriff of Nottinghamshire and Derbyshire.

[247]

DICKON The son of an ageing couple, Dickon had worked for PETER GREATREX, the armourer of NOTTINGHAM, but left to seek his fortune. Unfortunately he was arrested and locked in TICKHILL Castle, where he was secured by the ankle so tightly that his foot perished. His ageing parents travelled from Nottingham to Tickhill to secure his release, a goal which ROBIN HOOD promised them he would personally see achieved, though whether or not poor Dickon was ever released from Tickhill is unrecorded.

[319–20]

DICKON THE CARPENTER One of the original VILLEINs from the village of LOCKSLEY who joined the newly outlawed ROBERT OF LOCKSLEY after the burning of BIRKENCAR manor. As his epithet would suggest, Dickon was a carpenter by trade and taught his skills to the other members of the outlaw band so that they might make implements necessary to their survival, such as bows and arrows.

[50]

DICK THE REID One of the many scouts deployed by ROBIN HOOD throughout the forests so that intelligence on travellers might be relayed to him wherever he was. Dick the Reid, whose epithet means 'Red' (probably the colour of his hair), only appears once in the legends, when he passed on a message regarding the movements of Sir LAURENCE OF RABY to another scout, who then took the message on to Robin.

[238]

DODD, DUDDA A VILLEIN from the village of BLYTHE. The son of ALSTAN, he was pressed into service as a man-at-arms by Sir HUBERT OF LYNN, but yielded to ROBERT OF LOCKSLEY after Robert had killed Sir Hubert and four other men-at-arms during the rescue of SCADLOCK. Dodd only appears once more in the legends. In the company of BART and MICHAEL, he discovered Robin Hood after he had been knocked senseless by RICHARD MALBÊTE, and sent Bart and Michael

off to confront the beggar-spy while he helped Robin back to their camp.

[34, 94]

DONCASTER Town (OS111 SE5903) in South YORKSHIRE on the River Don, hence the name, which lies to the north of SHERWOOD FOREST and within the area known as BARNISDALE. Doncaster is known to have been the site of a Roman fort which was probably called *Danum*. The fort was located somewhere near the River Don and traces of a Roman iron and pottery industry have been found in the neighbourhood. In Anglo-Saxon times the kings of Northumbria are thought to have established a palace at Doncaster but this was attacked and destroyed by the Danes in a later century.

Doncaster was granted a charter by Richard I and became the site of a medieval friary, but its real heyday came in the eighteenth century. Horse-racing began at Doncaster in this period and races have been held in the town since at least 1703. The famous St Leger race, older than Epsom's Derby, commenced in 1778, two years after the Doncaster racecourse grandstand was built by John Carr, the famous Yorkshire architect.

The town was the administrative centre of Barnisdale, for it was to the courts at Doncaster that

The Aged Palmer gives young David of Doncaster news of Will Stuteley. Illustration from *The Merry Adventures of Robin Hood* by Howard Pyle.

WILL SCARLET was to be taken to be tried for the theft of one of the king's deer from the forest, a crime for which he would lose his right hand. It was also in Doncaster that ROBIN HOOD and MUCH THE MILLER'S SON learnt of the archery contest that the SHERIFF OF NOTTINGHAM was to stage.

[28, 39, 259] {K9}

DONCASTER, SIR ROGER OF See ROGER OF DONCASTER, Sir.

DOUBLET A man's close-fitting jacket or body-garment, with or without sleeves, extending from the neck to a little below the waist. It was worn by men of all ranks and ages. The doublet was introduced into England from France, and was originally padded for defence or warmth.

DOUGLAS One of the Scottish border clans which attacked Sir DROGO OF DALLAS TOWER but were subsequently put to flight by ROBIN HOOD, who instilled such fear into them that they never dared to venture south of the border again. The other three clans were ARMSTRONG, GRAHAM and JORDAN. The Douglas family are named after the River Douglas in Lanarkshire. One of their most famous members was Sir James Douglas (1286–1330), also known as Black Douglas or Good Sir James, the champion of Robert Bruce. He was called 'Black Douglas' by the English of the border counties, to whom he became a figure of dread. Sir Walter SCOTT, in his *Castle Dangerous*, refers to the family Douglas as 'Sholto Dhu Glass', which means 'Behold the dark grey man', Dhu Glass coming from *dhu glaise*, the Celtic for 'black stream':

> The complexion of the day is congenial with the original derivation of the name of the country, and the description of the chiefs to whom it belongs – Sholto Dhu Glass – (see yon dark grey man).
>
> Sir Walter Scott, *Castle Dangerous*, ch. iii.

[388]

DRAKENHOLE Unidentified castle at which RICHARD I lodged during his time in SHERWOOD FOREST looking for ROBIN HOOD. The king was at Drakenhole when Sir RALPH FITZSTEPHEN brought him the news that Robin and his men had been haunting the roads near OLLERTON. Sir Ralph then devised the plan to disguise the king and five members of his entourage as monks so that they might encounter the outlaw as they desired.

[314]

DRAYTON, MICHAEL (1563–1631) Born at Hartshill in Warwickshire in 1563, as a youth Michael Drayton became page to Sir Henry Goodeere of Polesworth, who can take the credit for the young man's education. Drayton fell in love with Sir Henry's daughter Anne, who served as an inspiration for *Idea*.

Drayton's career as a poet was long: his first published work appeared in 1591, his last in 1630. He constantly revised his works, rewriting and reissuing them, sometimes under different titles. His first published work was *Harmonie of the Church* (1591), a metrical rendering of scriptural passages, rife with alliteration. Soon thereafter he wrote *Idea, the Shepherd's Garland* (1593), consisting of nine eclogues or pastoral verse dialogues. Drayton revised and reissued this in 1606. Next Drayton published the historical poems *Piers Gaveston* (1593) and *Matilda* (1594). *Idea's Mirror* (1594) is a collection of love sonnets, the first version of his later sonnet sequence *Idea*. In 1595 Drayton published *Endymion and Phoebe*, one of the sources for Keats's *Endymion*. An erotic treatment of mythological narratives, this poem was also later revised and reissued as *The Man in the Moon* (1606 and 1619).

In 1596 Drayton published *Robert, Duke of Normandy* (revised 1605 and 1619), in which Fame and Fortune tell Robert's story in the presence of his ghost. In the same year Drayton also published the historical poem *Mortimeriados*, which underwent extensive rewriting and reappeared as *The Barons' Wars* in 1603. Both versions owe a debt to Marlowe's *Edward II*. The former was in rhyme royal, a series of scenes, the latter in *ottava rima*, several hundred lines longer and more serious in tone and in its interest in the nature of civil war. *The Barons' Wars* was itself revised in 1619.

One of Drayton's finest works, *England's Heroical Epistles* (1597), a collection of verse letters by lovers, earned Drayton the title of 'our English Ovid'. The work echoed Ovid's *Heroides*, but instead of mythological characters, Drayton's lovers were figures from English history.

Drayton's only extant play, *The First Part of Sir John Oldcastle* (1600), played on the popularity of Falstaff from Shakespeare's plays. It may have been a collaboration, like the now lost plays of which only mentions survive.

Drayton's *Poems Lyric and Pastoral* (1606) was the first to introduce imitations of Horace's *Odes*. The collection contains the odes 'To the Virginian Voyage' and 'The Battle of Agincourt'. Drayton's masterpiece, however, is the *POLYOLBION* (1612 and 1622), a 30,000-line historical-geographical poem celebrating all the counties of England and Wales.

In 1627 appeared *The Battle of Agincourt*, an attempt at epic poetry, *The Miseries of Queen Margaret* and *Nymphidia, the Court of Fairy*, Drayton's most popular work. *Nymphidia* is a mock-heroic series of fairy poems or 'Nimphalls', much influenced by Shakespeare's *A Midsummer Night's Dream*. Drayton's last published work, *The Muses' Elizium*, saw a return to the pastoral. Michael Drayton died in London on 2 December 1631 and was buried in Westminster Abbey. His monument bears an epitaph by Ben Jonson commissioned by the Countess of Dorset.

Drayton's connection with ROBIN HOOD lies in the *POLYOLBION*. Interestingly, his volume of poems entitled *The Harmonie of the Church*, published in 1591, was destroyed by order of the Archbishop of Canterbury.

DRING One of the younger members of ROBIN HOOD's band, Dring met KET THE TROW and MAID MARIAN by BRAMBURY BURN and said that he would take news of Marian's flight to Robin Hood. However, Dring had been seen talking to Ket the Trow by a VILLEIN in the pay of the EVIL HOLD, who killed the outlaw and stole his clothes so that he might more easily spy on the movements of Maid Marian and then take news of her whereabouts to Sir ISENBART DE BELAME. His plans came to nothing, though, as he was himself killed by Ket the Trow as he spied on his barrow home.

[287, 292]

DROGO OF DALLAS TOWER, SIR A knight who lived in the border regions of WESTMORLAND and was attacked by raiders from the clans ARMSTRONG, DOUGLAS, GRAHAM and JORDAN after he had punished one of their kinsmen. ROBIN HOOD and his men came to his aid and so utterly routed the attackers, and instilled in them such fear, that they never again sought to travel south of the border.

[388]

DROW Alternative form of TROW.

DUDDA Alternative name sometimes used by DODD, son of ALSTAN.

[34]

DUNN One of the villagers whom SCADLOCK said had come to his aid when Sir HUBERT OF LYNN

arrived to take possession of OUTWOODS on the orders of ABBOT ROBERT, after ROBERT OF LOCKSLEY had been proclaimed outlaw.

[35]

DYKEWALL, SIR FULK OF THE See FULK OF THE DYKEWALL, Sir.

EARLESS, COGG THE See COGG THE EARLESS.

ECTOR DE MALSTANE, SIR The real name of the knight more commonly known as Sir ECTOR OF THE HARELIP.

[149, 168]

ECTOR OF THE HARELIP, SIR The nephew of Sir RANULF DE GREASBY, his real name was Sir ECTOR DE MALSTANE. His reputation for cruelty was matched only by that of his uncle. After his uncle had been killed by an arrow shot from the rafters inside the church at CROMWELL on the occasion of his arranged marriage to ALICE DE BEAUFOREST, Sir Ector of the Harelip fought with ROBIN HOOD, the two men struggling long and hard until Robin managed to slip beneath Sir Ector's guard and strike him a fatal blow.

[149, 154, 158–9]

EDWARD THE CONFESSOR (*c.* 1003–66) The last Anglo-Saxon King of England, from 1042 to 1066, Edward's reputation for piety preserved his royal dignity despite his ineffectual leadership and the resulting difficulties with his nobles.

Edward was the son of King Æthelred II the Unready and Emma, daughter of Richard II, Duke of NORMANDY. The family was exiled to Normandy after the Danish invasion of 1013 but returned the following year and negotiated Æthelred's reinstatement. After Æthelred's death in 1016 the Danes again took control of England. Edward lived in exile during Cnut's reign until 1041, when he returned to the London court of his half-brother, King Hardecanute. He became king the following year.

Much of his reign was peaceful and prosperous. Skirmishes against the Scots and Welsh were infrequent and sound internal administration was maintained. The financial and judicial systems were efficient and trade was good. However, Edward brought to court some of his Norman friends, a move which prompted widespread resentment, particularly in the powerful houses of Mercia and Wessex.

For the first eleven years of Edward's reign the real ruler of England was Godwine, Earl of Wessex. Edward married Godwine's daughter Edith in 1045, but this could not prevent a breach between the two men in 1049. Two years later, with the support of Leofric of Mercia, Edward outlawed Godwine and his family.

However, Edward's continued favouritism caused problems with his nobles and in 1052 Godwine and his sons returned. The magnates were not prepared to engage them in civil war and forced the king to make terms. Godwine's lands were returned to him and many of Edward's Norman favourites were exiled.

When Godwine died in 1053, his son Harold became Earl of Wessex. It was he, rather than Edward, who subjugated Wales in 1063 and negotiated with the rebellious Northumbrians in 1065. Edward the Confessor was the founder of Westminster Abbey, but he was too ill to attend its consecration at Christmas 1065, and died in January of the following year. Although his legitimate heir was his grandson Edgar the Ætheling, Edward allegedly nominated Harold Godwinsson as his successor on his deathbed. It has also been suggested that he had already promised the crown to William of Normandy. William invaded England and killed Harold at the Battle of Hastings in October 1066, and just two months later ascended the throne.

Edward the Confessor was canonised in 1161, his feast day being 13 October.

[141]

ELDRITCH OAKS Unidentified section of BARNISDALE FOREST through which ROBIN HOOD travelled en route to meet FRIAR TUCK for the first time.

[119]

ELEANOR OF AQUITAINE (*c.* 1122–1204) Also called Eleanor of Guyenne, Éléonore d'Aquitaine and Aliénor d'Aquitaine, Eleanor was both Queen of France and later Queen of England, and arguably was the most powerful woman of high medieval Europe. The daughter of William X, Duke of AQUITAINE and Count of Poitiers, Eleanor inherited a domain larger than that of the French king. Aged 15, she married the future Louis VII of France, still a teenager himself, and a month later the adolescent couple became king and queen upon the death of King Louis VI.

Eleanor was famous for her beauty and wit. During their fifteen-year marriage she bore Louis two daughters and exercised considerable influence over her mild husband. In 1147 she coaxed him into going on a crusade, and boldly accompanied him to

Eleanor wall fresco in St Radegone Chapel, Chinon. (*Copyright Douglas Boyd*)

Alan-a-Dale singeth before our good Queen Eleanor. Illustration from *The Merry Adventures of Robin Hood* by Howard Pyle.

the Holy Land. There she easily stole the limelight and was rumoured to have carried on an affair with her uncle, Raymond of Poitiers.

A few years after their return from the Second Crusade, the royal couple's marriage was annulled and Eleanor regained control of her extensive lands in Aquitaine and Poitiers. Two months later, at the age of 30, she married 18-year-old Henry Plantagenet, Count of ANJOU, Duke of Normandy and grandson of Henry I of England. In 1154 he became HENRY II of England. Eleanor's French lands helped make Henry's lands in France greater than those of the French king.

The Plantagenets' stormy relationship resulted in eight children, two of whom (RICHARD and JOHN) would later become kings of England. Eleanor was an active participant in the affairs of state in both England and France, and was particularly involved in administrating Aquitaine and Poitiers. During a period of estrangement from her husband she spent some time turning Poitiers into a centre of culture, and had a hand in influencing the literary movement of courtly love.

In 1173 Eleanor supported her sons Henry and Richard in a revolt against their father, which failed; she was captured while seeking protection from her ex-husband and languished in prison until Henry's death in 1189. When Richard took the crown, Eleanor played a significant role in keeping England intact while the king spent years crusading. During John's reign she had considerable success guarding his interests on the continent.

Queen Eleanor died in the monastery at Fontevrault, Anjou, in April 1204. She was 82 years old.

ELF A supernatural or legendary being, usually characterised as small, human-like and mischievous, but with formidable magical powers that could be employed either benevolently or malevolently.

ELFWOOD SCAR Unidentified site within BARNISDALE FOREST. ROBIN HOOD and his men took shelter in the caves here whenever the weather turned bad.

[114]

ELIEZER, RABBI See RABBI ELIEZER.

ELY, LORD BISHOP OF A clerical post customarily held by the HIGH CHANCELLOR of England. A cathedral city in the east of England on the Great Ouse river, 15 miles north-east of Cambridge, Ely was the chief town of the former administrative district of the Isle of Ely. Its eleventh-century cathedral remains one of the largest in England and is famous for its wooden octagonal lantern. The legends state that the SHERIFF OF NOTTINGHAM had to buy his position from the Bishop of Ely.

[102, 279, 282] {U22}

EPHRAIM BEN ABEL Ageing Jew from YORK who was mercilessly killed by RICHARD MALBÊTE during the revolt against the Jews incited by ALBERIC DE WISGAR. His death was witnessed by REUBEN OF STAMFORD and his daughter RUTH.

[213]

ERMINE STREET The Anglo-Saxon name for the Roman road that runs from LONDON to LINCOLN, via Braughing and HUNTINGDON. It was constructed by legionary troops in the years immediately following the Roman occupation of AD 43. (Rather confusingly, the name is also sometimes applied to the Roman road that runs from Silchester to Cirencester and Gloucester.) The legends say that it was on this road that ROBIN HOOD and his men often stopped travellers and demanded a toll of them. They also say that it was on Ermine Street that LITTLE JOHN, WILL THE BOWMAN and MUCH THE MILLER'S SON came across Sir HERBRAND DE TRANMIRE en route to YORK to plead with ABBOT ROBERT for more time to repay a loan of 400 pounds. However, references to the Ermine Street in the legends are mistaken, for they often refer to that road in the context of BARNISDALE FOREST, where the true Roman road does not run. Rather, such references to Ermine Street really indicate the GREAT NORTH ROAD, better known today as the A1. However, later association has made the Great North Road cognate with Ermine Street, and some maps even label the Great North Road north of Lincoln as Ermine Street.

It is interesting to note that the three major Roman roads of Ermine Street, the FOSSE WAY and WATLING STREET, along with the prehistoric Icknield Way, are distinguished as *chimini regales* ('royal roads') in twelfth-century law books. These roads were under the king's protection, whereby an assault committed on them would be punishable by a

The gateway of Lincoln Cathedral. (*Mick Sharp Photography*)

fine of 100 shillings – a not inconsiderable sum. Additionally they had to be wide enough for two wagons to pass safely, for two oxherds to make their goads touch across them, or for sixteen armed knights to ride abreast.

[170, 248]

EVIL HOLD The name given not only to the castle of WRANGBY, but also to the knights who met within that castle under the leadership of Sir ISENBART DE BELAME. The knights of the Evil Hold named within the legends, in addition to Sir Isenbart, are: Sir BALDWIN THE KILLER, Sir BERNARD OF THE BRAKE, Sir BERTRAN LE NOIR, Sir ECTOR DE MALSTANE, Sir HAMO DE MORTAIN, Sir IVO DE RABY, Sir IVO LE RAVENER, Sir NIGER LE GRYM, Sir PHILIP DE SCROOBY, Sir RANULF DE GREASBY, Sir ROGER DE LONGCHAMP, Sir ROGER OF DONCASTER and Sir SCRIVEL OF CATSTY.

Associates and allies of the Evil Hold are named as: ABBOT ROBERT, BLACK HUGO, FULCO THE RED, GRAME GAPTOOTH, Sir GUY OF GISBORNE, Sir HUBERT OF LYNN, RALPH MURDACH, RICHARD MALBÊTE, Sir ROBERT DE LONGCHAMP, the SHERIFF OF YORK and Sir WILLIAM DE LONGCHAMP.

[25, 28, 55–6, 60–3, 135, 165, 167–9, 171, 176–7, 180–1, 195–6, 199, 200, 250, 257, 274, 290–1, 307, 331–2, 335, 338, 341, 344–5, 347–58, 366] {J8}

FANG One of the two merlin hawks, the other being GRIP, that were demanded as payment, along with the hunting hound ALISAUNDRE, by Sir PHILIP DE SCROOBY when Sir RANULF DE GREASBY asked him to go in search of the mysterious minstrel JOCELYN.

[155]

FANGTHIEF WOOD Unidentified wood that is recorded in the legends as lying on the edge of the lands of BIRKENCAR manor, the home of the evil, scheming Sir GUY OF GISBORNE.

[42]

FÉCAMP, BISHOP OF The primate of the Normandy town of Fécamp, which lies on the coast approximately 30 miles east of Dieppe and 20 miles north-east of Le Havre. Between the twelfth and seventeenth centuries the town was a major port. RICHARD I appointed his favourite WILLIAM DE LONGCHAMP, Bishop of Fécamp, HIGH CHANCELLOR when he came to the throne in 1189. William was the brother of Sir ROGER DE LONGCHAMP, who was killed by ROBERT OF LOCKSLEY as he tried to abduct the MAID MARIAN.

[15]

FENELLA The daughter of COLMAN GREY and thus the sister of KET THE TROW, HOB O'THE HILL and SIBBIE. Following the death of her mother, and the pardoning of ROBIN HOOD by RICHARD I, Fenella married WAT GRAHAM OF CAR PEEL, a borderlands fighter.

[333]

FERRERS, EARL OF WILLIAM, Earl of Ferrers was one of the party who accompanied RICHARD I to the forests in his attempts to meet ROBIN HOOD. He was also one of the five men chosen by the king to travel with him disguised as monks, so that Sir RALPH FITZSTEPHEN might lead the king and his party along the OLLERTON road where the outlaws were said to be waylaying travellers.

William de Ferrers (1168–1247), 4th Earl of Derby, was an historical character, who stood surety for King JOHN on 13 May 1213, and was thus loyal to both Richard I and his treacherous brother John.

[316]

FEUDALISM A system of land tenure that was characteristic of medieval Europe, its name being derived from the Latin *feodum*, meaning 'fief'. Under this system property is held by a vassal (the feudal inferior) of his lord (the feudal superior) in return for a pledge of homage and services. The system in England relied on the granting of land by the king to his tenants-in-chief in return for their services to the crown. They in turn could pass on a part of that land to tenants, and they could do likewise. All land was thus held directly, or indirectly, of the monarch, who was the feudal superior of all tenants.

FITZSTEPHEN, SIR RALPH See RALPH FITZSTEPHEN, Sir.

FITZWALTER The family name of MAID MARIAN. Her father was Sir RICHARD FITZWALTER, who held lands at MALASET in LANCASHIRE.

[330]

FITZWALTER, MARIAN See MAID MARIAN and MARIAN FITZWALTER.

FITZWALTER, SIR RICHARD See RICHARD FITZWALTER, Sir.

FOREST HERNE Unidentified spot between MANSFIELD and NOTTINGHAM where ROBIN HOOD arranged to meet BART and MICHAEL after they had secured the loan of the cart, pony and wares of the potter of WENTBRIDGE.

[100]

FOREST HOLD The unidentified home of PIERS THE LUCKY, ALAN-A-DALE's foster-brother.

[63]

FOREST LAW Forest Law consisted of a number of enactments made between 1066 and 1189 to maintain the right of the monarch alone to hunt in the royal forests. Penalties for infringement of these laws ranged from death to mutilation (as would have been the case for WILL SCARLET). The Forest Charter of 1217 abolished such punishments, though forest law continued to be enforced and was not repealed until 1817. The date of 1217 ties in nicely with ROBIN HOOD's second period as an outlaw, for all mention of fear of punishment for being caught stealing the royal meat occur during Robin's first period in the forests.

FOSS(E) WAY The Anglo-Saxon name for the Roman road running from the Devon coast at Axminster to LINCOLN, via Ilchester, Bath, Cirencester and Leicester. It derives its name from the ditches (Latin *fossa*) on each side of the road. It is quite possible that the Fosse Way has become confused with ERMINE STREET in the telling and retelling of the legends of ROBIN HOOD, but it still seems most likely that references to any Roman road in the legends should actually refer to the GREAT NORTH ROAD. The Fosse Way, Ermine Street, WATLING STREET and the prehistoric Icknield Way were classified as royal roads (*chemini regales*) during the twelfth century.

FOUNTAINS ABBEY St Mary of the Fountains was a twelfth-century Cistercian ABBEY in Skelldale, North YORKSHIRE, which was founded by a party of dissatisfied monks who left YORK in 1132. Its remains are now a scenic pivot between Fountains Hall, built in 1611 using stone from the dissolved abbey, and the wonderful eighteenth-century water gardens of Studley Royal, begun in 1718 by the disgraced Chancellor of the Exchequer, John Aislabie.

When the first monks arrived, the site was remote and wild – it had been deliberately chosen to underline their wish for a stricter rule. In 1133, by which time they were living in a thatched hut under an elm tree and eating little more than herbs and boiled leaves, they decided to adopt the Cistercian rule. St Bernard of Clairvaux sent one of his monks, Geoffrey, to teach them their new rule. Two years later the stone building began, funded by a rich newcomer, and the main surviving buildings bear testament to the skill of the masons from Burgundy. The long, vaulted cellarium, 302 feet long, survives little altered since its construction on beaten earth, the ribbed vault supported by nineteen central pillars. In the dormitory the monks slept in two rows, keeping their woollen cassocks on to be up and ready quickly for prayers at 2 a.m.

By the fifteenth century the monks' spartan rule had softened a little. The abbey possessed musical instruments and a paper map of the world, showing the altar of St Peter's in Rome at its centre. Excavations have revealed the remains of a rich diet of oysters, beef, mutton, pork and venison. By the time of its Dissolution in 1540, the abbey also possessed eighty copes, some of finely worked embroidery and six of

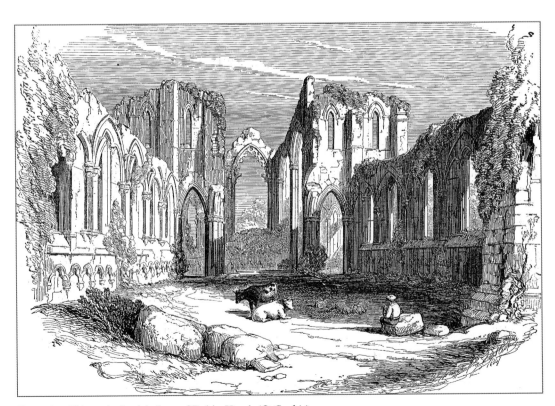

Fountains Abbey, the burial place of Robin Hood. (© *Corbis*)

cloth of gold. At the east end of the church a huge extra transept was built, called the Chapel of the Nine Altars. The only other thirteenth-century example is a later chapel at Durham Cathedral.

The legends say FRIAR TUCK belonged to the monastic order at Fountains Abbey, but was cast out because of his evil ways.

[114, 117]

FRIAR TUCK Portly monk who was said to have once been a member of the Cistercians at FOUNTAINS ABBEY, though the word friar usually indicates a Carmelite brother. Having been cast out of the abbey, allegedly for demonic worship, Friar Tuck took to living in a wooden house, or cell, beside a fast-flowing rivulet on the edge of BARNISDALE FOREST. This little house was protected by a moat on three sides, the fourth side being formed by the rivulet itself.

ROBIN HOOD heard about the monk from PETER THE DOCTOR, who said that the friar had forced him to consume all his own medicines, though NICK THE SMITH sought to protect the monk's honour by saying that he comforted the poor and tended the sick without any thought of reward. Robin Hood, having heard the varying reports, decided to meet the monk so that he might draw his own conclusions.

When Robin first came upon the fat friar he was asleep under a tree, so Robin rudely woke him and told him to carry him across the rivulet lest he get his feet wet. At first Friar Tuck ignored the man before him, but obediently bent his back and carried the outlaw across the water when Robin notched an arrow to his bowstring and threatened the monk. However, as Robin started to climb down again the monk caught him by his ankles and made him return the compliment, so Robin did get his feet wet.

As the pair once again reached dry land the monk laughed at how easily Robin had been taken, laughter which caused Robin to attack the monk. They rolled down the bank into the water. Freeing himself, Robin hurried to fetch his bow and arrows, but when he turned to fire he found that the monk had armed himself with a STAFF and was now wearing a helmet and carrying a shield. No matter how many arrows Robin fired at him the monk simply turned each one away with his shield.

Just then the two of them were startled by a youth crashing through the undergrowth towards them. This turned out to be none other than MAID MARIAN who had come to the forest to visit Robin, but who was now being pursued by BLACK HUGO and other men-at-arms in the employ of the EVIL HOLD.

Illustration from *Bold Robin Hood and his Outlaw Band* by Louis Read.

Robin blew on his horn to summon LITTLE JOHN and the other outlaws, while he and the friar attempted to hold back the men-at-arms. Robin killed several of them with well-aimed arrows, and Friar Tuck set his ten massive hounds on them, five of which were killed. The attackers were finally put to flight when Little John and the other outlaws arrived.

Friar Tuck took Marian and Robin back to his home, where Robin was introduced to ALICE DE BEAUFOREST. She told Robin that her love ALAN-A-DALE had been falsely outlawed and that she was to be forced to marry the evil old knight Sir RANULF DE GREASBY. Shortly afterwards, Robin, Marian, Alice de Beauforest and her maid NETTA O'THE MEERING took their leave of Friar Tuck and travelled to the castle of Sir RICHARD AT LEE, where the two ladies were staying.

It is a popular misconception that Friar Tuck was one of the band of outlaws living with Robin Hood, but the legends indicate that the monk never left his cell in the forest and continued to lead his own life, serving the spiritual needs of Robin and his men as necessary. He married Alice de Beauforest and Alan-a-Dale and later Robin and Marian. Friar Tuck plays only a small part in the legends, but he was called upon to bury Robin Hood after he had been so treacherously murdered by his aunt, Dame URSULA. As Michael DRAYTON wrote in the *POLYOLBION* (xxvi, 311–16):

> In this our spacious isle I think there is not one
> But he hath heard some talk of Hood and Little John;
> Of Tuck, the merry friar, which many a sermon made
> In praise of Robin Hood, his outlaws, and their trade.
> [115, 117, 120–33, 166, 277, 293, 399]

FULCO THE RED A mercenary from BRABANT in the pay of Sir ROGER OF DONCASTER. Fulco the Red led his forces into BEVERLEY GLADE as he searched for ROBIN HOOD, and there was set upon by Robin and twenty of his men. Though momentarily thrown off guard by the ambush, Fulco led his men against the outlaws with such gusto that a good number of outlaws fell, among them WILL THE BOWMAN, before Robin managed to kill Fulco and drive the rest of the Brabanters into the trap laid by LITTLE JOHN. None of them survived. For several years afterwards Beverley Glade was known as SLAUGHTER LEA.

[378–9, 381–4, 386–7]

FULK OF THE DYKEWALL, SIR One of the knights who came to the assistance of ROBIN HOOD as he and his men besieged the castle at WRANGBY. Something of a pessimist, he failed to see how the castle could be taken.

[344, 352]

G

GALLOW'S HILL Common name throughout England signifying the former location of a gallows. Another common name for Gallow's Hill was

Robin fights Will Gamwell. Illustration from *Bold Robin Hood and his Outlaw Band* by Louis Read.

DEAD MAN'S HILL. The Gallow's Hill at NOTTINGHAM, where WILL THE BOWMAN almost lost his life, was located to the north of the city just beyond the NORTHGATE.

[28, 229, 236] {K15}

GAM~MELL, ~WELL Unidentified home of ALFRED OF GAMMELL and STEPHEN OF GAMWELL. In all probability Gammell or Gamwell was the name of a manor rather than a village, and it may have been located in the vicinity of HUNTINGDON if the evidence contained within the legends is to be believed.

GAM~MELL, ~WELL, ALFRED OF See ALFRED OF GAM~MELL, ~WELL.

GAMWELL, STEPHEN OF See STEPHEN OF GAMWELL.

GAPTOOTH, GRAME See GRAME GAPTOOTH.

GEBUR The lowest class within Anglo-Saxon society, though the name is now incorrectly used for a CEORL or CHURL. More specifically, a gebur appears to have been given around 20 acres of land in return for often burdensome labours and rents, his land and tools reverting to the ownership of the lord upon his death. From this description it would appear as if JOHN A'GREEN was a gebur.

[6]

GENEAT A high-ranking CEORL who paid rent for his land and performed services that were commensurate with his position, such as horseman or armourer. It appears that a geneat (meaning 'companion') was originally a member of the lord's household and he would have ridden with his lord though he was still subject to the rules pertaining to a ceorl.

GEOFFREY OF BRITTANY (1158–86) Fourth son of HENRY II and ELEANOR OF AQUITAINE, he joined his brothers in their unsuccessful rebellion against their father in 1173. In 1182 he turned against his brother Richard (later RICHARD I) in Poitou, and retired to the court of PHILIP II of FRANCE. He died suddenly in Paris, trampled to death by his horse after a fall during a tournament. At the time he was plotting once more against his father. Geoffrey's death opened the way for JOHN to attain the throne after Richard I's death in 1199.

GEOFFREY PLANTAGENET Illegitimate son of HENRY II who, if legend and history are indeed compatible, might well have come into contact with ROBIN HOOD and his men as he was BISHOP of LINCOLN from 1173 to 1182, HIGH CHANCELLOR from 1182 to 1189, and Bishop (or Archbishop) of YORK from 1189 to 1207. His most likely contact with the outlaws would have resulted from this last post. He was forced to flee overseas after objecting to a tax on Church property, and died abroad in 1212.

GERMANY, KING OF The King of Germany receives only one mention in the legends, when Sir HERBRAND DE TRANMIRE recounts that he had fought a joust before the King of Germany to ABBOT ROBERT, who accused him of being a false and treacherous knight. If the legends follow history, then the most likely candidates for this role would be Henry the Lion (1129–95) or the emperor Henry VI (1165–97), the latter also being responsible for the imprisonment and ransom of RICHARD I.

[189]

GEST OF ROBYN HODE, A This late fourteenth- or early fifteenth-century serial attempts to draw together all the various strands of the legends of ROBIN HOOD as they were at that time, and arrange them in a single narrative. The title appears to be a corruption of *LYTELL GESTE OF ROBYN HODE*, as the two works are virtually identical. This work, which is possibly the earliest study of the life of Robin Hood, formed an important part of the research that led to the legends as they are told in Part One of this book.

GILBERT (OF THE WHITE ~HAND, ~HIND) Son of JOHN A'GREEN and nephew of WILL SCARLET, who raised the boy after his father had died and Sir GUY OF GISBORNE had evicted his mother, Will Scarlet's unnamed sister. Gilbert of the White Hand joined his uncle Will Scarlet as a member of ROBIN HOOD's outlaw band, and became so proficient with the longbow that he was almost as good as Robin Hood, a fact he proved at the archery contest at NOTTINGHAM, and again during the friendly archery tournament Robin and his men took part in to prove their mettle to the disguised RICHARD I.

Following the pardoning of Robin Hood and all his men by the king, Gilbert of the White Hand went to MALASET where he married SIBBIE and lived as a freeman on land given to him by Robin and MAID MARIAN. Later, during the siege of the EVIL HOLD, Gilbert of the White Hand led the forces across the moat along with LITTLE JOHN. Although almost killed by FULCO THE RED, Gilbert of the White Hand was still alive after the death of Robin Hood. He travelled to the border lands where he sought fame with the sword, stories of his deeds and exploits being told for generations to come.

History does not directly record Gilbert of the White Hand, though it does record one Gilbert of the White Hind, who is simply named as one of the best archers during the reign of HENRY II.

[8, 42–3, 113, 156, 263–4, 327, 333, 338, 347, 382, 402]

GILDINGCOTE Village on the borders of SHERWOOD FOREST that was home to an order of BLACK MONKS, with whom RICHARD I lodged while he was travelling through the forest in search of ROBIN HOOD. Unfortunately, no such place as Gildingcote exists today, so the location of the monastery cannot be accurately determined.

[313]

GISB~ORNE, ~URN(E) The native village (OS103 SD8348) in LANCASHIRE of the villainous

Sir GUY OF GISBORNE, his most likely home being Gisburne Park (OS103 SD8249) on the edge of the River Ribble.

{D5}

GISBORNE, SIR GUY OF See GUY OF GISBORNE, Sir.

GISORS Town in FRANCE, in the *département* of Eure, situated in the pleasant valley of the Epte, 44 miles north-west of Paris, approximately 30 miles south-east of Rouen and a few miles to the west of Chaumont. Gisors is dominated by a feudal stronghold built chiefly by the kings of England in the eleventh and twelfth centuries. The outer enceinte, to which is attached a cylindrical donjon erected by Philip Augustus, King of France, embraces an area of over 7 acres. On a mound in the centre of this space rises an older donjon, octagonal in shape, protected by another enceinte. The outer ramparts and the ground they enclose have been converted into promenades. The church of St Gervais dates in its oldest parts – the central tower, the choir and parts of the aisles – from the middle of the thirteenth century, when it was founded by Blanche of Castile. The rest of the church belongs to the Renaissance period. The Gothic and Renaissance styles mingle in the west façade, which, like the interior of the building, is adorned with a profusion of sculptures; the fine carving on the wooden doors of the north and west portals is particularly noticeable.

In the Middle Ages Gisors was capital of the Vexin. Its position on the frontier of Normandy caused its possession to be hotly contested by the kings of England and France during the twelfth century, at the end of which it and the dependent fortresses of Neaufles and Dangu were ceded by RICHARD I to PHILIP Augustus. During the wars of religion in the sixteenth century it was occupied by the Duke of Mayenne on behalf of the League, and in the seventeenth century, during the Fronde, by the Duke of Longueville. Gisors was given to Charles Auguste Fouquet in 1718 in exchange for Belle-Ile-en-Mer and made a duchy in 1742. It afterwards came into the possession of the Count of Eu and the Duke of Penthivre.

History records that the castle at Gisors was originally built by Robert de Bellême (see ISENBART DE BELAME), with a royal chamber specifically constructed in 1184. This alteration came after HENRY II had largely rebuilt the castle. Richard I once lodged in the castle, and while he slept RICHARD MALBÊTE stole a pair of his spurs, though it is not known whether these spurs were in the king's chamber or elsewhere in the castle. This part of the legends may be true, for Richard I was at Gisors in 1189 and again in 1190.

[245]

GLANVILLE, RANULF DE See RANULF DE GLANVILLE.

GODARD One of the villagers of LOCKSLEY who came to the aid of SCADLOCK when Sir HUBERT OF LYNN arrived to take possession of the manor of OUTWOODS after ROBERT OF LOCKSLEY had been outlawed.

[35]

GODMANCHESTER Small town just to the south of HUNTINGDON, to which REUBEN OF STAMFORD, his daughter RUTH and his son SILAS BEN REUBEN were escorted after they had been reunited after the hanging of RICHARD MALBÊTE.

[246] {R23}

GOSBERT DE LAMBLEY, SIR Sir Gosbert de Lambley plays no part in the legends, but a man-at-arms in his employ made it through one of the early rounds of the archery tournament at NOTTINGHAM.

[264]

GRAHAM One of the Scottish border clans which attacked Sir DROGO OF DALLAS TOWER but were subsequently put to flight by ROBIN HOOD, who instilled such fear into them that they never dared to venture south of the border again. The other three clans were ARMSTRONG, DOUGLAS and JORDAN.

[388]

GRAME GAPTOOTH Man-at-arms to the Lord of THURLSTAN, who captured MAID MARIAN and took her to the BLACK TOWER, from where she was rescued by KET THE TROW. Later Grame Gaptooth, by this time referred to as the Lord of Thurlstan, came to the assistance of the besieged Sir ISENBART DE BELAME and the knights of the EVIL HOLD, but was caught in a pincer movement by ROBIN HOOD's men and killed.

[290–1, 353, 355]

GREASBY Though no Greasby exists today, there is a Greasley to the north-west of NOTTINGHAM. It could be argued that this village (OS129 SK4947) is the Greasby of the legends as there are remains of a castle on the southern boundaries of the village. However, the legends distinctly refer to Greasby as lying on the fens to the east of the River TRENT.

{J15}

GREASBY, SIR RANULF DE See RANULF DE GREASBY, Sir and RANULF OF THE WASTE, Sir.

GREAT NORTH ROAD This famous road, today known simply as the A1, runs from LONDON to Scotland. It passes straight through the area of the legends, and doubtless would have been well known to ROBIN HOOD and his men. The legends often confuse this road with ERMINE STREET, but the latter lies much further to the east, and could not therefore have been reached in the short periods of time mentioned in the legends.

GREATREX, PETER See PETER GREATREX.

GREY, COLMAN See COLMAN GREY.

GRIMLEY MERE Unidentified lake in the vicinity of HAGTHORN WASTE, where the first wife of Sir RANULF DE GREASBY was found dead.

[147]

GRIMSBY Port (OS113 TA2810) on the north-eastern coast of LINCOLNSHIRE. It was to Grimsby that RICHARD MALBÊTE was being taken by the sons of JOHN LE MARCHANT to go into exile, but he never reached the port, having escaped from the sons by means unrecorded. Grimsby was also the port from which Sir ROGER OF DONCASTER fled the country after his part in the death of ROBIN HOOD, only narrowly escaping the determined pursuit of KET THE TROW and HOB O'THE HILL.

[183, 400] {R9}

GRIP One of the two merlin hawks, the other being FANG, that were demanded as payment, along with the hunting hound ALISAUNDRE, by Sir PHILIP DE SCROOBY when Sir RANULF DE GREASBY asked him to go in search of the mysterious minstrel JOCELYN.

[155]

GRULL A CHURL from EVIL HOLD, who spied on ROBIN HOOD and his men and led the knights of Sir ISENBART DE BELAME to CAMPSALL Church, where the outlaws had gone to celebrate mass and make their confessions. Grull was killed by HOB

O'THE HILL after the death of Sir IVO LE RAVENER at the hands of ALAN-A-DALE, and after he had failed in his own attempt to kill Robin Hood.

[62]

GRYM, SIR NIGER LE See NIGER LE GRYM, Sir.

GUY OF GISBORNE, SIR The lord of the manor of BIRKENCAR, he was hated by the VILLEINs under his control as he was a cruel and ruthless master. For a long time he had been in league with the monks of ST MARY'S ABBEY, especially ABBOT ROBERT, as they sought a way to dispossess ROBERT OF LOCKSLEY. Following Robert's outlawing, the villeins of Birkencar and LOCKSLEY turned against Sir Guy and burnt down his manor house. Sir Guy only just managed to escape with his life by disguising himself in the hide of a recently flayed horse as the SPECTRE MARE, frightening several of ROBIN HOOD's comrades as he fled. Subsequently he became a far more just lord as he had been blamed for the revolt by Abbot Robert, who threatened to take the manor from him.

Although Sir Guy of Gisborne is always considered a major character in the legends of Robin Hood, he does not actually play a major role in the early legends. Instead he is content to scheme with Abbot Robert and RALPH MURDACH, plotting to rid themselves of Robin Hood and his troublesome

Illustration from *The Merry Adventures of Robin Hood* by Howard Pyle.

Robin Hood and Sir Guy of Gisborne's head. Illustration from *A Book of Old English Ballads* by George Wharton Edwards.

band of outlaws, but Sir Guy himself took little active part in such schemes. He later aligned himself with Sir ROBERT DE LONGCHAMP, the new abbot of St Mary's Abbey, and latterly with the knights of the EVIL HOLD, but again there was no personal involvement.

Sir Guy's only contact with Robin Hood comes relatively late on in the legends, when both must have been in their late middle age. He confronted Robin on a forest path, still wearing the hide of the flayed horse, which gave him the peculiar appearance of a small brown horse walking on its hind legs. The two engaged in a bitter sword fight, and both managed to wound the other before Robin Hood finally ducked under Sir Guy's guard and embedded his sword almost to the hilt in the foul knight, who crumbled dead to the ground.

[6–7, 9, 29, 35, 37–9, 42–9, 88–9, 99, 104, 257, 335, 376, 386]

GUY OF WROTHSLEY, SIR The last legal owner of the manor of BIRKENCAR, his ancestors having held the lands since they were given them by WILLIAM II. Sir Guy bequeathed the land to the WHITE MONKS of ST MARY'S ABBEY, and since that time ROBERT OF LOCKSLEY's family had had to be on their guard as the monks greedily coveted the lands of LOCKSLEY, which were the most fertile in the entire manor.

[7]

H

HAGENAU A German town in the imperial province of Alsace-Lorraine. It is situated in the middle of the Hagenau Forest, on the River Moder approximately 50 miles east of Hamburg. Hagenau dates from the beginning of the twelfth century, and owes its origin to the erection of a hunting lodge by the dukes of Swabia. The emperor Frederick I surrounded it with walls and gave it town rights in 1154. On the site of the hunting lodge he founded an imperial palace, in which were preserved Charlemagne's jewelled imperial crown, sceptre, globe and sword. Subsequently it became the seat of the Landvogt of Hagenau, the imperial advocatus in Lower Alsace. Richard of Cornwall, King of the Romans, made it an imperial city in 1257. In 1648 it came into the possession of France, and in 1673 Louis XIV caused the fortifications to be razed. In 1675 it was captured by imperial troops, but two years later was retaken by the French and largely destroyed by fire. In 1871 it fell, with the rest of Alsace-Lorraine, into the possession of Germany. It was in the castle at Hagenau that RICHARD I was held to ransom.

[305]

HAGGAR SCAR A steep incline in the depths of CLUMBER FOREST where the SHERIFF OF NOTTINGHAM and his men were ambushed by ROBIN HOOD and eighty outlaws, who had come to rescue the sheriff's prisoner, Sir RICHARD AT LEE, who was being taken under guard to NOT-TINGHAM. Moments after RALPH MURDACH and his party had been called to a halt by Robin, the sheriff lay dead on the road andSir Richard at Lee had been liberated. Though the exact location of Haggar Scar is not known, it is possible that it can be identified with Hagg Hill (OS120 SK5774) at the western end of Clumber Forest. This location would fit in with the legends, which say that Sir Richard at Lee was taken captive at WOODSETT (probably Woodsetts to the north-west of WORKSOP at OS120 SK5583), which lies on a direct route through Clumber Forest at this point.

[282] {K12}

HAG'S WOOD Unidentified region of woodland through which the men-at-arms who had witnessed the death of Sir ROGER DE LONGCHAMP passed en route to the EVIL HOLD.

[28]

HAGTHORN ~CASTLE, ~WASTE The castle of Sir RANULF DE GREASBY, who was also known as Sir RANULF OF THE WASTE. Though the precise location of the castle cannot be pinpointed, it may have been at Greasley (OS129 SK4947), where there are remains of a castle on the southern boundaries of the village, although the legends clearly locate Greasby in the fenland to the east of the River TRENT.

[81–2, 130, 147, 149, 159] {J15}

HAMELIN, EARL DE WARENNE One of the king's treasurers, who heard of the exploits of ROBIN HOOD and his men to help raise the ransom required to release RICHARD I from his imprisonment in the castle of HAGENAU in Germany. Following the release of the king, Hamelin supported Robin Hood against the allegations levelled at him by WILLIAM DE LONGCHAMP, and it was this support, and the stories Hamelin told the king about the outlaw's loyalty that led the king to travel into the forests to meet him. Hamelin was one of the party chosen to go in disguise with the king under the direction of Sir RALPH FITZ-STEPHEN. He was present when the king revealed himself to Robin Hood and pardoned all those who had joined him in the greenwood, and received explicit orders from the king to see that the lands of MALASET were duly turned over to Robin and MAID MARIAN.

Hamelin was a historical character. He became the 5th Earl Warenne in 1163, following the death of William, the 4th earl, who died without issue in 1159. Hamelin was the son of Geoffrey of ANJOU, and thus the illegitimate half-brother of HENRY II, who made Hamelin the 5th earl when he married

Isabel, the widow of the 4th earl. In 1180 Hamelin ordered the building of stone castles at Conisbrough and Sandal, and in 1189 he and his wife jointly founded an endowment for a priest for the chapel of St Philip and St James within the castle at Conisbrough. In 1199 Hamelin witnessed the coronation of his nephew King JOHN and the following year travelled to LINCOLN to witness the King of Scotland's oath of homage. In 1201 he visited the castle at Conisbrough and granted a market charter for the town. He died in 1202 and was buried at Lewes Priory in Sussex.

[300, 304, 307, 316, 322, 330]

HAMO DE MORTAIN, SIR One of the knights of the EVIL HOLD. Very little is heard of him and it is assumed that he died during the fighting when ROBIN HOOD and his troops attacked and took the castle at WRANGBY.

[23, 56, 167]

HARELIP, SIR ECTOR OF THE See ECTOR OF THE HARELIP, Sir and ECTOR DE MALSTANE, Sir.

HARLOW WOOD Stretch of woodland leading to a road beyond which LITTLE JOHN and the other outlaws chased the men-at-arms led by BLACK HUGO, who had pursued MAID MARIAN through the woods and then attacked ROBIN HOOD and FRIAR TUCK. Though the wood cannot be located with certainty, there is a Harlow Wood (OS120 SK5457) to the south of MANSFIELD.

[132] {K14}

HAUBERK The name hauberk derives from the old German *halsberge*, meaning coat of mail. Simple hauberks were worn as early as the eighth century in Europe but didn't develop into what is now referred to as a hauberk (a chainmail coat) until the early Middle Ages. The first version of the hauberk, the 'small hauberk', was commonly worn by eighth-century European knights; it also became the dress of their squires. This early hauberk consisted of a padded cloth jacket covered in scales, reaching the hips and elbows in a rather loose-fitting style. The large hauberk was more of a frock/smock design and extended down to knees and elbows.

Before the construction of chainmail became the norm, hauberks were constructed by means of overlapping plates of bronze or iron and sewn-together rings, etc. Eventually, a hauberk became a complete suit of flexible armour which could be worn like a shirt without a 'wrong' side. Each ring in the garment was riveted to the others piece by piece, the final product being either of single- or double-layer construction. Commonly the sleeves were extended to cover the hands as well. The majority of crusader knights wore chainmail hauberks as plate-mail did not become common for a further two hundred years.

HAVELOND The lands of ALICE OF HAVELOND and her husband BENNETT. Regrettably modern maps give us no indication of where Havelond might have been.

[86–7, 392]

HAVELOND, ALICE OF See ALICE OF HAVELOND.

HENRY II, KING OF ENGLAND (1133–89) The son of Matilda, daughter of Henry I, and her second husband Geoffrey Plantagenet, Count of ANJOU, Henry was born in Le Mans and at 18 was invested with the duchy of NORMANDY, his mother's heritage. Within a year his father had died and Henry became Count of Anjou, while in 1152 his marriage to ELEANOR OF AQUITAINE added Poitou and Guienne to his dominions. In 1153 he landed in England and in November of that year signed with King Stephen the treaty of Winchester, whereby Henry was declared the king's successor. He was crowned on 19 December 1154 at Westminster Abbey.

Reverse of the royal seal of Henry II, depicting the king on horseback. (*Centre Historique des Archives Nationales, Paris/Bridgeman Art Library*)

Henry II was the first of the ANGEVIN kings and one of the most effective of all England's monarchs. He came to the throne amid the anarchy of Stephen's reign and promptly collared his errant barons. He refined Norman government and created a capable, self-standing bureaucracy. His energy was equalled only by his ambition and intelligence. Henry survived wars, rebellion and controversy to successfully rule one of the most powerful kingdoms in the Middle Ages. His continental empire included the French counties of Brittany, Maine, Poitou, Touraine, Gascony, Anjou, Aquitaine and Normandy.

Technically Henry was a feudal vassal of the King of France but in reality he owned more territory and was more powerful than his French lord. Although King JOHN (Henry's son) subsequently lost most of the English holdings in France, English kings continued to lay claim to the French throne until the fifteenth century. Henry also extended his territory in the British Isles in two significant ways. First, he retrieved Cumbria and Northumbria from Malcolm IV of Scotland and settled the Anglo-Scottish border in the north, and second, although his success with Welsh campaigns was limited, Henry invaded Ireland and secured an English presence there.

During Stephen's reign English and Norman barons had manipulated feudal law to undermine royal authority, so Henry instituted many reforms to weaken traditional feudal ties and strengthen his position. Unauthorised castles built during the previous reign were razed. Monetary payments replaced military service as the primary duty of vassals. The exchequer was revitalised to enforce accurate record-keeping and tax collection. Incompetent sheriffs were replaced and the authority of royal courts expanded. Henry empowered a new social class of government clerks who stabilised procedure – the government could thus operate effectively in the king's absence and would subsequently prove sufficiently tenacious to survive the reign of incompetent kings. Henry's reforms allowed the emergence of a body of common law to replace the disparate customs of feudal and county courts. Jury trials were initiated to end the old Germanic trials by ordeal or battle. Henry's systematic approach to law provided a common basis for the development of royal institutions throughout the entire realm.

The process of strengthening the royal courts, however, provoked an unexpected controversy. The Church courts instituted by William the Conqueror became a haven for criminals of varying degree and ability, for one in fifty of the English population qualified as clerics. Henry wished to transfer

Henry II is crowned, from *Flores Historiarum* by Matthew Paris, Ms 6712 (A.6.89), f.135v. (*Chetham's Library, Manchester/Bridgeman Art Library*)

Church courts. Beckett fled England in 1164, but through the intervention of Pope Adrian IV he returned in 1170. He greatly angered Henry by opposing the coronation of Prince Henry. Exasperated, Henry hastily and publicly conveyed his desire to be rid of the contentious archbishop. Four ambitious knights took the king at his word and murdered Beckett in his own cathedral on 29 December 1170. Henry endured a rather limited storm of protest over the incident and the controversy passed.

Henry's plans to divide his myriad lands and titles resulted in his sons' treachery. With the encouragement of their mother, they rebelled against their father several times, often with Louis VII of France as their accomplice. The deaths of Henry the Young King in 1183 and Geoffrey in 1186 brought no respite; RICHARD, with the assistance of Philip II Augustus of France, attacked and defeated Henry on 4 July 1189 and forced him to accept a humiliating peace. Henry II died two days later at Chinon in France and was succeeded by the eldest of his surviving sons, Richard.

Henry II does not directly feature in the legends of ROBIN HOOD, though it is now generally accepted that it was during the latter part of his reign, in a time of blossoming baronial power, that ROBERT OF LOCKSLEY was outlawed.

[169, 189, 303]

sentencing in such cases to the royal courts, since the church courts merely demoted clerics to laymen. Thomas Beckett, Henry's close friend and chancellor since 1155, was named Archbishop of Canterbury in June 1162 but distanced himself from Henry and vehemently opposed the weakening of

The coronation of Henry II's son, also called Henry, as co-monarch by Roger of Pont l'Eveque, Archbishop of York, in 1170. At right, Henry II serves the royal cup to his son at the coronation banquet in Westminster Palace. Becket Leaves f.3. (*British Library, London/Bridgeman Art Library*)

Henry III being crowned. Cott Vitt A XIII f.6. (*British Library, London/Bridgeman Art Library*)

HENRY III, KING OF ENGLAND (1207–72)
Born in Winchester, the son of King JOHN and ISABEL OF ANGOULÊME, Henry III inherited the throne at the age of 9. He was the first monarch to be crowned in his minority. His reign began immersed in the rebellion created by his father. London and most of the south-east were in the hands of the French Dauphin Louis while the northern regions were under the control of rebellious barons – only the Midlands and the south-west were loyal to the boy king. The barons, however, rallied under Henry's first regent, William the Marshall, and expelled the French Dauphin in 1217. William the Marshall governed until his death in 1219; HUBERT DE BURGH, the last of the justiciars to rule with the power of a king, took over until Henry came to the throne in earnest aged 25 in 1232, at which time he deprived Hubert de Burgh of all his offices. In 1236 he married Eleanor of Provence, by whom he had nine children: Edward (later King Edward I), Margaret, Beatrice, Edmund, Richard, John, Katherine, William and Henry.

A variety of factors coalesced in Henry's reign to plant the first seeds of English nationalism. Throughout his minority the barons held firm to the ideal of written restrictions on royal authority and reissued the MAGNA CARTA several times. The nobility wished to bind the king to the same feudal laws under which they were held. The emerging class of freemen also demanded protection from the king's excessive control. Barons, the nobility and freemen began viewing England as a community rather than a mere aggregation of independent manors, villages and outlying principalities. In addition to the restrictions outlined in the Magna Carta, the barons asked to be consulted in matters of state and called together as a Great Council. Viewing themselves as the natural counsellors of the king, they sought control over the machinery of government, particularly in the appointment of chief government positions. The exchequer and the chancery were separated from the rest of the government to decrease the king's chances of ruling irresponsibly.

Nationalism, such as it was at this early stage, manifested itself in the form of opposition to Henry's actions. He infuriated the barons by granting favours and appointments to foreigners rather than the English nobility. Peter des Roches, Bishop of Winchester and Henry's prime educator, introduced a number of Frenchmen from Poitou into the government, while many Italians entered English society through Henry's close ties to the papacy. His reign coincided with an expansion of papal power. The Church developed, in effect, into a massive European monarchy, and became as creative as it was excessive in extorting money from England. England was expected to assume a large portion of the financing of the myriad officials employed throughout Christendom as well as providing employment and parishes for Italians living abroad. Henry's acquiescence to Rome's demands initiated a backlash of protest from his subjects: laymen were denied the opportunity to be nominated for vacant ecclesiastical offices and clergymen lost any chance of advancement.

Matters came to a head in 1258. Henry levied extortionate taxes to pay for debts incurred through war with Wales, failed campaigns in France and an extensive programme of ecclesiastical building. Inept diplomacy and military defeat led Henry to sell his hereditary claims to all the ANGEVIN possessions in France except Gascony. When he assumed the considerable debts of the papacy in its fruitless war with Sicily, his barons demanded sweeping reforms and the king was in no position to offer resistance. He was forced to agree to the Provisions of Oxford, a document placing the barons in virtual control of the realm. A council of fifteen men, comprised of the king's supporters and detractors, brought about a situation whereby Henry could do nothing without the council's knowledge and consent. The magnates handled every level of government with great unity initially but gradually succumbed to petty bickering; the Provisions of Oxford remained in force for only a few years. Henry soon reasserted his authority and denied the Provisions, resulting in the outbreak of civil war in 1264, the so-called second BARONS' WAR. Edward, Henry's eldest son, led the king's forces against the opposition commanded by Simon de Montfort, Henry's brother-in-law. At the Battle of Lewes in Sussex de Montfort defeated Edward and captured both king and prince – and found himself in control of the government.

Simon de Montfort held absolute power after subduing Henry but was a champion of reform. The nobility supported him because of his royal ties and his belief in the Provisions of Oxford. Together with two close associates, he selected a council of nine (whose function was similar to the earlier council of fifteen) and ruled in the king's name. De Montfort recognised the need to gain the backing of smaller landowners and prosperous townsfolk: in 1264 he summoned knights from each shire in addition to the normal high churchmen and nobility to an early pre-Parliament, and in 1265 invited burgesses from selected towns. Although Parliament as an institution was yet to be formalised, the 1265 assembly was a precursor to both elements of Parliament: the House of Lords and the House of Commons.

In 1265 de Montfort lost the support of one of the most powerful barons, the Earl of Gloucester, and Edward managed to escape. The two men gathered an army and defeated de Montfort at the Battle of Evesham in Worcestershire. De Montfort was slain and the king was released; Henry resumed nominal control of the throne but for the remainder of his reign it was Edward who exercised the real power in his father's stead. The old king, after a long reign of fifty-six years, died in 1272. Although a failure as a politician and soldier, his reign was significant for defining the English monarchical position until the end of the fifteenth century: kingship limited by law.

Though Henry III does not directly feature in the legends of ROBIN HOOD, the outlaw would still have been active during the rule of Hubert de Burgh, and, if history serves us right, did not die until thirteen years after Henry III had taken over the administration of the country.

[366]

Effigy of Henry III, from his monument in the Chapel of Edward the Confessor. (*Private Collection/Bridgeman Art Library*)

HERBRAND DE TRANMIRE, SIR Husband of Dame JUDITH and father of ALAN DE TRANMIRE, the latter being better known as ALAN-A-DALE. The 'de Tranmire' part of his name means 'of Tranmire' or 'of Tranmere', which would seem to suggest that originally Sir Herbrand hailed from Merseyside, as Tranmere is part of Birkenhead.

Lord of the manor of WERRISDALE, Sir Herbrand was hounded by the knights of the EVIL HOLD after his son had killed Sir IVO LE RAVENER in a fair fight. Sir ISENBART DE BELAME plotted with ABBOT ROBERT to seize Sir Herbrand's lands, and even imposed a heavy fine on him of 400 pounds for Sir Ivo's death.

Sir Herbrand de Tranmire paid the first fine, so Sir Isenbart simply imposed a further fine, again of 400 pounds. This time Sir Herbrand could not raise the money, so he borrowed it from Abbot Robert on surety of his lands – and thus played straight into the hands of the wicked monk and his evil cohorts. Sir Herbrand would have forfeited his manor and his lands had he not been met on ERMINE STREET as he travelled from Werrisdale to YORK by LITTLE JOHN, WILL THE BOWMAN and MUCH THE MILLER'S SON. They brought the knight to ROBIN HOOD, who listened to his story; convinced that Sir Herbrand was a man of his word, Robin lent him the 400 pounds he needed to repay the abbot on surety of the VIRGIN MARY. This was even before Sir Herbrand had identified himself, and so Robin had yet to discover that he was Alan-a-Dale's father.

Sir Herbrand then travelled on to York in the company of Little John, who was to act as his squire. They went to the chapter house of ST MARY'S ABBEY and at first Sir Herbrand pleaded with the corpulent abbot to give him more time to repay the loan. All his various pleas were roughly turned down, and the abbot actually accused Sir Herbrand of being a false and treacherous knight. Then, unable to keep up the pretence any longer, Sir Herbrand threw the 400 pounds Robin had lent him onto the table, and demanded a receipt. Then he walked laughing out of the hall, and set off to return to Werrisdale.

During this journey Little John and Sir Herbrand were set upon by Sir NIGER LE GRYM, Sir BERNARD OF THE BRAKE and another knight. Little John killed Sir Niger le Grym, while Sir Herbrand dealt with the unnamed knight, and Sir Bernard of the Brake hurriedly retreated back to the Evil Hold to tell Sir Isenbart de Belame that they had been denied the lands of Werrisdale.

A year and a day after Robin had lent Sir Herbrand the 400 pounds under the surety of the Virgin Mary, the knight returned to Robin's camp to repay the outlaw. He also brought him a gift of 100 longbows and 200 steel-tipped arrows. However, even though Robin accepted the weapons, he would not accept a penny in repayment as earlier that day they had captured Abbot Robert himself, who had been carrying 800 pounds – a fact that Robin saw as the Virgin Mary overseeing her surety and repaying him twice what he was owed. The humiliation at learning that it was Robin Hood who had lent Sir Herbrand the 400 pounds he required made the abbot so ill that he died the following spring.

Very little else is heard of Sir Herbrand de Tranmire in the legends. He was too old to participate in the siege of WRANGBY, but he did send 10 knights and 100 men-at-arms to help Robin Hood and his troops. Later, following the death of Robin Hood, it is learnt that Sir Herbrand had also died, for his lands had passed to his son Alan-a-Dale.

[57, 134, 170–99, 248, 250, 253–5, 341, 353, 355, 401]

HERIOT A form of death duty paid by VILLEINs to the manorial lord, by which the heirs of the deceased villein were obliged to give the lord the best jewel, beast or chattel of the deceased. The word heriot is derived from the Old English *here geatu*, meaning 'army grant' or 'military apparel', which was originally on loan from the lord. The custom of presenting the lord with the best beast came about because many villeins had no armour or other valuable possessions.

HERNE THE HUNTER A legendary antlered giant said to live in the forests of Windsor Great Park. He probably owes his existence to the cult of Cernunnos, the Celtic antlered deity, of whom he is undoubtedly a lingering memory. Some sources have sought to link Herne the Hunter with ROBIN HOOD, a few even going so far as to make the legendary giant the father of the outlaw, but these links are dubious almost beyond belief, for Herne the Hunter is, without doubt, a far older figure.

HEXGROVE Unidentified section of BARNISDALE FOREST that was also known as the WITCHGROVE. It was to this part of the forest that ROBIN HOOD, in the guise of the potter of WENTBRIDGE, led the SHERIFF OF NOTTINGHAM and ten of his men-at-arms; having scared off the men-at-arms, he took the sheriff captive, feasted him, stripped him of his armour and sent him back to NOTTINGHAM on a PALFREY. Though the Hexgrove itself cannot be located, there is a Hexgreave (OS120 SK6558) about 12 miles to the south-east of MANSFIELD, though this would mean that the Hexgrove was in SHERWOOD FOREST rather than Barnisdale Forest.

[237–8] {L14}

HIGH CHANCELLOR Until the fourteenth century the High or Lord Chancellor was always an ecclesiastic, as portrayed in the legends where the position is held by successive bishops of ELY. An office that originated in the reign of EDWARD THE CONFESSOR, the High Chancellor was a royal secretary and effectively the second-in-command after the monarch. During the absence of RICHARD I, his High Chancellor WILLIAM DE LONGCHAMP acted as regent and was charged with all aspects of government, law and order. The word chancellor comes from the Latin *cancellarius*, a clerk in a Roman law court who sat at the railing – *ad cancellos* – separating the judges from the public.

[256, 276, 279, 294, 304]

HOAR THORN Tree in the village of CROMWELL beside which JACK, SON OF WILKIN, had his home. Today a Hoar Thorn tree would be known as a Hawthorn.

[137]

HOAR TREE A tree mentioned as part of the route that the men-at-arms fleeing from the killing of Sir ROGER DE LONGCHAMP followed on their way back to the castle at WRANGBY. Its location remains a mystery.

[28]

HOB O'THE HILL Son of COLMAN GREY and brother to KET THE TROW, SIBBIE and FENELLA. Though less active than Ket the Trow in the legends, Hob o'the Hill scouted for ROBIN HOOD, and on one occasion saved Robin from the knife of the CHURL GRULL. Following the pardoning of Robin Hood and the outlaws, which happened a short time after the death of his mother, his father having been burnt many years before by Sir RANULF DE GREASBY, Hob o'the Hill, his brother and his sisters travelled to MALASET with Robin and MAID MARIAN.

Taken captive by Sir ISENBART DE BELAME after that knight had come to Malaset and killed Marian with one of Hob's own arrows, Hob was held in the dungeons of the EVIL HOLD. He was eventually freed by his brother Ket after the castle had fallen to Robin and his troops. It was Hob who discovered where Robin Hood lay dying in KIRKLEES Abbey. Following the death of their friend, both Hob and Ket refused to leave the forests they loved, and instead, having hounded Sir ROGER OF DONCASTER out of the country, they tended their friend's grave until they too passed away.

It is interesting to note that Hob is a diminutive of Robin, and it might thus be suggested that Hob o'the Hill, in the context of the legends under consideration, represents an attempt to mythologise the historical character, or at least to connect him with folklore characters, thus removing him from the realm of reality and placing him firmly in the legendary mould. This argument may be taken a stage further by introducing the characterisation of the Hobgoblin, a name that is often applied to PUCK, and which actually means Rob-goblin or the

goblin Robin. The same might be said of ROBIN GOODFELLOW, for all of these may be used to link the historical figure of Robin Hood with the woodland folklore prevalent at the end of the twelfth and beginning of the thirteenth centuries.

[29, 62, 80–2, 132, 286, 333, 338–9, 361, 367, 377–8, 396, 400, 402]

HOLY LAND Euphemistic name for Palestine, where Christ was born, lived and died. It was the purpose of the CRUSADEs to free the Holy Land for all Christendom from the hands of the Muslim hordes.

[211, 230]

HOODMAN BLIND A game that is today known as Blind Man's Buff. Rather than wearing a blindfold, the hunter in Hoodman Blind wore over his head a hood with no eye-holes in it.

[26]

HOSE Garment for men that covered the legs and reached up to the waist. Usually, though not always, hose were woollen.

HUBERT DE BURGH The chief justiciar of England under JOHN and HENRY III, Hubert de Burgh entered royal service in the reign of RICHARD I. He traced his descent from Robert of Mortain, half-brother of William the Conqueror and 1st Earl of Cornwall, and in about 1200 he married the daughter of William de Vernon, Earl of Devon; thus, from the beginning of his career, he stood within the circle of the great ruling families. However, he owed his advancement to his exceptional abilities as an administrator and a soldier. By 1201 he was chamberlain to King John, the sheriff of three shires, the constable of Dover and Windsor castles, warden of the Cinque Ports and warden of the Welsh Marches. He served with John in the continental wars which led up to the loss of NORMANDY. It was to his keeping that the king first entrusted the captive ARTHUR OF BRITTANY. Hubert refused to permit the mutilation of his prisoner, but his loyalty was not shaken by the crime to which Arthur subsequently fell a victim. In 1204 Hubert distinguished himself by a long and obstinate defence of Chinon, at a time when nearly the whole of Poitou had passed into French hands. In 1213 he was appointed seneschal of Poitou.

Both before and after the issue of the Great Charter, Hubert adhered loyally to the king and was rewarded, in June 1215, with the office of chief justiciar. This office he retained after John's death, when William, the earl marshal, was elected as regent. However, until the expulsion of the French from England, Hubert was entirely engaged with military affairs. He had held Dover successfully through the darkest hour of John's misfortunes and restored Kent's allegiance to Henry III. In August 1217 he completed the discomfiture of the French and their allies by his naval victory over Eustace the Monk, the noted French privateer and admiral, in the Straits of Dover. This victory compelled King Louis to accept the treaty of Lambeth, under which he renounced his claims to the English crown and evacuated England. As the saviour of the national cause, the justiciar naturally assumed after William the Marshall's death (1219) the leadership of the English loyalists. He was opposed by the papal legate Pandulf, who claimed the guardianship of the kingdom for the Holy See; by the Poitevin Peter des Roches, Bishop of Winchester, the young king's tutor; by John's foreign mercenaries, primarily Falkes de Bréauté; and by the feudal party under the earls of Chester and Albemarle. On Pandulf's departure the Pope was induced to promise that no other legate should be appointed in the lifetime of Archbishop Stephen Langton. Other opponents were weakened by the audacious stroke of 1223, when the justiciar suddenly announced the resumption of all the castles, sheriffdoms and other grants made since the king's accession. A plausible excuse was found in the next year for issuing a sentence of confiscation and banishment against Falkes de Bréauté. Finally in 1227 Hubert proclaimed the king of age, and dismissed the Bishop of Winchester from his tutorship.

Hubert now stood at the height of his power. His possessions had been greatly enlarged by his four marriages, particularly by that which he contracted in 1221 with Margaret, the sister of Alexander II of Scotland; in 1227 he received the earldom of Kent, which had been dormant since the disgrace of Odo of Bayeux. However, the favour of Henry III was a precarious foundation on which to build. The king chafed against his justiciar's determined opposition to his wild plans of foreign conquest and inconsiderate concessions to the papacy. They quarrelled violently in 1229 at Portsmouth, when the king was with difficulty prevented from stabbing Hubert, because a sufficient supply of ships was not forthcoming for an expedition to France. In 1231 Henry lent an ear to those who asserted that the justiciar had secretly encouraged armed attacks upon the aliens to whom the Pope had given English benefices. Hubert was suddenly disgraced and required to render an account of his long administration. The blow fell suddenly, just a few weeks after his appointment as justiciar of Ireland. It was precipitated by one of those fits of passion to

which the king was prone, but Hubert's influence had for some time been waning before that of Peter des Roches and his nephew Peter des Rivaux. Some colour was given to their attacks by Hubert's injudicious plea that he held a charter from King John exempting him from any liability to produce accounts. But the other charges, far less plausible than that of embezzlement, which were heaped upon the head of the fallen favourite, are evidence of an intention to crush him at all costs. He was dragged from sanctuary at Bury St Edmunds and kept in confinement until Richard of Cornwall, the king's brother, and three other earls offered to act as his sureties. Under their protection he remained in honourable detention at Devizes Castle. On the outbreak of Richard Marshal's rebellion, Hubert was carried off by the rebels to the Marshal stronghold of Chepstow, in the hope that his name would enhance their cause. In 1234 he was admitted, along with the other supporters of the fallen Marshal, to the benefit of a full pardon. He regained his earldom and held it till his death (1243), although in 1239 the king's greed for Hubert's enormous wealth nearly tempted him to revive the charge of treason.

Hubert's earldom died with him, though he left two sons. In constitutional history he is remembered as the last of the great justiciars. After his death the office was shorn of its most important powers and became politically insignificant.

HUBERT OF LYNN, SIR An ally of the lords of the EVIL HOLD, this evil knight was sent to OUTWOODS by ABBOT ROBERT and the WHITE MONKS of ST MARY'S ABBEY the day after ROBERT OF LOCKSLEY had been declared outlaw, to take possession of the manor and lands. When Robert of Locksley returned home after it had been seized by Hubert of Lynn, he found SCADLOCK and three of the villagers tied to the door posts awaiting a whipping. Robert killed Hubert of Lynn and four of his men-at-arms before releasing Scadlock. Subsequently he led the villagers of LOCKSLEY and BIRKENCAR to the manor of Sir GUY OF GISBORNE, which they burnt, that evil knight only just escaping with his life.

[32–5, 40, 94]

HUBERT WALTER A leading figure during the reigns of both RICHARD I and JOHN, Hubert Walter was Archbishop of Canterbury from 1193 until his death in 1205, justiciar from 1193 to 1198 under Richard I, papal legate from 1195, and chancellor between 1199 and 1205 under John. He accompanied Richard I on the Third CRUSADE, and on his return, having been released from captivity with Richard I, raised the ransom required to release the king by means of the first tax for secular purposes. If ROBIN HOOD did indeed help to raise the ransom, then Hubert Walter would certainly have heard of him, and perhaps have come into direct contact with him. After Richard I's departure for his French campaign in 1194, Hubert Walter was the virtual ruler of England, and it was with his assistance that the accession of King John was assured. He had enormous power. In 1196, for example, it is recorded that he had provided from the royal demesne, and from taxes taken from the towns, the immense sum of 1,100,000 silver marks for Richard I's continental campaign.

HUGO, BLACK See BLACK HUGO.

HUNGER WOOD Unidentified area of SHER-WOOD FOREST where the forces of Sir ROGER OF DONCASTER under the command of FULCO THE RED set an ambush for ROBIN HOOD. Though Hunger Wood cannot today be identified, there is a Hunger Hill (OS129 SK6246) to the north-east of NOTTINGHAM that might be considered a likely contender.

[377–8] {L15}

HUNTINGDON Town on the River Ouse approx-imately 16 miles north-west of Cambridge. A fanciful pedigree found in the *Paleographica Brittanica* of 1788 by William Stukeley (see p. 11) asserts that ROBIN HOOD was the legitimate Earl of Hunting-don; several other sources suggest this may indeed have been the case, the earldom and lands of Huntingdon having been taken away from his family by the invading NORMANS. It is possible that the legends refer not to Huntingdon in Cambridgeshire but to Huntingdon Hall, ROBERT OF LOCKSLEY's

ancestral home (OS103 SD6638) some 12 miles to the south-west of GISBURN, the ancestral home of Sir GUY OF GISBORNE.

[16] {R22 and B6}

HUON DE BULWELL, SIR A friend of Sir RICHARD AT LEE, with whom he was staying when ROBERT OF LOCKSLEY escorted MAID MARIAN to the castle at LINDEN LEA after Sir ROGER DE LONGCHAMP's attempt to abduct her. This escapade resulted in the death of Sir Roger de Longchamp and the subsequent outlawing of Robert of Locksley.

[25]

I

INGELRAM The king's messenger at SEAFORD who was, according to Sir LAURENCE OF RABY, killed by RICHARD MALBÊTE. There are a large number of historical characters of this name who could easily fit into this role, but without further information it is impossible to determine which one is referred to here.

[245]

ISABEL OF ANGOULÊME (d. 1246) The second wife of King JOHN, whom she married on 30 August 1200 when she was aged just 12 or 13. Their marriage led to war between John and the

The tomb of Isabel of Angoulême in Fontevrault Abbey. (*Foutevrault Abbey, Fontevrault, France/Bridgeman Art Library*)

French king, and the subsequent loss of John's French possessions. Through her marriage to John, Isabel may well have come into contact with ROBIN HOOD and his men. In 1220 Isabel married Hugh of Lusignan, Count of La Marche, to whom she had been betrothed before her marriage to John.

ISENBART DE BELAME, SIR The wicked leader of the knights of the EVIL HOLD and lord of the castle at WRANGBY. Though Sir Isenbart de Belame was not often directly involved in the continuing struggle against the outlaws, more often as not trusting that task to his minions, he did venture forth from the castle on a number of occasions, though never coming into direct contact with ROBIN HOOD.

On one notable occasion he sent his men-at-arms after MAID MARIAN, who had travelled to BARNISDALE FOREST to visit Robin Hood. The men-at-arms on this occasion were led by BLACK HUGO, but they were forced to flee after Robin blew his horn and the clearing in which he, Marian and FRIAR TUCK were just about holding their own was overrun by outlaws led by LITTLE JOHN. Sir Isenbart de Belame waited eagerly for Black Hugo's return, but his hopes were thwarted. He only came into direct contact with any of the outlaws when Robin and his troops gathered outside the castle at Wrangby.

When the castle fell to Robin's victorious troops, Sir Isenbart de Belame and Sir BALDWIN THE KILLER were taken captive and hauled in bondage before Robin and his men who had gathered in the great hall to sit in judgement. There, by unanimous vote, Sir Isenbart and Sir Baldwin were condemned to be stripped of all the privileges of their rank, and hanged before the castle like common criminals.

History does not record an Isenbart de Belame. It is quite possible that he was a descendant of Robert de Bellême, though the association is by no means certain. Robert de Bellême was typical of a NORMAN baron at his worst. The eldest son of Roger de Montgomery and Mabel, heiress to the ill-famed house of Tavas, Robert succeeded first to the estates of his mother's family, which included large stretches of land and numerous castles on the borders of NORMANDY, Maine and Perche. He later added to these his father's English lands, which included the earldom of Shrewsbury, the lordship of Arundel (Sussex), and a number of castles and properties scattered through many counties. His most notable acquisition with regard to the legends was that of TICKHILL, for Sir Isenbart de Belame is described as 'the grandson of the fiend of Tickhill'.

Robert de Bellême became not only the most powerful of all the Norman barons, but also the most

repugnant in character, a family trait that seems to have been passed down through the generations. Robert de Bellême was a particularly nasty piece of work. He was an evil, treacherous man with an insatiable ambition and a lust for cruelty; even in such bloodthirsty times his sadism was unequalled. In 1102 he was indicted on forty-five separate charges, but rather than stand trial he put his English strongholds into a state of defence. One after another de Bellême's castles were overwhelmed by the king's forces, Tickhill among them. Robert himself surrendered at Shrewsbury, and was quickly banished. To avenge himself he went on the rampage in Normandy. Henry I decided that he could not allow these atrocities to continue and embarked on a conquest of Normandy.

Robert de Bellême sued for peace in 1105 and 1106 but his requests were turned down and the war continued unabated. In 1112 he came to Henry I's court as an envoy of King Louis VI and was promptly thrown into prison at Cherbourg. From there he was moved to Wareham (Dorset), where he spent the remainder of his life. The date of his death is unknown, but in 1130 the Sheriff of Dorset made accounts for his clothing and food, so it was certainly later than that.

It seems almost certain, therefore, that Sir Isenbart de Belame, if not an historical character, owes his origins to the bloodthirsty nature of a man who lived some eighty years before the period under consideration, and would appear, through the similarity of the two characters, to be a remembrance of the real Robert de Bellême.

[23, 56, 60–1, 133–5, 165–7, 169, 171, 176, 199, 200, 257, 291, 332, 335, 338–40, 342–3, 346, 355–63, 366]

IVO DE RABY, SIR A knight of the EVIL HOLD whose name appears only once. It can therefore be assumed that he was either killed fairly early on or remained very much in the background. Perhaps he left England to join RICHARD I on his CRUSADE. As 'de Raby' means 'of Raby', it is possible that Sir Ivo de Raby was related to Sir LAURENCE OF RABY, the marshal of the king's justice who helped ROBIN HOOD try to hang RICHARD MALBÊTE.

[23]

IVO LE RAVENER, SIR One of the knights of the EVIL HOLD, Sir Ivo and a companion attacked ROBIN HOOD and his men inside CAMPSALL Church. Sir Ivo fled after his horse had been shot out from underneath him. Later the same day Robin Hood and ALAN-A-DALE came across the horseless knight in the forest talking with GRULL the CHURL. Alan-a-Dale challenged the knight and killed him in a fair fight, but was none the less declared outlaw for the killing.

[58–9, 61, 134, 135, 168]

J

JACK ALICE'S SON Variant name sometimes used to refer to JACK, SON OF WILKIN, this variant naming him after his mother ALICE. Today he would be known as Jack Alison.

[140]

JACK-A-THORN Variant name for JACK, SON OF WILKIN, derived from the fact that Jack and his widowed mother lived beside the HOAR THORN in CROMWELL.

[140]

JACK, SON OF WILKIN A VILLEIN at the manor of Sir WALTER DE BEAUFOREST, where JOHN THE THINNE, STEWARD to Sir Walter, regarded him as one of the most willing of the younger workers on the manor. Jack had also come to the notice of ALICE DE BEAUFOREST, who had made him one of her falconers. However, upon the death of his father WILKIN, Jack had to give up this treasured position so that he might work the land in order to support his mother ALICE.

Although Jack fervently believed that spirits and demons dwelt in the forests, he had no hesitation at setting out to take messages from Alice de Beauforest to her outlawed love ALAN-A-DALE. Jack's first contact with the outlaws came when WILL THE BOWMAN brought him the rings of Alice de Beauforest and her maid NETTA O'THE MEERING, to whom Jack was betrothed, and asked him to lead him to Alan-a-Dale's hiding place.

Jack duly took Will the Bowman to Alan-a-Dale's hideout, and together they travelled back to the church at CROMWELL in time to participate in the battle that followed the death of Sir RANULF DE GREASBY. With a timely blow of his STAFF Jack saved the life of Alan-a-Dale, and then leapt onto the back of Sir BERTRAN LE NOIR's horse as he made

off with the unconscious Alice de Beauforest. He then stabbed that treacherous knight in the heart.

When Alice recovered her senses she thanked her saviour and promised that from that day on he would be a freeman living on lands that her father would give him, and thus Jack, son of Wilkin, lived out the remainder of his life in peace. Whether or not he actually married Netta o'the Meering is not recorded.

Jack, son of Wilkin, is known by a number of names. He is JACK WILL'S SON, JACK ALICE'S SON and JACK-A-THORN, the former two leading to the modern variants Jack Wilson and Jack Alison, while Jack, son of Wilkin, has been modernised to Jack Wilkinson.

[137–46, 161–4]

JACK WILL'S SON Variant by which JACK, SON OF WILKIN, is sometimes known. His father's name was really WILL, the name Wilkin actually being a nickname meaning Little Will.

[140]

JOCELYN The name used by ROBIN HOOD when he assumed the guise of a minstrel and went to the church at CROMWELL where ALICE DE BEAUFOREST was due to be married to Sir RANULF DE GREASBY. There he sang a song about COLMAN GREY, which so frightened Sir Ranulf that he rode wildly around the churchyard believing forest fiends were after him. Jocelyn disappeared shortly before the bride and her entourage arrived at the church, and even Sir PHILIP DE SCROOBY, whom Sir Ranulf had dispatched to find him at great personal cost, could not find the mysterious minstrel. Sir Philip had demanded the hound ALISAUNDRE and the hawks FANG and GRIP in payment.

[150–6]

JOCELYN OF THURGOLAND, SIR Lord of THURGOLAND, husband of AVIS and father of the uncharitable Squire STEPHEN.

[389]

JOHN One of the villagers of LOCKSLEY who came to the aid of SCADLOCK when Sir HUBERT OF LYNN arrived to take possession of the manor of OUTWOODS after ROBERT OF LOCKSLEY had been outlawed.

[35]

JOHN, DUKE/EARL OF MORTAIGNE The titles by which King JOHN was known prior to his coronation.

[198, 295, 301, 305, 331–2]

The royal seal of King John. (*Centre Historique des Archives Nationales, Paris/Bridgeman Art Library*)

JOHN, KING OF ENGLAND (1167–1216) The youngest and favourite son of HENRY II and ELEANOR OF AQUITAINE, he was the brother of RICHARD I and King of England himself from 1199 until his death in 1216. John was born in Oxford on Christmas Eve 1167. His parents drifted apart after his birth, his childhood being divided between his eldest brother Henry's house, where he learnt the art of knighthood, and the house of his father's JUSTICIAR, Ranulf Glanvil, where he learnt the business of government. As the fourth child, there was nothing left for him to inherit, leading his father to give him the nickname Lackland. His first marriage to Isabella of Gloucester lasted just ten years and was fruitless. In 1200 he married ISABEL OF ANGOULÊME, who bore him two sons, Henry (later HENRY III) and Richard, and three daughters, Joan, Isabella and Eleanor. He also had an illegitimate daughter, Joan, who married Llywelyn the Great of Wales. The survival of the English government during John's reign is a testament to the reforms of his father, as John ruthlessly taxed the system socially, economically and judicially.

The ANGEVIN family feuds profoundly marked John. He and Richard clashed in 1184 when the latter refused to honour his father's wishes for him to surrender AQUITAINE to John. The following year Henry II sent John to rule Ireland, but John alienated both the native Irish and the transplanted Anglo-Normans who emigrated to carve out new lordships for themselves. The experiment was a total failure and John returned home within six months.

After Richard gained the throne in 1189 he gave John vast estates in an unsuccessful attempt to appease his younger brother. John failed to overthrow Richard's administrators during his German captivity and conspired with PHILIP II in another failed coup. Upon Richard's release from captivity in 1194, John was forced to sue for pardon and he spent the next five years in his brother's shadow, though Richard obviously forgave his treacherous brother as on his deathbed he named John as his successor even though ARTHUR OF BRITTANY, the son of Henry II's eldest son Geoffrey, had a stronger claim.

John's reign was troubled in many respects, and as a king he proved extremely unpopular with his subjects. In addition to the Irish débâcle, he inflamed his French vassals by orchestrating the murder of his popular nephew Arthur of Brittany. In 1202 John went to war with PHILIP II of France after the latter had been petitioned by the Count of La Marche, who had been betrothed to Isabel of Angoulême, and by March 1204 only Aquitaine and a few other small areas of France remained in English hands. By the spring of 1205 he had lost the last of his French possessions and returned to England. A quarrel with the Church in 1205 resulted in England being placed under an interdict in 1207, with John himself being excommunicated two years

King John crowned, from *Flores Historiarum* by Matthew Paris, Ms 6712, f.144v. (*Chetham's Library, Manchester/Bridgeman Art Library*)

later. The dispute centred on John's stubborn refusal to install the papal candidate Stephen Langton as Archbishop of Canterbury. The issue remained unresolved until John surrendered to the wishes of Pope Innocent III in 1212 and paid tribute for England as the Pope's vassal, this tribute being an annual tax of 1,000 marks.

The final ten years of John's reign were occupied with failed attempts to regain the French territories he had lost. After he had levied a number of new taxes on the barons to pay for his dismal campaigns, and to cover the annual papal tribute, his discontented barons revolted and demanded that the king reinstate the laws of Henry I. John rejected the proposal and preparations for war began on both sides. The barons' army assembled at STAMFORD and marched on LONDON, capturing the city in May 1215. At Runnymede on 15 June 1215 John succumbed to pressure from the barons, the Church and the English people at large, and signed the MAGNA CARTA, the legends asserting that ROBIN HOOD himself attended that historic ceremony. The document, a declaration of feudal rights, stressed three points. First, the Church was free to make ecclesiastic appointments. Second, larger-than-

normal amounts of money could only be collected with the consent of the king's feudal tenants. Third, no freeman was to be punished except within the context of common law. Although a testament to John's complete failure as a monarch, Magna Carta was the forerunner of modern constitutions. John, however, only signed it as a means of buying time and his reluctance to implement its principles compelled the nobility to seek French assistance. The barons offered the English throne to Philip II's son Louis. John died at NEWARK on 19 October 1216, as the French invaded in the south and the barons rebelled in the north; some popular accounts say that he had been poisoned.

Popularisation of the legends made John a staunch ally of the SHERIFF OF NOTTINGHAM, but history does not seem to support this. Certainly the sheriff would have sought to ingratiate himself with the king, but there is little else to support a tenable and sustainable link between the king and the sheriff. His taxation policies undoubtedly made King John unpopular with the people, but his reign did see improvements in civil administration, the exchequer and the law courts.

[335–6, 365–6]

King John's tomb in the chancel of Worcester Cathedral. (*Worcester Cathedral/Bridgeman Art Library*)

JOHN, SON OF WILKIN Alternative name of JACK, SON OF WILKIN.

[137]

JOHN A'GREEN Brother-in-law of WILL SCARLET and the father of three children, one of whom was GILBERT OF THE WHITE HAND, whom Will Scarlet raised after the deaths of John a'Green and his sister, John a'Green's wife.

[6]

JOHN DE BIRKIN, SIR Ageing knight who told RICHARD I that no knight could take the lands of his friend Sir RICHARD AT LEE while ROBIN HOOD and his men protected it for its rightful owner who had been forced to live as an outlaw.

[311–12]

JOHN LE MARCHANT A merchant from MERCERS ROW in PONTEFRACT who took in and befriended RICHARD MALBÊTE, only to be killed by that treacherous man one night in his sleep. Richard Malbête made off with a great amount of money, but John le Marchant's five sons hounded him so hard that he was forced to seek sanctuary within ST MICHAEL'S, and then ABJURE before the coroner and swear to leave the country. By some unrecorded means Richard Malbête managed to escape from the five sons of John le Marchant, only to be hanged later for his crimes by ROBIN HOOD and Sir LAURENCE OF RABY, the marshal of the king's justice.

[183]

JOHN MARSHALL See MARSHALL, John.

JOHN O'THE STUBBS The true name of JOHN THE LITTLE, who became better known as LITTLE JOHN after he joined ROBIN HOOD and his band of outlaws.

[78]

JOHN THE LITTLE Nickname of JOHN O'THE STUBBS, which WILL THE BOWMAN soon altered to LITTLE JOHN.

[78–9]

JOHN THE STEWARD Name sometimes used to refer to JOHN THE THINNE, this variant coming about as he held the post of STEWARD to Sir WALTER DE BEAUFOREST.

[139]

JOHN THE THINNE The STEWARD to Sir WALTER DE BEAUFOREST, who was some-

times referred to as JOHN THE STEWARD. He thought highly of JACK, SON OF WILKIN, and regarded him as one of the most willing of the younger workers on the manor.

[139]

JOHN'S PALACE, KING A royal hunting lodge (OS120 SK6064) used by King JOHN. Its remains lie on the north-western edge of the present CLIPSTONE FOREST, but in its heyday it would have been within the boundaries of the ancient forest. The lodge is said to have been built on the site of a chapel raised by King Edwin of Northumbria. It was extended by HENRY I and given to John by his brother RICHARD I in 1189, but he took it back in 1194 after returning to England to find that his brother had attempted to usurp his throne. John regained the property in 1199 when he became king. It was destroyed by fire in 1220 and HENRY II re-erected it some fifty years later. Today only a few walls remain.

ROBIN HOOD and his men are said to have entered the palace and liberated all the prisoners in the dungeon while Prince John was off on a wild goose chase searching for the outlaws.

{L13}

The mighty fight betwixt Little John and the cook. Illustration from *The Merry Adventures of Robin Hood* by Howard Pyle.

JORDAN One of the Scottish border clans which attacked Sir DROGO OF DALLAS TOWER but were subsequently put to flight by ROBIN HOOD, who instilled such fear into them that they never dared to venture south of the border again. The other three clans were ARMSTRONG, DOUGLAS and GRAHAM.

[388]

JUDITH, DAME The wife of Sir HERBRAND DE TRANMIRE and mother of ALAN DE TRANMIRE, being better known as ALAN-A-DALE.

[197–8]

JUSTICIAR In English history, the title of the chief minister of the NORMAN and earlier ANGEVIN kings. The history of the title in this connotation is somewhat obscure. The Latin *justiciarius* meant simply judge, and was originally applied to any officer of the king's court, to the chief justice or in a very general way to all who possessed courts of their own or were qualified to act as judges in the shire courts. It was not until the reign of HENRY II that the title *justiciarius totius Angliae* was exclusively applied to the king's chief minister. The office, however, existed before the style of its holder was fixed, and later writers refer to them simply as *justiciarii*. Thus Ranulf Flambard, the chief minister of William II, who was probably the first to exercise the powers of a justiciar, is called *justiciarius* by Ordericus Vitalis.

The fact that English kings were often absent from England gave this office an importance that at times threatened to overshadow even that of the crown, and it was this circumstance that ultimately led to its abolition. HUBERT DE BURGH was the last of the great justiciars; after his fall (1231) the justiciarship was not again committed to a great baron, and the chancellor soon took the position formerly occupied by the justiciar as second to the king in dignity, as well as in power and influence. Under Edward I and his successor, the justiciar's responsibilities were divided between the justices of common pleas, the justices of the king's bench and the barons of the exchequer.

Outside England the title justiciar was given under Henry II to the seneschal of Normandy. In Scotland the title of justiciar was borne, under the earlier kings, by two high officials, one having his jurisdiction to the north, the other to the south of the Forth. They were the king's lieutenants for judicial and administrative purposes and were established in the twelfth century, either by Alexander I or by his successor David I. In the twelfth century a *magister*

justitiarius also appears in the Norman kingdom of Sicily, the title and office being probably borrowed from England; he presided over the royal court and was, with his assistants, empowered to decide all cases reserved to the crown.

KET THE TROW Son of COLMAN GREY and brother to HOB O'THE HILL, SIBBIE and FENELLA. Following the death of Colman Grey, who was burnt to death by Sir RANULF DE GREASBY, Ket, his brother, his sisters and his mother lived in a barrow in the heart of BARNISDALE FOREST. There they became the friends of ROBERT OF LOCKSLEY, after he had come across five knights who intended to burn Ket and his brother Hob. The two brothers managed to kill two of the knights, but the other three had all but killed them when their mother and sisters appeared and implored the knights to spare them. Instead the knights simply replied that the women should burn along with Ket and Hob. Robert could stand it no longer and quickly killed the three knights, thus saving the lives of Ket the Trow, Hob o'the Hill, Sibbie, Fenella and their mother.

Of the two brothers and two sisters, Ket is by far the most active in the legends. Always alert for trouble, he constantly brought ROBIN HOOD and his men intelligence on any travellers passing through the forest, as well as on the movements of the knights of the EVIL HOLD. In one of his most notable escapades he threw a stone at Captain BUSH, rendering him senseless, on the occasion when the SHERIFF OF NOTTINGHAM intended to hang WILL THE BOWMAN. While LITTLE JOHN and Will the Bowman fought off the sheriff's men-at-arms, Ket the Trow had the foresight to bind Captain Bush, for he had recognised him as RICHARD MALBÊTE.

Ket was also responsible for taking MAID MARIAN away from MALASET after her father had died. En route to Robin, Marian had been captured by GRAME GAPTOOTH and taken to the BLACK TOWER, from where Ket helped her to escape. The two made their way into the forest where they met DRING by BRAMBURY BURN, but they were seen by a spy from the Evil Hold who killed Dring, put on

Dring's clothes, and then followed Ket and Marian back to his barrow home. There Ket killed the spy just as Robin arrived. When Robin and all the outlaws were pardoned by RICHARD I, Ket the Trow, Hob o'the Hill, Sibbie and Fenella went with Robin and Marian to Malaset for they did not wish to stay in their barrow; their mother had died a short while before, and now the barrow served as her grave.

Ket the Trow was an excellent archer, firing his short black arrows with unerring accuracy. When Robin and his troops assembled on the ground before the castle at WRANGBY, even though the light was fading fast Ket the Trow managed to fire an arrow to the ramparts with such accuracy that it entered the eye-slit of the knight standing next to Sir ISENBART DE BELAME, though the angle meant that the arrow inflicted no more than a flesh wound. It was also during the siege of the Evil Hold that Ket the Trow, pondering on how he might release his brother from the dungeons of that dreadful place, spotted the signals being passed between the castle and Grame Gaptooth. By taking that intelligence to Robin he enabled a plan to be evolved which would ensure them victory. As the battle raged, Ket the Trow and Squire DENVIL OF TOOMLANDS entered the castle and quickly overcame the few men left within, and thus secured the castle for Robin and his troops.

Ket the Trow's loyalty to Robin Hood continued even after the outlaw had been murdered by his own aunt in KIRKLEES Abbey. Ket and Hob hounded Sir ROGER OF DONCASTER out of the country, and then, after the outlaws had gone their separate ways, Ket and his brother tended the grave of Robin Hood until their time also came to an end.

[26–9, 62, 81, 119–20, 126, 129, 132, 135, 200, 234–7, 244, 286–93, 333, 343, 345–6, 353, 359, 361, 363, 367–9, 400, 402]

KIRKLEES Site of the ABBEY at which Dame URSULA was the ABBESS. During the latter stages of his life ROBIN HOOD travelled there once every six months to visit his aunt Dame Ursula and his cousin ALICE OF HAVELOND, and to have his blood let as a cure for the ravages of old age. It was to Kirklees that Robin travelled in the company of LITTLE JOHN and others of his band to have his

Robin Hood's grave slab at Kirklees, drawn by Nathaniel Johnston, 1665.

blood let some months after Alice of Havelond had died, and there he died. Dame Ursula, in the pay of Sir ROGER OF DONCASTER, drugged the outlaw before opening a vein and allowing him to bleed to death.

The alleged grave of Robin Hood can still be visited at Kirklees (OS104 SE1721), a short distance to the north of the A664 between Brighouse and Mirfield. This grave is the subject of much controversy, and may or may not be the tomb erected over the site where Robin's last arrow fell, and where FRIAR TUCK spoke the appropriate words as his comrades-at-arms laid him to rest beneath the soil of the forest he loved so much.

[392–400] {G7}

KIRKSTALL Now a suburb of Leeds, Kirkstall (OS104 SE2635) was once the site of a Cistercian priory (OS104 SE2536) whose members on occasion provided ROBIN HOOD and his men with rich pickings.

Completed between 1152 and 1182, Kirkstall ABBEY still stands substantially to its full height, its massive structure presenting a unique example of early Cistercian architecture. Although its community was disbanded in 1539, it has continued to attract the attention of increasing numbers of visitors, for no other building so completely illustrates this early period of English monastic life.

The ideal of the monastic life is that a man who enters it gives up all interest in the affairs of the world and devotes his whole life to the service of God. About 525 St Benedict gathered together a community of such men at Monte Cassino between Rome and Naples, where he drew up a series of rules to guide their daily life and worship. Monasteries following the Benedictine rule were soon established in most European countries, but their increasing laxity led to a number of monastic revivals, the most important of these beginning in 1098 with the foundation of the Abbey of Citeaux in Burgundy in eastern France.

Kirkstall Abbey was founded by a group of monks who left FOUNTAINS ABBEY near Ripon in 1147. Under the leadership of Abbot Alexander, the monks first tried to settle on the lands of Henry de Lacy, Baron of PONTEFRACT, at Barnoldswick, a Pennine village near Skipton. Here both the climate and the local inhabitants proved so inhospitable that a new site had to be found. While passing through Airedale, Alexander came upon a pleasant stretch of country well stocked with timber, stone and water and inhabited by a group of hermits. As this land was in the ownership of William of Poitou, a vassal of Henry de Lacy, Abbot Alexander was able to use Henry's influence to gain possession of the site. On 19 May 1152 the monks transferred from Barnoldswick to Kirkstall, there to build their monastery dedicated to the Virgin Mary. At first all the buildings were of wood, but within a few years these were replaced by massive masonry structures in the local Bramley Fall gritstone. So quickly did the work progress that the church, the cloister and the surrounding buildings were all completed in the lifetime of Abbot Alexander, who died in 1182.

[118] {H6}

KIT THE SMITH One of the villagers of LOCKSLEY, he was one of the first to join the newly outlawed ROBERT OF LOCKSLEY, and took part in the attack on BIRKENCAR when they attempted to burn Sir GUY OF GISBORNE along with his manor. His trade is obvious from his epithet. Kit the Smith appears only fleetingly within the legends. He gave ALAN-A-DALE a bow and flight of arrows at CAMPSALL, and was the first to learn of the fate of WILL THE BOWMAN from the messenger sent by the innkeeper in NOTTINGHAM.

[44–5, 57, 224]

KNAVE A dishonest man or rogue. Derived from the Old English *cnafa*, the word later came to describe a page at court, as commonly depicted in a pack of cards.

KNIGHT The word knight is derived from the Old English *cniht*, and is today used to refer to the mounted warrior of medieval Europe, though the image most people have is far removed from fact. A knight was dubbed in a ceremony in which he was invested, by his father or lord, with a set of arms. Then, in return for field service for a stated period, garrison duty, payment of feudal dues and an obligation to give counsel and aid to his lord, a knight received land – his fee. In the late eleventh and early twelfth centuries most knights were relatively humble professional soldiers who held only one or two fees. However, their status rose during the twelfth century as they were called upon to serve in both local and central government. While a leading knight may have been so created by the monarch, that knight would have the ability to create subordinate knights, and each of them in turn could create knights, and so on *ad infinitum*. In this way a knight such as Sir ISENBART DE BELAME could create knights who would put their loyalty to him ahead of their loyalty to the monarchy, and thus build a corrupt dynasty. It was just such corruption that gave rise to the legends surrounding ROBIN HOOD.

KOTSETLA Also known as a COTSET, a kotsetla was a free peasant and thus ranked above a CEORL. In return for one day's labour a week for his lord (with extra at harvest time), the kotsetla was permitted to farm a small share of the common. The word comes from the Old English *cot-saeta*, a cottage-dweller.

L

LAMBLEY Village (OS129 SK6245) approximately 5 miles to the north-east of NOTTINGHAM close to the floodplain of the River TRENT. It appears to have been the home of Sir GOSBERT DE LAMBLEY.

{L15}

LAMBLEY, SIR GOSBERT DE See GOSBERT DE LAMBLEY, Sir.

LANCASHIRE County of north-west England not usually associated with the legends of ROBIN HOOD. However, it was the county in which MALASET was located, and was thus the home county of Sir RICHARD FITZWALTER and MAID MARIAN, as well as being the county from where Sir HERBRAND DE TRANMIRE, ALAN DE TRANMIRE and Sir GUY OF GISBORNE hailed.

[278, 280]

LANGLAND, WILLIAM (*c.* 1322–*c.* 1400) English poet, also known as William Langley. He was born probably at Ledbury near the Welsh Marches and may have gone to school at the Benedictine Great Malvern Priory. Although he took minor orders he never became a priest. Later in LONDON he apparently eked out his living by singing masses and copying documents as a clerk. His great work, *PIERS THE PLOWMAN*, or, more precisely, *The Vision of William concerning Piers the Plowman*, is an allegorical poem in unrhymed alliterative verse, which is widely regarded as the greatest Middle English poem before Chaucer. It is

both a social satire and a vision of the simple Christian life. Most scholars now believe that the majority of the text is by William Langland, although some still hold that the poem is the work of two or even five authors. The popularity of the poem is attested to by the large number of surviving manuscripts and by its many imitators. Although flawed as a work of art, the poem gives the first datable literary reference to ROBIN HOOD.

LANGTON, STEPHEN Born in about 1156 near Spilsby in Lincolnshire, Stephen Langton spent some time as a prebendary at York, before going to Paris to study. Having qualified, he stayed on to teach theology. It was Langton who organised the Holy Bible, placing the books into the order they remain in, as well as arranging the books into chapters.

Pope Innocent III created him Cardinal in 1206 and appointed him Archbishop of Canterbury in 1207, an appointment that was opposed by King JOHN until 1213. Langton played a central role in the drafting of the MAGNA CARTA, but was suspended shortly afterwards for his unwillingness to proclaim sentences of excommunication against the barons. He left England for Rome, returned in 1218 and died in 1228.

LAURENCE OF RABY, SIR The marshal of the king's justice who sat in judgement with ROBIN HOOD on the multifarious crimes of RICHARD MALBÊTE, and who with the outlaw condemned that murderous individual to be summarily hanged.

[240–7, 322]

LEE The ancestral home of Sir RICHARD AT LEE. There are a number of possible locations for Lee, or Lea as it appears more commonly today. Later legends suggest that Lee was in Wyredale in LANCASHIRE, and although this does not tally with the legendary picture, it would fit in with the home of Sir GUY OF GISBORNE at GISBURN (OS103 SD8248), and with the putative home of ROBERT OF LOCKSLEY at Huntingdon Hall (OS103 SD6638) some 12 miles to the south-west of Gisburn. The legends, however, say that Sir Richard at Lee lived in the castle at LINDEN LEA within sight of NOTTINGHAM. This leaves us with a quandary, for if Linden Lea were indeed within sight of the city walls then it has almost certainly been swallowed up by the developing suburbs. Perhaps the most likely site is Mapperley Park (OS129 SK5742).

{K15}

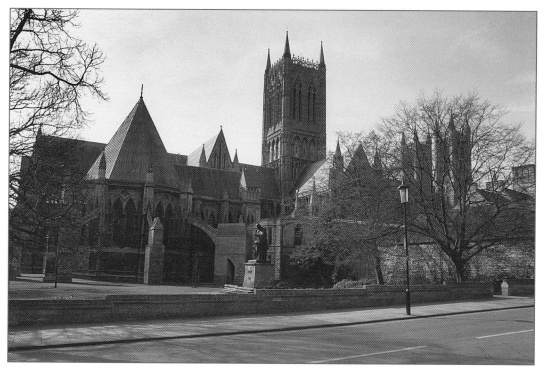

Lincoln Cathedral. (*Mick Sharp Photography*)

LEE, SIR RICHARD AT See RICHARD AT LEE, Sir.

LINCOLN City and county town (OS121 SK9771) of LINCOLNSHIRE. It was an important Roman town named *Lindum Colonia*, lying on both ERMINE STREET and the FOSSE WAY. Lincoln witnessed a massacre of its Jews, like LYNN, STAMFORD and YORK, that massacre being led by the evil RICHARD MALBÊTE. The medieval High Bridge in the High Street is the oldest surviving bridge in Britain still to have buildings on it. The city was the scene of the decisive battle of the first BARONS' WAR on 20 May 1217, when the forces of the future Louis VIII of France and the barons' rebellious English were defeated in the city streets by the supporters of the young HENRY III.

[211, 227, 245, 294, 322, 368] {O12}

LINCOLN GREEN Light-green cloth that was woven in LINCOLN. It was favoured by hunters and outlaws living in the forests of BARNISDALE, SHERWOOD and CLIPSTONE as the colour rendered them almost invisible among the leaves of the trees and the lush green undergrowth.

[287, 323, 365, 385]

LINCOLNSHIRE Large county in the east of England which is named after its administrative city of LINCOLN.

[247]

LINDEN LEA The name given to the lands held by Sir RICHARD AT LEE. The legends locate Linden Lea quite close to NOTTINGHAM, though other sources say that Linden Lea was at LEE in the Wyre Valley in LANCASHIRE.

[13, 24, 26, 310–11, 331] {K15}

LINDHURST WOOD Unidentified portion of the forests bordering the lands of NEWSTEAD ABBEY (OS120 SK5453), through which ROBIN HOOD passed en route to meet FRIAR TUCK for the first time.

[119] {K14}

LITTLE, JOHN THE See JOHN O'THE STUBBS, JOHN THE LITTLE and LITTLE JOHN.

LITTLE JOHN ROBIN HOOD's second-in-command. A giant of a man, some sources saying that he stood over 7 feet tall, Little John was originally called JOHN O'THE STUBBS, though

Little John sings at the banquet. From *Robin Hood* by N.C. Wyeth (1917), p. 327. (*Mary Evans Picture Library*)

those who knew him before he joined Robin Hood called him JOHN THE LITTLE. His surname was also said by some sources to have been NAILOR. Little John's first involvement in the legends came when he stole the meal of BLACK HUGO, whom he left tied to the post of a forester's hut as Robin and ALAN-A-DALE arrived on the scene, but they only caught a glimpse of him as he went. A short while later, in one of the most famous of all the incidents in the legends of Robin Hood, Little John confronted Robin Hood as the two of them attempted to cross the same fallen tree over a fast-flowing stream in opposite directions. They fought on the bridge with QUARTERSTAFFs until Little John managed to topple his opponent into the water.

However, rather than making his way off through the forest, John the Little sat down next to Robin Hood who congratulated him for having beaten him. Then others of Robin's band arrived on the scene and were about to throw John the Little into the water when Robin stopped them, and asked John the Little if he would like to join them. John the Little readily agreed, saying that he had run away from his master, whereupon WILL THE BOWMAN said that from that day forth John the Little would be known as Little John.

From that day until Robin Hood's death many years later, Little John was his right-hand man. He discussed tactics with him, cheered him up when he was low, watched over him, and became the most trusted friend any man could ever hope to have. He was later joined in the forests by his cousin ARTHUR-A-BLAND from NOTTINGHAM.

Little John once acted as squire to Sir HERBRAND DE TRANMIRE when that knight travelled to ST MARY'S ABBEY to repay ABBOT ROBERT the 400 pounds he had been forced to borrow after the knights of the EVIL HOLD had imposed fines on him for the death of Sir IVO LE RAVENER at the hands of Sir Herbrand's son Alan-a-Dale. Little John accompanied Sir Herbrand to YORK, supported him when he went to pay the abbot, and then helped Sir Herbrand fight off the ambush by Sir NIGER LE GRYM, Sir BERNARD OF THE BRAKE and a third unnamed knight. The latter was killed by Sir Herbrand, while Sir Niger le Grym was killed by an arrow fired by KET THE TROW.

Little John and Ket the Trow were major players in the rescue of Will the Bowman, who was to be hanged on GALLOW'S HILL by the SHERIFF OF NOTTINGHAM and Captain BUSH. While Ket the Trow dealt with Captain Bush, who was none other than RICHARD MALBÊTE in disguise, Little John freed Will the Bowman and the two stood back to back fighting off the sheriff's men-at-arms until Robin Hood and the other outlaws arrived on the scene.

Little John was also one of the archers in the tournament held at Nottingham by the sheriff, but he was eliminated in one of the early rounds, and after that kept a wary eye open for treachery. However, as the outlaws backed away towards the forests, Little John was hit in the leg and had to be carried to safety by MUCH THE MILLER'S SON. After the royal pardon had been received from RICHARD I, Little John went with Robin and MAID MARIAN to MALASET, where Robin made him his STEWARD.

Some years later, having accompanied Robin to LONDON to witness the signing of the MAGNA CARTA, Little John took part in the siege of the castle at WRANGBY. Together with GILBERT OF THE WHITE HAND, he led the forces whose job it was to cut the chains holding the drawbridge. During the battle that followed, when Sir ISENBART DE BELAME issued from the castle at the head of his forces, Little John wielded a double-headed axe as he protected Robin Hood, his mastery with that vicious weapon equalling his skills with his more normal weapon, the quarterstaff.

On the fateful day when Robin travelled to KIRKLEES abbey to have his blood let by the ABBESS Dame URSULA, Little John and a number of the other outlaws went with him. They remained within the forest as Robin travelled on alone, in the knowledge that should Robin have need of them he would blow his horn. That evening, as Little John and the others waited, he heard three weak blasts on the horn and rushed to the abbey where he found Robin in an upper room, his life almost spent after the treacherous abbess, in the pay of Sir ROGER OF DONCASTER, had drugged Robin and bled him to death. Lifting Robin from the bed he gave his friend his bow and arrows, and then, after Robin had fired an arrow from the abbey into the forest, laid his friend down to die, having promised to bury him where the arrow had fallen. Little John oversaw the burial of his friend and then travelled with WILL SCARLET to CROMWELL, where he was given lands by Alan-a-Dale. There he lived out the remaining years of his life.

> He was, I must tell you, but seven foot high,
> And, maybe, an ell in the waste;
> A sweet pretty lad;
> Much feasting they had;
> Bold Robin the christ'ning grac'd.
>
> Robin Hood and Little John
> (given in Ritson's *Robin Hood*)
> [64–9, 73–9, 82, 100, 111, 113, 119, 132–3, 136,
> 170–3, 175–6, 178–82, 184, 187, 192–9, 234–5,
> 248–50, 263, 270, 272, 333, 347, 356, 368–9,
> 378–9, 385, 393, 396–9, 401]

LITTLE JOHN'S WELL Well (OS119 SK2679) located approximately a third of a mile south of ROBIN HOOD'S WELL, both wells lying some 7 miles south-south-west of LOCKSLEY (Loxley). There is no evidence to suggest that this well was sunk by Little John, or indeed ever used by him, and it appears simply to follow the normal pattern of being named after characters from popular legend.

{H12}

LOCKSLEY Name of the village where ROBERT OF LOCKSLEY held the lands and manor of OUTWOODS. It was also the home village of a number of the outlaws who joined their master in the greenwood, among them WILL SCARLET and his nephew GILBERT OF THE WHITE HAND. Though there is no village with the name Locksley, there is a Loxley (OS110 SK3089) on the western outskirts of SHEFFIELD, a location

Little John fights with the cook in the sheriff's house. From *Robin Hood* by N.C. Wyeth (1917), p. 197. (*Mary Evans Picture Library*)

that would seem to fit in with the legends. It lies on the Loxley river, which runs into Sheffield from the Damflask Reservoir and merges in the city centre with the River Don. It seems likely, therefore, that this Loxley was the home of the young Robert of Locksley, a statement further supported by the fact that there is a Loxley Chase to the west (OS110 SK2990), where the young Robert and MAID MARIAN were said to have played as children.

[90] {I11}

LOCKSLEY, ROBERT OF See ROBERT OF LOCKSLEY.

LOCKSLEY CHASE Stretch of land near the village of LOCKSLEY where the young ROBERT OF LOCKSLEY and MAID MARIAN played together as children. A chase was an area of land where wild animals were preserved to be hunted. It was while in the chase that Robin and Marian fell in love with each other. Locksley Chase appears to be identifiable with Loxley Chase (OS110 SK2990), which lies a short distance from the village of Loxley (OS110 SK3089) on the western outskirts of SHEFFIELD.

[13] {I11}

LONDON Capital city of the United Kingdom that features in the legends of ROBIN HOOD. London was the first city to be plagued by the persecution of the Jews following the coronation of RICHARD I, and it was to London that Robin sent half of everything the outlaws had collected as toll to the LORD MAYOR with precise instructions that it was to be used towards the ransom required to effect the release of Richard I from his imprisonment in the castle of HAGENAU.

[256, 298, 300, 332, 336]

LONGBOW A light bow made of yew that possibly has a Welsh provenance, although some commentators say they originated in the Scandinavian countries. They were introduced into England in the late eleventh or early twelfth century. In the hands of a marksman the English longbow was a superb weapon: incredibly powerful, rapid in use and deadly. It was also a socially levelling force, as with it the yeoman became the equal, if not the superior, to the knight.

LONGCHAMP, ROBERT DE See ROBERT DE LONGCHAMP, Sir.

LONGCHAMP, SIR ROGER DE See ROGER DE LONGCHAMP, Sir.

LONGCHAMP, WILLIAM DE See WILLIAM DE LONGCHAMP, Sir.

LORD MAYOR Head of the administration in LONDON, to whom ROBIN HOOD sent half of all he and his men had collected as tolls from travellers through the forests to help towards the ransom required to effect the release of RICHARD I. The Lord Mayor subsequently received further payments from Robin and his men, who sent not just half of what they took as toll, but also what they had collected from those barons, knights and others who had been slow in paying the royal tax collectors.

The first Mayor of London was Henry FitzAilwin. He took up the position in 1191 and remained in it until his death. It therefore seems highly probable that it was to FitzAilwin that Robin sent his consignments of treasure under armed guard, and it was FitzAilwin who therefore acted as intermediary between the outlaw and the law.

[298, 304]

LUBBERFIEND Archaic name for a class of supernatural beings akin to the TROW. The name appears to come from the noun *lubber*, meaning a big, awkward or stupid person, thus suggesting that while they might have been terrifying, they were cumbersome and easily tricked. Some sources identify the lubberfiend with the leprechaun of Irish folk belief, in which case the lubberfiend was also called a lubberkin or lubrican.

[80]

LUKE THE RED One of the men-at-arms of the SHERIFF OF NOTTINGHAM, Luke the Red was the last man left in the archery tournament at NOTTINGHAM with ROBIN HOOD. They appeared to be equally matched, so the sheriff suggested that they should determine a method by which one could be declared the winner. Robin proposed that the wand they were to shoot at should be positioned while their backs were turned. Then

A hooded archer with hunting broadhead to his arrow. Drawing after a manuscript illustration from the *Luttrell Psalter, c.* 1340. British Library, Ms. Add 42130, f.307v.

they should turn and fire on the count of three. Luke the Red agreed, but added that he knew that he could not make the shot. He had only seen it accomplished once before, and that was by OLD BAT THE BANDY, chief archer to STEPHEN OF GAMWELL.

[266–8]

LUTE Plucked stringed instrument with a long fretted fingerboard and a pear-shaped body. During the Renaissance the lute was the most respected of all musical instruments. Delicacy, expressiveness and nuance of performance were made possible when fingers replaced the plectrum to pluck the strings. The lute was an ideal accompaniment for voice and other soft instruments, and the most eloquent of all solo instruments. In paintings and other artworks the lute is often associated with Apollo, angels or Orpheus, and it is often mentioned at climactic points in tragedies.

[151, 156]

LYNCHET LODGE Unidentified and probably no longer extant lodge located on WEARYALL HILL. ROBIN HOOD told WILL THE BOWMAN to take REUBEN OF STAMFORD and his daughter RUTH there so that they might recover their health.

[209]

LYNN Shortened version of King's Lynn, the home town of Sir HUBERT OF LYNN, which lies at the southernmost point of the Wash on the border between Norfolk and LINCOLNSHIRE. The town was the scene of one of the pogroms against the Jews, a persecution that had started at the coronation of RICHARD I and culminated in the massacre of 150 Jews in YORK in the middle of March 1190.

[211] {V17}

LYNN, SIR HUBERT OF See HUBERT OF LYNN, Sir.

LYTELL GESTE OF ROBYN HODE, A An early work, printed in about 1420 by Wynkyn de Worde, that relates the most important legends of ROBIN HOOD and his MERRY MEN. It is perhaps the earliest surviving narrative concerning the outlaw, and locates him firmly in South YORKSHIRE.

> Robyn was a proude outlaw,
> Whyles he walked on the ground,
> So curteyse an outlawe as he was one
> Was never none yfounde.

M

MACE A club, usually having a spiked head, that was a favourite weapon in the Middle Ages. Since then the mace has passed into ceremonial use. The mace was a simple development of the club, and is thought to have first appeared in ancient Egypt. Medieval improvements detached the head from the handle and joined the two with a short length of chain, allowing the heavy head to swing through an arc and thereby increasing its effectiveness.

[186]

MAGNA CARTA The charter granted by King JOHN in 1215 that is traditionally seen as guaranteeing human rights against the excessive use of royal power. Archbishop Stephen Langton proposed the drawing up of the charter to the barons in 1213 in response to the king's demands for excessive feudal dues and attacks on the privileges of the Church. John met the barons at RUNNYMEDE on 15 June 1215, and was forced to accept the terms of the charter. Legend says that ROBIN HOOD and his men attended the historic ceremony, but there is no evidence to support this.

The Magna Carta begins by reaffirming the rights of the Church. Certain clauses then guard against infringements of feudal custom, for example preventing the king from making excessive demands for money from his barons without their consent. Other clauses were designed to check extortion by officials or maladministration of justice. No freeman, for example, was to be arrested, imprisoned or punished except by the judgement of his peers or by the law of the land. The privileges of the cities and LONDON were also guaranteed. In all there were sixty-three clauses. The charter was to be enforced by a council of twenty-five barons, who if the king reneged on his promises, would declare war on him.

Within months of the signing of the charter John indeed reneged on the terms and conditions contained therein, and the country readied itself for civil war. Four original copies of the Magna Carta exist, one each in Salisbury and LINCOLN cathedrals, and two in the British Library. Several translations exist of the Magna Carta, which was originally in Latin. One such translation reads:

John, by the grace of God King of England, Lord of Ireland, Duke of Normandy and Aquitaine, and Count of Anjou, to his archbishops, bishops, abbots, earls, barons, justices, foresters, sheriffs, stewards, servants, and to all his officials and loyal subjects, greeting.

Know that before God, for the health of our soul and those of our ancestors and heirs, to the honour of God, the exaltation of the holy Church, and the better ordering of our kingdom, at the advice of our reverend fathers Stephen, archbishop of Canterbury, primate of all England, and cardinal of the holy Roman Church, Henry archbishop of Dublin, William bishop of London, Peter bishop of Winchester, Jocelin bishop of Bath and Glastonbury, Hugh bishop of Lincoln, Walter bishop of Worcester, William bishop of Coventry, Benedict bishop of Rochester, Master Pandulf sub-deacon and member of the papal household, Brother Aymeric master of the Knights of the Temple in England, William Marshal, earl of Pembroke, William earl of Salisbury, William earl of Warren, William earl of Arundel, Alan de Galloway constable of Scotland, Warin Fitz Gerald, Peter Fitz Herbert, Hubert de Burgh seneschal of Poitou, Hugh de Neville, Matthew Fitz Herbert, Thomas Basset, Alan Basset, Philip Daubeny, Robert de Roppeley, John Marshal, John Fitz Hugh, and other loyal subjects:

1. First, that we have granted to God, and by this present charter have confirmed for us and our heirs in perpetuity, that the English Church shall be free, and shall have its rights undiminished, and its liberties unimpaired. That we wish this so to be observed, appears from the fact that of our own free will, before the outbreak of the present dispute between us and our barons, we granted and confirmed by charter the freedom of the Church's elections – a right reckoned to be of the greatest necessity and importance to it – and caused this to be confirmed by Pope Innocent III. This freedom we shall observe ourselves, and desire to be observed in good faith by our heirs in perpetuity. We have also granted to all freemen of our realm, for us and our heirs for ever, all the liberties written out below, to have and to keep for them and their heirs, of us and our heirs.

2. If any earl, baron or other person that holds lands directly of the Crown, for military service, shall die, and at his death his heir shall be of full age and owe a 'relief', the heir shall have his inheritance on payment of the ancient scale of 'relief'. That is to say, the heir or heirs of an earl shall pay for the entire earl's barony, the heir or heirs of a knight 100 shillings at most for the entire knight's 'fee', and any man that owes less shall pay less, in accordance with the ancient usage of 'fees'.

3. But if the heir of such a person is under age and a ward, when he comes of age he shall have his inheritance without 'relief' or fine.

4. The guardian of the land of an heir who is under age shall take from it only reasonable revenues, customary dues and feudal services. He shall do this without destruction or damage to men or property. If we have given the guardianship of the land to a sheriff, or to any person answerable to us for the revenues, and he commits destruction or damage, we will exact compensation from him, and the land shall be entrusted to two worthy and prudent men of the same 'fee', who shall be answerable to us for the revenues, or to the person to whom we have assigned them. If we have given or sold to anyone the guardianship of such land, and he causes destruction or damage, he shall lose the guardianship of it, and it shall be handed over to two worthy and prudent men of the same 'fee', who shall be similarly answerable to us.

5. For so long as a guardian has guardianship of such land, he shall maintain the houses, parks, fish preserves, ponds, mills and everything else pertaining to it, from the revenues of the land itself. When the heir comes of age, he shall restore the whole land to him, stocked with plough teams and such implements of husbandry as the season demands and the revenues from the land can reasonably bear.

6. Heirs may be given in marriage, but not to someone of lower social standing. Before a marriage takes place, it shall be made known to the heir's next-of-kin.

7. At her husband's death, a widow may have her marriage portion and inheritance at

once and without trouble. She shall pay nothing for her dower, marriage portion or any inheritance that she and her husband held jointly on the day of his death. She may remain in her husband's house for forty days after his death, and within this period her dower shall be assigned to her.

8. No widow shall be compelled to marry, so long as she wishes to remain without a husband. But she must give security that she will not marry without royal consent, if she holds her lands of the Crown, or without the consent of whatever other lord she may hold them of.

9. Neither we nor our officials will seize any land or rent in payment of a debt, so long as the debtor has movable goods sufficient to discharge the debt. A debtor's sureties shall not be distrained* upon so long as the debtor himself can discharge his debt. If, for lack of means, the debtor is unable to discharge his debt, his sureties shall be answerable for it. If they so desire, they may have the debtor's lands and rents until they have received satisfaction for the debt that they paid for him, unless the debtor can show that he has settled his obligations to them.

10. If anyone who has borrowed a sum of money from Jews dies before the debt has been repaid, his heir shall pay no interest on the debt for so long as he remains under age, irrespective of whom he holds his lands. If such a debt falls into the hands of the Crown, it will take nothing except the principal sum specified in the bond.

11. If a man dies owing money to Jews, his wife may have her dower and pay nothing towards the debt from it. If he leaves children that are under age, their needs may also be provided for on a scale appropriate to the size of his holding of lands. The debt is to be paid out of the residue, reserving the service due to his feudal lords. Debts owed to persons other than Jews are to be dealt with similarly.

12. No 'scutage'† or 'aid' may be levied in our kingdom without its general consent,

unless it is for the ransom of our person, to make our eldest son a knight, and (once) to marry our eldest daughter. For these purposes only a reasonable 'aid' may be levied. 'Aids' from the city of London are to be treated similarly.

13. The city of London shall enjoy all its ancient liberties and free customs, both by land and by water. We also will and grant that all other cities, boroughs, towns and ports shall enjoy all their liberties and free customs.

14. To obtain the general consent of the realm for the assessment of an 'aid' – except in the three cases specified above – or a 'scutage', we will cause the archbishops, bishops, abbots, earls and greater barons to be summoned individually by letter. To those who hold lands directly of us we will cause a general summons to be issued, through the sheriffs and other officials, to come together on a fixed day (of which at least forty days' notice shall be given) and at a fixed place. In all letters of summons, the cause of the summons will be stated. When a summons has been issued, the business appointed for the day shall go forward in accordance with the resolution of those present, even if not all those who were summoned have appeared.

15. In future we will allow no one to levy an 'aid' from his free men, except to ransom his person, to make his eldest son a knight, and (once) to marry his eldest daughter. For these purposes only a reasonable 'aid' may be levied.

16. No man shall be forced to perform more service for a knight's 'fee', or other free holding of land, than is due from it.

17. Ordinary lawsuits shall not follow the royal court around, but shall be held in a fixed place.

18. Inquests of *novel disseisin*, *mort d'ancestor* and *darrein presentment* shall be taken only in their proper county court. We ourselves, or in our absence abroad our chief justice, will send two justices to each county four times a year, and these justices, with four knights of the county elected by the county itself, shall hold the assizes in the county court, on the day and in the place where the court meets.

19. If any assizes cannot be taken on the day of the county court, as many knights and

---

* Distrain: to take and keep any personal chattel in custody, as a distress.
† Scutage: in old English law, the name of a tax or contribution raised for the use of the king's armies by those who held lands by knight's service.

freeholders shall afterwards remain behind, of those who have attended the court, as will suffice for the administration of justice, having regard to the volume of business to be done.

20. For a trivial offence, a free man shall be fined only in proportion to the degree of his offence, and for a serious offence correspondingly, but not so heavily as to deprive him of his livelihood. In the same way, a merchant shall be spared his merchandise, and a husbandman the implements of his husbandry, if they fall upon the mercy of a royal court. None of these fines shall be imposed except by the assessment on oath of reputable men of the neighbourhood.

21. Earls and barons shall not be amerced save through their peers, and only according to the measure of the offence.

22. No clerk shall be amerced for his lay tenement except according to the manner of the other persons aforesaid; and not according to the amount of his ecclesiastical benefice.

23. Neither a town nor a man shall be forced to make bridges over the rivers, with the exception of those who, from of old and of right, ought to do it.

24. No sheriff, constable, coroners or other bailiffs of ours shall hold the pleas of our crown.

25. All counties, hundreds, wapentakes* and trithings† – our demesne manors being excepted – shall continue according to the old farms, without any increase at all.

26. If anyone holding from us a lay fee shall die, and our sheriff or bailiff can show our letters patent containing our summons for the debt which the dead man owed to us, – our sheriff or bailiff may be allowed to attach and enrol the chattels of the dead man to the value of that debt, through view of lawful men; in such way, however, that nothing shall be removed thence until the debt is paid which was plainly owed to us. And the residue shall be left to the executors that they may carry out the will of the dead man. And if nothing is owed to us by him, all the chattels shall go to the use prescribed by the deceased, saving their reasonable portions to his wife and children.

27. If any freeman shall have died intestate his chattels shall be distributed through the hands of his near relatives and friends, by view of the Church; saving to any one the debts which the dead man owed him.

28. No constable or other bailiff of ours shall take the corn or other chattels of any one except he straightway give money for them, or can be allowed a respite in that regard by the will of the seller.

29. No constable shall force any knight to pay money for castle-ward if he be willing to perform that ward in person, or – he for a reasonable cause not being able to perform it himself – through another proper man. And if we shall have led or sent him on a military expedition, he shall be quit of ward according to the amount of time during which, through us, he shall have been in military service.

30. No sheriff nor bailiff of ours, nor any one else, shall take the horses or carts of any freeman for transport, unless by the will of that freeman.

31. Neither we nor our bailiffs shall take another's wood for castles or for other private uses, unless by the will of him to whom the wood belongs.

32. We shall not hold the lands of those convicted of felony longer than a year and a day; and then the lands shall be restored to the lords of the fiefs.

33. Henceforth all the weirs in the Thames and Medway, and throughout all England, save on the sea-coast, shall be done away with entirely.

34. Henceforth the writ which is called Praecipe‡ shall not be served on anyone for any holding so as to cause a freeman to lose his court.

35. There shall be one measure of wine throughout our whole realm, and one measure of ale and one measure of corn – namely, the London quart; – and one width of dyed and russet and hauberk cloths – namely, two ells below the selvage. And with weights, moreover, it shall be as with measures.

---

* Wapentake: synonymous with a hundred – a district originally comprising a hundred families.

† Trithing: one of three ancient divisions of a county in England – now called riding.

‡ Praecipe: a writ commanding something to be done, or requiring an explanation for its neglect.

36. Henceforth nothing shall be given or taken for a writ of inquest in a matter concerning life or limb; but it shall be conceded gratis, and shall not be denied.

37. If anyone holds of us in fee-farm, or in socage,* or in burkage,† and holds land of another by military service, we shall not, by reason of that fee-farm, or socage, or burkage, have the wardship of his heir or of his land which is held in fee from another. Nor shall we have the wardship of that fee-farm, or socage, or burkage unless that fee-farm owes military service. We shall not, by reason of some petit-serjeanty which someone holds of us through the service of giving us knives or arrows or the like, have the wardship of his heir or of the land which he holds of another by military service.

38. No bailiff, on his own simple assertion, shall henceforth any one to his law, without producing faithful witnesses in evidence.

39. No freeman shall be taken, or imprisoned, or disseized,‡ or outlawed, or exiled, or in any way harmed – nor will we go upon or send upon him – save by the lawful judgment of his peers or by the law of the land.

40. To none will we sell, to none deny or delay, right or justice.

41. All merchants may safely and securely go out of England, and come into England, and delay and pass through England, as well by land as by water, for the purpose of buying and selling, free from all evil taxes, subject to the ancient and right customs – save in time of war, and if they are of the land at war against us. And if such be found in our land at the beginning of the war, they shall be held, without harm to their bodies and goods, until it shall be known to us or our chief justice how the merchants of our land are to be treated who shall, at that time, be found in the land at war against us. And if ours shall be safe there, the others shall be safe in our land.

42. Henceforth any person, saving fealty to us, may go out of our realm and return to it, safely and securely, by land and by water, except perhaps for a brief period in time of war, for the common good of the realm. But prisoners and outlaws are excepted according to the law of the realm; also people of a land at war against us, and the merchants, with regard to whom shall be done as we have said.

43. If anyone holds from any escheat – as from the honour of Wallingford, Nottingham, Boulogne, Lancaster, or the other escheats which are in our hands and are baronies – and shall die, his heir shall not give another relief, nor shall he perform for us other service than he would perform for a baron if that barony were in the hand of a baron; and we shall hold it in the same way in which the baron has held it.

44. Persons dwelling without the forest shall not henceforth come before the forest justices, through common summonses, unless they are in plead or are the sponsors of some person or persons attached for matters concerning the forest.

45. We will not make men justices, constables, sheriffs or bailiffs unless they are such as know the law of the realm, and are minded to observe it rightly.

46. All barons who have founded abbeys for which they have charters of the king of England, or ancient right of tenure, shall have, as they ought to have, their custody when vacant.

47. All forests constituted as such in our time shall straightway be annulled; and the same shall be done for river banks made into places of defence by us in our time.

48. All evil customs concerning forests and warrens, and concerning foresters and warreners,§ sheriffs and their servants, river banks and their guardians, shall straightway be inquired into in each county, through twelve sworn knights from that county, and shall be eradicated by them, entirely, so that they shall never be renewed, within forty days after the inquest has been made; in such manner that we shall first know about them, or our justice if we be not in England.

---

* Socage: land tenure by agricultural service or payment of rent, but not burdened with military service.

† Burkage: land tenure by agricultural service or payment of rent.

‡ Disseize: to deprive of possession; to dispossess or oust wrongfully (one in freehold possession of land).

§ Warrener: a game warden.

49. We shall straightway return all hostages and charters which were delivered to us by Englishmen as a surety for peace or faithful service.

50. We shall entirely remove from their bailiwicks* the relatives of Gerard de Athyes, so that they shall henceforth have no bailiwick in England: Engelard de Cygnes, Andrew Peter and Gyon de Chanceles, Gyon de Cygnes, Geoffrey de Martin and his brothers, Philip Mark and his brothers, and Geoffrey his nephew, and the whole following of them.

51. And straightway after peace is restored we shall remove from the realm all the foreign soldiers, crossbowmen, servants, hirelings, who may have come with horses and arms to the harm of the realm.

52. If anyone shall have been disseized by us, or removed, without a legal sentence of his peers, from his lands, castles, liberties or lawful right, we shall straightway restore them to him. And if a dispute shall arise concerning this matter it shall be settled according to the judgment of the twenty-five barons who are mentioned below as sureties for the peace. But with regard to all those things of which anyone was, by king Henry our father or king Richard our brother, disseized or dispossessed without legal judgment of his peers, which we have in our hand or which others hold, and for which we ought to give a guarantee: We shall have respite until the common term for crusaders, except with regard to those concerning which a plea was moved, or an inquest made by our order, before we took the cross. But when we return from our pilgrimage, or if, by chance, we desist from our pilgrimage, we shall straightway then show full justice regarding them.

53. We shall have the same respite, moreover, and in the same manner, in the matter of showing justice with regard to forests to be annulled and forests to remain, which Henry our father or Richard our brother constituted; and in the matter of wardships† of lands which belong to the fee of another – wardships of which kind

we have hitherto enjoyed by reason of the fee which someone held from us in military service; – and in the matter of abbeys founded in the fee of another than ourselves – in which the lord of the fee may say that he has jurisdiction. And when we return, or if we desist from our pilgrimage, we shall straightway exhibit full justice to those complaining with regard to these matters.

54. No one shall be taken or imprisoned on account of the appeal of a woman concerning the death of another than her husband.

55. All fines imposed by us unjustly and contrary to the law of the land, and all amercements‡ made unjustly and contrary to the law of the land, shall be altogether remitted, or it shall be done with regard to them according to the judgment of the twenty-five barons mentioned below as sureties for the peace, or according to the judgment of the majority of them together with the aforesaid Stephen archbishop of Canterbury, if he can be present, and with others whom he may wish to associate with himself for this purpose. And if he cannot be present, the affair shall nevertheless proceed without him; in such way that, if one or more of the said twenty-five barons shall be concerned in a similar complaint, they shall be removed as to this particular decision, and, in their place, for this purpose alone, others shall be substituted who shall be chosen and sworn by the remainder of those twenty-five.

56. If we have disseized or dispossessed Welshmen of their lands or liberties or other things without legal judgment of their peers, in England or in Wales, – they shall straightway be restored to them. And if a dispute shall arise concerning this, then action shall be taken upon it in the March through judgment of their peers – concerning English holdings according to the law of England, concerning Welsh holdings according to the law of Wales, concerning holdings in the March according to the law of the March. The Welsh shall do likewise with regard to us and our subjects.

---

* Bailiwick: the area over which a bailiff has jurisdiction.
† Wardship: the office of a ward or keeper; care and protection of a ward; guardianship; right of guardianship. Wardship is incident to tenure in socage.

‡ Amercement: money extracted as a penalty.

57. But with regard to all those things of which any one of the Welsh by king Henry our father or king Richard our brother, was disseized or dispossessed without legal judgment of his peers, which we have in our hand or which others hold, and for which we ought to give a guarantee: we shall have respite until the common term for crusaders, except with regard to those concerning which a plea was moved, or an inquest made by our order, before we took the cross. But when we return from our pilgrimage, or if, by chance, we desist from our pilgrimage, we shall straightway then show full justice regarding them, according to the laws of Wales and the aforesaid districts.

58. We shall straightway return the son of Llewellyn and all the Welsh hostages, and the charters delivered to us as surety for the peace.

59. We shall act towards Alexander king of the Scots regarding the restoration of his sisters, and his hostages, and his liberties and his lawful right, as we shall act towards our other barons of England; unless it ought to be otherwise according to the charters which we hold from William, his father, the former king of the Scots. And this shall be done through judgment of his peers in our court.

60. Moreover all the subjects of our realm, clergy as well as laity, shall, as far as pertains to them, observe, with regard to their vassals, all these aforesaid customs and liberties which we have decreed shall, as far as pertains to us, be observed in our realm with regard to our own.

61. Inasmuch as, for the sake of God, and for the bettering of our realm, and for the more ready healing of the discord which has arisen between us and our barons, we have made all these aforesaid concessions, – wishing them to enjoy for ever entire and firm stability, we make and grant to them the following security: that the barons, namely, may elect at their pleasure twenty-five barons from the realm, who ought, with all their strength, to observe, maintain and cause to be observed, the peace and privileges which we have granted to them and confirmed by this our present charter. In such wise, namely, that if we, or our justice, or our bailiffs, or any one of our servants shall have transgressed against anyone in any respect, or shall have broken one of the articles of peace or security, and our transgression shall have been shown to four barons of the aforesaid twenty-five: those four barons shall come to us, or, if we are abroad, to our justice, showing to us our error; and they shall ask us to cause that error to be amended without delay. And if we do not amend that error, or, we being abroad, if our justice do not amend it within a term of forty days from the time when it was shown to us or, we being abroad, to our justice: the aforesaid four barons shall refer the matter to the remainder of the twenty-five barons, and those twenty-five barons, with the whole land in common, shall distrain and oppress us in every way in their power, – namely, by taking our castles, lands and possessions, and in every other way that they can, until amends shall have been made according to their judgment. Saving the persons of ourselves, our queen and our children. And when amends shall have been made they shall be in accord with us as they had been previously. And whoever of the land wishes to do so, shall swear that in carrying out all the aforesaid measures he will obey the mandates of the aforesaid twenty-five barons, and that, with them, he will oppress us to the extent of his power. And, to anyone who wishes to do so, we publicly and freely give permission to swear; and we will never prevent any one from swearing. Moreover, all those in the land who shall be unwilling themselves and of their own accord, to swear to the twenty-five barons as to distraining and oppressing us with them: such ones we shall make to swear by our mandate, as has been said. And if any one of the twenty-five barons shall die, or leave the country, or in any other way be prevented from carrying out the aforesaid measures, – the remainder of the aforesaid twenty-five barons shall choose another in his place, according to their judgment, who shall be sworn in the same way as the others. Moreover, in all things entrusted to those twenty-five barons to be carried out, if those twenty-five shall be present and chance to disagree among themselves with

regard to some matter, or if some of them, having been summoned, shall be unwilling or unable to be present: that which the majority of those present shall decide or decree shall be considered binding and valid, just as if all the twenty-five had consented to it. And the aforesaid twenty-five shall swear that they will faithfully observe all the foregoing, and will cause them to be observed to the extent of their power. And we shall obtain nothing from anyone, either through ourselves or through another, by which any of those concessions and liberties may be revoked or diminished. And if any such thing shall have been obtained, it shall be vain and invalid, and we shall never make use of it either through ourselves or through another.

62. And we have fully remitted to all, and pardoned, all the ill-will, anger and rancour which have arisen between us and our subjects, clergy and laity, from the time of the struggle. Moreover we have fully remitted to all, clergy and laity, and – as far as pertains to us – have pardoned fully all the transgressions committed, on the occasion of that same struggle, from Easter of the sixteenth year of our reign until the re-establishment of peace. In witness of which, moreover, we have caused to be drawn up for them letters patent of lord Stephen, archbishop of Canterbury, lord Henry, archbishop of Dublin and the aforesaid bishops and Master Pandulf, regarding that surety and the aforesaid concessions.

63. Wherefore we will and firmly decree that the English Church shall be free, and that the subjects of our realm shall have and hold all the aforesaid liberties, rights and concessions, duly and in peace, freely and quietly, fully and entirely, for themselves and their heirs from us and our heirs, in all matters and in all places, forever, as has been said. Moreover it has been sworn, on our part as well as on the part of the barons, that all these above-mentioned provisions shall be observed with good faith and without evil intent. The witnesses being the above-mentioned and many others. Given through our hand, in the plain called Runnymede between Windsor and Staines, on the fifteenth day of June, in the seventeenth year of our reign.

[335–6]

MAID MARIAN The daughter of Sir RICHARD FITZWALTER and the childhood sweetheart of ROBERT OF LOCKSLEY, Maid Marian was a royal ward. This meant that her marriage required the blessing of the monarch, something she did not gain until long after the event. As a child she lived at MALASET in LANCASHIRE, where she and the young Robert had played together on LOCKSLEY CHASE. There they fell in love and swore they would marry none other. Maid Marian is almost as important to the legends of ROBIN HOOD as the outlaw himself. It is for her love that Robin fights the oppressors. Indeed it was while protecting his love that he was outlawed in the first place, as he killed Sir ROGER DE LONGCHAMP, who tried to abduct Marian on her way to LINDEN LEA to stay with her uncle Sir RICHARD AT LEE.

Throughout Robin's time as an outlaw in the forest Marian was kept abreast of all he did by FRIAR TUCK, who introduced her to KET THE TROW and HOB O'THE HILL. Indeed, she was visiting Friar Tuck when Robin came to meet him, and the two of them have to fight off the attentions of the men-at-arms of the EVIL HOLD under the leadership of BLACK HUGO.

Sometime later, following the archery tournament in NOTTINGHAM, Robin learnt from Sir Richard at Lee that Marian's father had died and that Marian herself was under threat from her neighbours, who sought to seize the lands of Malaset. Robin quickly travelled to Malaset but found out from WALTER the STEWARD that Marian had disappeared. Robin set out to find her, but could not find hide nor hair of her. He returned to BARNISDALE FOREST, where he was reunited with her in the barrow home of Ket the Trow, who told him that he had helped Marian escape from Malaset, and subsequently from the BLACK TOWER, after she had been captured by GRAME GAPTOOTH. Immediately Robin left to have Friar Tuck prepare for their marriage, and a short time later Robin and Marian FitzWalter were married. From that date on they lived together in the forests.

A short while later, after RICHARD I had returned from his imprisonment in the castle of HAGENAU, Marian and Robin were pardoned by the king and returned to Malaset. Robin reverted to his true name, and he and Marian lived in peace and contentment. That peace, however, was not to be long-lived, for in 1215 Robin travelled south to witness the signing of the MAGNA CARTA, and afterwards stayed on in LONDON until the early winter, when, having heard of the wholesale

Robin finds Maid Marian dressed as a boy. Illustration by Petherick in *Robin Hood's Ballads* (1867), p. 266. (*Mary Evans Picture Library*)

slaughter brought about by King JOHN's treachery, he travelled back to Malaset. He arrived a day too late, for Marian had been killed by Sir ISENBART DE BELAME. Robin laid her to rest in the churchyard of Malaset alongside her father, and then set out to destroy the EVIL HOLD, and all those who had for so long terrorised the land.

Later tradition makes Maid Marian the Queen of May in the old May Day celebrations at which Robin Hood plays were often performed. Some sources erroneously state that Maid Marian only became associated with Robin Hood through the performance of such plays, but history and legend do not support this view, and it seems most likely that the May Day plays were a celebration of the life of Robin Hood and Maid Marian who had, by that time, already passed into legend.

[13, 15–17, 20–5, 29, 125–7, 129–30, 132–6, 138, 277–80, 285, 287–94, 297, 327, 329–30, 333, 335, 338–40, 342, 353, 361]

MAJOR OAK Oak tree near Edwinstowe in NOTTINGHAMSHIRE (OS120 SK6267), that is supposed to have been full-grown by the time of the reign of King JOHN, and was the hiding place of ROBIN HOOD and his followers. The hollow in the centre of the tree could at one time comfortably accommodate fifteen people, and the huge canopy of the tree many, many more. However, there is no evidence that Robin Hood or any of his men ever hid in the tree, its association with the outlaws arising from the publication of *A History of Greater Britain, both England and Scotland*, by John Major (hence the Major Oak) in 1521.

{L13}

MALASET The LANCASHIRE manor of Sir RICHARD FITZWALTER, father of MAID MARIAN. Malaset fell into the hands of Sir SCRIVEL OF CATSTY after Sir Richard FitzWalter died, but he had to hand the castle and lands over to ROBIN HOOD and his wife Marian after RICHARD I had returned to

The Major Oak, Birklands Wood, Sherwood Forest, Edwinstowe, Nottinghamshire. (*Mick Sharp Photography*)

England, pardoned Robin Hood and all his men, and 'sentenced' Robin to live a quiet and law-abiding life as lord over the lands of Malaset. The king instructed HAMELIN, EARL DE WARENNE to ensure the lands were duly and properly turned over to Robin and Marian. There is no way today to determine the location of Malaset, though it is likely to be in the vicinity of Wyredale, as that is where tradition places the home of Sir RICHARD AT LEE.

[13, 17, 278, 280, 290, 330, 333–7, 340, 365]

MALBÊTE, RICHARD See RICHARD MALBÊTE.

MA(L)KIN The housekeeper of the manor at BIRKENCAR. She was given free passage out of the manor when the newly outlawed ROBIN HOOD and those men who had chosen to follow him attempted to burn Sir GUY OF GISBORNE inside his manor. The name Malkin was a diminutive of Matilda and was used as a generic term for a kitchen-wench, but was also sometimes given to the Queen of May.

[46–7]

MALSTANE, SIR ECTOR DE See ECTOR DE MALSTANE, Sir and ECTOR OF THE HARELIP, Sir.

MANOR A landholding unit of medieval England that was normally, though not always, divided into two: the DEMESNE land kept under the direct control of the lord and cultivated for his profit; and the tenants' holdings granted in return for service, either free (for money rent) or unfree (for labour provided on the lord's demesne). The proportion of demesne and tenants' holdings varied widely. Some manors had no demesne, others no tenants. Additionally, a manor was not always coterminous with a village. Some manors were made up of several villages, or conversely one village might be shared between several manors. Thus when a manor is referred to in the legends it does not necessarily follow that the manor in question was named after the nearest village, and indeed many manors had names that did not relate which village or villages might be within their jurisdiction. The word manor comes from the Old French *manoir*, which in turn comes from the Latin *manere*, 'to remain'.

MANSFIELD Town of NOTTINGHAMSHIRE (OS120 SK5461) lying on the River Maun 14 miles north of NOTTINGHAM. Though the town does not feature widely in the legends, it is mentioned in passing, and certainly would have been known to ROBIN HOOD and his men.

[100, 201, 261] {K13}

MARCHANT, JOHN LE See JOHN LE MARCHANT.

MARGARET, DAME The wife of RALPH MURDACH, the SHERIFF OF NOTTINGHAM. She met with ROBIN HOOD twice, first when he had travelled to NOTTINGHAM disguised as the potter of WENTBRIDGE, when she invited him to eat with her and her husband at the market table, and the second time when she awarded Robin the golden arrow for winning the archery tournament. On this occasion she recognised Robin but bit her lip so as not to give him away, but something in her actions gave the game away to her husband, who ordered WATKIN the bailiff to arrest Robin Hood.

[101–3, 111, 269]

MARIAN, MAID See MAID MARIAN.

MARIAN FITZWALTER Full name of MAID MARIAN.

[294, 307, 309]

MARK OAK Unidentified tree a short distance from the castle at WRANGBY. It features as a marker on the route taken by the men-at-arms fleeing from the killing of Sir ROGER DE LONGCHAMP. Much later ROBIN HOOD and his troops hold council under its spreading limbs to discuss their tactics for storming and taking the EVIL HOLD.

[28, 341, 344, 364]

MARSHALL, JOHN SHERIFF OF YORK until 1190 when he was replaced by Osbert de Longchamp, the brother of the justiciar WILLIAM DE LONGCHAMP. His summary dismissal came about after the Jews of York sought refuge in York Castle, and he did not have a clue what to do. He tried persuasion; he tried force; he tried turning the Jews out of the castle; but whatever he did he just made things worse. The Jews defended themselves in the castle for two days, but then decided that suicide was preferable to the murder the mob outside was inevitably going to inflict on them. Many of the families in the castle killed themselves, but a few left the castle and were murdered by the mob. In the mêlée the king's castle, which was still of timber construction, was burnt down.

When RICHARD I heard about the massacre he was furious. The Jews enjoyed the king's special protection in return for providing a lucrative source of revenue. He was losing money as well as being challenged by the locals, so he sent William de Longchamp back to England to settle things. Longchamp picked up his brother Henry, who was sheriff in another county, and a military company on the way to York. When they got to York they followed the orders of the king and fired John Marshall, replacing him with Osbert.

MEERING, NETTA O'THE See NETTA O'THE MEERING.

MEIN~IE, ~Y Followers who have sworn an oath of allegiance to an individual. The word is derived from the Old French *meyné* or *mesne*, which is in turn derived from the Latin *mansio*, 'a house'.

[15]

MERCERS ROW Street in PONTEFRACT where JOHN LE MARCHANT owned a shop, and where that man was killed after he had befriended RICHARD MALBÊTE.

[183]

MERRY MEN Nickname given to the outlaws who followed ROBIN HOOD, though the name does not appear anywhere in the legends, and it is highly doubtful if they ever had anything to be merry about. Those men specifically named in the legends, and in this dictionary, as members of the Merry Men are given below, but they are only a small proportion of the total, which the legends say numbered in excess of eighty:

ARTHUR-A-BLAND, BA(R)T, BAT THE CHARCOAL-BURNER, DICKON THE CARPENTER, DICK THE REID, DODD or DUDDA, DRING, GILBERT OF THE WHITE HAND, KIT THE SMITH, LITTLE JOHN, MICHAEL, MUCH THE MILLER'S SON, NICK THE SMITH, PETER THE DOCTOR, RAFE THE CARTER, REYNOLD, SCADLOCK, WILL SCARLET and WILL THE BOWMAN.

Robin Hood and his Merry Men hunting in Sherwood Forest. Illustration in *Aunt Louisa's Keepsake*. (*Mary Evans Picture Library*)

Others who were allied to the outlaws but not actually members of the group, no matter what popular legend says, were:

ALAN-A-DALE, ALFRED OF GAMMELL, ALICE DE BEAUFOREST, ALICE OF HAVELOND, BENNETT, COLE THE REEVE, CRIPPS, Squire DENVIL OF TOOMLANDS, DUNN, FENELLA, FRIAR TUCK, GODARD, Sir HERBRAND DE TRANMIRE, HOB O'THE HILL, Sir HUON DE BULWELL, JACK, SON OF WILKIN, JOHN, Dame JUDITH, KET THE TROW, MAID MARIAN, RAFE OF THE BILLHOOK, Sir RICHARD AT LEE, Sir RICHARD FITZWALTER, SIBBIE, Sir WALTER DE BEAUFOREST, WARD and the potter of WENTBRIDGE.

The term Merry Men does not actually denote gaiety or happiness. Rather it denotes the companions at arms of another, and is really a form of Merry MEINIE.

MICHAEL One of the younger members of ROBIN HOOD's band of outlaws, though why he became an outlaw is not made clear. He features in the story of RICHARD MALBÊTE, along with

BART. The two young outlaws, in the company of DODD, came across a senseless Robin in the forest. Dodd stayed with him while the two younger men went after the beggar they saw leaving the scene down the forest path. They stopped and disarmed the beggar, who was Richard Malbête in disguise, but he persuaded them he had money in his bags. Thus he distracted the inexperienced outlaws, and then managed to blind them temporarily with a cloud of flour, and then beat them with his STAFF before they could clear their eyes sufficiently to make their escape.

Though beaten, they went back to Robin and told him all that had passed, and gave him the pouch they took from the beggar. This pouch contained a letter from Sir GUY OF GISBORNE to the SHERIFF OF NOTTINGHAM. Robin told the youthful outlaws that he would overlook the episode and promised to set them a task to test their mettle. Soon he sent them to find the potter of WENTBRIDGE and obtain from him the loan of his cart, pony and pots so that Robin might travel into NOTTINGHAM in disguise to learn more about the sheriff's plans to capture Robin and his men. The task was not a hard one, though Bart and Michael did not know that, for the potter and Robin were already on good terms following a meeting in the forest some time earlier.

[93–101]

MONK A monk may be defined as a member of a community of men, leading a more or less contemplative life apart from the world, under the vows of poverty, chastity and obedience, according to a rule characteristic of the particular order to which he belongs. The word monk is not itself a term commonly used in the official language of the Church. It is a popular rather than a scientific designation, but is at the same time very ancient, so much so that its origin cannot be precisely determined. The English form of the word undoubtedly comes from the Anglo-Saxon *munuc*, which in turn derived from the Latin *monachus*. The female counterpart of a monk is a NUN.

MORTAI(G)N(E) County in NORMANDY of which Prince JOHN was once the earl or duke, being granted the territory in 1177 by his father HENRY II. Following his attempt to seize the throne in the absence of his brother RICHARD I, John had the earldom of Mortain stripped from him at Easter 1194, though it was restored in 1195, and he retained the earldom until 1198 when it was granted to the Duchess of Louvain. It seems that Sir HAMO DE MORTAIN was also from this county in northern France, as his epithet simply means 'of Mortain'.

MORTAIN, SIR HAMO DE See HAMO DE MORTAIN, Sir.

MOUND FOLK HOB O'THE HILL and KET THE TROW called themselves Mound Folk, referring to the fact that they dwelt in an earthen barrow. Popular belief of the late twelfth and early thirteenth centuries held that supernatural beings lived in the many earthen barrows to be found all over the countryside, and it is thus unsurprising to find characters such as Ket the Trow and his brother in the legends of ROBIN HOOD.

[82]

MUCH THE MILLER'S SON Much was one of the first men to join the newly outlawed ROBERT OF LOCKSLEY. When the men were debating whether or not they should take to the forests, Much brought the news that ten of them were to be sold the following day by Sir GUY OF GISBORNE to the savage Lord ARNALD OF SHOTLEY HAWE – news that made up the minds of many of them there and then.

Much, whose position in life is obvious from his epithet, appears throughout the legends of ROBIN HOOD. He travelled with LITTLE JOHN and WILL THE BOWMAN when they brought Sir HERBRAND DE TRANMIRE back to Robin's camp, and he was with Robin in DONCASTER when they learnt of the archery tournament to be held by the SHERIFF OF NOTTINGHAM. At that contest Much himself participated, as he had grown almost as competent with bow and arrow as Robin himself. After the outlaws had been rumbled, it was Much who bodily carried the wounded Little John to safety across his shoulders.

Following the royal pardon granted by RICHARD I in the forests, Much travelled to France with the king. Having survived that campaign, he returned to England and went to MALASET, where Robin and MAID MARIAN gave him lands of his own. Following the death of Robin Hood, Much travelled to WERRISDALE, where ALAN-A-DALE made him his bailiff, and there he presumably lived out the remainder of his days.

[38, 44, 52–3, 55, 80, 170–2, 248, 259, 263, 272, 334, 401]

MURDACH, RALPH See RALPH MURDACH.

NAILOR The surname, according to some sources, of LITTLE JOHN.

NEIF A female VILLEIN.

[389]

NETTA O'THE MEERING The maid of ALICE DE BEAUFOREST, with whom she travelled to meet FRIAR TUCK. She gave her ring to WILL THE BOWMAN, when he was sent to seek out JACK, SON OF WILKIN, who gave her the ring and to whom she was betrothed, with a message from Alice de Beauforest for her love ALAN-A-DALE. Three days later Netta o'the Meering accompanied her lady to the church in CROMWELL, where she was to be married to Sir RANULF DE GREASBY, and there tried to stop Sir BERTRAN LE NOIR making off with Alice de Beauforest. The knight knocked her senseless, but was himself killed a few minutes later by Jack, son of Wilkin, who was made a freeman for his gallant actions by Alice de Beauforest. That is the last time the legends mention either Netta o'the Meering or Jack, son of Wilkin, and it can only be assumed that they married and lived together on the lands that Sir WALTER DE BEAUFOREST bestowed on Jack for saving his daughter.

[137, 144, 155, 159, 164]

NEWARK Market town in NOTTINGHAMSHIRE (OS121 SK7953), sited where the GREAT NORTH ROAD crosses the River TRENT, though it is in fact on the River Devon.

The church of St Mary Magdalene is a gem, very large and one of the grandest parish churches in England. It is 222 feet long and the spire is 252 feet high. The oldest parts are the crypt, believed to be twelfth century, and the tower, built in 1227. The church contains one of the largest monumental brasses in England, in memory of Alan Fleming (d. 1363).

The best building in the town is the White Hart Inn in the Market Square. It is a highly decorated, late fifteenth-century timber-framed building that is perhaps the best of its age in the country. Newark also has one of the finest Georgian town halls in Britain.

{N14}

Newark-on-Trent, Nottinghamshire. (*Mary Evans Picture Library*)

NEWARK CASTLE Newark Castle (OS121 SK7954) was built between 1133 and 1148. It is very large and dominates the rivers. The remains are substantial, mainly high curtain walling with towers and a magnificent gatehouse, all set in a public park. It was here that King JOHN died on 19 October 1216. Some sources say he was poisoned. It was a royalist stronghold during the Civil War but surrendered after King Charles was taken and the Parliamentarians destroyed it.

[366] {N14}

NEWSTEAD Village in NOTTINGHAMSHIRE midway between NOTTINGHAM to the south and MANSFIELD to the north (OS120 SK5252).

{K14}

NEWSTEAD ABBEY Abbey (OS120 SK5453) approximately 8 miles to the north of NOTTING-HAM, near the village of NEWSTEAD, where NICK THE SMITH had once worked as COTTER and smith to the abbot. His harsh treatment drove Nick the Smith into the forests as an outlaw. It was also on the boundaries of the lands of this abbey that FRIAR TUCK was said to have had his cell.

Founded as a monastic house in the late twelfth century (*c.* 1170), Newstead became the seat of the

Byron family in 1540. The abbey's most famous owner, the poet Lord Byron, sold the property in 1818 to his friend Colonel Thomas Wildman. Newstead Abbey remained a private country house until 1931, when it was presented to the Nottingham Corporation for the public to enjoy.

[114, 119] {K14}

NICHOLAS The real name of NICK THE SMITH.

[113–14]

NICHOLAS O'THE CLIFFE Though not directly connected with the legends of ROBIN HOOD, Nicholas o'the Cliffe was JACK, SON OF WILKIN's role model, for he was once a VILLEIN and managed to become a freeman. This is Jack's dearest ambition.

[141]

NICK THE SMITH Name given to NICHOLAS, the former COTTER and smith to the abbot of NEWSTEAD ABBEY, who had fled to the forests to escape the abbot's harsh treatment. There he had joined up with ROBIN HOOD and become a member of his outlaw band. Nick the Smith knew of FRIAR TUCK and defended him against the accusations of PETER THE DOCTOR, thus bringing the friar to the attentions of Robin Hood.

[114, 117, 119]

NIGER LE GRYM, SIR One of the knights of the EVIL HOLD. Although he does not feature widely in the legends, it was Sir Niger who commended the evil RICHARD MALBÊTE to Sir GUY OF GISBORNE. He also accompanied Sir ISENBART DE BELAME himself to the fringes of the forests on the occasion when BLACK HUGO chased MAID MARIAN through the woods to FRIAR TUCK's cell, where she ran straight into the arms of ROBIN HOOD.

However, Sir Niger le Grym played an important part in the story of Sir HERBRAND DE TRANMIRE. He travelled to the chapter house of ST MARY'S ABBEY on the day that Sir Herbrand de Tranmire was due to repay the loan of 400 pounds to ABBOT ROBERT or lose his lands, in order to take possession of those lands when Sir Herbrand defaulted. All did not go according to the plans of the Evil Hold, when Sir Herbrand repaid the loan with money lent to him by Robin Hood. Sir Niger le Grym, in the company of Sir BERNARD OF THE BRAKE and another unnamed knight, ambushed Sir Herbrand de

Tranmire and LITTLE JOHN, but he was killed during his battle with Little John by a short black arrow shot from the bushes by KET THE TROW.

[23, 56, 98, 133, 167, 186, 192, 196–9]

NOBLE Early British gold coin having a value of one-third of a pound (6 shillings and 8 pence). Its appearance in the legends of ROBIN HOOD seems to be an anachronism, especially if that outlaw lived at the end of the twelfth and beginning of the thirteenth centuries, as the coin was not introduced until the reign of Edward III (1312–77). However, it is quite probable that the coin became included simply because many of the legends were not recorded until after the reign of Edward III.

[98]

NOIR, SIR BERTRAN LE See BERTRAN LE NOIR, Sir.

NORMANDY Region of north-west France divided into Haute-Normandie and Basse-Normandie. The region has played a significant role in history throughout the ages. Conquered by the Romans, who founded the cities of Rouen, Lisieux and Evreux among others, Normandy was invaded by Christian Nordic tribes during the second century and was occupied by them until the Franks came to prominence two centuries later.

The Middle Ages witnessed the creation of the many monasteries and abbeys that still adorn the countryside. In 800 all of Normandy was overrun by the Vikings – the Northmen from whom the region's name derives – who later ceded the region to Rollo, the 1st Duke of Normandy, in 911. Normandy remained an independent kingdom for three centuries, a period that saw the invasion of England by William the Conqueror, who successfully defended his claim to the throne bequeathed him by his cousin.

Normandy was united with England from 1100 to 1135, and was successfully invaded by PHILIP II of France in 1202, after which only the Channel Islands remained in British hands. During the Hundred Years War the city of Rouen was the infamous site of the trial and torture of Joan of Arc. Shortly thereafter Normandy was united with the French crown when the last Duke of Normandy was dispossessed of his domain in 1204. It was partially recovered over the next 250 years, but was finally lost in 1449/50 to Charles VII.

The 1870 Franco-Prussian War led to the occupation of the Seine Valley area, but Normandy's most crucial military role came in the Second World War. On 6 June 1944 the coast was the setting for the D-Day landings, when 135,000 men of the Allied Forces stepped onto European soil to begin the big push to Berlin.

[331, 334–5]

NORMANS Name given to the inhabitants of NORMANDY, as well as the ruling classes that came to England with William the Conqueror. The name Norman is a corruption of Northmen, from the Viking people who conquered Normandy during the ninth century under the leadership of Rollo.

[16]

NORTHGATE The northernmost gate to the city of NOTTINGHAM, beyond which lay GALLOW'S HILL where WILL THE BOWMAN almost lost his life. A little further away was the flat piece of land on which the archery tournament arranged by the SHERIFF OF NOTTINGHAM took place.

[228–9]

NORWELL Village in NOTTINGHAMSHIRE (OS120 SK7761), a short distance due west of CROMWELL, and therefore possibly within the manor of BEAUFOREST. It was also the home village of STURT OF NORWELL.

[142] {M13}

NORWELL, STURT OF See STURT OF NORWELL.

NOTTINGHAM City and administrative centre of NOTTINGHAMSHIRE (OS129 SK5739). The city of Nottingham was dominated by NOTTINGHAM CASTLE, the home in the legends of RALPH MURDACH, the SHERIFF OF NOTTINGHAM. While the city undoubtedly features in a great many of the legends, it is not central to most of the stories. In fact, almost the only time the outlaws entered the city was when WILL THE BOWMAN took a message to SILAS BEN REUBEN, which resulted in that outlaw's capture and almost his death. Although they travelled *en masse* to the archery tournament arranged by the sheriff, that tournament was held outside the city walls, and thus they did not actually have to enter the city. Under the circumstances, given that many of them had a price on their heads, such a move would have been extremely foolish.

Robin and his men had no quarrel with the people of Nottingham itself. Their fight was with the man who sat in the castle, and those he sought to ally himself with. Thus Robin and his men tended to leave the city very much alone, though they did frequently 'tax' people from the city as they passed through the forests.

[13, 91, 98, 100–1, 109, 111–13, 207–8, 214–16, 226–7, 230, 235, 261–2, 265, 276, 281, 284, 294–5, 301–2, 310, 317, 319, 321, 325, 331–2, 346] {K15}

NOTTINGHAM, SHERIFF OF See SHERIFF OF NOTTINGHAM.

NOTTINGHAM CASTLE Castle (OS129 SK5639) that dominated the twelfth- and thirteenth-century city of NOTTINGHAM, though today it is somewhat disappointing, the site now being occupied by a seventeenth- or eighteenth-century mansion with very little of the original castle remaining. The legends make the castle the home of RALPH MURDACH (both of them), the SHERIFF OF NOTTINGHAM, and his wife, Dame MARGARET. They also say that Nottingham and TICKHILL were the only castles to refuse to submit to the authority of RICHARD I after his release from imprisonment, and remained staunchly allied to Earl JOHN of Mortaigne. When Richard I marched against them, Tickhill readily surrendered but Nottingham Castle still held out, so the king laid siege to it, reducing its outer walls to rubble before those inside gave in. History says that during this siege in 1194 'Greek Fire' – a mixture thought to consist of sulphur, pitch and naphtha – was used to breach the outer walls. History also says that a council was held at Nottingham Castle after it had fallen, and it was at this castle that John's fate was decided, and his lands and titles stripped from him.

[303, 313] {K15}

NOTTINGHAMSHIRE County of central England that most people associate exclusively with the legends of ROBIN HOOD, though the majority of the legends, excepting those that involve the SHERIFF OF NOTTINGHAM, appear to come from South YORKSHIRE and even LANCASHIRE and LINCOLNSHIRE.

[12, 247]

NUN Female member of a religious order bound by vows of poverty, chastity and obedience. Her male counterpart is a MONK.

The remains of the bailey of Nottingham Castle, looking south. (*Mick Sharp Photography*)

O

OLD BAT THE BANDY Chief archer to STEPHEN OF GAMWELL. LUKE THE RED said Old Bat was the last person he had seen hit a target set up in secret, after being given just a count to three to judge the distance and wind, aim and then shoot. ROBIN HOOD achieved the same feat.

[267–8]

OLD NICK'S PIECE Unidentified area of the forests near OUTWOODS where KET THE TROW once met SCADLOCK, when the latter was still the STEWARD of Outwoods.

[29]

OLLERTON Village in NOTTINGHAMSHIRE (OS120 SK6567) approximately 6 miles north-east of MANSFIELD. The village does not feature directly in the legends of ROBIN HOOD, but is often used to describe direction.

[91, 118, 230, 261, 315, 323] {L13}

OSBERT DE SCOFTON, SIR One of the party chosen by RICHARD I to accompany him into the forests disguised as monks so that they might encounter ROBIN HOOD.

[316]

OUTLAW An outlaw was a person who had been placed outside the protection of the law for failing to answer a charge of felony. Before the Norman Conquest an outlaw was described as a *caput lupinum* ('wolf's head'), and might be killed by anyone with impunity. However, during the reign of Edward III (1327–77) the laws concerning outlawry were repealed so that only a sheriff had the power to put an outlaw to death. The possessions of any person outlawed were forfeited to the crown, and his lands to his lord. Outlawry was abolished in civil proceedings in 1879, but not until 1938 in criminal proceedings.

OUTWOODS The name of ROBERT OF LOCKSLEY's manor, which lay a short way from the village of LOCKSLEY beyond the boundaries of the forests, hence the name. There are several locations that might be considered as the location of Outwoods simply for etymological reasons. They are:

1. The village of Outwood (OS104 SE3223) just to the north of WAKEFIELD. Perhaps the naming of this village is trying to allude to the home of Robert of Locksley, for a short distance to the east is the village of STANLEY (OS104 SE3523) which would align itself nicely with the name of ROBIN HOOD's hiding place at STANE LEA. Additionally, a few miles to the north there is a village named Robin Hood (OS104 SE3227). Perhaps the people who named these villages in centuries gone by knew something we don't! {I7}
2. The village of Outwoods (OS129 SK4018) approximately 17 miles south-west of NOTTINGHAM. This would place it well outside the area normally associated with Robert of Locksley. {J18}
3. Outwoods Wood (OS129 SK5116), approximately 16 miles south of Nottingham, is again possibly too far south. {K18}

[1, 9, 11, 29, 34, 42, 83, 88]

OVERWORLD The way in which KET THE TROW and HOB O'THE HILL referred to the land above their subterranean realm.

[82]

P

Merry Robin clad as a beggar stops the corn engrosser by the cross nigh Ollerton. Illustration from *The Merry Adventures of Robin Hood* by Howard Pyle.

PALFREY A light saddle horse that was especially ridden by women.

PAPPLEWICK Village in NOTTINGHAMSHIRE (OS120 SK5451) approximately 5 miles north of the city of NOTTINGHAM, and just to the south of NEWSTEAD ABBEY, to which the village was granted in 1120. The abbey retained control over the village until the Dissolution of the monasteries in 1539, whereafter the abbey, and the village, passed into the hands of the Byron family.

Papplewick is described as lying near the HEXGROVE, to which WILL THE BOWMAN had arranged for SILAS BEN REUBEN to travel to be reunited with his father REUBEN OF STAMFORD and his sister RUTH. It is also therefore the nearest village to the place where ROBIN HOOD and Sir LAURENCE OF RABY passed judgment on and then hanged RICHARD MALBÊTE.

[237] {K14}

PATHERLEY, THOMAS OF See THOMAS OF PATHERLEY.

PEAK Castle lying in the Peak District of DERBYSHIRE, to which WILLIAM DE LONG-CHAMP threatened to dispatch part of a huge army to destroy ROBIN HOOD and his men, but the threat came to nothing. Though not named as such, it is now generally regarded that Peak Castle is none other than Peveril Castle (OS110 SK1482) at Castleton in the Peak District.

[294] {G11}

PETER GREATREX The armourer of NOTTINGHAM from whose employ one DICKON had run away, only to be subsequently captured as a vagrant and imprisoned in TICKHILL Castle.

[319]

PETER THE DOCTOR One of ROBIN HOOD's men who had once been forced by FRIAR TUCK to consume all his own medicines – a fact that did not dispose Peter the Doctor kindly towards that portly monk.

[113–17, 119]

PHILIP DE SCROOBY, SIR Knight who accompanied Sir RANULF DE GREASBY, Sir BERTRAN LE NOIR and Sir ECTOR DE MALSTANE to CROMWELL for Sir Ranulf's wedding to ALICE DE BEAUFOREST. After the mysterious minstrel JOCELYN had disappeared, Sir Ranulf asked Sir Philip to search for him, a task Sir Philip agreed to – but only after Sir Ranulf had grudgingly agreed to pay him with his hunting hound ALISAUNDRE and his merlin hawks GRIP and FANG. Needless to say, Sir Philip did not find the minstrel, who was none other than ROBIN HOOD in disguise.

Sir Philip was still searching for the minstrel when Sir Ranulf met his end inside the church, but he subsequently became engaged in a fight to the death with ALAN-A-DALE outside the church, and very nearly succeeded in killing his opponent when Sir Bertran le Noir carried Alice de Beauforest away. However, his killing stroke was deflected by JACK,

SON OF WILKIN, and a few minutes later Sir Philip himself lay dead outside the church gates, Alan-a-Dale having ducked under his guard and struck him straight through the heart.

[155, 160, 163, 168]

PHILIP II, KING OF FRANCE (1165–1223) The son of Louis VII, he is also known as Philip Augustus, and was King of France from 1180 until his death. During his reign the royal domains were more than doubled, and royal power was consolidated at the expense of the feudal lords. Philip defeated a coalition of Flanders, Burgundy and Champagne (1181–6), securing Amiens, Artois and part of Vermandois from the Count of Flanders. He then attacked (1187) the English territories in France. Allied (November 1188) with RICHARD, the rebellious son of HENRY II of England, Philip compelled Henry to cede several territories to him. After Henry's death (1189), Philip and Richard, now King of England, left on the Third Crusade. They quarrelled in Sicily, and after the capture of Acre Philip returned (1191) to France. Richard also left the crusade but was captured on his way home by Leopold V of Austria and held in the castle at HAGENAU. During Richard's captivity (1192–4), Philip conspired against him with his youngest brother John. After his release Richard made war on Philip (1194–9), compelling him to surrender most of his annexations. When John acceded to the English throne on Richard's death at Chaluz (1199), Philip championed the cause of Arthur I of Brittany, whose murder in 1203 gave him the excuse he had been looking for to invade John's French domains, forcing him to surrender NORMANDY, Brittany, ANJOU, Maine and Touraine. Philip later conquered Poitou. In 1214, at Bouvines, the French defeated the combined forces of John, the Holy Roman Emperor Otto IV and the Count of Flanders; it was a victory that established France as a leading European power. When the English barons revolted against John (1215), they invited Philip's son Louis (later Louis VIII of France) to invade England and take the English throne; the venture failed. During Philip's reign the Pope proclaimed the crusade against the Albigenses. Although Philip did not participate directly in this crusade, he allowed his vassals to do so. Their victories prepared the ground for the annexation of southern France by Louis IX. In internal affairs Philip's most important reform was the creation of a class of salaried administrative officers, the *baillis* (bailiffs), to supervise local administration of the domain. Philip also systematised the collection of customs, tolls, fines

The conquest of Acre (1191) and the return to France of Philip II Augustus (1165–1223). Illustration from Vincent of Beauvais's *Speculum Maius*, fifteenth century. (© *Archivo Iconografico, S.A./Corbis*)

and fees due to the crown. He supported the towns of France against the royal barons, thereby increasing their power and prosperity. In Paris he continued the construction of Nôtre-Dame de Paris, built the first Louvre, paved the main streets and walled the city.

[331]

PIERS THE LUCKY Foster-brother of ALAN-A-DALE who lived at FOREST HOLD.

[63]

PIERS (THE) PLOWMAN Popular name for the long allegorical poem in Middle English alliterative verse written by William LANGLAND in 1362 that gives the first literary reference to ROBIN HOOD. It is possible that Piers the Plowman is none other than PIERS THE LUCKY, the foster-brother of ALAN-A-DALE. The full title of the poem is *The Vision of William concerning Piers the Plowman*.

POLYOLBION The greatest poetic work of Michael DRAYTON (1563–1631). The first eighteen books, or 'songs', were published in 1613, while the finished poem of thirty books did not appear for a further nine years, in 1622. The *Polyolbion* was Drayton's attempt to give 'a chronographical

description of all the tracts, rivers, mountains, forests and other parts of Great Britain'. See FRIAR TUCK for a sample of this epic work.

PONTEFRACT Town in West YORKSHIRE (OS105 SE4622) that lies within the borough of WAKEFIELD. The legends say that ROBERT OF LOCKSLEY was declared outlaw on the steps of the cross at Pontefract, so the town would appear to have been an important administrative centre for the BARNISDALE area at that time. It was also the home of JOHN LE MARCHANT, who had a shop in MERCERS ROW where he was killed by the evil RICHARD MALBÊTE.

[35, 91, 172, 183] {J7}

PRESTBURY, ROBERT OF See ROBERT OF PRESTBURY.

PRIOR Usually the second-in-command to the ABBOT in a monastery or an ABBEY, though in certain religious orders the prior was the superior.

Prior William provides a feast for the king and the bishop. Illustration from *Bold Robin Hood and his Outlaw Band* by Louis Read.

PUCK A peculiarly British earth-spirit who is a definite but distant relation of the Pan of classical mythology. He had various names – Gruagach, Urisk, BOGGART, Dobie, ROBIN GOODFELLOW and Hob – all of which reflect his earthy quality. His most famous appearance is as the impish servant to Oberon in Shakespeare's *A Midsummer Night's Dream*.

Puck is described in a biography of him written in 1588 as the child of a young girl and a *hee-fayrie*. He confines his mischief to the house, doing housework in exchange for cream or cake, and has the ability to change himself into any animal at will. One tale says that weary travellers tempted to mount a strange horse on a wild moor have often found themselves in the middle of a stream with nothing between their legs save a saddle!

Although Puck does not himself feature in the legends of ROBIN HOOD, MUCH THE MILLER'S SON likens the small man he had sighted in the forests, actually HOB O'THE HILL, to Puck, or else to Puck's brother.

[53]

Q

QUARTERSTAFF Stout, iron-tipped wooden staff, usually between 6 and 8 feet in length, that was the simplest form of polearm weapon in medieval Europe. Not particularly effective in a fight against an opponent in armour or wielding anything other than a wooden weapon, the quarterstaff was an excellent weapon for travellers as it doubled both as a walking stick and as a deterrent against brigands. The quarterstaff was used more in fencing and brawling than mêlée combat. The quarterstaff favoured by LITTLE JOHN would, in all probability, not have been tipped, and would rather have been a stout branch, the straightest he could find. The quarterstaff is frequently referred to simply as a STAFF.

[50, 67, 69, 74–5, 77]

R

RABBI ELIEZER Leading member of the Jewry of YORK, who was alleged to have hidden his huge fortune a short while before the riots in that city led by RICHARD MALBÊTE. Rabbi Eliezer lost his life in the riots, but Richard Malbête believed REUBEN OF STAMFORD knew the whereabouts of the dead man's wealth.

[212, 228]

RABY, SIR IVO DE See IVO DE RABY, Sir.

RABY, SIR LAURENCE OF See LAURENCE OF RABY, Sir.

RAFE Man to the STEWARD of Lord ARNALD OF SHOTLEY HAWE, from whom MUCH THE MILLER'S SON said that he had learnt of the deal made by Sir GUY OF GISBORNE to sell ten of the VILLEINs of the manor of BIRKENCAR to Lord Arnald, a piece of intelligence he had gathered in the alehouse at BLYTHE. This news was instrumental in persuading the men of the village of LOCKSLEY to follow the newly outlawed ROBERT OF LOCKSLEY into the forests to live as outlaws.

[38]

RAFE OF THE BILLHOOK Old man who took part in the archery contest at NOTTINGHAM. Many years later Rafe of the Billhook came to ROBIN HOOD's assistance as his men made ready to storm the EVIL HOLD. He persuaded the villagers of WRANGBY to lend their weight to the coming battle, and there he was identified as THURSTAN of STONE COT, a man of Danish lineage whom Sir ISENBART DE BELAME and his evil horde had attacked and displaced some thirty years before, killing his wife and baby. During the final battle for the castle at Wrangby, Rafe of the Billhook – so named as his weapon was a huge curved knife – wounded Sir Isenbart de Belame and would have killed him had Robin not thrown his shield in the path of the blow, an honourable death in battle being too good for the likes of de Belame.

[264, 346, 356–8]

RAFE THE CARTER One of the outlaw followers of ROBIN HOOD who, when confronted by his first sight of HOB O'THE HILL, said that evil spirits such as Hob made green rings in the meadow that would poison any beast who ate them – a statement which earned him a stern rebuff from Robin.

[80–1]

RALPH FITZSTEPHEN, SIR Chief forester of SHERWOOD FOREST, whom RICHARD I charged with locating ROBIN HOOD. Sir Ralph searched for two days before returning to the king and his party at the castle at DRAKENHOLE, where he told the king that Robin and his men were on the OLLERTON road. He then suggested that the king and five of his party should disguise themselves as monks, and he would lead them along the road where they were sure to come into contact with the outlaw and his men.

Though history does not mention Ralph FitzStephen, it is quite possible that he was related to the half-brothers Robert FitzStephen and Maurice FitzGerald, Anglo-NORMAN lords who played a prominent part in Welsh politics and took part in HENRY II's Irish campaign. Robert FitzStephen was awarded the kingdom of Cork in 1177, along with one Miles of Cogan.

[314–15, 322]

RALPH MURDACH

1. The husband of Dame MARGARET, the SHERIFF OF NOTTINGHAM, a rich CORDWAINER who bought his position from the Bishop of ELY. He is not often named as such within the legends, which usually simply refer to him as the sheriff. The sworn enemy of ROBIN HOOD, he met his death at the hands of that outlaw after he had taken Sir RICHARD AT LEE prisoner and was leading him back to NOTTINGHAM.

[88, 98, 101–12]

2. Brother of RALPH MURDACH,[1] who became Sheriff of Nottingham after the death of his brother. Remaining loyal to Duke JOHN, Ralph held out for several days in Nottingham Castle until he was forced to surrender after RICHARD I had reduced the outer walls to ruins, and hanged those he had taken captive in full sight of those still holding out.

[302]

RAN(N)ULF, EARL OF CHESTER One of the five companions of RICHARD I chosen to accompany the king in the guise of monks, so that they might be led along the OLLERTON road by Sir RALPH FITZSTEPHEN to meet ROBIN HOOD. Ranulf was an historical character. His full name was Ranulf de Blundeville (also known as Ralph and Randulph), and he succeeded his father Hugh de Kevelioc as the 4th earl in 1181, and was created Earl of Lincoln in 1217. He was born in about 1172 and died in 1232. He married Constance de Bretagne, the widow of HENRY II's son Geoffrey of Brittany, some time between February 1186 and February 1188, but they were divorced in 1199 after Constance deserted him. Ranulf was loyal to both Richard I and King JOHN, fighting for the latter during his struggle with the barons over the MAGNA CARTA. Following John's death he was one of the king's executors.

Staunchly loyal to the crown, he fought for the young king HENRY III against the French invaders and their allies, and in 1218 he left on a crusade to the Holy Land where he took part in the battle at Damietta. On his return to England he started the construction of Beeston Castle in Cheshire, using a unique design that was probably based on the castles he had seen during his campaign in the Middle East. He died at Wallingford in October 1232. His memory lives on in some lines of *PIERS THE PLOWMAN* (v. II, 401–2):

> I can nougte perfectly my pater-noster as be
> prest it syngeth
> But I can rymes of Robyn hood and Randolf
> erle of Chestre.

[316]

RANULF DE GLANVILL(E) Chief JUSTICIAR of England. He was born at Stratford in Suffolk into a baronial family that derived its name from Glanville in NORMANDY and held property in Norfolk and Suffolk. His father was William de Glanville. After the death of his elder brother he inherited the family estates and honours. Both before and after his appointments to the judicial bench, he held the shrievalty of various counties, which seems to betoken employment in the exchequer. In particular he was Sheriff of YORK from 1163, or 1164, until the death of HENRY II in 1189 save for a short break, and in 1173 he became Sheriff of LANCASHIRE. In the latter year there broke out the great rebellion of Henry II's sons against their father, and in the following year the Scottish king entered England with a mighty army while Henry was in Poitou. However, in July, Robert Stuteville, Sheriff of Yorkshire, and Glanville, the latter doubtless at the head of the men of Lancashire, encountered the invaders near Alnwick and utterly routed them, King William himself becoming Glanville's prisoner.

In 1176 Glanville was a justice itinerant, and in 1180 he became Chief Justiciar of England. He had now reached the zenith of royal favour. He held the position throughout the remainder of Henry's reign, being on occasion employed on various embassies, negotiations and warlike expeditions, and in 1182 was appointed an executor of the king's will. Chief Justiciar Glanville was present at the coronation of Henry's successor RICHARD I in 1189, and when that prince took the cross, Glanville joined him, contributing a large sum towards the CRUSADE. In the autumn of 1190 he died at or near the siege of Acre, a victim of the unwholesomeness of the climate. By his wife Bertha, a daughter of a neighbouring Suffolk landowner, Theobald de Valognes, he left three daughters.

Glanville is considered to have been a great lawyer and teacher, at one time tutoring the young Duke JOHN as well as HUBERT WALTER. He is the reputed author of the celebrated treatise *Tractatus de Leibus et Consuetudinibus Regni Angliae (Treatise of the Laws and Customs of England)*, a book of English law little affected by foreign jurisprudence which is the first reasoned account of legal procedure. However, this work was more probably written by his illustrious nephew and secretary, Hubert Walter. Glanville also founded two abbeys, both in Suffolk, namely Butley, for Black Canons, in 1171, and Leiston, for White Canons, in 1183. He also founded a leper hospital at Somerton in Norfolk.

The young ROBERT OF LOCKSLEY may well have come into contact with Ranulf de Glanville, especially in his role as justiciar, which coincided with the traditional period of ROBIN HOOD's time as an outlaw.

RANULF DE GREASBY, SIR Wicked, ageing knight of the EVIL HOLD. His first wife fled from his castle, HAGTHORN WASTE (from which he was also known as Sir RANULF OF THE WASTE), after two years and was found dead in GRIMLEY MERE. Following that, Sir Ranulf sought the hand of ALICE DE BEAUFOREST, but her father would not agree to the suit. Thus Sir Ranulf had Sir ISENBART DE BELAME threaten Sir WALTER DE BEAUFOREST that, unless his daughter married Sir Ranulf, his lands at BEAUFOREST would be seized, the manor burnt, and Sir Walter and his household evicted. As a result, after successfully putting off the dreaded day for some time, the marriage of Sir Ranulf de Greasby and Alice de Beauforest was arranged to take place in the church at CROMWELL.

Sir Ranulf arrived at the church in the company of Sir ECTOR DE MALSTANE, Sir PHILIP DE SCROOBY and Sir BERTRAN LE NOIR, and was extremely displeased to find that his bride had not yet arrived. He was only prevented from going to bring her to the church by force by the mysterious minstrel JOCELYN, who sang a song about COLMAN GREY. This filled Sir Ranulf with such dread that he rode uncontrollably around the churchyard trying to fight off the invisible spirits he felt certain had come to kill him. However, when his bride arrived he dispatched Sir Philip de Scrooby to find the minstrel, though the young knight demanded Sir Ranulf's favourite hunting animals, the hound ALISAUNDRE and the merlin hawks GRIP and FANG, as payment.

Inside the church Sir Ranulf was confronted by the minstrel Jocelyn, who had now removed his disguise and revealed himself to be none other than ROBIN HOOD, though Sir Ranulf thought he was ALAN-A-DALE, the beloved of Alice de Beauforest. Sir Ranulf drew his sword to dash at the outlaw, but as he did so a voice from the rafters above croaked 'Colman Grey' – and as he looked up he was shot dead by a short black arrow. One of the sons of Colman Grey had finally gained his revenge on Sir Ranulf, who had burnt to death his father some years before.

[130, 134, 137, 147–50, 152–8, 167–9]

RANULF OF THE WASTE, SIR Alternative name for Sir RANULF DE GREASBY, this variant deriving from the fact that his castle was known as HAGTHORN WASTE.

[82, 361]

RAVENER, SIR IVO LE See IVO LE RAVENER, Sir.

RED STONES, LANE OF THE Unidentified lane, presumably graced with standing stones, that is mentioned as forming part of the route followed by the men-at-arms fleeing from the killing of Sir ROGER DE LONGCHAMP back to the EVIL HOLD.

[28]

REEVE An official having local jurisdiction under his lord, the word being derived from the Old English *gerefa*. The shire reeves (or SHERIFFs) administered justice and collected revenues for the king in the counties they were appointed to govern. The manorial reeve acted as a farm manager, organised the year's work on the DEMESNE (see MANOR), managed the lord's livestock and supervised the VILLEINs in their labour on the lord's land. The villeins usually elected the reeve from among their number. The reeve witnessed all contracts and bargains, brought offenders to justice and delivered them to punishment, took bail for such as were to appear at the county court, and presided at the court or *folcmote*.

REEVE, COLE THE See COLE THE REEVE.

REUBEN, SILAS BEN See SILAS BEN REUBEN.

REUBEN OF STAMFORD Ageing Jew from STAMFORD who fled with his daughter RUTH from LINCOLN to YORK to escape the persecution of the Jews. Their relief was only temporary as the baron ALBERIC DE WISGAR stirred up trouble in York, and all the Jews were forced to seek refuge in YORK CASTLE, where they were besieged by the people under the leadership of RICHARD MALBÊTE. They managed to hold out for three days, armed with nothing more than lumps of rock torn from the castle walls, but eventually they were overrun and mercilessly slaughtered. Many of the Jews preferred to take their own lives rather than be killed by the rabble.

Reuben of Stamford had been unable to kill his daughter and then take his own life, so they hid and hoped that they would not be discovered, and from their hiding place they saw Richard Malbête, who obviously enjoyed his work, mercilessly killing men, women and children. They were finally discovered in their hiding place by a man-at-arms who had wanted no part in the massacre; he disguised Reuben and Ruth as soldiers so that they might escape the city, and then put them on the road to NOTTINGHAM, where Reuben's son SILAS BEN REUBEN lived.

They set out for Nottingham, but Reuben's health was rapidly failing, and so he and his daughter took refuge in a cave in SHERWOOD FOREST. Ruth was discovered foraging for food by WILL THE BOWMAN, who took news of the pair to ROBIN HOOD. Then, upon Robin's instructions, he took the old man and his daughter to the LYNCHET LODGE on WEARYALL HILL, where they were nursed back to health. Reuben told Robin and his men all that had befallen them and then asked if Robin could get word to his son Silas ben Reuben in Nottingham. Robin dispatched Will the Bowman, who met with Silas but was then taken captive and almost hanged by the SHERIFF OF NOTTINGHAM, into whose employ Richard Malbête had moved after fleeing York just ahead of the king's justices.

Silas ben Reuben was reunited with his father at the HEXGROVE where, minutes before, after hearing the evidence of Reuben of Stamford, Robin Hood and Sir LAURENCE OF RABY, marshal of the king's justice, had sat in judgment on and then hanged Richard Malbête. Reuben of Stamford, Ruth and Silas ben Reuben then travelled on to GODMANCHESTER escorted by twelve of Robin's men, and there Reuben presumably lived out the last few years of his life.

There is a great deal of historical evidence to support Reuben of Stamford's story, particularly the persecution of the Jews during the twelfth century and the massacre of 150 Jews in York in 1190. This part of the story seems to support the existence of Robin Hood and his men during the latter part of the twelfth century.

[203–17, 228, 237, 244]

REYNOLD Outlaw about whom very little is known. He took part in the archery tournament in NOTTINGHAM, but did not progress very far.

[263–4]

RICHARD, DUKE Title by which the young RICHARD I was known during the reign of his father HENRY II.

[15]

RICHARD I, KING OF ENGLAND (1157–99) The third son of HENRY II and ELEANOR OF AQUITAINE, Richard was born at Beaumont Palace, Oxford, on 8 September 1157 and became King of

Statue of Richard the Lionheart, Parliament Square, London. Sculpted by Carlo Marochetti, 1860. (© *WildCountry/Corbis*)

England in 1189, his reign coinciding with the most important years in the life of ROBIN HOOD and his men.

As a child Richard was invested with the duchy of AQUITAINE, and in all his life he spent no more than six months in England. It may even be reasonably doubted whether he could speak English. The young prince spent much of his youth at his mother's court at Poitiers, and under her influence came to care far more for his mother than for his father, as well as preferring his continental possessions to England. His preference towards his mother is well illustrated by the fact that he fought alongside his brothers in their rebellion of 1173–4. However, he fought for his father against his brothers when they supported a revolt in Aquitaine in 1183, and then promptly switched sides again to join PHILIP II of France against his father in 1188, defeating Henry in 1189.

On 5 July 1189 Richard became King of England, Duke of NORMANDY and Count of ANJOU, but he had already taken the crusader's vow and in early 1190 left on the Third CRUSADE (1190–1) in the company of Philip of France, during which time he earned his well-known sobriquet *Cœur de Lion* (Lionheart). In 1191 he conquered Cyprus en route to Jerusalem, and performed admirably against

Saladin, twice nearly taking the holy city. While in Cyprus he married Berengaria, the daughter of Sancho IV, King of Navarre, on 12 May 1191. There were no offspring from the union.

Richard and Philip quarrelled while wintering in Sicily, whereupon Philip returned to France and schemed with Richard's brother JOHN. The crusade failed in its primary objective of liberating the Holy Land from Muslim Turks, but did have a positive result – a truce with Saladin which brought easier access to the region for Christian pilgrims. Richard received word of John's treachery and decided to return home, but was captured by Leopold V of Austria and imprisoned by the Holy Roman Emperor Henry VI at HAGENAU. Richard finally made it back to England in 1194 and promptly crushed John's coup attempt and regained the lands lost to Philip during his period of German captivity. The war with Philip continued sporadically until the French were finally defeated near Gisors in 1198. Richard was killed at the siege of the castle of CHALUZ on 6 April 1199 and was buried at Fontevrault ABBEY in ANJOU.

The legends only involve Richard I during the latter part of Robin Hood's first period of living in the forests. Robin and his men learnt of the king's imprisonment and then set about helping to raise

Decorated tiles showing Richard I and Saladin, from the Benedictine Abbey at Chertsey, Surrey. (*British Museum, London/Bridgeman Art Library*)

Robin wagers his head. Illustration from *Bold Robin Hood and his Outlaw Band* by Louis Read.

the required ransom, even though Richard's brother JOHN did everything in his power to prevent the raising of the ransom, and aligned himself to many of the most powerful lords in the land in his efforts to seize the throne. Robin and his men sent half of everything they had collected as tolls from travellers through the forests, and then sent half of everything they collected from that day forth, each casket of money being sent to the LORD MAYOR of LONDON under heavy guard. They even acted as unofficial tax collectors and forced many who were reluctant to pay to cough up; some were even made to pay twice, as they were subsequently visited by the official tax collectors.

Eventually Richard I returned to England, landing at SANDWICH, where he discovered that many castles remained loyal to John. He marched on them, and only NOTTINGHAM CASTLE refused to surrender. He laid siege to the castle, and two days later, having reduced the outer walls to piles of rubble, took the castle. It was there that he learnt of the actions of Robin Hood and his men to free him, and set out into the forests in an attempt to personally thank the outlaw. At first unsuccessful, he charged Sir RALPH FITZSTEPHEN with locating the outlaw. Two days later, while staying at the castle of DRAKENHOLE, he was told that Robin Hood and his men had been steering clear of the king and were to be found taking tolls from travellers along the road by OLLERTON. Richard went disguised as an abbot, in the company of five of his most trusted knights disguised as monks, along that road, where he was duly stopped by Robin Hood.

Robin Hood did not see through the disguise and invited the 'abbot' and his companions to dine with him and his men in the forest. He then put on a display of archery so that the 'abbot' might take news to the king of what kind of men they were. Just as Robin had failed in his allotted shot, and had received a buffet from the king's forearm, Sir RICHARD AT LEE, MAID MARIAN, ALAN-A-DALE and ALICE DE BEAUFOREST rode into the camp. Sir Richard at Lee immediately recognised the king. His true identity discovered, Richard made himself known to the outlaws whom he pardoned there and then, sentencing Robin to live a quiet and law-abiding life on the lands of MALASET with his wife Marian. Shortly after this meeting Richard left England for France, taking many of Robin's men with him. He never again set foot on English soil.

[169, 198, 210, 256, 295, 301–26, 328–32, 334]

RICHARD AT LEE, SIR Lord of the castle and lands of LINDEN LEA near NOTTINGHAM and husband of Lady ALICE. A close friend of Sir RICHARD FITZWALTER, Sir Richard at Lee was the uncle of Maid Marian and a good friend to ROBIN HOOD, whose fight against injustice he firmly supported, even though his support brought him powerful enemies. Sir Richard remains a fleeting character until just after the archery contest at Nottingham, when he insisted that Robin and his men seek sanctuary with him, for they had no other route of escape from the SHERIFF OF NOTTING-HAM's men. Reluctantly Robin took up the offer, for he knew that by sheltering the outlaws Sir Richard would put himself on the wrong side of the law.

Some time later Sir Richard had gone hunting from his lodge at WOODSETT, and been seized by the sheriff who sought to take him back to false justice in Nottingham. Lady Alice took news of his arrest to Robin, who set out to free his friend, which he did, killing the sheriff into the bargain. Sir Richard and Lady Alice were then obliged to live with Robin and his men in the forests until they were pardoned by RICHARD I.

[13, 25–6, 29, 129, 133, 138, 272–4, 276–7, 280, 284–5, 310–11, 327–8, 331]

RICHARD CŒUR DE LION 'Richard the Lionheart', the nickname by which RICHARD I became popularly known.

[169]

RICHARD FITZWALTER, SIR The lord of the castle and lands of MALASET in LANCASHIRE and the father of the MAID MARIAN. Sir Richard plays no active part in the legends, and is simply mentioned in his capacity as Maid Marian's father and the lord of Malaset.

[13, 15, 277, 279, 365]

RICHARD MALBÊTE Richard Illbeast if his surname is translated, this evil character is one of the most unlikeable of all the characters in the legends of ROBIN HOOD, far surpassing even Sir GUY OF GISBORNE, the SHERIFF OF NOTTINGHAM and Sir ISENBART DE BELAME.

Richard Malbête's first contact with Robin Hood came when he was passing through SHERWOOD FOREST en route for NOTTINGHAM in the disguise of a beggar. He was accosted by Robin but managed to knock out the outlaw, and was about to kill him when he was disturbed by DODD, BART and MICHAEL, three of Robin's men. Malbête quickly left the unconscious Robin Hood and

Illustration from *Bold Robin Hood and his Outlaw Band* by Louis Read.

continued on his way through the forest, but was pursued by Bart and Michael. Aware of the danger, Malbête knew that his only chance of escape lay in stealth, but before he could escape from the clutches of the outlaws Bart stole his pouch containing a letter of introduction to the Sheriff of Nottingham from Sir Guy of Gisborne. Richard Malbête did escape, but he could not gain access to the sheriff without the letter of introduction, and was mercilessly beaten from Nottingham.

Malbête is next heard of when LITTLE JOHN and Sir HERBRAND DE TRANMIRE came across the sons of JOHN LE MARCHANT leading him under guard to GRIMSBY, where he was to leave the country after being forced to ABJURE before the coroner for the murder of John le Marchant in PONTEFRACT. However, by some means unrecorded Malbête managed to escape, and is next heard of during the persecution of the Jews.

He was responsible for leading the revolt against the Jews in LINCOLN, from which REUBEN OF STAMFORD and his daughter RUTH fled to YORK, where the massacre of 150 Jews is recorded as occurring in 1190. Richard Malbête again led the uprising against the Jews in York, where Reuben and Ruth saw him kill EPHRAIM BEN ABEL, who pleaded for his life to be spared, and then murder men, women and children with relish. Richard Malbête fled from York just ahead of the king's justices and travelled to Nottingham, where he entered the employ of the sheriff under the alias Captain BUSH. There he was responsible for the capture of WILL THE BOWMAN, but was taken captive by Robin and his men after he had been knocked out and bound by KET THE TROW.

Back in the forest, Richard Malbête was tried at the HEXGROVE before Robin and Sir LAURENCE OF RABY, marshal of the king's justice, and summarily hanged for his crimes.

History does not record Richard Malbête. However, Richard Malebysse is recorded as having led the massacre of the Jews at York in 1190, and it thus seems inconceivable that this Malebysse is not one and the same as the legendary Malbête. Malebysse was heavily fined for his part in the massacre and had his lands confiscated. He may have been in league with John MARSHALL, the SHERIFF OF YORK at this time, though this is by no means certain.

[98, 103–4, 183, 204, 212–14, 236, 238–40, 242–6, 321–2]

RIDGEWAY, THE Unidentified feature on the route taken by the men-at-arms fleeing from the killing of Sir ROGER DE LONGCHAMP as they returned to the castle at WRANGBY, the so-called EVIL HOLD.

[28]

ROBERT, ABBOT See ABBOT ROBERT.

ROBERT DE LONGCHAMP, SIR An historical character, the nephew of WILLIAM DE LONG-CHAMP and one-time ABBOT of ST MARY'S ABBEY. The legends say that his appointment came about following the death of ABBOT ROBERT and at the insistence ofSir ISENBART DE BELAME. Immediately he began to plot against ROBIN HOOD and the other outlaws, and within the space of a few short weeks his allies included the lords of the EVIL HOLD, Sir GUY OF GISBORNE and RALPH MURDACH, the SHERIFF OF NOTTINGHAM.

[257]

ROBERT OF LOCKSLEY The true name of ROBIN HOOD, Robert held the lands and manor of LOCKSLEY. Following RICHARD I's pardon, he reverted to using his true name, but once again became Robin Hood following the death of MAID MARIAN.

ROBERT OF PRESTBURY One of the neighbours of ALICE OF HAVELOND, who, along with THOMAS OF PATHERLEY, seized the lands of HAVELOND and evicted Alice after her husband BENNETT had been taken prisoner and held to ransom by a Scottish knight. Alice of Havelond raised the ransom required to free her husband, but when he returned to reclaim his lands he was set upon by the two robbers, who crippled him. When the king would not hear Alice's appeal, she went to ALFRED OF GAMWELL, but although he offered to appeal for her, she sought out her cousin ROBIN HOOD. A few days later the men of SCAURDALE saw two houses burning in the distance, and immediately knew that vengeance had been wreaked on the robbers.

[86–8]

ROBERT OF STAITHES, SIR A knight who came to the assistance of ROBIN HOOD and his men during the siege of the castle at WRANGBY.

[352]

ROBIN AND THE MONK A dubious source of dubious date. It may be pre-sixteenth century, but is also quite possibly a great deal later. The story is not a ballad as the other sources are, but is rather a genre story, akin to a modern thriller, in which ROBIN HOOD is betrayed by a monk in NOTTINGHAM and subsequently rescued by LITTLE JOHN.

ROBIN AND THE POTTER Pre-sixteenth-century comedy in which ROBIN HOOD assumes the guise of the potter of WENTBRIDGE and so travels unrecognised into NOTTINGHAM before leading the SHERIFF OF NOTTINGHAM back to the forest where he is humiliated by Robin and his men.

ROBIN GOODFELLOW Alternative name for PUCK, and by that association also for HOB O'THE HILL. Some dubious sources have even said that Robin Goodfellow was none other than ROBIN HOOD himself, but this is nonsense. The character and activities of Robin Goodfellow, and thus also of Puck, Hob o'the Hill and, to some extent KET THE TROW, are related in the ballad that carries his name, as typified in the following verse:

> When house or harth doth sluttish lye,
> I pinch the maidens black and blue;
> The bed-clothes from the bedd pull I,
> And lay them naked all to view.
> 　　　'Twixt sleepe and wake,
> 　　　I do them take,
> And on the key-cold floor them throw.
> 　　　If out they cry
> 　　　Then forth I fly,
> And loudly laugh out, ho, ho, ho!
> Thomas Percy, *Reliques of Ancient English Poetry*,
> 1765

ROBIN (O'THE) HOOD The name used by ROBERT OF LOCKSLEY during the two periods he spent living in SHERWOOD FOREST, CLIPSTONE FOREST and BARNISDALE FOREST. He had always been known as Robin by those who knew and trusted him, and he chose to add 'Hood' as he would have to hide his head, as if under a hood, until he could once more live as a freeman. A discussion of the historicity of the character may be found in Part Four of this book.

Interestingly the village named Robin Hood (OS104 SE3227) about 7 miles north of WAKEFIELD lies just over 2 miles north of another village named Outwood (see OUTWOODS), and just over 2 miles north-west of one called STANLEY. It is most likely that these villages were simply named after the legendary character and places associated with him, but who knows? There is another similarly named village to the south-west of SHEFFIELD.

{I7 and H12}

ROBIN HOOD AND GUY OF GISBORNE Pre-sixteenth-century source that tells the story of ROBIN HOOD and his battle with Sir GUY OF GISBORNE.

ROBIN HOOD AND THE CURTAL FRIAR Pre-sixteenth-century source that tells the famous story of the meeting between ROBIN HOOD and FRIAR TUCK, and how each has the other carry him across a fast-flowing stream. This source is undoubtedly based on an earlier story, though how early is difficult to determine.

ROBIN HOOD HILL Hill (OS120 SK6353) on the summit of which is an Iron Age settlement that may well have been used at some time by ROBIN HOOD and his men, though there is absolutely no evidence to support this. The hill lies approximately 11 miles north-east of NOTTINGHAM and 8 miles south-east of MANSFIELD.

{L14}

Robin Hood statue in Nottingham. (*Getty Images*)

Robin Hood's Bay, North Yorkshire. (*Mary Evans Picture Library*)

ROBIN HOOD'S BAY Bay on the east coast of North YORKSHIRE approximately 5 miles south of Whitby and 15 miles north of Scarborough. It was named after the battle between ROBIN HOOD and the pirate DAMON THE MONK, who had been harrying the north Yorkshire coast. Robin killed Damon the Monk and all his crew and hanged them from their own yard-arm before beaching the ship. Since that time the bay has been known as Robin Hood's Bay.

[391]

ROBIN HOOD'S CAVE There are several caves named after ROBIN HOOD. While there is no evidence that the outlaw ever took shelter in any of them, some of them are in the right geographical location, and must therefore be worthy of serious consideration, particularly as the legends mention Robin Hood and his men taking shelter in caves during periods of inclement weather. The three most interesting examples of caves named after Robin Hood are:

1. (OS110 SK2483) on the south-western border of Hallam Moors approximately 6 miles south-west of LOCKSLEY (Loxley), and thus some 8 miles south-west of SHEFFIELD. {H11}
2. (OS120 SK6670) on the banks of the River Whitewater approximately 8 miles south-east of WORKSOP and 10.5 miles north-east of MANSFIELD. {L12}
3. (OS120 SK5154) at the western end of ROBIN HOOD'S HILLS approximately 2 miles north-north-west of NEWSTEAD ABBEY. {K14}

ROBIN HOOD'S CROSS Monument (OS110 SK1880) approximately 2 miles to the west of ROBIN HOOD'S STOOP, some 4.5 miles south-west of ROBIN HOOD'S CAVE[1] (OS110 SK2483), 10.5 miles south-west of LOCKSLEY (Loxley) and 12.5 miles south-south-west of SHEFFIELD.

{G11}

ROBIN HOOD'S DEATH Early source that tells the story of ROBIN HOOD's betrayal and death at KIRKLEES.

ROBIN HOOD'S HILLS Range of hills at the western end of which lies ROBIN HOOD'S CAVE[3] (OS120 SK5154).

{K14}

ROBIN HOOD'S LARDER An oak in SHERWOOD FOREST, the hollow trunk of which was used to conceal deer and other animals killed in the forest, though the legends contain no references to this popular belief. Late in the nineteenth century a large part of the tree was burnt down when some schoolgirls tried to boil a kettle in it. It was finally blown down in 1966.

ROBIN HOOD'S PICKING RODS Unusual feature (OS110 SK0091) approximately 21 miles to the west of SHEFFIELD, though why they should be so named remains a mystery.

{F10}

ROBIN HOOD'S STOOP Hunting hide (OS110 SK2180) about 2 miles to the east of ROBIN HOOD'S CROSS.

{H11}

ROBIN HOOD'S WELL There are several wells named after ROBIN HOOD. While there is no evidence that the outlaw ever sank any of them, or even drank from them, some of them are in the right geographical location and must therefore be worthy of consideration. The three most interesting examples of wells named after Robin Hood are:

1. (OS129 SK4949) approximately 7.5 miles north-north-west of NOTTINGHAM and 4 miles south-south-west of NEWSTEAD ABBEY. {J15}
2. (OS111 SK5111) approximately 2 miles south-south-west of CAMPSALL, and thus plum in the area Robin and his men lived in immediately after they had taken to life in the forests. {K8}
3. (OS119 SK2679) approximately ⅓ mile north-east of LITTLE JOHN'S WELL. {H12}

ROCHE ABBEY The ABBEY of St Mary of Roche, a Cistercian house founded in 1147 by Richard de Bully, Lord of TICKHILL, and Richard FitzTurgis. There are many charters detailing the landed property of the abbey but no chronicle of the house survives. The abbey is situated in a deep and narrow valley in South YORKSHIRE (OS120 SK5489), approximately 1.5 miles south of Maltby,

roughly 6 miles to the west of BLYTHE and 9 and 13 miles from DONCASTER and SHEFFIELD respectively.

[370] {K11}

ROGER BIGOT One of the party chosen by RICHARD I to accompany him in the guise of monks into the forests so that they might meet ROBIN HOOD. It is quite possible that Roger Bigot is meant to refer to Roger Bigod, the Earl of Norfolk, who took a prominent role in securing the MAGNA CARTA, his family having secured the earldom of Norfolk in 1136. This is pure supposition, but the similarity of name is remarkable, as is a position that would place him within the central core of the monarch's coterie.

Roger Bigod was born about 1150 and succeeded as the 2nd Earl of Norfolk and Suffolk. It is thus fitting that, after Richard's return to England after his captivity in Germany, Roger Bigod was chosen to be one of the four earls who carried the king's silken canopy, as Hugh Bigod had borne the royal sceptre in the royal procession.

In 1189 Richard I appointed Roger Bigod one of the ambassadors to Philip of France, charged with obtaining aid for the recovery of the Holy Land. In 1191 he was keeper of Hereford Castle and chief judge in the King's Court from 1195 to 1202. In 1200 he was sent by King JOHN as one of his messengers to summon William the Lion, King of Scotland, to do homage to him in the Parliament held at LINCOLN, and subsequently attended John into Poitou. On his return the rebellious barons won him over, and he became one of the strongest advocates of the Charter of Liberty, for which he was excommunicated by Pope Innocent III. He died before August 1221. His first wife was Isabella, daughter of Hameline Plantagenet, who was descended from the earls of Warenne.

[316]

ROGER DE LONGCHAMP, SIR One of the knights of the EVIL HOLD, who coveted MAID MARIAN and attempted to abduct her, but was killed during the attempt by ROBERT OF LOCKSLEY, who shot him in the eye through the narrow eye-slit of his visor. His death led to Robert of Locksley being proclaimed outlaw, and thereafter he was a constant thorn in the side of WILLIAM DE LONGCHAMP, the HIGH CHANCELLOR. It is entirely possible that Roger de Longchamp was an historical character, though it is equally likely that the authors of the legends simply picked up on the name de Longchamp and invented a character who could be associated with the historical family.

[15, 17–21, 23, 28, 168, 306–8]

ROGER OF DONCASTER, SIR Cowardly knight of the EVIL HOLD. He was the only one to escape from the battle at WRANGBY, having fled from the scene at the earliest opportunity. From then on he sought only to destroy ROBIN HOOD and allied himself with Sir GUY OF GISBORNE and a group of BRABANT mercenaries under the command of FULCO THE RED. After the deaths of Sir Guy of Gisborne, Fulco the Red and all the mercenaries, Sir Roger sought a more underhand method of killing Robin Hood.

To achieve his end he paid Dame URSULA, Robin's aunt and the ABBESS of KIRKLEES priory, to bleed her cousin to death when he made one of his regular visits to the priory. After Robin Hood's death, Sir Roger of Doncaster was hounded by KET THE TROW and HOB O'THE HILL, and only just managed to escape on a ship from GRIMSBY to France, where he died as a lonely and bitter old man.

[167, 335, 358, 367–9, 377–9, 385–6, 395, 400]

ROME Capital city of Italy and head of the Roman Catholic Church. The city is only mentioned in the legends once. WILL THE BOWMAN's elder brother travelled there to expiate the crime of having killed a man.

[230]

RUFFORD BRAKES Location within SHERWOOD FOREST where RICHARD I and his party startled a hart while hunting. Today Rufford is the location of a country park (OS120 SK6465).

[313] {L13}

RUNNYMEDE A meadow on the south bank of the River Thames near Egham, Surrey, where on 15 June 1215 King JOHN put his seal to the MAGNA CARTA. The legends say ROBIN HOOD (as ROBERT OF LOCKSLEY and MALASET) was present on this occasion, along with a great many of his followers. The site is now owned and administered by the National Trust.

Runnymede was originally one of three individual 'medes', the others being Long Mede and Yard Mede. The name Runnymede may originate from the Anglo-Saxon *runieg* (regular meeting) and *mede* (mead or meadow). The pre-Norman form of government, the Witan Council, was held here during the reign of Alfred the Great, whose castle was in Old Windsor.

The precise place on the meads where the parties to these proceedings met is not recorded. The king and his entourage came to Runnymede for the negotiations from Windsor Castle and apparently returned there nightly. The headquarters of the disaffected barons was at Staines. Eight bishops were also present, including the Archbishop of Canterbury Stephen Langton, and most of the nobles of the land, with their followers. Runnymede was chosen because it was a conveniently large meeting place for so great a throng. It is now thought that 15 June 1215 was not the date of the signing of the final charter, but that of the sealing of the preliminary draft, known as the Articles of the Barons, which is now housed in the British Museum.

[335]

RUTH Daughter of REUBEN OF STAMFORD and sister of SILAS BEN REUBEN. She fled with her father from LINCOLN to YORK to escape the persecution of the Jews. The persecution spread, and Ruth, along with her father and all the Jewry of York, was forced to seek refuge in YORK CASTLE. The terrified Jews barricaded themselves in and held their attackers off for three days armed with nothing more than lumps of rock torn from the walls of the castle itself.

When the castle fell Ruth and her father were discovered by a kindly man-at-arms who disguised them as soldiers and took them out of the city, and then put them on the road to NOTTINGHAM. With her father's health failing, Ruth hid him in a cave and then went to forage for food in the forest where she was discovered by WILL THE BOWMAN. Following instructions from ROBIN HOOD, he took them to the LYNCHET LODGE on WEARYALL HILL, where they were nursed back to health. Later, Will the Bowman had taken a message to Silas ben Reuben in Nottingham, but had then been captured. He was rescued from the gallows during a struggle in which RICHARD MALBÊTE was captured. Ruth witnessed the trial and summary execution of Richard Malbête before she, her father and her brother travelled to GODMANCHESTER under outlaw guard, and there she presumably lived in peace and safety with her family.

[202–9, 237, 244, 246]

RYE Town in East Sussex, originally one of the Cinque Ports but now 3 miles inland. SCADLOCK, returning from the French campaign of RICHARD I, drowned in a storm off the coast near Rye.

[334]

S

SACRIST(AN) An officer charged with the care of the sacristy, the church and their contents. In ancient times many of the sacristan's duties were performed by the doorkeepers (*ostiarii*), later by the *mansionarii* and the treasurers. Nowadays the sacristan is elected or appointed. The *Cæremoniale episcoporum* prescribed that in cathedral and collegiate churches the sacristan should be a priest, and describes his duties in regard to the sacristy, the Blessed Eucharist, the baptismal font, the holy oils, the sacred relics, the decoration of the church for the different seasons and feasts, the preparation of what is necessary for the various ceremonies, the pregustation in pontifical mass, the ringing of the church bells, the preservation of order in the church and the distribution of masses. Finally it suggests that one or two canons should be appointed each year to supervise the work of the sacristan and his assistants.

The under-sacristan (*custos*) or sacristan's assistant was subject to the archdeacon and discharged duties very similar to those of the sacristan. Now the office is hardly ever attached to a benefice, but is usually a salaried position. The Council of Trent desired that, according to the old canons, clerics should hold such offices; but in most churches, on account of the difficulty or impossibility of obtaining clerics, laymen perform many of the duties of the sacristan and under-sacristan.

ST MARY'S ABBEY Abbey in YORK (OS105 SE5952) of which the corrupt ABBOT ROBERT was primate. Throughout the legends the abbey is referred to as the enemy of the common man and all those who refused to kowtow to the abbot's wishes. However, not all the members of the monastic order of St Mary's were corrupt, as the actions of the PRIOR clearly demonstrated when Sir HERBRAND DE TRANMIRE arrived to pay off the loan made to him by the abbot. Following the death of Abbot Robert, the new abbot chosen by the WHITE MONKS of the order was sent to LONDON to be approved by WILLIAM DE LONGCHAMP, the HIGH CHANCELLOR, but he, under the direction of Sir ISENBART DE BELAME, refused to accept the choice of the monks, and instead appointed ROBERT DE LONGCHAMP, his nephew, to the

post. Thus he gave the abbey a new and equally corrupt abbot.

The ruins of St Mary's, probably the most important and influential monastery in the north of England, stand serenely among the brightly coloured flowers and neatly cut lawns of the Museum Gardens. This Benedictine house was founded in 1086 by Stephen of Lastingham on land granted by Alan, Earl of Richmond, the foundation stone being laid in 1088 by William Rufus. As well as the picturesque ruins of the thirteenth-century abbey church, there are several monastic buildings scattered around the park, including a timber-framed guest house that dates from around 1300.

[7, 35, 89, 127, 176, 181, 185, 249, 254, 257, 279, 306] {L4}

ST MICHAEL'S Church in PONTEFRACT (OS105 SE4521) in which RICHARD MALBÊTE was forced to seek sanctuary after he had killed JOHN LE MARCHANT.

[183] {J7}

SANDWICH Coastal town in Kent, midway between Ramsgate to the north and Deal to the south, where RICHARD I landed after being released from imprisonment in the castle of HAGENAU.

[302]

SAYLES Meeting place of five roads on ERMINE STREET. ROBIN HOOD sent LITTLE JOHN, WILL THE BOWMAN and MUCH THE MILLER'S SON there to see if they could find some traveller to entertain; they returned with Sir HERBRAND DE TRANMIRE. The legends say that this was 7 miles from PONTEFRACT, but that must be incorrect as Ermine Street runs nowhere near Pontefract. In fact the legends should be referring to the GREAT NORTH ROAD, which does. The name Sayles does not appear on any modern map within a 7 mile radius of Pontefract. However, as the location was on Ermine Street, which is here taken to refer to the Great North Road, the most favourable siting for Sayles might be Barnsdale Bar (OS111 SE5113), about 2 miles to the west of CAMPSALL. This would fit nicely into the framework of the legends, as Robin Hood and his men were meant to have celebrated mass at Campsall Church.

[170] {K8}

SCADLOCK STEWARD to ROBERT OF LOCKSLEY at OUTWOODS. A good friend to all the villagers of LOCKSLEY, Scadlock was tied to a post in front of the manor by HUBERT OF LYNN to be whipped after Robert of Locksley had been outlawed, but he was set free when Hubert of Lynn and four of his men-at-arms were killed by his master. Scadlock then joined Robert and the other outlaws living in the forests, and only appears occasionally in the legends. Most notably he was one of those who took part in the archery tournament at NOTTINGHAM. Following the pardon handed out by RICHARD I, Scadlock went with the king on his French campaign, which he survived, but was drowned while returning to England in a storm just off RYE.

[9, 29, 32, 34–5, 43, 263–4, 334]

SCARLET, WILL See WILL SCARLET.

SCAURDALE Valley in YORKSHIRE that was close to the homes of THOMAS OF PATHERLEY and ROBERT OF PRESTBURY.

[87]

SCOFTON Village (OS120 SK6280) that can be identified as the home of Sir OSBERT DE SCOFTON, a claim that is further supported by the presence of Osberton Hall to the south of the village (OS120 SK6279) and Osberton Mill to the east (OS120 SK6480), both of which doubtless owe their names to Sir Osbert.

{L11}

SCOFTON, SIR OSBERT DE See OSBERT DE SCOFTON, Sir.

SCOTT, SIR WALTER (1771–1832) Scottish novelist and poet and a national figure who became an advocate in 1792. His first publication was a volume of rhymed versions of the ballads of Schiller Bürger (1796), the ballad becoming his main area of interest from that time until 1814 when he embarked on a successful career as a novelist. After losing financial control of his publications, Scott was made bankrupt in 1826. The Waverley Novels, for which Scott is perhaps today best remembered, started with *Waverley* in 1814. *Ivanhoe* (possibly his most famous) came in 1820, while *Castle Dangerous* (see DOUGLAS) came in the year of Scott's death, 1832.

SCRIVEL OF CATSTY, SIR One of the wicked knights of the EVIL HOLD, whom WILLIAM DE LONGCHAMP, Bishop of ELY and HIGH CHANCELLOR of England, sent to MALASET to act as MAID MARIAN's guardian after her father, Sir RICHARD FITZWALTER, had died. Later,

following the pardon of RICHARD I, the lands of Malaset were handed back to Marian and her husband ROBIN HOOD by order of the king, those orders being overseen by HAMELIN, Earl de WARENNE.

Sir Scrivel of Catsty soon returned to the fold at WRANGBY, but no more is heard of him, and it can only be assumed that he met his end when Robin Hood stormed and took the castle.

[279–80, 333, 335]

SCROOBY Village (OS111 SK6590) approximately 4 miles south-east of TICKHILL and 3 miles northeast of BLYTHE, that can be identified as the home of Sir PHILIP DE SCROOBY. His home within the village may have been the castle or manor that was once protected by the moat to the east of the village.

{L10}

SCROOBY, SIR PHILIP DE See PHILIP DE SCROOBY, Sir.

SEAFORD Town on the coast of Sussex between Brighton and Eastbourne, where RICHARD MALBÊTE killed the king's messenger INGELRAM.

[245]

SENESCHAL Alternative name for a STEWARD.

SERF An unfree peasant. A serf was bound to the land which he cultivated in return for paying a fee either in cash or in kind by providing services to his lord. His binding to the land was so complete that a serf could be sold along with the land to which he was attached.

[51, 171, 389]

SERVITOR Archaic term for a waiter, though the servitor was much more than simply a person employed to wait on table. Such men carried out any number of tasks within the household that involved fetching and carrying, as well as acting as henchmen when required.

[103–4]

SHEFFIELD Large city (OS111 SK3587) in South YORKSHIRE that is referred to in the legends of ROBIN HOOD as a small town to the north-east of LOCKSLEY. Famous for its steel and cutlery, Sheffield is only mentioned in passing in the legends.

[90] {I11}

SHERIFF Royal official who, from the early eleventh century, came to replace the earl as the king's chief agent in the shire counties. In Latin he is called *vice comes*, because in England he represented the *comes* or earl. His name is said to be derived from the Saxon *seyre*, shire or county, and REEVE, meaning keeper, bailiff or guardian. In Old English he was the *scir gerefa* (or 'shire reeve').

The general duties of the sheriff were to keep the peace within the county, and in so doing he could apprehend and commit to prison any persons who broke the peace or attempted to break it, and bind anyone in a recognisance to keep the peace. He was required to pursue and take all traitors, murderers, felons and rioters, and he had the keeping of the county gaol, which he was bound to defend against all attacks. He sat in the shire court but did not preside over the court until after the NORMAN Conquest.

In his ministerial capacity the sheriff was bound to execute within his county or bailiwick all process issuing from the courts of the commonwealth. He was responsible for financial administration, the collection and assessment of royal taxes and the supervision of royal estates and DEMESNE in the shire. An inquest in 1170 into abuse of power led to the dismissal of a great many sheriffs.

SHERIFF MURDACH Unusual way of referring to the SHERIFF OF NOTTINGHAM.

[111]

SHERIFF OF NOTTINGHAM(SHIRE AND DERBYSHIRE) One of the main protagonists in the legends of ROBIN HOOD and his band of outlaws. There are actually two sheriffs mentioned in those legends, brothers who are both called RALPH MURDACH. The first was the husband of Dame

The Sheriff of Nottingham cometh before the king at London. Illustration from *The Merry Adventures of Robin Hood* by Howard Pyle.

MARGARET. A rich CORDWAINER, he bought his position from the Bishop of ELY, and thus embarked on a relentless campaign of high taxation to repay his debt to that grasping bishop, a campaign that made him increasingly unpopular with the people. It should be noted that although he is usually referred to as the Sheriff of Nottingham, he was actually the sheriff of the entire county of NOTTINGHAMSHIRE along with neighbouring DERBYSHIRE.

The sheriff was undoubtedly keen to rid himself of the outlaws that infested the forests but he had very little direct contact with them. In fact, the first Ralph Murdach only met Robin Hood three times, and there is no evidence to suggest that his brother, who succeeded him as sheriff, ever met Robin at all.

The first meeting between Robin and the sheriff was when the former went to NOTTINGHAM disguised as the potter of WENTBRIDGE, and subsequently led the sheriff into the forest where he was fed and then stripped of his armour and horse before being sent back to Nottingham riding a PALFREY. The second meeting was when Robin accepted the Golden Arrow from the sheriff after he had won the archery tournament in Nottingham. Finally the sheriff was stopped by Robin Hood en route back to Nottingham with Sir RICHARD AT LEE, this third meeting resulting in the sheriff's death.

The choice of the second Ralph Murdach as sheriff may be a story invented to cover the fact that the sheriff was dead, but enabling the animosity between Robin and the sheriff to continue through the legends until Robin's death, though it would have been this Ralph Murdach who would have held NOTTINGHAM CASTLE against RICHARD I.

[88, 98, 101–12, 131, 214, 224, 226–7, 230, 232–7, 257, 259–60, 262, 264–6, 268–74, 276, 281–4, 302, 309, 311]

SHERIFF OF YORK The administrative head of the city of YORK and a friend of ABBOT ROBERT. He appears only once in the legends: he was present with the abbot in ST MARY'S ABBEY on the occasion when Sir HERBRAND DE TRANMIRE came to repay the loan of 400 pounds. Historical records suggest that the Sheriff of York at this time was one Osbert de Longchamp, the brother of the justiciar WILLIAM DE LONGCHAMP. Records also show that he assumed his illustrious position through his brother, following the failure of the outgoing SHERIFF, one John MARSHALL, to halt the massacre of the Jews in 1190. Records also show that in 1201 one William de Stuteville paid 1,000 pounds to purchase the office of Sheriff of York.

[185, 189]

SHERWOOD District of NOTTINGHAMSHIRE that includes SHERWOOD FOREST as well as CLIPSTONE FOREST.

[142, 314]

SHERWOOD FOREST The king's forest within the county of NOTTINGHAMSHIRE. Most people associate it solely with ROBIN HOOD, though the legends suggest he was more active in BARNISDALE FOREST to the north. Today Sherwood Forest has been largely deforested, and most of the places actually mentioned within the legends as lying within the boundaries of the forest now lie well outside the wooded areas. Additionally CLIPSTONE FOREST, which was once a separate entity, is today considered part of the forest, the entire area today being referred to as the Dukeries.

Sherwood is not the original name of the forest, which was Shirewood – that is, the 'wood of the shire'. Cartographic study of the area may be performed on OS120. By the time of Robin Hood and his contemporaries, Sherwood Forest would not have been simply a vast tract of trees, but rather areas of dense oak and birch woodland along with open areas of heathland, woodland pastures and numerous small settlements, man being responsible

A stag-headed oak in Sherwood Forest. (*Mick Sharp Photography*)

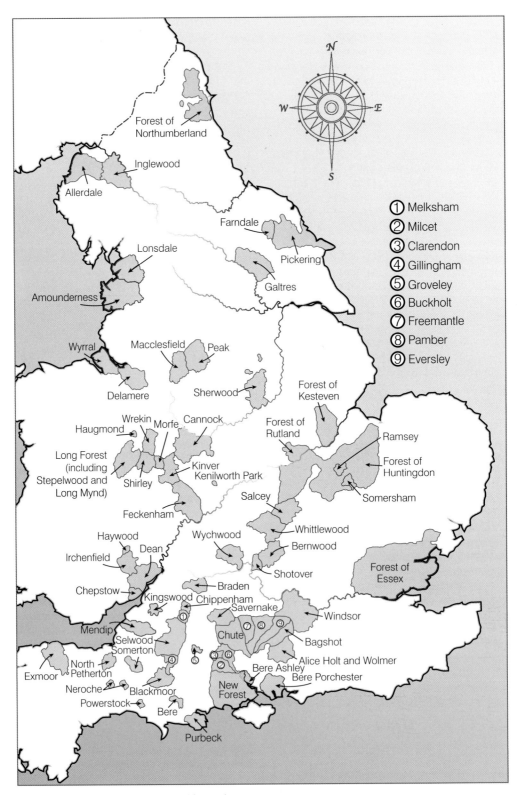

The royal forests at the start of the thirteenth century.

Four kings of England, left to right: Henry II, Richard I, below: John, Henry II. From the *Historia Anglorum* by Matthew Paris, thirteenth century. Roy 14 C VII f.9. (*British Library, London/Bridgeman Art Library*)

Henry II. French school, fifteenth century. Ms 722/1196 fol.146r. (*Musée Conde, Chantilly, France/ Bridgeman Art Library*)

Richard I enthroned from *Historia Major* by Matthew Paris, *c.* 1240. Ms.Royal.20.A.II. (*British Library, London/Bridgeman Art Library, BL 51331*)

Richard I the Lionheart, by M.J. Blondel, 1841. (*Château de Versailles, France/Bridgeman Art Library*)

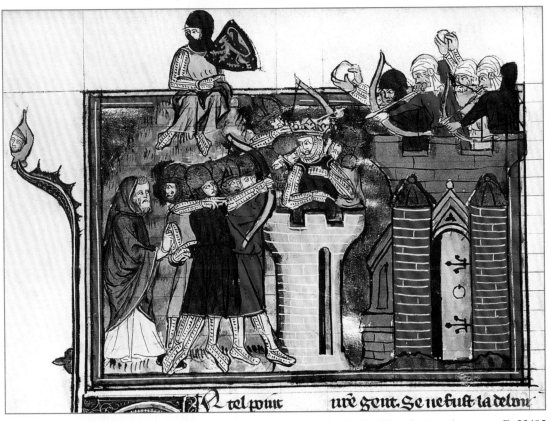

The Crusader assault on Jerusalem, 1099, from *Le Roman de Godefroi de Bouillon*, fourteenth century. Fr 22495 f.69v. (*Bibliotheque Nationale, Paris/Bridgeman Art Library*)

Decorated tile with roundel of Richard I from the Benedictine Abbey at Chertsey, Surrey, thirteenth century. (*British Museum, London/Bridgeman Art Library*)

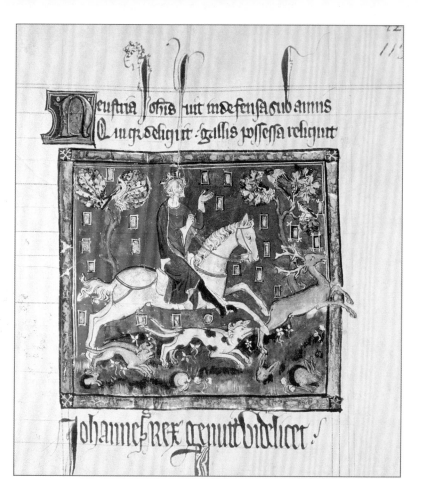

King John hunting, from the
*Liber Legum Antiquorum
Regum*, *c.* 1321. Cott Claud
D II f.113. (*British Library,
London/Bridgeman Art
Library*)

The tombs of Henry II, Eleanor of Aquitaine and Richard I in Fontevrault Abbey. (*Bridgeman Art Library*)

Above: The Major Oak, Birklands Wood, Sherwood Forest, Edwinstowe, Nottinghamshire. (*Mick Sharp Photography*)
Below: Lincoln Castle. (*Mick Sharp Photography*)

Lincoln Cathedral. (*Mick Sharp Photography*)

Above: Oak and birch trees in Birklands Wood, Sherwood Forest, Edwinstowe, Nottinghamshire. (*Mick Sharp Photography*)
Below: A multangular tower in York. (*Mick Sharp Photography*)

The outer bailey and gatehouse of Nottingham Castle, looking south. (*Mick Sharp Photography*)

Fountains Abbey by J.M.W. Turner. (*York City Art Gallery, North Yorkshire/Bridgeman Art Library*)

An archery match for which the competitors dress like Robin Hood and his Merry Men. Illustration by Robert Cruikshank, 1828. (*Mary Evans Picture Library*)

Robin meets Maid Marian at the royal tourney. From *Robin Hood* by N.C. Wyeth (1917), page 116. (*Mary Evans Picture Library*)

Robin Hood and Little John; characters for a toy theatre. (*Mary Evans Picture Library*)

Robin Hood & Little John.

Maid Marian joins Robin Hood and his Merry Men. Colour illustration by Joyce Merier, early twentieth century. (*Mary Evans Picture Library/Thomas Gilmor*)

Having bound the forester and stolen his dinner, Little John eats it in front of him. Illustration by Walter Crane in *Stories of Robin Hood and His Merry Men* by Henry Gilbert. (*Mary Evans Picture Library/Edwin Wallace*)

Robin Hood and Maid Marian on a hunting trip in the forest. Lithographed music cover by P. Hacker, *Maid Marian Quadrilles* by H.T. Swatton, *c*. 1860. (*Mary Evans Picture Library*)

A young tourist hugs a Robin Hood character at Walt Disney World, Florida. (© *Kelly-Mooney Photography/Corbis*)

Errol Flynn as Robin Hood in the film *The Adventures of Robin Hood*, 1938. (*Mary Evans Picture Library*)

Errol Flynn as Robin Hood and Olivia de Havilland as Maid Marian in the film *The Adventures of Robin Hood*, 1938. (*Mary Evans Picture Library*)

The Edge of Sherwood Forest by Andrew Maccallum, 1878. (*Phillips, The International Fine Art Auctioneers, UK/Bridgeman Art Library*)

for the felling of the trees and the clearing of the land to support feudal agriculture.

The term 'forest' was by and large a legal term to define an area in which the FOREST LAWS held sway. These laws were strictly enforced throughout the medieval period, and punishments for cutting timber or poaching the king's deer were severe in the extreme.

Around the time of the NORMAN Conquest Sherwood Forest would have covered almost a fifth of Nottinghamshire. As a royal hunting preserve its heaths and thickets provided an ideal venue for the aristocratic sports of hunting and falconry. Many English kings came to the forest to enjoy the pleasures of the chase – notably Prince JOHN, James I and his son Charles I. Richard III was hunting in Sherwood when he received the fateful news that Henry Tudor had landed, and rode south to meet his death at the Battle of Bosworth.

[60, 294–5, 303, 332, 334, 366, 368, 387, 401]
{K11–M16}

SHOTLEY HAWE Manor of Lord ARNALD OF SHOTLEY HAWE, an evil knight to whom Sir GUY OF GISBORNE intended to sell the ten most troublesome VILLEINs of the manor of BIRKENCAR. This plan was discovered by MUCH THE MILLER'S SON, who brought the intelligence to ROBERT OF LOCKSLEY as the villagers were debating whether or not to join him as outlaws. The news instantly made up the minds of those still wavering.

[38–9]

SHOTLEY HAWE, LORD ARNALD OF See ARNALD OF SHOTLEY HAWE, Lord.

SIBBIE The beautiful daughter of COLMAN GREY and sister to KET THE TROW, HOB O'THE HILL and FENELLA. Following the pardoning of ROBIN HOOD and his men, Sibbie went to live at MALASET, where she married GILBERT OF THE WHITE HAND and thereafter acted as lady-in-waiting to MAID MARIAN.

[333, 338–9]

SILAS BEN REUBEN A leading member of the Jewry of NOTTINGHAM, the son of REUBEN OF STAMFORD and brother of RUTH. WILL THE BOWMAN brought him news of his father's escape from YORK, and arranged for him to come to the forest to be reunited with his father at the HEXGROVE on the high road by PAPPLEWICK. Silas ben Reuben duly followed these instructions and was reunited with his father and his sister in the WITCHGROVE, where RICHARD MALBÊTE had been summarily hanged moments before.

[216–19, 228, 237, 246]

SIM OF WAKEFIELD One of the members of ROBIN HOOD's outlaw band, who evidently came from WAKEFIELD. He is only mentioned once in the legends, and nothing more is known about him.

[113]

SIMON Clerk to ALFRED OF GAMWELL, who travelled with his master to meet ROBIN HOOD and warn him of the plans of Sir GUY OF GISBORNE and the SHERIFF OF NOTTINGHAM to disguise men-at-arms as beggars so as to gather intelligence on the whereabouts of Robin and his men.

[83]

SIMON THE FLETCHER Freeman from the village of CROMWELL, whose life was an example to JACK, SON OF WILKIN, who hoped that one day he too would become a freeman.

[141]

SLAUGHTER LEA Name by which BEVERLEY GLADE was known for many years after ROBIN HOOD and his men had killed FULCO THE RED and all his BRABANT mercenaries there.

[386]

SPECTRE ~BEAST, ~MARE Supernatural beast which the men at BIRKENCAR manor thought had confronted them when they tried to kill Sir GUY OF GISBORNE by burning down his manor. What they actually saw was the fleeing Sir Guy draped in the hide of a recently flayed horse. Thus apparelled, he had charged out of the burning barn at the men.

[47]

SQUIRE Originally esquire, from the Old French *esquier*, which in turn comes from the Latin *scutarius*, meaning shield-bearer, the squire was a young man of good birth attendant upon a knight, though he could also be regarded as a knight in training.

STAFF Popular shortening of QUARTERSTAFF.

STAITHES, ROBERT OF See ROBERT OF STAITHES.

STAKES, THE Unidentified location on the route taken by the men-at-arms fleeing from the killing of Sir ROGER DE LONGCHAMP, where they were reported to have forded a brook.

[28]

STAMFORD Town in south LINCOLNSHIRE near the borders of Cambridgeshire and Leicestershire. It was the home of the Jew REUBEN OF STAMFORD and his daughter RUTH, and was one of the towns plagued by the barbaric persecution of the Jews. It is unrecorded if the attacks at Stamford were led by RICHARD MALBÊTE, as they were at LYNN, LINCOLN and YORK.

[211] {P19}

STAMFORD, REUBEN OF See REUBEN OF STAMFORD.

STANE LEA Unidentified site of ROBIN HOOD's camp within BARNISDALE FOREST, also referred to as STANLEY. There is no mention in the legends of the MAJOR OAK, the popular site of Robin's headquarters in SHERWOOD FOREST, and it seems doubtful that there is any link between that legendary tree and the camp at the Stane Lea.

[49, 55, 62, 72, 79, 259, 280–1, 285, 293, 369, 392]

STANLEY Alternative name for the STANE LEA. There are a great number of Stanleys to be found on modern maps. Those that fall roughly within the area in which ROBIN HOOD is said to have operated are:

1. Village on the River Calder (OS104 SE3523) just to the east of the village of Outwood. {I7}
2. Stanley House (OS103 SD6429) approximately 5 miles south of Huntingdon House (see HUNTINGDON). {B7}
3. Village (OS120 SK4662) approximately 4.5 miles to the west of MANSFIELD. {J13}
4. Village (OS129 SK4140) approximately 15 miles to the west of NOTTINGHAM {J15}

[49]

STEPHEN, SQUIRE Son of Sir JOCELYN OF THURGOLAND and AVIS his wife. A cruel and harsh boy, he evicted his mother from the manor after the death of his father and returned her to a life of villeinage. News of her ordeal soon spread far and

Here the merry men enjoyed the long evening. Illustration from *Tales and Plays of Robin Hood* by Eleanor L. Skinner.

wide until one day Squire Stephen was abducted from his manor by thirty men in hooded robes. For a while no one knew what had become of him, but it soon became known that he had been taken by ROBIN HOOD so that he could be taught how to treat his mother and those who worked for him. Many months later Squire Stephen returned to THURGOLAND, where he immediately sought out his mother and begged her forgiveness. From that day forth he lived as a true noble and treated all those on his manor with due respect and attention, especially his mother, whom he returned to her rightful place in the manor.

[389–90]

STEPHEN OF GAMWELL Ancestor of ROBERT OF LOCKSLEY, who had told his nephew that Robert's family had once been the lords of HUNTINGDON, but the NORMANS drove them from their home, lands and title.

[16, 267]

STEWARD A steward was the keeper of a court of justice, who served as an officer either of the crown

or of a feudal lord, in which case he also administered the lord's property, house and finances, as well as presiding over the manorial court. Also known as a SENESCHAL.

STEWARD, JOHN THE See JOHN THE STEWARD.

STONE COT THURSTAN's former home in BARNISDALE FOREST. He was driven out by Sir ISENBART DE BELAME, who killed his wife and baby. Thurstan took to the forests, where he assumed the name RAFE OF THE BILLHOOK.

[346]

STONE FOLK Name by which HOB O'THE HILL referred to the spirits who inhabited standing stones.

[82]

STONE HOUSE Unidentified house by BARNIS-DALE FOUR WENTS, towards which KET THE TROW reported that Sir ROGER OF DONCASTER and his troops were moving.

[368]

STUBBS, JOHN O'THE See JOHN O'THE STUBBS.

STURT OF NORWELL Serf who had gone to the aid of a fairy, whose daughter he subsequently married. His descendants still lived in the village of NORWELL, where they were counted among the most respected citizens.

[142]

STUTELEY, WILL OF THE See WILL (OF THE) STUTELEY.

SUMPTER A baggage- or pack-horse.

SURTOUT A man's overcoat in the style of a frock-coat.

SYKE Manor belonging to Sir ROGER OF DONCASTER. That evil knight and his men set out from Syke in an attempt to trap ROBIN HOOD and his men, but instead Robin killed Sir GUY OF GISBORNE, and then the outlaw and his men killed FULCO THE RED and all his BRABANT mercenaries. There is one possible location for the manor of this cowardly knight. This is the hamlet of Sykes (OS103 SD6351) approximately 12 miles to the west of GISBORNE, and thus well into Lancashire – though by the same token well outside the area of the legends.

[368] {A4}

T

THICKET HOLLOW Unidentified location on the route followed by the men-at-arms fleeing from the killing of Sir ROGER DE LONGCHAMP back to the castle at WRANGBY.

[28]

THINNE, JOHN THE See JOHN THE THINNE.

THOMAS OF PATHERLEY One of the neighbours of ALICE OF HAVELOND, who, along with ROBERT OF PRESTBURY, seized the lands of HAVELOND and evicted Alice after her husband

BENNETT had been taken prisoner and held to ransom by a Scottish knight. Alice of Havelond raised the ransom required to free her husband, but when he returned to reclaim his lands he was set upon by the two robbers, who crippled him. When the king would not hear Alice's appeal, she went to ALFRED OF GAMWELL, but although he offered to appeal for her, she sought out her cousin ROBIN HOOD. A few days later the men of SCAURDALE saw two houses burning in the distance, and immediately knew that vengeance had been wreaked on the robbers.

[86–8]

THREE STANE RIGG The name of three standing stones. ROBIN HOOD told the SHERIFF OF NOTTINGHAM, whom he was escorting through the forest in the guise of the potter of WENTBRIDGE, that according to legend they were simply stones by day but at night they became three hags who did the bidding of the witch who lived in the WITCH WOOD. Unfortunately there is no way today of identifying these stones, or where they might have stood.

[110]

THURGOLAND Village (OS110 SE2901) in South YORKSHIRE approximately 5 miles to the north-west of SHEFFIELD. It was known as Turgesland in Saxon times. The legends say that the village was the manor of Sir JOCELYN OF THURGOLAND who married AVIS, a NEIF. Their son was the cruel and harsh Squire STEPHEN.

[389–90] {H9}

THURGOLAND, SIR JOCELYN OF See JOCELYN OF THURGOLAND, Sir.

THURLSTAN During the first period of ROBIN HOOD's life as an outlaw GRAME GAPTOOTH was man-at-arms to the lord of Thurlstan manor. By the time of the storming of the EVIL HOLD he had become the lord of the manor, though by what means, fair or foul, he achieved that status is not recorded. Though the location of Thurlstan cannot be accurately determined, it is quite possible that it was in or near the village of Thurlstone (OS110 SE2303), which lies on the course of the River Don approximately 7 miles north-west of SHEFFIELD.

[290, 353] {H9}

THURSTAN Freeman of Danish lineage who was unjustly forced from his land by Sir ISENBART DE BELAME, who killed his wife and baby. Thurstan took to the forests vowing that one day he would return and have his vengeance, which he did when he helped ROBIN HOOD and his troops storm the castle at WRANGBY. It was not until he told his story to Robin that he was recognised, for in the thirty years between his eviction and the taking of the EVIL HOLD, Thurstan had gone by the name of RAFE OF THE BILLHOOK, and had even competed against Robin during the archery tournament at NOTTINGHAM.

[171, 346]

TICKHILL Small town (OS111 SK5993) in south YORKSHIRE approximately 7 miles south of DONCASTER on the route of the GREAT NORTH ROAD. Historically the town is of great importance as just to the south of the town, between Tickhill and BLYTHE, lay one of the five tilting-grounds licensed by RICHARD I in 1194. Tickhill Castle passed into the ownership of Robert de Bellême, who may perhaps have been an ancestor of Sir ISENBART DE BELAME.

William the Conqueror gave the original wooden castle at Tickhill (the stone castle not being started until around 1100) to Roger de Busli, along with forty-nine manors including, interestingly, the land around LOXLEY. This large estate was styled the honour of Tickhill. Henry I seized on this honour, and other succeeding kings did likewise. Edward III gave it to John of Gaunt, Duke of Lancaster, from whom it passed to Henry IV, remaining part of the Duchy of Lancaster ever since. In the reign of Charles I it was regarded as a strong fortress, and was garrisoned by the king's troops. After the battle of Marston Moor, and the surrender of YORK to Parliament's forces, the Earl of Manchester sent Colonel Lilburn to reduce the castle, following complaints from the inhabitants of the surrounding country that it was exceedingly oppressive. After two days' siege the garrison capitulated.

In 1646–7 Parliament ordered that Tickhill Castle, with several others, should be dismantled and rendered untenable. The circular tower was, in consequence, demolished. It is still, however, an impressive example of a Norman stone motte and bailey fortress partly enclosed by a large wet ditch. The curtain wall sits on top of the massive bailey rampart and is flanked by a simple but interesting gatehouse, with a small barbican. On top of the high motte are the remains of the eleven-sided keep, with projecting buttresses at the angles.

The castle at Tickhill is mentioned several times in the legends. ALAN-A-DALE refers to Sir Isenbart de Belame as the grandson of the fiend of Tickhill, though nothing else is said about this 'fiend'. However, as the castle had once been owned by the historical Robert de Bellême, it seems quite probable, thanks to that character's reprehensible nature, that the fiend of Tickhill was none other than Robert de Bellême himself. Later the castle, along with NOTTINGHAM CASTLE, fell into the hands of Earl JOHN, and there one DICKON, the son of an old couple from NOTTINGHAM, who had once worked for PETER GREATREX, the armourer of Nottingham, had been imprisoned so securely that one foot had perished. History says that from 1189 to 1194 Tickhill and Nottingham Castles were held by John, though the government kept a check on him by retaining overall authority over those castles and others in his hands. This, however, did not stop John taking direct control of the castles, a rebellious move that led, following the release of his brother, to Tickhill being stormed. Nottingham Castle was also stormed a short time later.

[56, 294–5, 319, 321] {K10}

TITHE A levy of one-tenth of all produce, income or profits that was used for the support of the Church or clergy, though often as not the tithe would be retained by the lord whose responsibility it was to collect it. Originally voluntary, tithes became compulsory in the mid-tenth century and were always unpopular.

TOOMLANDS, SQUIRE DENVIL OF See DENVIL OF TOOMLANDS, Squire.

TRANMIRE The epithet of ALAN DE TRANMIRE and his father Sir HERBRAND DE TRANMIRE. It would seem to indicate that ALAN-A-DALE and his father came from Tranmere on Merseyside, though this is by no means certain.

TRANMIRE, ALAN DE See ALAN DE TRANMIRE and ALAN-A-DALE.

TRANMIRE, SIR HERBRAND DE See HERBRAND DE TRANMIRE, Sir.

TREE FOLK The name by which HOB O'THE HILL referred to supernatural beings who inhabited the upper reaches of the trees in the forests.

[82]

TRENT, RIVER Major river, the third longest in England at 170 miles. It rises in the south Pennines and discharges into the River Humber. Both NOTTINGHAM and NEWARK lie on the course of the river, which is used in the legends as a demarcation boundary.

[138, 259]

TROLL Scandinavian supernatural beings that live in caves or mountains and are depicted either as dwarfs or giants. Wonderfully skilled in metalworking, they had a penchant for stealing, even carrying off women and children. Their British equivalent was the TROW, which was always depicted as small and human-like.

[80]

TROW Also DROW. The British version of the Scandinavian TROLL, though technically the name originated in the Shetlands and Orkneys. Unlike the troll, which could be either giant or dwarf, the trow was always small, a fully grown trow being no taller than an early teenage youth. The word seems to derive from the archaic verb *trow*, meaning to think, believe or trust, thus indicating that a trow, once its friendship had been won, could always be trusted. KET THE TROW admirably displayed just such a trait.

TROW, KET THE See KET THE TROW.

TUCK, FRIAR See FRIAR TUCK.

UNDERWORLD The land of the dead, that world to which all things pass after their time on Earth. It is neither heaven nor hell, but rather a realm divided into various regions to which each person is allocated according to their actions during life. The Underworld occurs only once in the legends.

[82]

URSULA, DAME The aunt of ROBIN HOOD and ALICE OF HAVELOND and the ABBESS of the priory at KIRKLEES. Towards the end of his life, when he was growing weary with age, Robin used to travel to Kirklees every six months or so to have his blood let. When he went there after the death of Alice of Havelond, Dame Ursula drugged him and then bled him to death, her treacherous act being paid for by the cowardly Sir ROGER OF DONCASTER who, when urged to finish the outlaw with his own knife, turned and fled. Even though LITTLE JOHN wanted to burn down the abbey after finding his friend close to death, Robin would not allow him, for he had never harmed women, and anyway there would have been no point as Dame Ursula would already have been many miles away. What became of her after the death of Robin Hood is not recorded.

[392, 394–5]

VILLEIN A medieval peasant personally bound to his lord or to his manor, to whom he pays dues and services in return for his land. The name comes from the late Latin *villanus*, meaning a farm-servant. By the thirteenth century the villein had become an unfree peasant bound to his lord by rigid legal and economic ties; in effect, he was no better than a slave. Such repressive restrictions led to great unrest among the villeins and other classes of peasant, and it was amid this unrest that the legends of ROBIN HOOD and his band of outlaws rose to prominence.

VIRGIN MARY The mother of Jesus Christ, she appears in the story of Sir HERBRAND DE TRANMIRE. She represented the best surety Robin could have hoped for when he lent that knight the 400 pounds he needed to pay off ABBOT ROBERT. The Virgin Mary did indeed stand surety for Robin, for, according to the legends, it was she who caused Abbot Robert to travel through the forests carrying 800 pounds on the very day Sir Herbrand de Tranmire was due to repay the loan to Robin. Thus, when that knight arrived Robin would not accept repayment as he had already been paid twice over by the corpulent abbot.

[32, 177, 179, 250, 254]

Wakefield from the south. Engraving from Nathaniel Buck, *Antiquities of England*, 1774.

WAKEFIELD City and administrative headquarters of West YORKSHIRE (OS104 SE3320), delightfully situated on the side of a hill that gently slopes down to the River Calder south of Leeds. It only appears once in the legends of ROBIN HOOD as the home of SIM OF WAKEFIELD, who joined Robin and his men sometime during their first year as outlaws. It was also the home of George a'Green, the 'Jolly Pinder [or Pound Keeper] of Wakefield', according to some early ballads. If the name is anything to go by he would have lived near the present-day Pinderfields Hospital.

[113] {I7}

WAKEFIELD ABBEY Abbey at WAKEFIELD that only appears once in the legends of ROBIN HOOD. A bishop's convoy was to set out from the abbey to travel to LINCOLN, and Robin and KET THE TROW thought Sir ROGER OF DONCASTER aimed to ambush it.

[368] {I7}

WALSINGHAM Site of a holy shrine in Norfolk approximately 25 miles north-east of King's Lynn, between Wells-next-the-Sea and Fakenham. It is mentioned as the goal of WILL THE BOWMAN while he is in NOTTINGHAM in the guise of a pilgrim, having taken a message from REUBEN OF STAMFORD to SILAS BEN REUBEN.

Walsingham has been a place of pilgrimage since medieval times. In 1061 the lady of the manor Richeldis de Faverches had a series of visions, or dreams, in which the Virgin Mary came to her and showed her the house in Nazareth where the Annunciation took place. She was instructed to build a replica of the holy house in Walsingham, which she duly did. The site of the holy house can still be seen in the ABBEY grounds.

In about 1153 the Augustinian canons established the Augustinian Priory to the Annunciation of the Blessed Virgin Mary adjacent to the holy house. By the fourteenth century so many pilgrims were visiting the site that the priory was enlarged, and the little wooden holy house encased in a larger stone chapel, described by William of Worcester in 1479 as the *Novum Opus*.

The medieval village of Walsingham developed to cater for the increasing number of pilgrims and to meet local needs. By 1252 a charter had been granted to hold a weekly market and an annual fair. At about this time the village was laid out in a grid pattern. The fine medieval timber-framed jetted buildings, still visible today, provided hostelries and shops for visiting pilgrims, as they continue to do today. Pilgrims came from all over Britain and Europe, including the kings and queens of England from HENRY III (*c.* 1226) to Henry VIII (1511). However, Walsingham's life as a flourishing medieval pilgrimage centre came to an end in 1538 when Henry VIII's commissioners dissolved the priory and the friary.

The pilgrimage revival began in the late nineteenth century, with the first modern pilgrimage taking place on 20 August 1897 to the Slipper

Chapel at Houghton St Giles, now the Roman Catholic shrine to Our Lady of Walsingham. The Anglican shrine was built by Father Alfred Hope Patten in 1933–7.

[221] {Y16}

WALTER The STEWARD to Sir RICHARD FITZWALTER at MALASET. He appears twice in the legends. The first time he was accompanying MAID MARIAN through the forests en route for LINDEN LEA when Sir ROGER DE LONG-CHAMP attempted to abduct her, and the second time was when he greeted ROBIN HOOD at Malaset following the death of Sir Richard FitzWalter, and told him that Marian had vanished.

[17–18, 21–2, 24, 277–80]

WALTER, HUBERT See HUBERT WALTER.

WALTER DE BEAUFOREST, SIR The lord of BEAUFOREST, as his epithet indicates, and father of ALICE DE BEAUFOREST. For some time he managed to resist Sir ISENBART DE BELAME's orders to marry his daughter to Sir RANULF DE GREASBY, even though Sir Isenbart had threatened to seize his lands and burn his manor. When he was eventually forced to accede, ROBIN HOOD interrupted the wedding, Sir Ranulf de Greasby and his comrades were killed, and Sir Walter agreed to his daughter marrying her beloved, ALAN-A-DALE. Robin offered Sir Walter the sanctuary of the forest, but he refused, saying that with friends like Robin he had nothing to fear from the knights of the EVIL HOLD – a sentiment apparently upheld by the legends as there is no evidence that those knights ever moved against Sir Walter de Beauforest after the deaths of their comrades.

Sir Walter de Beauforest joined Robin and his troops for the storming of the castle at WRANGBY, but nothing more is heard of him, and between that time and the death of Robin Hood Sir Walter de Beauforest must have died. The lands of Beauforest passed to Alan-a-Dale and his wife Alice, who gave land to LITTLE JOHN and WILL SCARLET at CROMWELL after they had buried their friend and leader.

[139, 155, 159, 164–6, 201, 352]

WARD One of the villagers of LOCKSLEY who came to the aid of SCADLOCK when Sir HUBERT OF LYNN arrived to take possession of the manor of OUTWOODS after ROBERT OF LOCKSLEY had been outlawed.

[35]

WARENNE, EARL OF Title of one of the king's treasurers. The title Earl of Warenne, or de Warenne, is certainly historical, being founded between 1087 and 1089. History records one John de Warenne, Earl of Surrey and Sussex, who was also simply known as Earl Warenne; he was the Warden of Scotland from 1296. However, this is too late to coincide with the traditional period ascribed to the legends of ROBIN HOOD, and it seems more likely that the Earl of Warenne depicted in the legends is HAMELIN, who stood surety for King JOHN on 13 May 1213 along with the Earl of FERRERS, the Earl of Salisbury and the Count of Boulogne.

Hamelin was an historical character, who became the 5th Earl Warenne in 1163 following the death of William, the 4th earl, who died without issue in 1159. Hamelin was the son of Geoffrey of ANJOU, and thus the illegitimate half-brother of HENRY II; when Hamelin married Isabel, the widow of the 4th earl, Henry made him the 5th earl. In 1180 Hamelin ordered the building of stone castles at Conisbrough and Sandal, and in 1189 he and his wife jointly founded an endowment for a priest for the chapel of St Philip and St James within the castle at Conisbrough. In 1199 Hamelin witnessed the coronation of his nephew King John and the following year travelled to LINCOLN to witness the King of Scotland's oath of homage. The year 1201 saw him visiting the castle at Conisbrough, during which visit he granted a market charter for the town. He died in 1202 and was buried at Lewes Priory in Sussex.

[300, 304, 307, 316, 322, 366]

WARSOP Small town in NOTTINGHAMSHIRE (OS120 SK5767) approximately 4 miles north of MANSFIELD on the River Meden. Following the NORMAN Conquest, Warsop became one of the 174 manors held by Baron Roger de Busli, who was responsible for the building of TICKHILL Castle. Lying on the edge of the forests, the town is only mentioned once in the legends as the place where BART and MICHAEL had served an evil master before fleeing to join Robin's band of outlaws in the forests.

[99] {K13}

WASTE, SIR RANULF OF THE See RANULF OF THE WASTE, Sir.

WAT GRAHAM OF CAR PEEL Borderlands fighter of some repute whom FENELLA, sister of SIBBIE, HOB O'THE HILL and KET THE TROW, married after the pardon of RICHARD I. This happened a short time after her mother had died and been buried in the barrow within BARNISDALE FOREST that had been their home.

[333]

WATKIN The bailiff of NOTTINGHAM, who was in charge of the archery tournament arranged by the SHERIFF OF NOTTINGHAM. He did his best to see that LUKE THE RED, who was one of the sheriff's men, won the contest by counting to three very slowly when it was Luke the Red's turn to make the blind shot, and very quickly to three when it was ROBIN HOOD's turn. Following the contest the sheriff told Watkin to stop the mysterious archer who had just won, and Watkin pushed his way through the throng calling out that he was arresting Robin Hood in the name of the king. As he spoke the words the outlaws formed ranks and fought off the sheriff's men, Watkin himself being dashed to the ground by LITTLE JOHN. Later Watkin led a troop of horsemen up to the castle of Sir RICHARD AT LEE at LINDEN LEA, but was forced to retreat when Robin's archers cut them down. What happened to Watkin after that is not recorded.

[265, 268–70, 275]

WATLING STREET Roman road extending east and west across England. Starting at Reculver near Dover on the Kent coast, Watling Street passed through Canterbury and LONDON, thence through St Albans (Roman *Verulamium*), Dunstable, along the boundaries of Leicester, where it intersected the FOSSE WAY, and Warwick, to Wroxeter on the Severn (Roman *Viroconium*). The origin of the name is not known, but the road was, along with ERMINE STREET, the Fosse Way and the Icknield Way, one of the royal roads. The section of Watling Street between London and Dover is also Roman in origin, but was almost certainly a later addition to the road.

WEARYALL HILL Unidentified hill on which stood the LYNCHET LODGE, where REUBEN OF STAMFORD and his daughter RUTH were taken by WILL THE BOWMAN to recover their strength.

[209]

WENTBRIDGE Village of West YORKSHIRE (OS111 SE4917) to the south of PONTEFRACT, from which the potter of WENTBRIDGE hailed. It was also here that LITTLE JOHN is thought to have first met ROBIN HOOD and the pair had their famous QUARTERSTAFF contest for the right to cross the bridge.

[100–1, 107] {J8}

Little John's view of Wentbridge. Photograph by J.C. Holt.

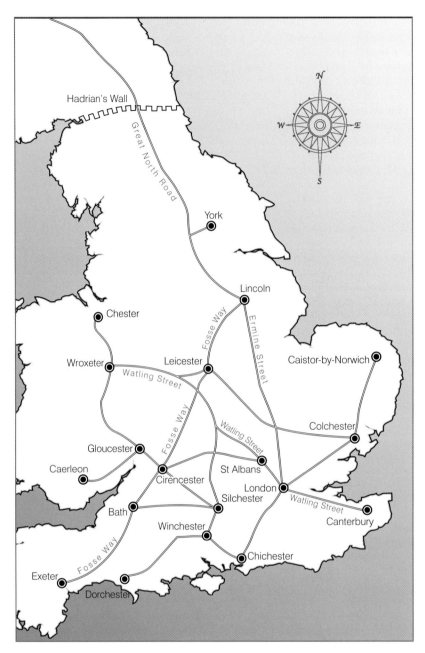

Principal Roman roads.

WENTBRIDGE, POTTER OF Potter from WENTBRIDGE who was stopped for toll in the forest by ROBIN HOOD, but courageously told the outlaw he paid no one except the king's representative. He was challenged to an archery contest in which he acquitted himself so admirably that Robin granted him free passage through the forests, and thus cemented his friendship with the potter. This was to prove useful to Robin when he borrowed the potter's cart, pony and wares in order to travel into NOTTINGHAM incognito.

[100–1, 107]

WERRISDALE Lands and manor of Sir HERBRAND DE TRANMIRE, his wife Dame JUDITH and their son ALAN DE TRANMIRE. Following the death of Sir IVO LE RAVENER, who was killed in a fair fight by ALAN-A-DALE, the knights of the EVIL HOLD imposed a fine on Sir Herbrand that was so heavy that he looked likely to be ruined. He paid the first demand for 400 pounds, but then had to borrow, on the surety of his manor of Werrisdale, a further 400 pounds from ABBOT ROBERT. Sir ISENBART DE BELAME and his horde were denied possession of Werrisdale after ROBIN HOOD lent Sir Herbrand the money he needed. The legends point to Werrisdale being to the north and west of SHEFFIELD, but study of modern maps does not reveal the manor's whereabouts.

[63, 72, 142, 186, 192, 197, 401]

WESTMORLAND Former county of England in the Lake District, that is today a part of Cumbria. ROBIN HOOD is recorded as having travelled here to help Sir DROGO OF DALLAS TOWER against the border clans who were raiding his manor. Robin and his men so utterly routed the raiders that the men of the clans ARMSTRONG, DOUGLAS, GRAHAM and JORDAN never again dared to travel south of the Scottish border.

[388]

WHITE HAND, GILBERT OF THE See GILBERT (OF THE WHITE HAND).

WHITE MONKS The monastic order of ST MARY'S ABBEY, so-called as they wore white habits. This would identify them as Cistercians, though they are also sometimes incorrectly called Carmelites. The Carmelites did indeed wear white habits, but they were normally referred to as Whitefriars.

[7]

WICKET A small door or gate near or within a larger one, though the term also applies to a small window or opening within a door, especially one fitted with glass or a grating, through which visitors can be viewed and questioned before admittance.

WILKIN Father of JACK, SON OF WILKIN. His true name was WILL, Wilkin being a nickname reflecting his small size.

[139–40]

WILL True name of WILKIN, the father of JACK, SON OF WILKIN.

[140]

WILL (OF THE) STUTELEY True name of WILL THE BOWMAN, reflecting that he came from a village or district known as STUTELEY. This may have been an error, for there are two villages called Stukeley just to the north of HUNTINGDON.

[36, 231–3]

Illustration from *Bold Robin Hood and his Outlaw Band* by Louis Read.

WILL SCARLET The name of a VILLEIN from LOCKSLEY village, whom ROBERT OF LOCKS-LEY found hunting deer in the royal forest as he was en route through the forest to guard MAID MARIAN as she travelled to LINDEN LEA. Will Scarlet is popularly thought to have gained his surname through wearing a red or scarlet tunic, but there is no evidence in the early sources to support this, and it seems more likely that the name is a reflection of his ruddy complexion or red hair.

The brother-in-law of JOHN A'GREEN, Will Scarlet had taken in his widowed sister and her three children after John a'Green's death, but his sister died a short while afterwards, forcing Will Scarlet to find suitable homes for two of his three nephews. He decided to care for GILBERT OF THE WHITE

Illustration from *Bold Robin Hood and his Outlaw Band* by Louis Read.

HAND himself. Will was taken prisoner by Sir GUY OF GISBORNE for hunting royal deer, but was released from his prison by Robert of Locksley when he led the villagers to the manor at BIRKENCAR to burn it down in an attempt to kill Sir Guy of Gisborne.

Very little is heard of Will Scarlet in the legends following that time, but he was still with ROBIN HOOD when they stormed the castle at WRANGBY. During that siege, along with WILL THE BOWMAN, he was in charge of the archers keeping the castle's bowmen at bay. He survived the day and outlived Robin Hood, finally settling on land at CROMWELL that was given to him by ALAN-A-DALE.

[4–12, 29, 39, 42–3, 347, 368–9, 401]

WILL THE BOWMAN One of the major characters within the legends of ROBIN HOOD, who is sometimes confused with WILL SCARLET. Will the Bowman was also known as WILL OF THE STUTELEY. He was the first to suggest that the villagers of LOCKSLEY and the manor of BIRKENCAR should follow the newly outlawed ROBERT OF LOCKSLEY into the forests. He then went with the villagers to Birkencar manor and chased after the fleeing figure of Sir GUY OF GISBORNE, but in vain. Having taken to life as an outlaw, Will the Bowman used his skills to teach those not used to the longbow how to use that weapon, his young nephew being among those who excelled under his tuition. A natural leader, he appears to have been Robin's second-in-command before the arrival of JOHN THE LITTLE, whom Will the Bowman rechristened LITTLE JOHN.

Will the Bowman is perhaps remembered best for two missions he carried out for Robin. On the first he was dispatched to CROMWELL carrying the rings of ALICE DE BEAUFOREST and her maid NETTA O'THE MEERING to find JACK, SON OF WILKIN, the purpose of the mission being to persuade that young man to lead him to the hideout of ALAN-A-DALE so that they could stop the forced marriage of Alice de Beauforest to

Merry Robin stops a stranger in scarlet. Illustration from *The Merry Adventures of Robin Hood* by Howard Pyle.

Sir RANULF DE GREASBY. Will succeeded in his allotted task, and the wedding was duly interrupted and Sir Ranulf and his three companions killed.

The second memorable event in the career of Will the Bowman was when he came across RUTH, the daughter of REUBEN OF STAMFORD, foraging for food. When she took him to her dying father, he gave them food and then took them to the LYNCHET LODGE on WEARYALL HILL where they were nursed back to health. Then, after Reuben of Stamford had told Robin of the slaughter of the Jews at the hands of RICHARD MALBÊTE, Will the Bowman travelled in the disguise of a pilgrim to NOTTINGHAM to take a message to SILAS BEN REUBEN, Reuben's son. However, as Will the Bowman attempted to leave the city he was captured and sentenced to be hanged on GALLOW'S HILL.

The SHERIFF OF NOTTINGHAM refused his request to be allowed to die with a sword in his hand, but even as the noose tightened around his neck he was rescued by Little John and KET THE TROW, and together he and Little John held off the sheriff's men-at-arms until Robin and the rest of the outlaws arrived.

Following the pardon of RICHARD I, Will the Bowman accompanied the king on his French campaign, and when he returned to England he was given land at MALASET by Robin and MAID MARIAN. There he lived in peace until after the signing of the MAGNA CARTA when he joined Robin and his troops in the siege and taking of the castle at WRANGBY, his task during that battle being, along with Will Scarlet, to hold off the archers of the EVIL HOLD. Afterwards he returned to a life in the forests with Robin and the other outlaws.

Will the Bowman met his death during the battle with FULCO THE RED and his BRABANT mercenaries. Rushing to the aid of Robin Hood, who was about to be struck down from behind, Will the Bowman was hacked down by another mercenary, but with his dying breath he managed to warn Robin of his danger. Robin's would-be attacker was killed along with the man who had disposed of Will the Bowman.

[36, 40, 44–7, 50, 78–9, 138, 145–6, 202–9, 216–26, 228, 230–5, 237, 248, 261, 334, 347, 369, 377–9, 383]

WILLIAM, EARL OF FERRERS One of the party chosen by RICHARD I to travel with him disguised as monks through the forest so that they might encounter ROBIN HOOD. The others chosen were HAMELIN, Earl de WARENNE, RANULF, Earl of CHESTER, Sir OSBERT DE SCOFTON and one ROGER BIGOT.

[316]

WILLIAM, KING OF ENGLAND Although the legends mention King William they fail to specify which is meant. It seems most likely that this was William II (*c*. 1056–1100), also known as William Rufus ('the Red'), as it was under his rule that the NORMAN conquest of the north of England was completed.

[7]

WILLIAM DE LONGCHAMP, SIR The Lord Bishop of ELY, JUSTICIAR and HIGH CHANCELLOR of England, who acted as regent in the absence of RICHARD I. An historical character, William de Longchamp was in the service of GEOFFREY OF BRITTANY when he sided with the Princes Richard and JOHN against their father. He was appointed Bishop of Ely in 1189, upon Richard's accession to the throne, and was also appointed High Chancellor at the same time. Becoming justiciar and papal legate in NORMANDY in March 1190, he administered England in Richard I's absence until Earl John engineered his fall from power in 1191 when he fled the country (29 October), though he had at first stood up to the tyrant with a certain degree of success. He continued to serve his king abroad, helping to negotiate his release in 1193 from the castle at HAGENAU. He returned to England and was reinstated as chancellor, but left again with Richard I in 1194, never to return. He died in 1197. His brother Osbert de Longchamp is mentioned as having at one time held the post of SHERIFF OF YORK, while his elder brother was justiciar, his appointment coming in the wake of the Jewish massacre in 1190. William de Longchamp was one of the signatories to the 'Charter by Which Many Liberties are Granted and Confirmed to the Jews', which was signed on 22 March 1190 as a result of the massacre. This important document read:

Richard, by the grace of God, King of England, duke of Normandy, &c., to his archbishops, bishops, &c., greeting:
I. Know ye that we have granted and, by the present charter, confirmed, to Ysaac, son of Rabbi Joe, and his sons and their men, all their customs and liberties just as the Lord King Henry, our father, granted and by his charter confirmed to the Jews of England and Normandy, namely: to reside in our land freely and honourably, and to hold all those things from us which the aforesaid Isaac and his sons held in the time of Henry the King, our father, in lands, and fiefs, and pledges, and gifts, and purchases, viz., Hame, which Henry, our father, gave them for their service, and Thurroc, which

the said Isaac bought of the Count of Ferrars, and all the houses, and messages, and pledges which the said Isaac and his sons had in our land in the time of King Henry, our father.

II. And if any quarrel arise between a Christian and Ysaac, or any of his children or heirs, he that appeals the other to determine the quarrel shall have witnesses, viz., a lawful Christian and a lawful Jew. And if the aforesaid Ysaac, or his heirs, or his children, have a writ about the quarrel, the writ shall serve them for testimony; and if a Christian have a quarrel against the aforesaid Jews let it be adjudicated by the peers of the Jews.

III. And if any of the aforesaid Jews shall die let not his body be kept above ground, but let his heir have his money and his debts so that he be not disturbed if he has an heir who can answer for him and do right about his debts and his forfeits, and let the aforesaid Jews receive and buy at any time whatever is brought them except things of the church and bloodstained garments.

IV. And if they are appealed by any one without a witness let them be quits of that appeal on their own oath upon their book [of the Law] and let them be quits from an appeal of those things which pertain to our crown on their own oath on their roll [of the Law]. And if there be any dissension between a Christian and any of the aforesaid Jews or their children about the settlement of any money, the Jew shall prove the capital and the Christian the interest.

V. And the aforesaid Jews may sell their pledges without trouble after it is certified that they have held them a year and a day, and they shall not enter into any pleadings except before us or before those who guard our castles in whose bailiwicks they themselves remain wherever they may be.

VI. Let them go whithersoever they will with all their chattels just like our own goods and let no one keep them or prevent them. And if a Christian debtor dies, who owes money to a Jew, and the debtor has an heir, during the minority of the heir let not the Jew be disturbed of his debt unless the land of the heir is in our hands.

VII. And we order that the Jews through all England and Normandy be free of all customs and of tolls and modiation of wine just like our own chattels, and we command and order you to ward and defend and protect them, and we forbid any one against this charter about the aforesaid to put the said Jews into plea on our forfeit.

Witnesses: Will. de Hum.', constable of Normandy, &c., &c. Given by the hand of William de Longchamp, our Chancellor, Bishop of Ely, at Rouen, on the twenty-second day of March, in the first year of our reign.

The legends make William de Longchamp a disagreeable character, though the reality was not much better, for he would willingly descend on a monastery with his entire retinue and stay there until the house could no longer support them before moving on. One of his duties was to approve the new abbot of ST MARY'S ABBEY, but he turned down the choice of the monks there and instead appointed his nephew ROBERT DE LONGCHAMP at the insistence of his cousin Sir ISENBART DE BELAME (a relationship that has no historical foundation if Sir Isenbart is indeed a descendant of Robert de Bellême). Although the legends do not mention any relationship between Robert and William de Longchamp, it seems likely that Sir William was related in some way to Sir ROGER DE LONGCHAMP, whom ROBIN HOOD had killed, this hidden relationship perhaps explaining Sir William's animosity towards the outlaw.

One thing that is certain is that, for all his shortcomings, Sir William de Longchamp was loyal to Richard I, to such an extent that he was forced to flee the country by those who favoured Earl JOHN, though his enemies ranged far and wide and included many of those closest to Richard I himself. However, Sir William returned to England with the king after his release from the castle at Hagenau, and sought any means possible to turn the king against Robin Hood and the outlaws. He almost succeeded when he mentioned that Sir RICHARD AT LEE had deserted his lands and taken to a life in the forests, but HAMELIN, Earl de WARENNE, vociferously defended the actions of the outlaws, much to William de Longchamp's chagrin.

[256–7, 279, 294–5, 303–6, 308–10]

WINDLESWISP MARSH Unidentified marsh in which PETER THE DOCTOR said he wished to bury FRIAR TUCK, whom he did not like after that portly friar had forced him to consume all his own quack medicines.

[115]

WISGAR, ALBERIC DE See ALBERIC DE WISGAR.

WITCHGROVE Alternative name for the HEXGROVE.

[237]

WITCH WOOD Unidentified part of SHERWOOD FOREST, where ROBIN HOOD, in the guise of the Potter of WENTBRIDGE, led the SHERIFF OF NOTTINGHAM into a trap. En route Robin told the sheriff that the Witch Wood was an evil place, the abode of a vile witch who could use her powers to kill any man or imprison him for all time under her spell.

[108–10]

WOODSETT(S) Village (OS120 SK5583) just to the north and west of WORKSOP where Sir RICHARD AT LEE had a hunting lodge, and where he was taken captive by the SHERIFF OF NOTTINGHAM.

[281] {K11}

WOOLGAR Neighbour of THURSTAN, and like him of Danish lineage. When Sir ISENBART DE BELAME unjustly seized the lands of Woolgar and Thurstan, Woolgar was killed as his family were dragged from their home, and Thurstan fled to the forests after his wife and baby were murdered. Woolgar's wife and children became serfs at the EVIL HOLD.

[171]

WORKSOP Market town of north NOTTINGHAMSHIRE (OS120 SK5879) on the River Ryton. The town does not feature widely in the legends of ROBIN HOOD, but as it lies on the edge of CLUMBER FOREST, it must have been visited on more than one occasion by Robin and his men.

[282] {K12}

WRANGBY Village and manor of Sir ISENBART DE BELAME, the castle of Wrangby being widely referred to as the EVIL HOLD, though that term was also applied to the knights who allied themselves with Sir Isenbart. There are numerous mentions of the castle and village, either as Wrangby or as the Evil Hold, throughout the legends of ROBIN HOOD, especially when Robin and his troops stormed and took the castle, hanged Sir Isenbart de Belame and then burnt the castle to the ground.

Though there is no Wrangby to be found on modern maps, there is one possible location for the dreaded Evil Hold. This is the village of Wragby (OS111 SE4117) approximately 5 miles south-east of WAKEFIELD, and today famous as the location of Nostell Priory. This village is a likely contender due to its location and to the fact that there are lakes in the vicinity, one of which might have been called WRANGBY MERE. If Nostell Priory is indeed the location of the Evil Hold, it would seem to suggest that Sir Isenbart de Belame's castle became a priory after the siege. None of this is certain, but Wragby would certainly locate the Evil Hold in the right geographical location for the legends.

[25, 167, 195, 200, 251, 255, 273, 291, 331, 335, 341, 345–60, 363–4, 366–7] {J8}

WRANGBY MERE Lake at WRANGBY beside which stood the MARK OAK, ROBIN HOOD's chosen rallying point for the men he had brought together to storm the EVIL HOLD.

[341]

WROTHSLEY, SIR GUY OF See GUY OF WROTHSLEY, Sir.

YEOMAN Either a member of a middle class of small freeholders who cultivated their own land, or an attendant or lesser official in a royal or noble household. ROBERT OF LOCKSLEY would have been the former, his qualification for the position being his possession of free land of sufficient value.

YORK Cathedral city and administrative centre of YORKSHIRE (OS105 SE6051) which features extensively in the legends of ROBIN HOOD and his band of outlaws.

The Roman name for York was *Eboracum*, which was derived from a native British name for the ancient site. It is thought that the root of the early name was *Eburos*, an Ancient British personal name, which suggests that the site was founded by someone called Eburos. However, the Ancient British word *Eburos* also means yew, a sacred Celtic tree from which the personal name derives. In Roman times there was a Gaulish tribe called the *Eburorovices*, or the 'Warriors of the Yew Tree'.

When the Anglo-Saxons arrived in the north from Germany and Denmark in the sixth century they made *Eboracum* the capital of Deira, a Northumbrian sub-kingdom. *Eboracum* was corrupted by Anglo-Saxon speech into *Eoforwic*, meaning 'wild boar settlement'. The Anglo-Saxons confused the

Clifford's Tower, York, looking east-south-east.
(*Mick Sharp Photography*)

Celtic word *Ebor* meaning yew tree with their own word *Eofor* meaning 'wild boar'.

In AD 865 the Danes captured the north and in 876 Halfdene the Dane made *Eoforwic* the capital of the Viking kingdom of York. Later in 918 a mixed race of Norwegian–Irish Vikings settled at York and for many years the settlement was subordinated to the Viking stronghold at Dublin. Viking influence can still be detected in the street names of York, where the suffix 'gate' – as in Stonegate or Goodramgate – derives from the Old Norse *gata* meaning road or way. Stonegate follows the course of a Roman road through the city, while Goodramgate is named after Guthrum, a Viking leader.

The Vikings interpreted *Eoforwic*, the Anglo-Saxon name for York, as *Jorvik*. In the late Viking period it is thought that the name *Jorvik* was shortened to something resembling its present form, and in the medieval age the name York was generally used, although the form 'Yerk' is also known to have existed at this time. One of the problems of studying York's name is that many early records are written in Latin and thus still use the Roman name *Eboracum* in periods when *Eoforwic* or *Jorvik* were used in everyday speech.

Due to its strategic position on the River Ouse, York was the northern capital of England until the nineteenth century, and a rival in importance to LONDON. York was the home city of the WHITE MONKS of ST MARY'S ABBEY, and thus also of the scheming ABBOT ROBERT. It was to York that Sir HERBRAND DE TRANMIRE travelled in the company of LITTLE JOHN to repay the loan to Abbot Robert, and it was at York that REUBEN OF STAMFORD and his daughter RUTH hid from the slaughter of the Jews led by RICHARD MALBÊTE. The massacre of 150 Jews in York is recorded in 1190, so this part of the legends locates Robin Hood and his followers firmly in the latter part of the twelfth century.

[184, 186, 204, 208, 210–14, 227, 244–5, 294, 322] {L4}

YORK, BISHOP OF The head of the Church in YORK, he appears only once in the legends of ROBIN HOOD when his convoy through the forest on the road between KIRKSTALL and OLLERTON was waylaid by Robin's men. They replenished their stores from the bishop's goods, as well as lightening his coffers into the bargain.

[118]

YORK, SHERIFF OF See SHERIFF OF YORK.

YORK CATHEDRAL York's cathedral, although known as York Minster, is officially the Cathedral and Metropolitical Church of St Peter in York (OS105 SE6052). By definition a cathedral is the site of a bishop's throne (a *cathedra*) but the word cathedral did not come into use until after the Norman conquest. In Anglo-Saxon times important churches were known as minsters, but not all were bishops' seats.

York Minster's history began in AD 627 when King Edwin of Northumbria was baptised in a simple wooden church at York within the site of the old Roman fort. The church was approved by the Pope and its dedication to St Peter reflected its links with Rome. The wooden church was rebuilt in stone and completed by King Oswald but the bishop's seat was transferred for a time to Lindisfarne. The minster was rebuilt in 664 and again after a fire in 741. It was eventually destroyed during the Norman siege of the city in 1069.

The cathedral at York is only mentioned in one brief passage in the legends when the people of York, having massacred the Jews under the direction of RICHARD MALBÊTE, ran there to destroy the Jews' money-lending records and thus free themselves of all obligations.

[213] {L4}

YORKSHIRE Large county in north-east England that features extensively in the legends of ROBIN HOOD. In fact the legends suggest that the outlaw was more active in South Yorkshire than he was in NOTTINGHAMSHIRE, the county most people associate with him and his men.

[247, 391]

PART THREE

He smote Eric full and square on his skull.
Illustration from *Bold Robin Hood and his Outlaw Band* by Louis Read.

Robin Hood, in armour and on horseback, is thanked by the peasants for rescuing them from oppression. Illustration by Walter Crane in *Stories of Robin Hood and His Merry Men* by Henry Gilbert. (*Mary Evans Picture Library/Edwin Wallace*)

SOURCE TEXTS

For a researcher into Robin Hood, whether the legendary character or the 'real' man, the bulk of literature available sometimes makes it difficult to track down the key source texts around which the majority of these works appear to be based, and indeed upon which many of the multitude of early texts have themselves been based. This section is intended to redress that situation, by bringing together all these key source texts in a single reference collection. There are, of course, many other texts that some readers might consider 'essential', but I have had to draw the line somewhere, and my rule of thumb has been the texts I have personally used.

Each text within this small but essential reference library is presented in its original form, or at least as near to its original form as possible. In this way it is hoped that they will foster new research and debate, but if not, at least they should make an enjoyable collection for readers. Many eminent historians have, over many years, written innumerable words on the content of the Robin Hood texts, and it is far beyond the scope of this book to add to these already excellent commentaries, many of which may be found in the books listed in the bibliography at the back of this book. Rather, this section is solely intended to present these texts in the hope that the reader will first and foremost derive some degree of pleasure from them, and second that they may foster in some readers a desire to conduct further research. A glossary of terms can be found at the end of this part.

The texts contained within this section are as follows:

A Gest of Robyn Hode
The Jolly Pinder of Wakefield
Little John Goes a-Begging
Robin Hood and Allin a Dale
Robin Hood and Guy of Gisborne
Robin Hood and Little John
Robin Hood and Maid Marian
Robin Hood and Queen Catherin
Robin Hood and the Bishop
Robin Hood and the Curtal Friar
Robin Hood and the Golden Arrow
Robin Hood and the Monk

Robin Hood and the Pedlars
Robin Hood and the Potter
Robin Hood and Will Scarlet
Robin Hood Rescues Three Young
  Men
Robin Hood's Birth, Breeding, Valour
  and Marriage
Robin Hood's Fishing
Robin Hood's Golden Prize
Robin Hood's Progress to Nottingham
Robyn and Gandelyn
The Death of Robin Hood

There were, of course, other texts that presented themselves as perhaps worthy of inclusion in this section, but upon further deliberation I concluded that they were not 'source' texts but rather texts that owed their existence to one or more of the texts presented here.

A GEST OF ROBYN HODE

This late fourteenth- or early fifteenth-century serial attempts to draw together all the various strands of the legends of Robin Hood current at that time and arrange them in a single narrative. The first printed form of the *Gest* appeared in the mid-sixteenth century and met with such popular acclaim that a dozen more printed editions appeared in the sixteenth and seventeenth centuries.

No single manuscript copy of the work exists, and the best extant text is a set of substantial fragments printed by Jan van Doesbroch in Antwerp around 1510 (formerly called the Lettersnijder edition) and now in the National Library of Scotland, Edinburgh. A second famous early edition was that printed by Wynkyn de Worde, which may have been in print before the Antwerp text.

THE FIRST FYTTE
Lythe and listin, gentilmen,
That be of frebore blode;
I shall you tel of a gode yeman,
His name was Robyn Hode.

5   Robyn was a prude outlaw,
Whyles he walked on grounde:
So curteyse an outlawe as he was one
Was nevere non founde.

Robyn stode in Bernesdale,
10   And lenyd hym to a tre,
And bi hym stode Litell Johnn,
A gode yeman was he.

And alsoo dyd gode Scarlok,
And Much, the millers son:
15   There was none ynch of his bodi
But it was worth a grome.

Than bespake Lytell Johnn
All untoo Robyn Hode:
'Maister, and ye wolde dyne betyme
20   It wolde doo you moche gode.'

The title page of Wynkyn de Worde's edition of *The Lytell Geste of Robin Hode*, Cambridge University Library Ms Sel. 5.18, *c.* 1515. *(By permission of Cambridge University Library)*

Than bespake hym gode Robyn:
'To dyne have I noo lust,
Till that I have som bolde baron,
Or som unkouth gest.

25   'Here shal come a lord or sire
That may pay for the best,
Or som knyght or squyer,
That dwelleth here bi west.'

A gode maner than had Robyn;
30   In londe where that he were,
Every day or he wold dyne
Thre messis wolde he here.

The one in the worship of the Fader,
And another of the Holy Gost,
35   The thirde of Our dere Lady,
That he loved allther moste.

Robyn loved Oure dere Lady:
For dout of dydly synne,
Wolde he never do compani harme
40   That any woman was in.

'Maistar,' than sayde Lytil Johnn,
'And we our borde shal sprede,
Tell us wheder that we shal go,
And what life that we shall lede.

45   'Where we shall take, where we shall leve,
Where we shall abide behynde;
Where we shall robbe, where we shal reve,
Where we shall bete and bynde.'

'Therof no force,' than sayde Robyn;
50   'We shall do well inowe;
But loke ye do no husbonde harme,
That tilleth with his ploughe.

'No more ye shall no gode yeman
That walketh by grene wode shawe,
55   Ne no knyght ne no squyer
That wol be a gode felawe.

The four yeomen have merry sport with a stout miller. Illustration from *The Merry Adventures of Robin Hood* by Howard Pyle.

'These bisshoppes and these archebishoppes,
Ye shall them bete and bynde;
The hye sherif of Notyingham,
60   Hym holde ye in your mynde.'

'This worde shalbe holde,' sayde Lytell Johnn,
'And this lesson we shall lere;
It is fer dayes, God sende us a gest,
That we were at oure dynere!'

65   'Take thy gode bowe in thy honde,' sayde Robyn;
'Late Much wende with the:
And so shal Willyam Scarlok,
And no man abyde with me.

'And walke up to the Saylis,
70   And so to Watlinge Strete,
And wayte after some unkuth gest,
Up chaunce ye may them mete.

'Be he erle, or ani baron,
Abbot, or ani knyght,
75   Bringhe hym to lodge to me;
His dyner shall be dight.'

They wente up to the Saylis,
These yeman all thre;
They loked est, they loke weest;
80   They myght no man see.

But as they loked in to Bernysdale,
Bi a derne strete,
Than came a knyght ridinghe,
Full sone they gan hym mete.

85   All dreri was his semblaunce,
And lytell was his pryde;
His one fote in the styrop stode,
That othere wavyd beside.

His hode hanged in his iyn two;
90   He rode in symple aray,
A soriar man than he was one
Rode never in somer day.

Little John in the guise of a friar stops three lasses.
Illustration from *The Merry Adventures of Robin Hood* by Howard Pyle.

Litell Johnn was full curteyes,
And sette hym on his kne:
95 'Welcom be ye, gentyll knyght,
Welcom ar ye to me.

'Welcom be thou to grene wode,
Hende knyght and fre;
My maister hath abiden you fastinge,
100 Syr, al these oures thre.'

'Who is thy maister?' sayde the knyght;
Johnn sayde, 'Robyn Hode.'
'He is gode yoman,' sayde the knyght,
'Of hym I have herde moche gode.

105 'I graunte,' he sayde, 'with you to wende,
My bretherne, all in fere;
My purpos was to have dyned to day
At Blith or Dancastere.'

Furth than went this gentyl knight,
110 With a carefull chere;
The teris oute of his iyen ran,
And fell downe by his lere.

They brought hym to the lodge door,
Whan Robyn hym gan see,
115 Full curtesly dyd of his hode
And sette hym on his knee.

'Welcome, sir knight,' than sayde Robyn,
'Welcome art thou to me;
I have abyden you fastinge, sir,
120 All these ouris thre.'

Than answered the gentyll knight,
With wordes fayre and fre:
'God the save, goode Robyn,
And all thy fayre meyné.'

125 They wasshed togeder and wyped bothe,
And sette to theyr dynere;
Brede and wyne they had right ynoughe,
And noumbles of the dere.

Swannes and fessauntes they had full gode,
130 And foules of the ryvere;
There fayled none so litell a birde
That ever was bred on bryre.

'Do gladly, sir knight,' sayde Robyn;
'Gramarcy, sir,' sayde he,
135 'Such a dinere had I nat
Of all these wekys thre.

'If I come ageyne, Robyn,
Here by thys contré,
As gode a dyner I shall the make
140 As that thou haest made to me.'

'Gramarcy, knyght,' sayde Robyn,
'My dyner whan that I it have;
I was never so gredy, bi dere worthy God,
My dyner for to crave.

145 'But pay or ye wende,' sayde Robyn;
'Me thynketh it is gode ryght;
It was never the maner, by dere worthi God,
A yoman to pay for a knyght.'

'I have nought in my coffers,' saide the knyght,
150 'That I may profer for shame.'
'Litell Johnn, go loke,' sayde Robyn,
'Ne let nat for no blame.

'Tel me truth,' than saide Robyn,
'So God have parte of the.'
155 'I have no more but ten shelynges,' sayde the knyght,
'So God have part of me.'

'If thou hast no more,' sayde Robyn,
'I woll nat one peny,
And yf thou have nede of any more,
160 More shall I lend the.

'Go nowe furth, Littell Johnn,
The truth tell thou me:
If there be no more but ten shelinges,
No peny that I se.'

165   Lyttell Johnn sprede downe hys mantell
      Full fayre upon the grounde,
      And there he fonde in the knyghtes cofer
      But even halfe pounde.

      Littell Johnn let it lye full styll,
170   And went to hys maysteer lowe;
      'What tidynges Johnn?' sayde Robyn;
      'Sir, the knyght is true inowe.'

      'Fyll of the best wine,' sayde Robyn,
      'The knyght shall begynne;
175   Moche wonder thinketh me
      Thy clothynge is so thin.

      'Tell me one worde,' sayde Robyn,
      'And counsel shal it be:
      I trowe thou warte made a knyght of force,
180   Or ellys of yemanry.

      'Or ellys thou hast bene a sori husbande,
      And lyved in stroke and stryfe,
      An okerer or ellis a lechoure,' sayde Robyn,
      'Wyth wronge hast led thy lyfe.'

185   'I am none of those,' sayde the knyght,
      'By God that made me;
      An hundred wynter here before
      Myn auncetres knyghtes have be.

      'But oft it hath befal, Robyn,
190   A man hath be disgrate,
      But God that sitteth in heven above
      May amende his state.

      'Withyn this two yere, Robyne,' he sayde,
      'My neghbours well it wende,
195   Foure hundred pounde of gode money
      Ful well than myght I spende.

      'Nowe have I no gode,' saide the knyght,
      'God hath shaped such an ende,
      But my chyldren and my wyfe,
200   Tyll God yt may amende.'

'In what maner,' than sayde Robyn,
'Hast thou lorne thy rychesse?'
'For my greate foly,' he sayde,
'And for my kyndnesse.

205   'I hade a sone, forsoth, Robyn,
That shulde have ben myn ayre,
Whanne he was twenty wynter olde,
In felde wolde just full fayre.

'He slewe a knyght of Lancaster,
210   And a squyer bolde;
For to save hym in his ryght
My godes beth sette and solde.

'My londes beth sette to wedde, Robyn,
Untyll a certayn day,
215   To a ryche abbot here besyde
Of Seynt Mari Abbey.'

'What is the som?' sayde Robyn;
'Trouth than tell thou me.'
'Sir,' he sayde, 'foure hundred pounde;
220   The abbot told it to me.'

'Nowe and thou lese thy lond,' sayde Robyn,
'What woll fall of the?'
'Hastely I wol me buske,' sayde the knyght,
'Over the salte see,

225   'And se where Criste was quyke and dede,
On the mount of Calveré;
Fare wel, frende, and have gode day;
It may no better be.'

Teris fell out of hys iyen two;
230   He wolde have gone hys way.
'Farewel, frende, and have gode day;
I ne have no more to pay.'

'Where be thy frendes?' sayde Robyn.
'Syr, never one wol me knowe:
235   While I was ryche ynowe at home
Great boste than wolde they blowe.

'And nowe they renne away fro me,
As bestis on a rowe;
They take no more hede of me
240   Thanne they had me never sawe.'

For ruthe thanne wept Litell Johnn,
Scarlok and Muche in fere;
'Fyl of the best wyne,' sayde Robyn,
'For here is a symple chere.

245   'Hast thou any frende,' sayde Robyn,
'Thy borowe that wolde be?'
'I have none,' than sayde the knyght,
'But God that dyed on tree.'

'Do away thy japis,' than sayde Robyn,
250   'Thereof wol I right none;
Wenest thou I wolde have God to borowe,
Peter, Poule, or Johnn?

'Nay, by Hym that me made,
And shope both sonne and mone,
255   Fynde me a better borowe,' sayde Robyn,
'Or money getest thou none.'

'I have none other,' sayde the knyght,
'The sothe for to say,
But yf yt be Our dere Lady;
260   She fayled me never or thys day.'

'By dere worthy God,' sayde Robyn,
'To seche all Englonde thorowe,
Yet fonde I never to my pay
A moche better borowe.

265   'Come nowe furth, Litell Johnn.
And go to my tresouré,
And bringe me foure hundered pound,
And loke well tolde it be.'

Furth than went Litell Johnn,
270   And Scarlok went before;
He tolde oute foure hundred pounde
By eightene and two score.

'Here's money enough master,' quoth little
John, 'to pay the reckoning.' Illustration from
Bold Robin Hood and his Outlaw Band by
Louis Read.

'Is thys well tolde?' sayde litell Much;
Johnn sayde, 'What greveth the?
275   It is almus to helpe a gentyll knyght,
That is fal in poverté.

'Master,' than sayde Lityll John,
'His clothinge is full thynne;
Ye must gyve the knight a lyveray,
280   To lappe his body therin.

'For ye have scarlet and grene, mayster,
And many a riche aray;
Ther is no marchaunt in mery Englond
So ryche, I dare well say.'

285   'Take hym thre yerdes of every colour,
And loke well mete that it be.'
Lytell Johnn toke none other mesure
But his bowe-tree.

And at every handfull that he met
290   He leped footes three.
'What devylles drapar,' sayid litell Muche,
'Thynkest thou for to be?'

Scarlok stode full stil and loughe,
And sayd, 'By God Almyght,
295   Johnn may gyve hym gode mesure,
For it costeth hym but lyght.'

'Mayster,' than said Litell Johnn
To gentill Robyn Hode,
'Ye must give the knight a hors,
300   To lede home this gode.'

'Take hym a gray coursar,' sayde Robyn,
'And a saydle newe;
He is Oure Ladye's messangere;
God graunt that he be true.'

305   'And a gode palfray,' sayde lytell Much,
'To mayntene hym in his right.'
'And a peyre of botes,' sayde Scarlock,
'For he is a gentyll knight.'

'What shalt thou gyve hym, Litell John?' said Robyn;
310 'Sir, a peyre of gilt sporis clene,
To pray, for all this company,
God bringe hym oute of tene.'

'Whan shal mi day be,' said the knight,
'Sir, and your wyll be?'
315 'This day twelve moneth,' saide Robyn,
'Under this grene-wode tre.

'It were greate shame,' sayde Robyn,
'A knight alone to ryde,
Withoute squyre, yoman, or page,
320 To walke by his syde.

'I shall the lende Litell John, my man,
For he shalbe thy knave;
In a yemans stede he may the stande,
If thou greate nede have.'

THE SECONDE FYTTE
325 Now is the knight gone on his way:
This game hym thought full gode;
Whanne he loked on Bernesdale
He blessyd Robyn Hode.

And whanne he thought on Bernysdale,
330 On Scarlok, Much, and Johnn,
He blyssyd them for the best company
That ever he in come.

Then spake that gentyll knyght,
To Lytel Johan gan he saye,
335 'To-morrowe I must to Yorke toune,
To Saynt Mary abbay.

'And to the abbot of that place
Foure hondred pounde I must pay;
And but I be there upon this nyght
340 My londe is lost for ay.'

The abbot sayd to his covent,
There he stode on grounde,
'This day twelfe moneth came there a knyght
And borrowed foure hondred pounde.

Little John knoweth not which road to take. Illustration from *The Merry Adventures of Robin Hood* by Howard Pyle.

345   'He borrowed foure hondred pounde,
        Upon all his londe fre;
        But he come this ylke day
        Dysheryte shall he be.'

        'It is full erely,' sayd the pryoure,
350   'The day is not yet ferre gone;
        I had lever to pay an hondred pounde,
        And lay downe anone.

        'The knyght is ferre beyonde the see,
        In Englonde ryght,
355   And suffreth honger and colde,
        And many a sory nyght.

        'It were grete pyté,' said the pryoure,
        'So to have his londe;
        And ye be so lyght of your consyence,
360   Ye do to hym moch wronge.'

        'Thou arte ever in my berde,' sayd the abbot,
        'By God and Saynt Rychere.'
        With that cam in a fat-heded monke,
        The heygh selerer.

365   'He is dede or hanged,' sayd the monke,
        'By God that bought me dere,
        And we shall have to spende in this place
        Foure hondred pounde by yere.'

        The abbot and the hy selerer
370   Sterte forthe full bolde,
        The justyce of Englonde
        The abbot there dyde holde.

The hye justyce and many mo
Had take in to theyr honde
375   Holy all the knyghtes det,
To put that knyght to wronge.

They demed the knyght wonder sore,
The abbot and his meyné:
'But he come this ylke day
380   Dysheryte shall he be.'

'He wyll not come yet,' sayd the justyce,
'I dare well undertake.'
But in sorowe tyme for them all
The knyght came to the gate.

385   Than bespake that gentyll knyght
Untyll his meyné:
'Now put on your symple wedes
That ye brought fro the see.'

They put on their symple wedes,
390   They came to the gates anone;
The porter was redy hymselfe,
And welcomed them everychone.

'Welcome, syr knyght,' sayd the porter;
'My lorde to mete is he,
395   And so is many a gentyll man,
For the love of the.'

The porter swore a full grete othe,
'By God that made me,
Here be the best coressed hors
400   That ever yet sawe I me.

'Lede them in to the stable,' he sayd,
'That eased myght they be.'
'They shall not come therin,' sayd the knyght,
'By God that dyed on a tre.'

405   Lordes were to mete isette
In that abbotes hall;
The knyght went forth and kneled downe,
And salued them grete and small.

'Do gladly, syr abbot,' sayd the knyght,
410 'I am come to holde my day.'
The fyrst word the abbot spake,
'Hast thou brought my pay?'

'Not one peny,' sayd the knyght,
'By God that maked me.'
415 'Thou art a shrewed dettour' sayd the abbot;
'Syr justyce, drynke to me.

'What doost thou here,' sayd the abbot,
'But thou haddest brought thy pay?'
'For God,' than sayd the knyght,
420 'To pray of a lenger daye.'

'Thy daye is broke,' sayd the justyce,
'Londe getest thou none.'
'Now, good syr justyce, be my frende,
And fende me of my fone!'

'I come to pray thee that thou wilt give me a little time of grace.' Illustration from *Bold Robin Hood and his Outlaw Band* by Louis Read.

425 'I am holde with the abbot,' sayd the justyce,
'Both with cloth and fee.'
'Now, good syr sheryf, be my frende!'
'Nay, for God,' sayd he.

'Now, good syr abbot, be my frende,
430 For thy curteysé,
And holde my londes in thy honde
Tyll I have made the gree!

'And I wyll be thy true servaunte,
And trewely serve the,
435 Tyl ye have foure hondred pounde
Of money good and free.'

The abbot sware a full grete othe,
'By God that dyed on a tree,
Get the londe where thou may,
440 For thou getest none of me.'

'By dere worthy God,' then sayd the knyght,
'That all this worlde wrought,
But I have my londe agayne,
Full dere it shall be bought.

445 'God, that was of a mayden borne,
Leve us well to spede!
For it is good to assay a frende
Or that a man have need.'

The abbot lothely on hym gan loke,
450 And vylaynesly hym gan call:
'Out,' he sayd, 'thou false knyght,
Spede the out of my hall!'

'Thou lyest,' then sayd the gentyll knyght,
'Abbot, in thy hall;
455 False knyght was I never,
By God that made us all.'

Up then stode that gentyll knyght,
To the abbot sayd he,
'To suffre a knyght to knele so longe,
460 Thou canst no curteysye.

'In joustes and in tournement
Full ferre than have I be,
And put my selfe as ferre in press
As ony that ever I se.'

465 'What wyll ye gyve more,' sayd the justice,
'And the knyght shall make a releyse?
And elles dare I safly swere
Ye holde never your londe in pees.'

'An hondred pounde,' sayd the abbot;
470 The justice sayd, 'Gyve hym two.'
'Nay, be God,' sayd the knyght,
'Yit gete ye it not so.'

'Though ye wolde gyve a thousand more,
Yet were ye never the nere;
475 Shall there never be myn heyre
Abbot, justice, ne frere.'

He stert hym to a borde anone,
Tyll a table rounde,
And there shoke oute of a bagge
480 Even four hundred pound.

'Have here thi golde, sir abbot,' saide the knight,
'Which that thou lentest me;
Had thou ben curtes at my comynge,
Rewarded shuldest thou have be.'

485 The abbot sat styll, and ete no more,
For all his ryall fare;
He cast his hede on his shulder,
And fast began to stare.

'Take me my golde agayne,' saide the abbot,
490 'Sir justice, that I toke the.'
'Not a peni,' said the justice,
'Bi God that dyed on tree.'

'Sir abbot and ye men of lawe,
Now have I holde my daye;
495 Now shall I have my londe agayne,
For ought that you can saye.'

The knyght stert out of the dore,
Awaye was all his care,
And on he put his good clothynge,
500   The other he lefte there.

He wente hym forth full mery syngynge,
As men have tolde in tale;
His lady met hym at the gate,
At home in Verysdale.

505   'Welcome, my lorde,' sayd his lady;
'Syr, lost is all your good?'
'Be mery, dame,' sayd the knyght,
'And pray for Robyn Hode,

'That ever his soule be in blysse:
510   He holpe me out of tene;
Ne had be his kyndenesse,
Beggers had we bene.

'The abbot and I accorded ben,
He is served of his pay;
515   The god yoman lent it me,
As I cam by the way.'

This knight than dwelled fayre at home,
The sothe for to saye.
Tyll he had gete four hundred pound,
520   Al redy for to pay.

He purveyed him an hundred bowes,
The strynges well ydyght,
An hundred shefe of arowes gode,
The hedys burneshed full bryght;

525   And every arowe an elle longe,
With pecok wel idyght,
Inocked all with whyte silver;
It was a semely syght.

He purveyed hym an hundreth men,
530   Well harnessed in that stede.
And hym selfe in that same sete,
And clothed in whyte and rede.

He bare a launsgay in his honde,
And a man ledde his male,
535   And reden with a lyght songe
Unto Bernsydale.

But at Wentbrydge ther was a wrastelyng,
And there taryed was he,
And there was all the best yemen
540   Of all the west countree.

A full fayre game there was up set,
A whyte bulle up i-pyght,
A grete courser, with sadle and brydil,
With golde burnyssht full bryght.

545   A payre of gloves, a rede golde rynge,
A pype of wyne, in fay;
What man that bereth hym best i-wys
The pryce shall bere away.

There was a yoman in that place,
550   And best worthy was he,
And for he was ferre and frembde bested,
Slayne he shulde have be.

The knight had ruthe of this yoman,
In place where he stode;
555   He sayde that yoman shulde have no harme,
For love of Robyn Hode.

The knyght presed in to the place,
An hundreth folowed hym in fere,
With bowes bent and arowes sharpe,
560   For to shende that companye.

They shulderd all and made hym rome,
To wete what he wolde say;
He toke the yeman bi the hande,
And gave hym al the play.

565   He gave hym fyve marke for his wyne,
There it lay on the molde,
And bad it shulde be set a broche,
Drynke who so wolde.

Thus longe taried this gentyll knyght,
570 Tyll that play was done;
So longe abode Robyn fastinge,
Thre houres after the none.

THE THIRDE FYTTE
Lyth and lystyn, gentilmen,
All that nowe be here,
575 Of Litell Johnn, that was the knightes man,
Goode myrth ye shall here.

It was upon a mery day
That yonge men wolde go shete,
Lytell Johnn fet his bowe anone,
580 And sayde he wolde them mete.

Thre tymes Litell Johnn shet aboute,
And alwey he slet the wande:
The proude sherif of Notingham
By the markes can stande.

585 The sherif swore a full great othe:
'By Hym that dyede on a tre,
This man is the best arschere
That ever yet sawe I me.

'Say me nowe, wight yonge man,
590 What is nowe thy name?
In what countré were thou borne,
And where is thy wonynge wane?'

'In Holdernes, sir, I was borne,
Iwys al of my dame;
595 Men cal me Reynolde Grenelef
Whan I am at hame.'

'Sey me, Reynolde Grenelefe,
Wolde thou dwell with me?
And every yere I woll the gyve
600 Twenty marke to thy fee.'

'I have a maister,' sayde Litell Johnn,
'A curteys knight is he;
May ye leve gete of hym,
The better may it be.'

'My freedom have I won through my staff, and not by grace of thee.' Illustration from *Bold Robin Hood and his Outlaw Band* by Louis Read.

249

605 The sherif gate Litell John
Twelve monethes of the knight;
Therefore he gave him right anone
A gode hors and a wight.

Nowe is Litell John the sherifes man
610 God lende us well to spede!
But alwey thought Lytell John
To quyte hym wele his mede.

'Nowe so God me helpe,' sayde Litell John,
'And by my true leutye,
615 I shall be the worst servaunt to hym
That ever yet had he.'

It fell upon a Wednesday
The sherif on huntynge was gone,
And Litel John lay in his bed,
620 And was foriete at home.

Therefore he was fastinge
Til it was past the none.
'God sir stuarde, I pray to the,
Gyve me my dynere,' saide Litell John.

625 'It is longe for Grenelefe
Fastinge thus for to be;
Therfor I pray the, sir stuarde,
Mi dyner gif thou me.'

'Shalt thou never ete ne drynke,' saide the stuarde,
630 'Tyll my lorde be come to towne.'
'I make myn avowe to God,' saide Litell John,
'I had lever to crake thy crowne.'

The boteler was full uncurteys,
There he stode on flore;
635 He start to the botery
And shet fast the dore.

Lytell Johnn gave the boteler suche a tap
His backe were nere in two;
Though he lived an hundred ier,
640 The wors shuld he go.

He sporned the dore with his fote,
It went open wel and fyne,
And there he made large lyveray,
Bothe of ale and of wyne.

645 'Sith ye wol nat dyne,' sayde Litell John,
'I shall gyve you to drinke,
And though ye lyve an hundred wynter,
On Lytel Johnn ye shall thinke.'

Litell John ete, and Litel John drank,
650 The while that he wolde;
The sherife had in his kechyn a coke,
A stoute man and a bolde.

'I make myn avowe to God,' saide the coke,
'Thou arte a shrewde hynde
655 In ani hous for to dwel,
For to aske thus to dyne.'

And there he lent Litell John
God strokis thre;
'I make myn avowe to God,' sayde Lytell John,
660 'These strokis lyked well me.

'Thou arte a bolde man and hardy,
And so thinketh me;
And or I pas fro this place
Assayed better shalt thou be.'

665 Lytell Johnn drew a ful gode sworde,
The coke toke another in hande;
They thought no thynge for to fle,
But stifly for to stande.

There they faught sore togedere
670 Two myle way and well more;
Myght neyther other harme done,
The mountnaunce of an owre.

'I make myn avowe to God,' sayde Litell Johnn,
'And by my true lewté,
Thou art one of the best swordemen
675 That ever yit sawe I me.

Little John overcomes Eric o'Lincoln.
Illustration from *The Merry Adventures of Robin Hood* by Howard Pyle.

'Cowdest thou shote as well in a bowe,
To grene wode thou shuldest with me,
And two times in the yere thy clothinge
680   Chaunged shulde be,

'And every yere of Robyn Hode
Twenty merke to thy fe.'
'Put up thy swerde,' saide the coke,
'And felowes woll we be.'

685   Thanne he fet to Lytell Johnn,
The nowmbles of a do,
Gode brede, and full gode wyne;
They ete and drank theretoo.

And when they had dronkyn well,
690   Theyre trouthes togeder they plight,
That they wolde be with Robyn
That ylke same nyght.

They dyd them to the tresoure hows,
As fast as they myght gone;
695   The lokkes, that were of full gode stele,
They brake them everichone.

They toke away the silver vessell,
And all that thei might get;
Pecis, masars, ne sponis,
700   Wolde thei not forget.

Also they toke the gode pens,
Three hundred pounde and more,
And did them streyte to Robyn Hode,
Under the grene wode hore.

705   'God the save, my dere mayster,
And Criste the save and se!'
And thanne sayde Robyn to Litell Johnn,
'Welcome myght thou be.'

'Also be that fayre yeman
710   Thou bryngest there with the;
What tydynges fro Notyngham?
Lytill Johnn, tell thou me.'

'Well the gretith the proude sheryf,
And sende the here by me
715   His coke and his silver vessell,
And thre hundred pounde and thre.'

'I make myne avowe to God,' sayde Robyn,
'And to the Trenyté,
It was never by his gode wyll
720   This gode is come to me.'

Lytyll Johnn there hym bethought
On a shrewde wyle;
Fyve myle in the forest he ran;
Hym happed all his wyll.

725   Than he met the proude sheref,
Huntynge with houndes and horne;
Lytell Johnn coude of curtesye,
And knelyd hym beforne.

'God the save, my dere mayster,
730   And Criste the save and se!'
'Reynolde Grenelefe,' sayde the shyref,
'Where hast thou nowe be?'

'I have be in this forest;
A fayre syght can I se;
735   It was one of the fayrest syghtes
That ever yet sawe I me.

'Yonder I sawe a ryght fayre harte,
His coloure is of grene;
Seven score of dere upon a herde
740   Be with hym all bydene.

'Their tyndes are so sharpe, maister,
Of sexty, and well mo,
That I durst not shote for drede,
Lest they wolde me slo.'

745   'I make myn avowe to God,' sayde the shyref,
'That syght wolde I fayne se.'
'Buske you thyderwarde, mi dere mayster,
Anone, and wende with me.'

The first encounter between Robin Hood and Little John. Illustration by Walter Crane in *Stories of Robin Hood and His Merry Men* by Henry Gilbert. (*Mary Evans Picture Library/Edwin Wallace*)

The sherif rode, and Litell Johnn
750   Of fote he was full smerte,
And whane they came before Robyn,
'Lo, sir, here is the mayster-herte.'

Still stode the proude sherief,
A sory man was he;
755   'Wo the worthe, Raynolde Grenelefe,
Thou hast betrayed nowe me.'

'I make myn avowe to God,' sayde Litell Johnn,
'Mayster, ye be to blame;
I was mysserved of my dynere
760   Whan I was with you at home.'

Sone he was to souper sette,
And served well with silver white,
And whan the sherif sawe his vessell,
For sorowe he myght nat ete.

765   'Make glad chere,' sayde Robyn Hode,
'Sherif, for charité,
And for the love of Litill Johnn
Thy lyfe I graunt to the.'

Whan they had souped well,
770   The day was al gone;
Robyn commaunded Litell Johnn
To drawe of his hosen and his shone,

His kirtell, and his cote of pie,
That was fured well and fine,
775   And toke hym a grene mantel,
To lap his body therin.

Robyn commaundyd his wight yonge men,
Under the grene wode tree,
They shulde lye in that same sute,
780   That the sherif myght them see.

All nyght lay the proude sherif
In his breche and in his schert;
No wonder it was, in grene wode,
Though his sydes gan to smerte.

785 'Make glade chere,' sayde Robyn Hode,
'Sheref, for charité,
For this is our ordre iwys,
Under the grene wode tree.'

'This is harder order,' sayde the sherief,
790 'Than any ankir or frere;
For all the golde in mery Englonde
I wolde nat longe dwell her.'

'All this twelve monthes,' sayde Robyn,
'Thou shalt dwell with me;
795 I shall the teche, proude sherif,
An outlawe for to be.'

'Or I be here another nyght,' sayde the sherif,
'Robyn, nowe pray I the,
Smythe of mijn hede rather to-morowe,
800 And I forgyve it the.

'Lat me go,' than sayde the sherif,
'For saynte charité,
And I woll be thy best frende
That ever yet had ye.'

805 'Thou shalt swere me an othe,' sayde Robyn,
'On my bright bronde:
Shalt thou never awayte me scathe,
By water ne by lande.'

'And if thou fynde any of my men,
810 By nyght or day,
Upon thyn othe thou shalt swere
To helpe them that thou may.'

Now hathe the sherif sworne his othe,
And home he began to gone;
815 He was as full of grene wode
As ever was hepe of stone.

THE FOURTH FYTTE
The sherif dwelled in Notingham
He was fayne he was agone,
And Robyn and his mery men
820 Went to wode anone.

'Go we to dyner,' sayde Littell Johnn,
Robyn Hode sayde, 'Nay,
For I drede Our Lady be wroth with me,
For she sent me nat my pay.'

825   'Have no doute, maister,' sayde Litell Johnn,
'Yet is nat the sonne at rest;
For I dare say, and savely swere,
The knight is true and truste.'

'Take thy bowe in thy hande,' sayde Robyn,
830   'Late Much wende with the,
And so shal Wyllyam Scarlok,
And no man abyde with me.

'And walke up under the Sayles,
And to Watlynge-strete,
835   And wayte after such unketh gest;
Up-chaunce ye may them mete.

'Whether he be messengere,
Or a man that myrthes can,
Of my good he shall have some,
840   Yf he be a pore man.'

Forth then stert Lytel Johan,
Half in tray and tene,
And gyrde hym with a full good swerde,
Under a mantel of grene.

845   They went up to the Sayles,
These yemen all thre;
They loked est, they loked west,
They myght no man se.

But as they loked in Bernysdale,
850   By the hye waye,
Than were they ware of two blacke monkes,
Eche on a good palferay.

Then bespake Lytell Johan,
To Much he gan say,
855   'I dare lay my lyfe to wedde,
The monkes have brought our pay.

'Make glad chere,' sayd Lytell Johan,
'And drese our bowes of ewe,
And loke your hertes be seker and sad,
860   Your strynges trusty and trewe.

'The monke hath two and fifty
And seven somers full stronge;
There rydeth no bysshop in this londe
So ryally, I understond.

865   'Brethern,' sayd Lytell Johan,
'Here are no more but we thre;
But we brynge them to dyner,
Our mayster dare we not se.

'Bende your bowes,' sayd Lytell Johan,
870   'Make all yon prese to stonde;
The formost monke, his lyfe and his deth,
Is closed in my honde.

'Abyde, chorle monke,' sayd Lytell Johan,
'No ferther that thou gone;
875   Yf thou doost, by dere worthy God,
Thy deth is in my honde.

'And evyll thryfte on thy hede,' sayd Litell Johan,
'Ryght under thy hattes bonde,
For thou hast made our mayster wroth,
880   He is fastynge so longe.'

'Who is your mayster?' sayd the monke;
Lytell Johan sayd, 'Robyn Hode.'
'He is a stronge thefe,' sayd the monke,
'Of hym herd I never good.'

885   'Thou lyest,' than sayd Lytell Johan,
'And that shall rewe the;
He is a yeman of the forest,
To dyne he hath bode the.'

Much was redy with a bolte,
890   Redly and anone;
He set the monke to-fore the brest,
To the grounde that he can gone.

Of two and fyfty wyght yonge yemen
There abode not one,
895   Saf a lytell page and a grome,
To lede the somers with Lytel Johan.

They brought the monke to the lodge dore,
Whether he were loth or lefe,
For to speke with Robyn Hode,
900   Maugré in theyr tethe.

Robyn dyde adowne his hode,
The monke whan that he se;
The monke was not so curteyse,
His hode then let he be.

905   'He is a chorle, mayster, by dere worthy God,'
Than sayd Lytell Johan.
'Thereof no force,' sayd Robyn,
'For curteysy can he none.

'How many men,' sayd Robyn,
910   'Had this monke, Johan?'
'Fyfty and two whan that we met,
But many of them be gone.'

'Let blowe a horne,' sayd Robyn,
'That felaushyp may us knowe.'
915   Seven score of wyght yemen
Came pryckynge on a rowe.

And everych of them a good mantell
Of scarlet and of raye,
All they came to good Robyn,
920   To wyte what he wolde say.

They made the monke to wasshe and wype,
And syt at his denere,
Robyn Hode and Lytell Johan
They served him both in fere.

925   'Do gladly, monke,' sayd Robyn.
'Gramercy, syr,' sayd he.
'Where is your abbay, whan ye are at home,
And who is your avowé?'

'Saynt Mary abbay,' sayd the monke,
930   'Though I be symple here.'
'In what offyce?' sayd Robyn,
'Syr, the hye selerer.'

'Ye be the more welcome,' sayd Robyn,
'So ever mote I the.
935   Fyll of the best wyne,' sayd Robyn,
'This monke shall drynke to me.

'But I have grete mervayle,' sayd Robyn,
'Of all this longe day,
I drede Our Lady be wroth with me,
940   She sent me not my pay.'

'Have no doute, mayster,' sayd Lytell Johan,
'Ye have no nede, I saye;
This monke it hath brought, I dare well swere,
For he is of her abbay.'

945   'And she was a borowe,' sayd Robyn,
'Betwene a knyght and me,
Of a lytell money that I hym lent,
Under the grene wode tree.

'And yf thou hast that sylver i-brought,
950   I pray the let me se,
And I shall helpe the eftsones,
Yf thou have nede to me.'

The monke swore a full grete othe,
With a sory chere,
955   'Of the borowehode thou spekest to me,
Herde I never ere.'

'I make myn avowe to God,' sayd Robyn,
'Monke, thou art to blame,
For God is holde a ryghtwys man,
960   And so is His dame.

'Thou toldest with thyn owne tonge,
Thou may not say nay,
How thou arte her servaunt,
And servest her every day.

965 'And thou art made her messengere,
 My money for to pay;
 Therfore I cun the more thanke
 Thou arte come at thy day.

 'What is in your cofers?' sayd Robyn,
970 'Trewe than tell thou me.'
 'Syr,' he sayd, 'twenty marke,
 Al so mote I the.'

 'Yf there be no more,' sayd Robyn,
 'I wyll not one peny;
975 Yf thou hast myster of ony more,
 Syr, more I shall lende to the.

 'And yf I fynde more,' sayd Robyn,
 'Iwys thou shalte it for gone,
 For of thy spendynge sylver, monke,
980 Thereof wyll I ryght none.

 'Go nowe forthe, Lytell Johan,
 And the trouth tell thou me;
 If there be no more but twenty marke,
 No peny that I se.'

985 Lytell Johan spred his mantell downe,
 As he had done before,
 And he tolde out of the monkes male
 Eyght hundred pounde and more.

 Lytell Johan let it lye full styll,
990 And went to his mayster in hast.
 'Syr,' he sayd, 'the monke is trewe ynowe,
 Out Lady hath doubled your cast.'

 'I make myn avowe to God,' sayd Robyn,
 'Monke, what tolde I the?
995 Our Lady is the trewest woman
 That ever yet founde I me.

 'By dere worthy God,' sayd Robyn,
 'To seche all Englond thorowe,
 Yet founde I never to my pay
1000 A moche better borowe.

'Fyll of the best wyne, and do hym drynke,' sayd Robyn,
'And grete well thy lady hende,
And yf she have nede to Robyn Hode,
A frende she shall hym fynde.

1005   'And yf she nedeth ony more sylver,
Come thou agayne to me,
And, by this token she hath me sent,
She shall have such thre.'

The monke was goynge to London-ward,
1010   There to holde grete mote,
The knyght that rode so hye on hors,
To brynge hym under fote.

'Whether be ye away?' sayd Robyn.
'Syr, to maners in this londe,
1015   Too reken with our reves,
That have done moch wronge.

'Come now forth, Lytell Johan,
And harken to my tale;
A better yeman I knowe none,
1020   To seke a monkes male.

Illustration from *The Merry Adventures of Robin Hood* by Howard Pyle.

'How moch is in yonder other corser?' sayd Robyn,
'The soth must we see.'
'By Our Lady,' than sayd the monke,
'That were no curteysye,

1025 'To bydde a man to dyner,
And syth hym bete and bynde.'
'It is our olde maner,' sayd Robyn,
'To leve but lytell behynde.'

The monke toke the hors with spore,
1030 No lenger wolde he abyde:
'Aske to drynke,' than sayd Robyn,
'Or that ye forther ryde.'

'Nay, for God,' than sayd the monke,
'Me reweth I cam so nere;
1035 For better chepe I myght have dyned
In Blythe or in Dankestere.'

'Grete well your abbot,' sayd Robyn,
'And your pryour, I you pray,
And byd hym send me such a monke
1040 To dyner every day.'

Now lete we that monke be styll,
And speke we of that knyght:
Yet he came to holde his day,
Whyle that it was lyght.

1045 He dyde him streyt to Bernysdale,
Under the grene wode tre,
And he founde there Robyn Hode,
And all the mery meyné.

The knyght lyght doune of his good palfray;
1050 Robyn whan he gan see,
So curteysly he dyde adoune his hode,
And set hym on his knee.

'God the save, Robyn Hode,
And all this company.'
1055 'Welcome be thou, gentyll knyght,
And ryght welcome to me.'

Than bespake hym Robyn Hode,
To that knyght so fre:
'What nede dryveth the to grene wode?
1060 I praye the, syr knyght, tell me.

'And welcome be thou, gentyll knyght,
Why hast thou be so longe?'
'For the abbot and the hye justyce
Wolde have had my londe.'

1065 'Hast thou thy londe agayne?' sayd Robyn;
'Treuth than tell thou me.'
'Ye, for God,' sayd the knyght,
'And that thanke I God and the.

'But take not a grefe, that I have be
    so longe;
1070 I came by a wrastelynge,
And there I holpe a pore yeman,
With wronge was put behynde.'

'Nay, for God,' sayd Robyn,
'Syr knyght, that thanke I the;
1075 What man that helpeth a good yeman,
His frende than wyll I be.'

'Have here foure hondred pounde,'
    than sayd the knyght,
'The whiche ye lent to me,
And here is also twenty marke
1080 For your curteysy.'

Merry Robin stops a sorrowful knight. Illustration from *The Merry Adventures of Robin Hood* by Howard Pyle.

'Nay, for God,' than sayd Robyn,
'Thou broke it well for ay,
For Our Lady, by her selerer,
Hath sent to me my pay.

1085 'And yf I toke it i-twyse,
A shame it were to me,
But trewely, gentyll knyght,
Welcom arte thou to me.'

Whan Robyn had tolde his tale,
1090   He leugh and had good chere:
'By my trouthe,' then sayd the knyght,
'Your money is redy here.'

'Broke it well,' sayd Robyn,
'Thou gentyll knyght so fre,
1095   And welcome be thou, gentyll knyght,
Under my trystell-tre.

'But what shall these bowes do?' sayd Robyn,
And these arowes ifedred fre?'
'By God,' than sayd the knyght,
1100   'A pore present to the.'

'Come now forth, Lytell Johan,
And go to my treasuré,
And brynge me there foure hondred pounde;
The monke over-tolde it me.

1105   'Have here foure hondred pounde,
Thou gentyll knyght and trewe,
And bye hors and harnes good,
And gylte thy spores all newe.

'And yf thou fayle ony spendynge,
1110   Com to Robyn Hode,
And by my trouth thou shalt none fayle,
The whyles I have any good.

'And broke well thy foure hondred pound,
Whiche I lent to the,
1115   And make thy selfe no more so bare,
By the counsell of me.'

Thus than holpe hym good Robyn,
The knyght all of his care:
God, that syt in heven hye,
1120   Graunte us well to fare!

THE FYFTH FYTTE

Now hath the knyght his leve i-take,
And wente hym on his way;
Robyn Hode and his mery men
Dwelled styll full many a day.

1125 Lyth and lysten, gentil men,
And herken what I shall say,
How the proud sheryfe of Notyngham
Dyde crye a full fayre play,

That all the best archers of the north
1130 Sholde come upon a day,
And that shoteth allther best
The game shall bere away.

He that shoteth allther best,
Furthest, fayre and lowe,
1135 At a payre of fynly buttes,
Under the grene wode shawe,

A ryght good arowe he shall have,
The shaft of sylver whyte,
The hede and the feders of ryche rede golde,
1140 In Englond is none lyke.

This than herde good Robyn,
Under his trystell-tre:
'Make you redy, ye wyght yonge men;
That shotynge wyll I se.

1145 'Buske you, my mery yonge men,
Ye shall go with me,
And I wyll wete the shryves fayth,
Trewe and yf he be.'

Whan they had theyr bowes i-bent,
1150 Theyr takles fedred fre,
Seven score of wyght yonge men
Stode by Robyns kne.

Whan they cam to Notyngham,
The buttes were fayre and longe,
1155 Many was the bolde archere
That shot with bowes stronge.

'There shall but syx shote with me;
The other shal kepe my hede,
And stande with good bowes bent,
1160   That I be not desceyved.'

The fourth outlawe his bowe gan bende,
And that was Robyn Hode,
And that behelde the proud sheryfe,
All by the but he stode.

1165   Thryes Robyn shot a bout,
And alway he slist the wand,
And so dyde good Gylberte
Wyth the Whyte Hande.

Lytell Johan and good Scatheloke
1170   Were archers good and fre;
Lytell Much and good Reynolde,
The worste wolde they not be.

Whan they had shot a boute,
These archours fayre and good,
1175   Evermore was the best,
For soth, Robyn Hode.

Hym was delyvered the good arowe,
For best worthy was he;
He toke the yeft so curteysly,
1180   To grene wode wolde he.

They cryed out on Robyn Hode,
And grete hornes gan they blowe:
'Wo worth the, treason!' sayd Robyn,
'Full evyl thou art to knowe.

1185   'And wo be thou! thou proude sheryf,
Thus gladdynge thy gest;
Other wyse thou behote me
In yonder wylde forest.

'But had I the in grene wode,
1190   Under my trystell-tre,
Thou sholdest leve me a better wedde
Than thy trewe lewté.

Full many a bowe there was bent,
And arowes let they glyde;
1195   Many a kyrtell there was rent,
And hurt many a syde.

The outlawes shot was so stronge
That no man myght them dryve,
And the proud sheryfes men,
1200   They fled away full blyve.

Robyn sawe the busshement to-broke,
In grene wode he wolde have be;
Many an arowe there was shot
Amonge that company.

1205   Lytell Johan was hurte full sore,
With an arowe in his kne,
That he myght neyther go nor ryde;
It was full grete pyté.

'Mayster,' then sayd Lytell Johan,
1210   'If ever thou lovest me,
And for that ylke Lordes love
That dyed upon a tre,

'And for the medes of my servyce,
That I have served the,
1215   Lete never the proude sheryf
Alyve now fynde me.

'But take out thy browne swerde,
And smyte all of my hede,
And gyve me woundes depe and wyde,
1220   No lyfe on me be lefte.'

'I wolde not that,' sayd Robyn,
'Johan, that thou were slawe,
For all the golde in mery Englonde,
Though it lay now on a rawe.'

1225   'God forbede,' sayd Lytell Much,
'That dyed on a tre,
That thou sholdest, Lytell Johan,
Parte our company.'

Up he toke hym on his backe,
1230   And bare hym well a myle;
Many a tyme he layd hym downe,
And shot another whyle.

Then was there a fayre castell,
A lytell within the wode;
1235   Double-dyched it was about,
And walled, by the Rode.

And there dwelled that gentyll knyght,
Syr Rychard at the Lee,
That Robyn had lent his good,
1240   Under the grene wode tree.

In he toke good Robyn,
And all his company:
'Welcome be thou, Robyn Hode,
Welcome arte thou to me,

1245   'And moche I thanke the of thy confort,
And of thy curteysye,
And of thy grete kyndenesse,
Under the grene wode tre.

'I love no man in all this worlde
1250   So much as I do the;
For all the proud sheryf of Notyngham,
Ryght here shalt thou be.

'Shyt the gates, and drawe the brydge,
And let no man come in,
1255   And arme you well, and make you redy,
And to the walles ye wynne.

'For one thynge, Robyn, I the behote;
I swere by Saynt Quyntyne,
These forty dayes thou wonnest with me,
1260   To soupe, ete, and dyne.'

Bordes were layde, and clothes were spredde,
Redely and anone;
Robyn Hode and his mery men
To mete can they gone.

THE SIXTH FYTTE

1265   Lythe and lysten, gentylmen,
     And herkyn to your songe,
     Howe the proude shyref of Notyngham,
     And men of armys stronge

     Full fast cam to the hye shyref,
1270   The contré up to route,
     And they besette the knyghtes castell,
     The walles all aboute.

     The proude shyref loude gan crye,
     And sayde, 'Thou traytour knight,
1275   Thou kepest here the kynges enemys,
     Agaynst the lawe and right.'

     'Syr, I wyll avowe that I have done,
     The dedys that here be dyght,
     Upon all the landes that I have,
1280   As I am a trewe knyght.

     'Wende furth, sirs, on your way,
     And do no more to me
     Tyll ye wyt oure kynges wille,
     What he wyll say to the.'

1285   The shyref thus had his answere,
     Without any lesynge;
     Furth he yede to London towne,
     All for to tel our kinge.

     Ther he telde him of that knight,
1290   And eke of Robyn Hode,
     And also of the bolde archars,
     That were soo noble and gode.

     'He wyll avowe that he hath done,
     To mayntene the outlawes stronge;
1295   He wyll be lorde, and set you at nought,
     In all the northe londe.'

     'I wyl be at Notyngham,' saide our kynge,
     'Within this fourteenyght,
     And take I wyll Robyn Hode,
1300   And so I wyll that knight.

'Go nowe home, shyref,' sayde our kynge,
'And do as I byd the,
And ordeyn gode archers ynowe,
Of all the wyde contré.'

1305   The shyref had his leve i-take,
And went hym on his way,
And Robyn Hode to grene wode,
Upon a certen day.

And Lytel John was hole of the arowe
1310   That shot was in his kne,
And dyd hym streyght to Robyn Hode,
Under the grene wode tree.

Robyn Hode walked in the forest,
Under the levys grene;
1315   The proude shyref of Notyngham
Thereof he had grete tene.

The shyref there fayled of Robyn Hode,
He myght not have his pray;
Than he awayted this gentyll knight,
1320   Bothe by nyght and day.

Ever he wayted the gentyll knyght,
Syr Richarde at the Lee,
As he went on haukynge by the ryver-syde,
And lete haukes flee.

1325   Toke he there this gentyll knight,
With men of armys stronge,
And led hym to Notyngham warde,
Bounde bothe fote and hande.

The sheref sware a full grete othe,
1330   Bi Hym that dyed on Rode,
He had lever than an hundred pound
That he had Robyn Hode.

This harde the knyghtes wyfe,
A fayr lady and a free;
1335   She set hir on a gode palfrey,
To grene wode anone rode she.

Whanne she cam in the forest,
Under the grene wode tree,
Fonde she there Robyn Hode,
1340   And al his fayre mené.

'God the save, gode Robyn,
And all thy company;
For Our dere Ladyes sake,
A bone graunte thou me.

1345   'Late never my wedded lorde
Shamefully slayne be;
He is fast bowne to Notingham warde,
For the love of the.'

Anone than saide goode Robyn
1350   To that lady so fre,
'What man hath your lorde take?'
'The proude shirife,' than sayd she.

'The shirife hatt hym take,' she sayd,
'For soth as I the say;
1355   He is nat yet thre myles
Passed on his way.'

Up than sterte gode Robyn,
As man that had ben wode:
'Buske you, my mery men,
1360   For Hym that dyed on Rode.

'And he that this sorowe forsaketh,
By hym that dyed on tre,
Shall he never in grene wode
No lenger dwel with me.'

1365   Sone there were gode bowes bent,
Mo than seven score;
Hedge ne dyche spared they none
That was them before.

'I make myn avowe to God,' sayde Robyn,
1370   'The sherif wolde I fayne see,
And if I may hym take,
I-quyte shall it be.'

And whan they came to Notingham,
They walked in the strete,
1375 And with the proude sherif iwys
Sone can they mete.

'Abyde, thou proude sherif,' he sayde,
'Abyde, and speke with me;
Of some tidinges of oure kinge
1380 I wolde fayne here of the.

'This seven yere, by dere worthy God,
Ne yede I this fast on fote;
I make myn avowe to God, thou proude sherif,
It is nat for thy gode.'

1385 Robyn bent a full goode bowe,
An arrowe he drowe at wyll;
He hit so the proude sherife
Upon the grounde he lay full still.

And or he myght up aryse,
1390 On his fete to stonde,
He smote of the sherifs hede
With his bright bronde.

'Lye thou there, thou proude sherife,
Evyll mote thou cheve!
1395 There myght no man to the truste
The whyles thou were a lyve.'

His men drewe out theyr bryght swerdes,
That were so sharpe and kene,
And layde on the sheryves men,
1400 And dryved them downe bydene.

Robyn stert to that knyght,
And cut a two his bonde,
And toke hym in his hand a bowe,
And bad hym by hym stonde.

1405 'Leve thy hors the behynde,
And lerne for to renne;
Thou shalt with me to grene wode,
Through myre, mosse, and fenne.

'Thou shalt with me to grene wode,
1410   Without ony leasynge,
Tyll that I have gete us grace
Of Edwarde, our comly kynge.'

THE SEVENTH FYTTE
The kynge came to Notynghame,
With knyghtes in grete araye,
1415   For to take that gentyll knyght
And Robyn Hode, yf he may.

He asked men of that countré
After Robyn Hode,
And after that gentyll knyght,
1420   That was so bolde and stout.

Whan they had tolde hym the case
Our kyng understode ther tale,
And seased in his honde
The knyghtes londes all.

1425   All the compasse of Lancasshyre
He went both ferre and nere,
Tyll he came to Plomton Parke;
He faylyd many of his dere.

There our kynge was wont to se
1430   Herdes many one,
He coud unneth fynde one dere,
That bare ony good horne.

The kynge was wonder wroth withall,
And swore by the Trynyté,
1435   'I wolde I had Robyn Hode,
With eyen I myght hym se.

'And he that wolde smyte of the knyghtes hede,
And brynge it to me,
He shall have the knyghtes londes,
1440   Syr Rycharde at the Le.

'I gyve it hym with my charter,
And sele it my honde,
To have and holde for ever more,
In al mery Englonde.'

1445 Than bespake a fayre olde knyght,
   That was treue in his fay:
   'A, my leege lorde the kynge,
   One worde I shall you say.

   'There is no man in this countré
1450 May have the knyghtes londes,
   Whyle Robyn Hode may ryde or gone,
   And bere a bowe in his hondes,

   'That he ne shall lese his hede,
   That is the best ball in his hode:
1455 Give it no man, my lorde the kynge,
   That ye wyll any good.'

   Half a yere dwelled our comly kynge
   In Notyngham, and well more;
   Coude he not here of Robyn Hode,
1460 In what countré that he were.

   But alwey went good Robyn
   By halke and eke by hyll,
   And alway slewe the kynges dere,
   And welt them at his wyll.

1465 Than bespake a proude fostere,
   That stode by our kynges kne:
   'Yf ye wyll se good Robyn,
   Ye must do after me.

   'Take fyve of the best knyghtes
1470 That be in your lede,
   And walke downe by yon abbay,
   And gete you monkes wede.

   'And I wyll be your bedesman,
   And lede you the way,
1475 And or ye come to Notyngham.
   Myn hede then dare I lay,

   'That ye shall mete with good Robyn,
   On lyve yf that he be;
   Or ye come to Notyngham,
1480 With eyen ye shall hym se.'

Richard I and his barons. (*British Library, London/Bridgeman Art Library*)

Full hastly our kynge was dyght,
So were his knyghtes fyve,
Everych of them in monkes wede,
And hasted them thyder blyve.

1485   Our kynge was grete above his cole,
A brode hat on his crowne,
Ryght as he were abbot-lyke,
They rode up into the towne.

Styf botes our kynge had on,
1490   Forsoth as I you say;
He rode syngynge to grene wode,
The covent was clothed in graye.

His male-hors and his grete somers
Folowed our kynge behynde,
1495   Tyll they came to grene wode,
A myle under the lynde.

There they met with good Robyn,
Stondynge on the waye,
And so dyde many a bolde archere,
1500   For soth as I you say.

Robyn toke the kynges hors,
Hastely in that stede,
And sayd, 'Syr abbot, by your leve,
A whyle ye must abyde.

1505   'We be yemen of this foreste,
Under the grene wode tre;
We lyve by our kynges dere,
Under the grene wode tre.

'And ye have chyrches and rentes both,
1510   And gold full grete plenté;
Gyve us some of your spendynge,
For saynt charyté.'

Than bespake our cumly kynge,
Anone than sayd he:
1515   'I brought no more to grene wode
But forty pounde with me.

'I have layne at Notyngham
This fourtynyght with our kynge,
And spent I have full moche good,
1520   On many a grete lordynge.

'And I have but forty pounde,
No more than have I me;
But yf I had an hondred pounde,
I vouch it halfe on the.'

1525   Robyn toke the forty pounde,
And departed it in two partye;
Halfendell he gave his mery men,
And bad them mery to be.

Full curteysly Robyn gan say;
1530 'Syr, have this for your spendyng;
We shall mete another day.'
'Gramercy,' than sayd our kynge.

'But well the greteth Edwarde, our kynge,
And sent to the his seale,
1535 And byddeth the com to Notyngham,
Both to mete and mele.'

He toke out the brode targe,
And sone he lete hym se;
Robyn coud his courteysy,
1540 And set hym on his kne.

'I love no man in all the worlde
So well as I do my kynge;
Welcome is my lordes seale;
And, monke, for thy tydynge,

1545 'Syr abbot, for thy tydynges,
To day thou shalt dyne with me,
For the love of my kynge,
Under my trystell-tre.'

Forth he lad our comly kynge,
1550 Full fayre by the honde;
Many a dere there was slayne,
And full fast dyghtande.

Robyn toke a full grete horne,
And loude he gan blowe;
1555 Seven score of wyght yonge men
Came redy on a rowe.

All they kneled on theyr kne,
Full fayre before Robyn;
The kynge sayd hym selfe untyll,
1560 And swore by Saynt Austyn,

'Here is a wonder semely syght;
Me thynketh, by Goddes pyne,
His men are more at his byddynge
Then my men be at myn.'

1565   Full hastly was theyr dyner idyght,
        And therto gan they gone;
        They served our kynge with al theyr myght,
        Both Robyn and Lytell Johan.

        Anone before our kynge was set
1570   The fatte venyson,
        The good whyte brede, the good rede wyne,
        And therto the fyne ale and browne.

        'Make good chere,' said Robyn,
        'Abbot, for charyté,
1575   And for this ylke tydynge,
        Blyssed mote thou be.

        'Now shalte thou se what lyfe we lede,
        Or thou hens wende;
        Than thou may enfourme our kynge,
1580   Whan ye togyder lende.'

        Up they sterte all in hast,
        Theyr bowes were smartly bent;
        Our kynge was never so sore agast,
        He wende to have be shente.

1585   Two yerdes there were up set,
        Thereto gan they gange;
        By fyfty pase, our kynge sayd,
        The merkes were to longe.

        On every syde a rose-garlonde,
1590   They shot under the lyne;
        'Who so fayleth of the rose-garlonde,' sayd Robyn,
        'His takyll he shall tyne,

        'And yelde it to his mayster,
        Be it never so fyne;
1595   For no man wyll I spare,
        So drynke I ale or wyne:

        'And bere a buffet on his hede,
        Iwys ryght all bare.'
        And all that fell in Robyns lote,
1600   He smote them wonder sare.

Twyse Robyn shot a boute,
And ever he cleved the wande,
And so dyde good Gylberte
With the Whyte Hande.

1605   Lytell Johan and good Scathelocke,
For nothynge wolde they spare;
When they fayled of the garlonde,
Robyn smote them full sore.

At the last shot that Robyn shot,
1610   For all his frendes fare,
Yet he fayled of the garlonde,
Thre fyngers and mare.

Than bespake good Gylberte,
And thus he gan say:
1615   'Mayster,' he sayd, 'your takyll is lost,
Stande forth and take your pay.'

'If it be so,' sayd Robyn,
'That may no better be,
Syr abbot, I delyver the myn arowe,
1620   I pray the, syr, serve thou me.'

'It falleth not for myn ordre,' sayd our kynge,
'Robyn, by thy leve,
For to smyte no good yeman,
For doute I sholde hym greve.'

1625   'Smyte on boldely,' sayd Robyn,
'I give the large leve.'
Anone our kynge, with that worde,
He folde up his sleve,

And sych a buffet he gave Robyn,
1630   To grounde he yede full nere:
'I make myn avowe to God,' sayd Robyn,
'Thou arte a stalworthe frere.

'There is pith in thyn arme,' sayd Robyn,
'I trowe thou canst well shete.'
1635   Thus our kynge and Robyn Hode
Togeder gan they mete.

Robyn behelde our comly kynge
Wystly in the face,
So dyde Syr Rycharde at the Le,
1640   And kneled downe in that place.

And so dyde all the wylde outlawes,
Whan they see them knele:
'My lorde the kynge of Englonde,
Now I knowe you well.'

1645   'Mercy then, Robyn,' sayd our kynge,
'Under your trystyll-tre,
Of thy goodnesse and thy grace,
For my men and me!'

'Yes, for God,' sayd Robyn,
1650   'And also God me save,
I aske mercy, my lorde the kynge,
And for my men I crave.'

'Yes, for God,' than sayd our kynge,
'And therto sent I me,
1655   With that thou leve the grene wode,
And all thy company,

'And come home, syr, to my courte,
And there dwell with me.'
'I make myn avowe to God,' sayd Robyn,
1660   'And ryght so shall it be.

'I wyll come to your courte,
Your servyse for to se,
And brynge with me of my men
Seven score and thre.

1665   'But me lyke well your servyse,
'I come agayne full soone,
And shote at the donne dere,
As I am wonte to done.'

THE EIGHTH FYTTE
'Haste thou ony grene cloth,' sayd our kynge,
1670   'That thou wylte sell nowe to me?'
'Ye, for God,' sayd Robyn,
'Thyrty yerdes and thre.'

'Robyn,' sayd our kynge,
'Now pray I the,
1675 Sell me some of that cloth,
To me and my meyné.'

'Yes, for God,' then sayd Robyn,
'Or elles I were a fole:
Another day ye wyll me clothe,
1680 I trowe, ayenst the Yole.'

The kynge kest of his cole then,
A grene garment he dyde on,
And every knyght had so, iwys,
Another hode full sone.

1685 Whan they were clothed in Lyncolne grene,
They keste away theyr graye:
'Now we shall to Notyngham,'
All thus our kynge gan say.

Theyr bowes bente, and forth they went,
1690 Shotynge all in fere,
Towarde the towne of Notyngham,
Outlawes as they were.

Our kynge and Robyn rode togyder,
For soth as I you say,
1695 And they shote plucke buffet,
As they went by the way.

And many a buffet our kynge wan
Of Robyn Hode that day,
And nothynge spared good Robyn
1700 Our kynge in his pay.

'So God me helpe,' sayd our kynge,
'Thy game is nought to lere;
I sholde not get a shote of the,
Though I shote all this yere.'

1705 All the people of Notyngham
They stode and behelde;
They sawe nothynge but mantels of grene
That covered all the felde.

Than every man to other gan say,
1710 'I drede our kynge be slone:
Come Robyn Hode to the towne, iwys
On lyve he lefte never one.'

Full hastly they began to fle,
Both yemen and knaves,
1715 And olde wyves that myght evyll goo,
They hypped on theyr staves.

The kynge loughe full fast,
And commaunded theym agayne;
When they se our comly kynge,
1720 I wys they were full fayne.

They ete and dranke and made them glad,
And sange with notes hye;
Than bespake our comly kynge
To Syr Rycharde at the Lee.

1725 He gave hym there his londe agayne,
A good man he bad hym be;
Robyn thanked our comly kynge,
And set hym on his kne.

Had Robyn dwelled in the kynges courte
1730 But twelve monethes and thre,
That he had spent an hondred pounde,
And all his mennes fe.

In every place where Robyn came
Ever more he layde downe,
1735 Both for knyghtes and for squyres,
To gete hym grete renowne.

By than the yere was all agone
He had no man but twayne,
Lytell Johan and good Scathelocke,
1740 With hym all for to gone.

Robyn sawe yonge men shote
Full ferre upon a day;
'Alas!' than sayd good Robyn,
'My welthe is went away.

1745 'Somtyme I was an archere good,
A styffe and eke a stronge;
I was comted the best archere
That was in mery Englonde.

'Alas!' then sayd good Robyn,
1750 'Alas and well a woo!
Yf I dwele lenger with the kynge,
Sorowe wyll me sloo.'

Forth than went Robyn Hode
Tyll he came to our kynge:
1755 'My lorde the kynge of Englonde,
Graunte me myn askynge.

'I made a chapell in Bernysdale,
That semely is to se,
It is of Mary Magdaleyne,
1760 And thereto wolde I be.

'I myght never in this seven nyght
No tyme to slepe ne wynke,
Nother all these seven dayes
Nother ete ne drynke.

1765 'Me longeth sore to Bernysdale,
I may not be therfro;
Barefote and wolwarde I have hyght
Thyder for to go.'

'Yf it be so,' than sayd our kynge,
1770 'It may no better be,
Seven nyght I gyve the leve,
No lengre, to dwell fro me.'

'Gramercy, lorde,' then sayd Robyn,
And set hym on his kne;
1775 He toke his leve courteysly,
To grene wode then went he.

Whan he came to grene wode,
In a mery mornynge,
There he herde the notes small
1780 Of byrdes mery syngynge.

'It is ferre gone,' sayd Robyn,
'That I was last here;
Me lyste a lytell for to shote
At the donne dere.'

1785   Robyn slewe a full grete harte,
His horne than gan he blow,
That all the outlawes of that forest
That horne coud they knowe,

And gadred them togyder,
1790   In a lytell throwe;
Seven score of wyght yonge men
Came redy on a rowe.

And fayre dyde of theyr hodes,
And set them on theyr kne:
1795   'Welcome,' they sayd, 'our mayster,
Under this grene wode tre.'

Robyn dwelled in grene wode,
Twenty yere and two;
For all drede of Edwarde our kynge,
1800   Agayne wolde he not goo.

Yet he was begyled, iwys,
Through a wycked woman,
The pryoresse of Kyrkely,
That nye was of hys kynne,

1805   For the love of a knyght,
Syr Roger of Donkesly,
That was her owne speciall;
Full evyll mote they the!

They toke togyder theyr counsell
1810   Robyn Hode for to sle,
And how they myght best do that dede,
His banis for to be.

Than bespake good Robyn,
In place where as he stode,
1815   'To morow I muste to Kyrkely,
Craftely to be leten blode.'

Syr Roger of Donkestere,
By the pryoresse he lay,
And there they betrayed good Robyn Hode,
1820   Through theyr false playe.

Cryst have mercy on his soule,
That dyded on the Rode!
For he was a good outlawe,
And dyde pore men moch god.

THE JOLLY PINDER OF WAKEFIELD

A pinder is 'an officer of a manor, having duty of impounding stray beasts' (OED), and may also be spelled 'pinner'. The green would be the pinfold, the place where the pinder would pin or pen the stray animals. Although the date of this text remains unclear, it certainly existed by the middle of the sixteenth century, as a ballad with this title was recorded in the Stationers' Register in 1557–9.

In Wakefield there lives a jolly pinder,
In Wakefield, all on a green.

'There is neither knight nor squire,' said
    the pinder,
'Nor barron that is so bold,
5   Dare make a trespasse to the town of
    Wakefield,
But his pledge goes to the pinfold.'

All this beheard three wight young men,
'Twas Robin Hood, Scarlet, and John;
With that they spyed the jolly pinder,
10   As he sate under a thorn.

'Now turn again, turn again,' said the
    pinder,
'For a wrong way have you gone;
For you have forsaken the king his high
    way,
And made a path over the corn.'

15   'O that were great shame,' said jolly Robin,
'We being three, and thou but one.'
The pinder leapt back then three good foot,
'Twas three good foot and one.

Robin Hood's encounter with the pinder of Wakefield. Etching by A.H. Tourrier. (*Mary Evans Picture Library*)

He leaned his back fast unto a thorn,
20   And his foot unto a stone,
And there he fought a long summer's day,
A summer's day so long.

Till that their swords, on their broad bucklers,
Were broken fast unto their hands.
25   'Hold thy hand, hold thy hand,' said Robin Hood,
'And my merry men every one.

Robin's encounter with the shepherd. Illustration by Petherick in *Robin Hood's Ballads* (1867), p. 188. (*Mary Evans Picture Library*)

'For this is one of the best pinders
That ever I saw with eye.
And wilt thou forsake the pinder his craft,
30   And live in green wood with me?'

'At Michaelmas next my cov'nant comes out,
When every man gathers his fee;
I'le take my blew blade all in my hand,
And plod to the green wood with thee.'
35   'Hast thou either meat or drink,' said Robin Hood
'For my merry men and me?'

'I have both bread and beef,' said the pinder,
'And good ale of the best.'
'And that is meat good enough,' said Robin Hood,
40   'For such unbidden guest.

'O wilt thou forsake the pinder his craft,
And go to the green wood with me?
Thou shalt have a livery twice in the year,
The one green, the other brown.'

45   'If Michaelmas day were once come and gone
And my master had paid me my fee,
Then would I set as little by him
As my master doth set by me.
I'le take my benbowe in my hand,
50   And come into the grenwode to thee.'

LITTLE JOHN GOES A-BEGGING

The earliest broadside of *Little John Goes a-Begging* was printed for William Gilbertson, who was active between 1640 and 1663. This text describes it as a 'merry new song', and although broadside publishers were not above claiming modernity for something borrowed, it does have the characteristics of a new creation, the refrain line 'With a hey down down a down down' being common to many of the mid-century ballads.

All you that delight to spend some time
    With a hey down down a down down
A merry song for to sing,
Unto me draw near, and you shall hear
5   How Little John went a-begging.

Robin and the beggar fight with quarterstaffs. Illustration in *Robin Hood's Ballads* (1867), p. 208. (*Mary Evans Picture Library*)

As Robin Hood walked the forrest along,
And all his yeomandree,
Sayes Robin, 'Some of you must a-begging go,
And Little John, it must be thee.'

10   Sayes John, 'If I must a-begging go,
I will have a palmers weed,
With a staff and a coat, and bags of all sort,
The better then shall I speed.

      'Come give me now a bag for my bread,
15   And another for my cheese,
And one for a peny, when as I get any,
That nothing I may leese.'

      Now Little John he is a-begging gone,
Seeking for some relief,
20   But of all the beggers he met on the way,
Little John he was the chief.

But as he was walking himself alone
Four beggers he chanced to spy,
Some deaf and some blind, and some came behind:
25   Says John, 'Here's brave company!

'Good morrow,' said John, 'my brethren dear,
Good fortune I had you to see;
Which way do you go? Pray let me know,
For I want some company.

30   'O what is here to do?' then said Little John,
'Why rings all these bells?' said he,
'What dog is a-hanging? Come let us be ganging,
That we the truth may see.'

'Here is no dog a-hanging,' then one of them said,
35   'Good fellow, we tell unto thee;
But here is one dead wil give us cheese and bread,
And it may be one single peny.'

'We have brethren in London,' another he said,
'So have we in Coventry,
40   In Barwick and Dover, and all the world over,
But nere a crookt carril like thee.

'Therefore stand thee back, thou crooked carel,
And take that knock on the crown.'
'Nay,' said Little John, 'I'le not yet be gone,
45   For a bout will I have with you round.

'Now have at you all,' then said Little John,
'If you be so full of your blows;
Fight on all four, and nere give ore,
Whether you be friends or foes.'

50   John nipped the dumb, and made him to rore,
And the blind that could not see,
And he that a cripple had been seven years,
He made him run faster than he.

And flinging them all against the wall,
55   With many a sturdie bang,
It made John sing, to hear the gold ring,
Which against the walls cryed 'Twang.'

Then he got out of the beggers cloak
Three hundred pound in gold.
60   'Good fortune had I,' then said Little John.
'Such a good sight to behold.'

But what found he in a beggers bag,
But three hundred pound and three?
'If I drink water while this doth last,
65   Then an ill death may I dye!

'And my begging-trade I will now give ore,
My fortune hath bin so good,
Therefore I'le not stay, but I will away,
To the forrest of merry Sherwood.'

70   And when to the forrest of Sherwood he came,
He quickly there did see,
His master good, bold Robin Hood,
And all his company.

'What news? What news?' then said Robin Hood,
75   'Come, Little John, tell unto me,
How hast thou sped with thy beggers trade?
For that I fain would see.'

'No news but good,' then said Little John,
'With begging ful wel I have sped;
80   Six hundred and three I have here for thee,
In silver and gold so red.'

Then Robin took Little John by the hand
And danced about the oak tree.
'If we drink water while this doth last,
85   Then an il death may we die!'

So to conclude my merry new song,
All you that delight it to sing,
'Tis of Robin Hood, that archer good,
And how Little John went a-begging.

ROBIN HOOD AND ALLIN A DALE

This ballad appears in seventeenth-century broadsides but did not find a place in the garland collections, possibly owing to the fact that Allin a Dale (Allen in the later texts) was not a well-known member of the outlaw band.

Come listen to me, you gallants so free,
All you that love mirth for to hear,
And I will tell of a bold outlaw,
That lived in Nottinghamshire.

5   As Robin Hood in the forrest stood,
All under the green-wood tree,
There was he ware of a brave young man,
As fine as fine might be.

The youngster was clothed in scarlet red,
10   In scarlet fine and gay,
And he did frisk it over the plain,
And chanted a roundelay.

Robin and Alan-a-Dale. Illustration in *Robin Hood's Ballads* (1867), p. 230. (*Mary Evans Picture Library*)

As Robin Hood next morning stood,
Amongst the leaves so gay,
15   There did he espy the same young man,
Come drooping along the way.

The scarlet he wore the day before,
It was clean cast away;
And every step he fetcht a sigh,
20   'Alack and a well a day!'

Then stepped forth brave Little John,
And Nick the millers son,
Which made the young man bend his bow,
When as he see them come.

25   'Stand off, stand off,' the young man said,
'What is your will with me?'
'You must come before our master straight,
Under yon green-wood tree.'

And when he came bold Robin before,
30   Robin askt him courteously,
'O hast thou any money to spare
For my merry men and me?'

'I have no money,' the young man said,
'But five shillings and a ring;
35   And that I have kept this seven long years,
To have it at my wedding.

'Yesterday I should have married a maid,
But she is now from me tane,
And chosen to be an old knights delight,
40   Whereby my poor heart is slain.'

'What is thy name?' then said Robin Hood,
'Come tell me, without any fail.'
'By the faith of my body,' then said the young man,
'My name it is Allin a Dale.'

45   'What wilt thou give me,' said Robin Hood,
'In ready gold or fee,
To help thee to thy true love again,
And deliver her unto thee?'

'I have no money,' then quoth the young man,
50   'No ready gold nor fee,
But I will swear upon a book
Thy true servant for to be.'

'How many miles is it to thy true love?
Come tell me without any guile.'
55   'By the faith of my body,' then said the young man,
'It is but five little mile.'

Then Robin he hasted over the plain,
He did neither stint nor lin,
Until he came unto the church,
60   Where Allin should keep his wedding.

'What dost thou here?' the bishop he said,
'I prethee now tell to me.'
'I am a bold harper,' quoth Robin Hood,
'And the best in the north countrey.'

65   'O welcome, O welcome,' the bishop he said,
'That musick best pleaseth me.'
'You shall have no musick,' quoth Robin Hood,
'Till the bride and the bridegroom I see.'

With that came in a wealthy knight,
70   Which was both grave and old,
And after him a finikin lass,
Did shine like glistering gold.

'This is no fit match,' quoth bold Robin Hood,
'That you do seem to make here;
75   For since we are come unto the church,
The bride she shall chuse her own dear.'

Then Robin Hood put his horn to his mouth,
And blew blasts two or three;
When four and twenty bowmen bold
80   Came leaping over the lee.

And when they came into the church-yard,
Marching all on a row,
The first man was Allin a Dale,
To give bold Robin his bow.

85   'This is thy true love,' Robin he said,
    'Young Allin, as I hear say,
    And you shall be married at this same time,
    Before we depart away.'

    'That shall not be,' the bishop he said,
90   'For thy word shall not stand;
    They shall be three times askt in the church,
    As the law is of our land.'

    Robin Hood pulld off the bishops coat,
    And put it upon Little John;
95   'By the faith of my body,' then Robin said,
    'This cloath doth make thee a man.'

    When Little John went into the quire,
    The people began for to laugh;
    He askt them seven times in the church,
100   Least three times should not be enough.

    'Who gives me this maid,' then said Little John;
    Quoth Robin, 'That do I,
    And he that doth take her from Allin a Dale
    Full dearly he shall her buy.'

105   And thus having ended this merry wedding,
    The bride lookt as fresh as a queen,
    And so they returnd to the merry green wood,
    Amongst the leaves so green.

ROBIN HOOD AND GUY OF GISBORNE

This ballad survives only in the folio manuscript acquired by Thomas Percy (British Library Add. MS 27879), which is dated to the mid-seventeenth century and is clearly a collection of pre-existing materials. Percy gave the ballad its present title, perhaps omitting the honorific 'Sir' as the text states that both he and Robin were yeomen (line 87).

    When shawes beene sheene and shradds full fayre,
    And leeves both large and longe,
    Itt is merry, walking in the fayre forrest,
    To heare the small birds singe.

5   The woodweele sang, and wold not cease,
    Amongst the leaves a lyne.
    'And it is by two wight yeoman,
    By deare God, that I meane.

Robin's encounter with Sir Guy of Gisborne. Illustration by Petherick in *Robin Hood's Ballads* (1867), p. 84. (*Mary Evans Picture Library*)

>   'Me thought they did mee beate and binde,
> 10   And tooke my bow mee froe;
>   If I bee Robin a-live in this lande,
>   Ile be wrocken on both them towe.'
>
>   'Sweavens are swift, master,' quoth John,
>   'As the wind that blowes ore a hill,
> 15   For if itt be never soe lowde this night,
>   To-morrow it may be still.'
>
>   'Buske yee, bowne yee, my merry men all,
>   For John shall goe with mee,
>   For Ile goe seeke yond wight yeomen
> 20   In greenwood where the bee.'

The cast on their gowne of greene,
A-shooting gone are they,
Untill they came to the merry greenwood,
Where they had gladdest bee;

25   There were the ware of wight yeoman,
His body leaned to a tree.

A sword and a dagger he wore by his side,
Had beene many a mans bane,
And he was cladd in his capull-hyde,
30   Topp, and tayle, and mayne.

'Stand you still, master,' quoth Litle John,
'Under this trusty tree,
And I will goe to yond wight yeoman,
To know his meaning trulye.'

35   'A, John, by me thou setts noe store,
And thats a farley thinge;
How offt send I my men beffore,
And tarry myselfe behinde?

'It is noe cunning a knave to ken,
40   And a man but heare him speake;
And itt were not for bursting of my bowe,
John, I wold thy head breake.'

But often words they breeden bale,
That parted Robin and John;
45   John is gone to Barnsdale,
The gates he knowes eche one.

And when hee came to Barnesdale,
Great heavinesse there hee hadd;
He found two of his owne fellowes
50   Were slaine both in a slade,

And Scarlett afoote flyinge was,
Over stockes and stone,
For the sheriffe with seven score men
Fast after him is gone.

55   'Yett one shoote Ile shoote,' sayes Little John,
       'With Crist his might and mayne;
       Ile make yond fellow that flyes soe fast
       To be both glad and faine.'

       John bent up a good yeiwe bow,
60   And fetteled him to shoote;
       The bow was made of a tender boughe,
       And fell downe to his foote.

       'Woe worth thee, wicked wood,' sayd
         Litle John,
       'That ere thou grew on a tree!
65   For this day thou art my bale,
       My boote when thou shold bee!'

       This shoote it was but looselye shott,
       The arrowe flew in vaine,
       And it mett one of the sheriffes men;
70   Good William a Trent was slaine.

       It had beene better for William a Trent
       To hange upon a gallowe
       Then for to lye in the greenwoode,
       There slaine with an arrowe.

75   And it is sayd, when men be mett,
       Six can doe more than three:
       And they have tane Litle John,
       And bound him fast to a tree.

       'Thou shalt be drawen by dale and
         downe,' quoth the sheriffe,
80   'And hanged hye on a hill.'
       'But thou may fayle,' quoth Litle John,
       'If itt be Christs owne will.'

       Let us leave talking of Litle John,
       For hee is bound fast to a tree,
85   And talke of Guy and Robin Hood,
       In the green woode where they bee.

Robin learns to shoot. From *Robin Hood* by
N.C. Wyeth (1917). (*Mary Evans Picture Library*)

How these two yeomen together they mett,
Under the leaves of lyne,
To see what marchandise they made
90   Even at that same time.

'Good morrow, good fellow,' quoth Sir Guy;
'Good morrow, good felow,' quoth hee,
'Methinkes by this bow thou beares in thy hand,
A good archer thou seems to be.'

95   'I am wilfull of my way,' quoth Sir Guye,
'And of my morning tyde.'
'Ile lead thee through the wood,' quoth Robin,
'Good felow, Ile be thy guide.'

'I seeke an outlaw,' quoth Sir Guye,
100   'Men call him Robin Hood;
I had rather meet with him upon a day,
Then forty pound of golde.'

'If you tow mett, itt wold be seene whether were better
Afore yee did part awaye;
105   Let us some other pastime find,
Good fellow, I thee pray.

'Let us some other masteryes make,
And wee will walke in the woods even;
Wee may chance meet with Robin Hoode
110   Att some unsett steven.'

They cutt them downe the summer shroggs
Which grew both under a bryar,
And sett them three score rood in twinn,
To shoote the prickes full neare.

115   'Leade on, good fellow,' sayd Sir Guye,
'Lead on, I doe bidd thee.'
'Nay, by my faith,' quoth Robin Hood,
'The leader thou shalt bee.'

The first good shoot that Robin ledd
120   Did not shoote an inch the pricke froe;
Guy was an archer good enoughe,
But he cold neere shoote soe.

The second shoote Sir Guy shott,
He shott within the garlande;
125   But Robin Hoode shott it better than hee,
For he clove the good pricke-wande.

'Gods blessing on thy heart!' sayes Guye,
'Goode fellow, thy shooting is goode,
For an thy hart be as good as thy hands,
130   Thou were better then Robin Hood.

'Tell me thy name, good fellow,' quoth Guy,
'Under the leaves of lyne.'
'Nay, by my faith,' quoth good Robin,
'Till thou have told me thine.'

135   'I dwell by dale and downe,' quoth Guye,
'And I have done many a curst turne;
And he that calles me by my right name
Calles me Guye of good Gysborne.'

'My dwelling is in the wood,' sayes Robin,
140   'By thee I set right nought;
My name is Robin Hood of Barnesdale,
A fellow thou has long sought.'

He that had neither beene a kithe nor kin
Might have seene a full fayre sight,
145   To see how together these yeomen went,
With blades both browne and bright.

To have seene how these yeomen together fought,
Two howers of a summers day;
Itt was neither Guy nor Robin Hood
150   That fettled them to flye away.

Robin was reachles on a roote,
And stumbled at that tyde,
And Guy was quicke and nimble with-all,
And hitt him ore the left side.

155   'Ah, deere Lady!' sayd Robin Hoode,
'Thou art both mother and may!
I thinke it was never mans destinye
To dye before his day.'

Robin thought on Our Lady deere,
160   And soone leapt up againe,
And thus he came with an awkwarde stroke;
Good Sir Guy hee has slayne.

He tooke Sir Guys head by the hayre,
And sticked itt on his bowes end:
165   'Thou hast beene traytor all thy liffe,
Which thing must have an ende.'

Robin pulled forth an Irish kniffe,
And nicked Sir Guy in the face,
That hee was never on a woman borne
170   Cold tell who Sir Guye was.

Saies, 'Lye there, lye there, good Sir Guye,
And with me be not wrothe;
If thou have had the worse stroakes at my hand,
Thou shalt have the better cloathe.'

175   Robin did his gowne of greene,
On Sir Guye it throwe;
And hee put on that capull-hyde,
That cladd him topp to toe.

'The bowe, the arrowes, and litle horne,
180   And with me now Ile beare;
For now I will goe to Barnsdale,
To see how my men doe fare.'

Robin sett Guyes horne to his mouth,
A lowd blast in it he did blow;
185   That beheard the sheriffe of Nottingham,
As he leaned under a lowe.

'Hearken! hearken!' sayd the sheriffe,
'I heard noe tydings but good,
For yonder I heare Sir Guyes horne blowe,
190   For he hath slaine Robin Hoode.

'For yonder I heare Sir Guyes horne blow,
Itt blowes soe well in tyde,
For yonder comes that wight yeoman,
Cladd in his capull-hyde.

195 'Come hither, thou good Sir Guy,
Aske of mee what thou wilt have.'
'Ile none of thy gold,' sayes Robin
Hood,
'Nor Ile none of itt have.'

'But now I have slaine the master,' he
sayd,
200 'Let me goe strike the knave;
This is all the reward I aske,
Nor noe other will I have.'

'Thou art a madman,' said the shiriffe,
'Thou sholdest have had a knights fee;
205 Seeing thy asking bee soe badd,
Well granted it shall be.'

But Litle John heard his master speake,
Well he knew that was his steven;
'Now shall I be loset,' quoth Little Iohn,
210 'With Christs might in heaven.'

But Robin hee hyed him towards Litle
John,
Hee thought hee wold loose him
belive;
The sheriffe and all his companye
Fast after him did drive.

215 'Stand abacke! stand abacke!' sayd
Robin;
'Why draw you mee soe neere?
Itt was never the use in our countrye
One's shrift another shold heere.'

But Robin pulled forth an Irysh kniffe,
220 And losed John hand and foote,
And gave him Sir Guyes bow in his hand,
And bade it be his boote.

But John tooke Guyes bow in his hand
His arrowes were rawstye by the roote;
225 The sherriffe saw Little John draw a bow
And fettle him to shoote.

Illustration from *Bold Robin Hood and his
Outlaw Band* by Louis Read.

Towards his house in Nottingam
He fled full fast away,
And soe did all his companye,
230   Not one behind did stay.

But he cold neither soe fast goe,
Nor away soe fast runn,
But Litle John, with an arrow broade,
Did cleave his heart in twinn.

ROBIN HOOD AND LITTLE JOHN

This ballad was perhaps first printed by W. Onley in London in 1680–5. As with *Robin Hood and the Curtal Friar* and *The Jolly Pinder of Wakefield*, there is clear evidence of the much earlier existence of this story. A play called *Robin Hood and Little John* was registered in 1594 but has sadly not survived, and there was another from 1640, though these may of course have been general dramas based on sources like the *Gest* or even *Robin Hood and the Monk*. A ballad with this title was registered in 1624, and that date is quite possible for the original version of this text.

When Robin Hood was about twenty years old,
With a hey down, down, and a down
He happen'd to meet Little John,
A jolly brisk blade, right fit for the trade,
5   For he was a lusty young man.

Though he was call'd Little, his limbs they were large,
And his stature was seven foot high;
Whereever he came, they quak'd at his name,
For soon he wou'd make them to flie.

10   How they came acquainted, I'll tell you in brief,
If you will but listen a while;
For this very jest, amongst all the rest,
I think it may cause you to smile.

Bold Robin Hood said to his jolly bowmen,
15   'Pray tarry you here in this grove;
And see that you all observe well my call,
While through the forest I rove.

'We have had no sport for these fourteen long days,
Therefore now abroad will I go;
20   Now should I be beat, and cannot retreat,
My horn I will presently blow.'

Then did he shake hands with his merry men all,
And bid them at present good by;
Then, as near a brook his journey he took,
25   A stranger he chanc'd to espy.

They happen'd to meet on a long narrow bridge,
And neither of them wou'd give way;
Quoth bold Robin Hood, and sturdily stood,
'I'll show you right Nottingham play.'

30   With that from his quiver an arrow he drew,
A broad arrow with a goose-wing:
The stranger replyd, 'I'll licker thy hide,
If thou offer to touch the string.'

Quoth bold Robin Hood, 'Thou dost prate like an ass,
35   For were I to bend but my bow,
I could send a dart quite through thy proud heart,
Before thou couldst strike me one blow.'

'You talk like a coward,' the stranger reply'd;
'Well arm'd with a long bow you stand,
40   To shoot at my breast, while I, I protest,
Have naught but a staff in my hand.'

'The name of a coward,' quoth Robin, 'I scorn,
Wherefore my long bow I'll lay by;
And now, for thy sake, a staff will I take,
45   The truth of thy manhood to try.'

Then Robin Hood stept to a thicket of trees,
And chose him a staff of ground oak;
Now this being done, away he did run
To the stranger and merrily spoke:

50   'Lo! see my staff; it is lusty and tough,
Now here on the bridge we will play;
Whoever falls in, the other shall win
The battle, and so we'll away.'

'With all my whole heart to thy humor I yield,
55   I scorn in the least to give out.'
This said, they fell to't without more dispute,
And their staffs they did flourish about.

And first Robin he gave the stranger a bang,
So hard that it made his bones ring:
60   The stranger he said, 'This must be repaid;
I'll give you as good as you bring.

'So long as I am able to handle my staff,
To die in your debt, friend, I scorn.'
Then to it both goes, and follow'd their blows,
65   As if they'd been thrashing of corn.

The stranger gave Robin a crack on the crown,
Which caused the blood to appear;
Then Robin, enrag'd, more fiercely engag'd,
And follow'd his blows more severe.

70   So thick and so fast did he lay it on him,
With a passionate fury and eyre,
At every stroke he made him to smoke,
As if he had been all on fire.

O then into a fury the stranger he grew
75   And gave him a damnable look,
And with it a blow that laid him full low
And tumbl'd him into the brook.

'I prithee, good fellow, O where art thou now?'
The stranger in laughter he cry'd;
80   Quoth bold Robin Hood, 'Good faith, in the flood,
And floting along with the tide.

'I needs must acknowledge thou art a brave soul;
With thee I'll no longer contend;
For needs must I say, thou hast got the day,
85   Our battle shall be at an end.'

Then, then, to the bank he did presently wade,
And pull'd himself out by a thorn;
Which done, at the last, he blow'd a loud blast
Straitways on his fine bugle-horn.

90   The eccho of which through the vallies did flie,
At which his stout bowmen appear'd,
All cloathed in green, most gay, to be seen;
So up to their master they steer'd.

'O what's the matter?' quoth William Stutely,
95   'Good master, you are wet to the skin.'
'No matter,' quoth he, 'the lad which you see,
In fighting he tumbl'd me in.'

'He shall not go scot free,' the others reply'd;
So straight they were seising him there,
100   To duck him likewise, but Robin Hood cries,
'He is a stout fellow, forbear.

'There's no one shall wrong thee, friend, be not afraid;
These bowmen upon me do wait;
There's threescore and nine; if thou wilt be mine,
105   Thou shalt have my livery strait.

'And other accoutrements fit for my train,
Speak up, jolly blade, ne'r fear;
I'll teach thee also the use of the bow,
To shoot at the fat fallow-deer.'

110   'O here is my hand,' the stranger reply'd,
'I'll serve you with all my whole heart;
My name is John Little, a man of good mettle;
Ne'r doubt me, for I'll play my part.'

'His name shall be alter'd,' quoth William Stutely,
115   'And I will his godfather be;
Prepare then a feast, and none of the least,
For we will be merry,' quoth he.

They presently fetch'd in a brace of fat does,
With humming strong liquor likewise;
120   They lov'd what was good, so in the greenwood,
This pritty sweet babe they baptize.

He was, I must tell you, but seven foot high,
And may be an ell in the waste;
A pritty sweet lad, much feasting they had;
125   Bold Robin the christ'ning grac'd,

With all his bowmen, which stood in a ring,
And were of the Nottingham breed;
Brave Stutely comes then, with seven yeomen,
And did in this manner proceed:

130   'This infant was called John Little,' quoth he,
         'Which name shall be changed anon;
         The words we'll transpose, so where-ever he goes,
         His name shall be call'd Little John.'

         They all with a shout made the elements ring,
135   So soon as the office was o're;
         To feasting they went, with true merriment,
         And tipl'd strong liquor gallore.

         Then Robin he took the pritty sweet babe,
         And cloath'd him from top to the toe
140   In garments of green, most gay to be seen,
         And gave him a curious long bow.

         'Thou shalt be an archer as well as the best,
         And range in the green wood with us;
         Where we'll not want gold nor silver, behold,
145   While bishops have ought in their purse.

         'We live here like esquires, or lords of renown,
         Without e're a foot of free land;
         We feast on good cheer, with wine, ale and beer,
         And ev'ry thing at our command.'

150   Then musick and dancing did finish the day
         At length when the sun waxed low,
         Then all the whole train the grove did refrain,
         And unto their caves they did go.

         And so ever after, as long as he liv'd,
155   Although he was proper and tall,
         Yet nevertheless, the truth to express,
         Still Little John they did him call.

ROBIN HOOD AND MAID MARIAN

This ballad appears only once, in a broadside ballad that may well be post-Restoration. Much about this ballad suggests that it was deliberately constructed to add an element to the Robin Hood tradition. It is the only ballad where Maid Marian plays a part, though she is briefly mentioned in *Robin Hood and Queen Catherin* and *Robin Hood's Golden Prize*.

A bonny fine maid of a noble degree,
With a hey down down a down down
Maid Marian calld by name,
Did live in the North, of excellent
    worth,
5   For she was a gallant dame.

For favour and face, and beauty most rare,
Queen Hellen shee did excell;
For Marian then was praisd of all men
That did in the country dwell.

10   'Twas neither Rosamond nor Jane
     Shore,
Whose beauty was clear and bright,
That could surpass this country lass,
Beloved of lord and knight.

The Earl of Huntington, nobly born,
15   That came of noble blood,
To Marian went, with a good intent,
By the name of Robin Hood.

Robin Hood and Marian in their bower. Illustration from *Bold Robin Hood and his Outlaw Band* by Louis Read.

With kisses sweet their red lips meet,
For shee and the earl did agree;
20   In every place, they kindly imbrace,
With love and sweet unity.

But fortune bearing these lovers a spight,
That soon they were forced to part;
To the merry green wood then went Robin Hood,
25   With a sad and sorrowfull heart.

And Marian, poor soul, was troubled in mind,
For the absence of her friend;
With finger in eye, shee often did cry,
And his person did much comend.

30   Perplexed and vexed, and troubled in mind,
Shee drest her self like a page,
And ranged the wood to find Robin Hood,
The bravest of men in that age.

With quiver and bow, sword, buckler, and all,
35   Thus armed was Marian most bold,
Still wandering about to find Robin out,
Whose person was better then gold.

But Robin Hood, hee, himself had disguisd,
And Marian was strangly attir'd,
40   That they provd foes, and so fell to blowes,
Whose vallour bold Robin admir'd.

They drew out their swords, and to cutting they went,
At least an hour or more,
That the blood ran apace from bold Robins face,
45   And Marian was wounded sore.

'O hold thy hand, hold thy hand,' said Robin Hood,
'And thou shalt be one of my string,
To range in the wood with bold Robin Hood,
To hear the sweet nightingall sing.'

50   When Marian did hear the voice of her love,
Her self shee did quickly discover,
And with kisses sweet she did him greet,
Like to a most loyall lover.

When bold Robin Hood his Marian did see,
55   Good lord, what clipping was there!
With kind imbraces, and jobbing of faces,
Providing of gallant cheer.

For Little John took his bow in his hand,
And wandring in the wood,
60   To kill the deer, and make good chear,
For Marian and Robin Hood.

A stately banquet they had full soon,
All in a shaded bower,
Where venison sweet they had to eat,
65   And were merry that present hour.

Great flaggons of wine were set on the board,
And merrily they drunk round
Their boules of sack, to strengthen the back,
Whilst their knees did touch the ground.

70   First Robin Hood began a health
To Marian his onely dear,
And his yeomen all, both comly and tall,
Did quickly bring up the rear.

For in a brave veine they tost off the bouls,
75   Whilst thus they did remain,
And every cup, as they drunk up,
They filled with speed again.

At last they ended their merryment,
And went to walk in the wood,
80   Where Little John and Maid Marian
Attended on bold Robin Hood.

In sollid content together they livd,
With all their yeomen gay;
They livd by their hands, without
    any lands,
85   And so they did many a day.

But now to conclude, an end I will
    make
In time, as I think it good,
For the people that dwell in the
    North can tell
Of Marian and bold Robin Hood.

Robin Hood, Maid Marian, Friar Tuck and some of their fellow outlaws. Seventeenth-century woodcut in *Robin Hood's Ballads* (1867). (*Mary Evans Picture Library*)

ROBIN HOOD AND QUEEN CATHERIN

This was a popular ballad in the seventeenth century. A closely related version, entitled *Renowned Robin Hood*, exists in six separate broadsides and the two early garlands of 1663 and 1670. The earliest full text of this version – now in the Wood collection in the Bodleian Library, Oxford – dates from before 1655 when Grove, the printer, ceased operations.

FITT 1

Gold taken from the kings harbengers
As seldom hath been seen
And carryed by bold Robin Hood
A present to the queen.

5   'If that I live a year to an end,'
Thus gan Queen Catherin say,
'Bold Robin Hood, I'le be thy friend,
And all thy yeomen gay.'

The king and queen to th' gardens gon,
10   To passe the time away,
And lovingly with one another
Till evening they did stay.

'What game, what game, my queen,' he said
'For game or also for glee?'
15   'I'de have a shooting,' she reply'd
'So please your majestie.'

'Ile have a shooting for your sake,
The best in Christentie.'
'Make lite the wager, sir,' she said,
20   'And holden you shall bee.'

'Ile make the wager light, my queen,
For that you need not fear,
Three hundred tunn of Renish wine,
Three hundred tunn of beer.

25   'Three hundred of the fattest harts
That run on Dalum Lee.'
'That's a princly wager,' said our queen,
'Bravly holden you shall bee.'

The queen is to her chamber gon
30   As fast as she can wend,
She calls to her her lovely page,
His name was Patrington.

'Com hether to me my lovely page,
Com hether unto me,
35   For thou must post to Notingham
As fast as thou canst dree.

'And when thou comst to Notingham
Search all that English wood;
Enquire of each good yeoman thou meetst
40   To finde out Robin Hood.

'And whan thou comst Robin Hood before
Deliver him this ringe,
And bid him post to London towne
And not fear any thing.

45 'I've made a shooting with the king
    The best in Christentee,
    And I have chosen bold Robin Hood
    To be of my partie.'

    He tooke his leave of the royall queen
50 And fast away is gan,
    Somtimes he rode, sometimes he rann,
    Till he came to Nottingham.

    And when he came to Nottingham
    And there took up his inn,
55 He call'd for a pottle of Renish wine
    And dranck a health to his queen.

    Then sate a yeoman by his side
    'Tell me, sweet page,' said hee,
    'What is thy businesse or thy cause
60 So farr in the North contrie?'

    'This is my business and my cause
    I tell it you for good;
    I com from London,' said the page,
    'To seeke bold Robin Hood.'

65 'Ile take my horse betimes i'th morn
    Be it by break of day,
    And Ile show thee bold Robin Hood
    And all his yeomen gay.'

    He took his horse betimes i'th morne
70 As soon as he could see,
    And had him to bold Robin Hood
    And all his archerie.

    When the page came to Robin Hood
    He fell downe on his knee.
75 'Queen Catherin she doth greet you well
    She greets you well by mee.

    'Queen Catherin she dooth greet you well
    And sends you here her ring,
    She bids you post to London towne
80 And not fear any thing.

'She hath made a shooting with our king
The best in Christentee,
And desires you, bold Robin Hood,
To be of her partie.'

85   Robin tooke his mantle from his back,
It was of Lincolne green;
'Here take my mantle,' said Robin Hood,
'A present for the queen.

And go thy way thou lovely page
90   And to Queen Catherin say
"If Robin Hood doth loose the match
He will the wager pay."'

FITT 2
In summer time when leaves grow green
'Twas a seemly sight to see
95   How Robin Hood himselfe had drest
And all his yeomandrie.

He clad himselfe in scarlett red
His men in Lincoln green
And so prepars for London towne,
100   To shoot before the lovly queen.

They had bows of ewe and strings of silke
Arrows of silver chest,
Black hats, white feathers all alike
Full deftly they were drest.

105   'Com Little John, thou shalt be one,
One Clifton thou shall bee,
And so shall Midge the Millers son
To bere us companie.

'Will Scathlock to shall go alonge
110   For he will never faile,
But Renett Browne shall stay behinde
And look to Brensdale.'

Robin came before the queen,
He kneeld downe on his knee.
115   'Thou'rt welcome, Loxley,' said our queen
And these thy yeomandrie.

Robin and his huntsmen kill game in Sherwood Forest. Illustration in *Robin Hood's Ballad*s (1867), p. 155. (*Mary Evans Picture Library*)

        'Thou'rt welcom,' said the queen,
        And these thy archers good.
        I hope ere this day be at an end
120   To call thee Robin Hood.'

        The queen's to the king's chamber gon,
        As fast as she can dree,
        'God save you lovly prince,' she said,
        'Welcom, my queen,' quoth he.

125   'Our match goes ill and please your grace,
        As far as I can ken,
        Ther's not an archer in all my court,
        Will shoot against your men.'

        'I knew it very well,' said our king,
130   'My archers are so good,
        That never a man durst shoott with them
        Except it were Robin Hood.'

'Double the wager,' said the queen,
'Brave holden you shall bee.'
135 'No, by my truth,' then said our king,
'Woman's full of subteltie.'

FITT 3
Our king is unto Finsbury gon
In all his best array,
The queen she follows after him,
140 With all her archers gay.

'Come hether, Tempest,' said the king,
'Bow berer unto mee,
Ther's not in England, France, nor Spaine
An archer like to thee.'

145 The queen took Loxly by the hand
And gave him on his head tapps three,
'Look wel to this man, my leig,' she said,
'Hee'l prove as good as hee.'

'Com hether, Tempest,' said the king,
150 'The best in Christentie,
And measure out here with thy line
How long the marks shall bee.'

With that bespoke bold Loxly then,
Full quickly and full soon,
155 'Mesure no marks for us, my leige,
Wee'l shoot at sun and moon.'

'Full fifteen score your marks shall bee,
Full fifteen score shall stand.
I'le lay my bow,' quoth Clifton then,
160 'I'le cleave the willow wand.'

Then the king's archers led about
Till it was three and none.
With that the ladys began to pout,
'Madam, the game is gon.'

165 'A boon, a boon,' then sais the queen,
'Please your grace grant to mee.
Two of your privy councellors
To be of my partie.'

'Have I two in my privy councell,
170   This day will pleasure thee,
If they bett any thing on thy side,
Right welcom shall they bee.'

'Com hether then Sir Richard Lee,
Thou art a knight right good,
175   Full well I know thy pedigree
Thou'rt sprung from Gawain's blood.

'And come hether thou Bishop of Hereford',
A noble preist was hee.
'By my silver myter,' said the bishop,
180   'I'le not bett one penny.

'Our king hath archers of his owne
Full redy and full light,
But these are strangers every one
I know not how they height.'

185   'What wilt thou bett,' said Robin Hood,
'Thou seest our gam's the worse.'
'By my silver myter,' said the Bishop,
'All the money in my purse.'

'What's in thy purse?' quoth Robin tho,
190   'Tell it downe on the ground.'
'Fifteen score of nobles,' quoth the bishop,
'It's neer a hundred pounds.'

Robin tooke his mantle from his back,
And threw it on the mould,
195   Forth he pluck'd a velvett pouch,
It was well lin'd with gold.

Forth he pluck'd his velvet pouch
He told the gold on the green,
Then cry'd Midge the Millers son,
200   'I know who the gold will win.'

In came Will Scathlock to the rest
And to Little John did thrust,
'They shall not gett another shoot
And all their hearts would brust.'

205   Then the queen's archers led aboute
       Till it was three and three,
       And then the ladies gave a shoute,
       'Woodcock, bewere thine eye.'

       'Tis three and three now,' says our king,
210   'The next three pays for all.'
       Then Robin whisper'd to the queen
       'The king's part will be but small.'

       Then shot Tempest for the king
       He led it gallantly,
215   Then shott Loxly for our queen
       And clove his arrow in three.

       Then shott Midge the Millers son,
       He was not far the worse,
       Within a finger of the pegg,
220   'Bishop, bewere thy purse.'

       The yeoman of the crowne who stod him by
       Hee shott underhand,
       But Clifton with a bearded arrow
       He clove the willow wand.

225   'The upshott now,' said Will Scathlock,
       'For the honor o'th queen and mee',
       Hee tooke the prick on arrow poynt
       The king and all did see.

       Then spoke Tempest to our king,
230   'These archers are so good,
       I'm sore affraid and like your grace,
       They learn'd of Robin Hood.'

       'But fear not that,' our king did say
       For 'twas told me of late
235   That Robin Hood and his wel wight men
       Were slaine at pallas gate.'

       'A boon, a boon,' Queen Catherin cry'd,
       'I aske it on my knee,
       Your grace will angry be with none
240   That are of my partie.'

'They shal have forty days to come
And forty days to go
Twice forty days to sport and play
Then welcom friend or foe.'

245   'Welcom Robin Hood,' then said the queen,
'And so is Little John,
And so is Midge the Millers son,
Will Scathlock every one.'

'Is this Robin Hood,' then said the bishop,
250   'As it seems well to bee?
Had I knowne t'had bin that bold outlaw
I'de not bett one penny.

'Hee tooke me late one Satterday night,
And bound me to a tree,
255   And made me sing a masse, God wott,
To him and's companie.'

'What if I did?' said Robin tho;
'Of that masse I was full faine.
To recompence thee for that deed,
260   Heers halfe thy gold again.'

'Now nay, now nay,' sais Little John,
'Master, that may not bee.
Wee must give gifts to th' kings officers
'Twill serve both you and wee.'

ROBIN HOOD AND THE BISHOP

This ballad is found in seventeenth-century broadsides and early garland collections, and while there is no clear indication that it existed before then, the incidents have an air of familiarity, being variations on a theme of disguise found in many of the ballads. They also express the hostility to the established Church found in the *Gest* and *Robin Hood and the Monk*.

Come, gentlemen all, and listen a while,
Hey down down an a down
And a story I'le to you unfold:
I'le tell you how Robin Hood served the Bishop,
5   When he robbed him of his gold.

Robin Hood and the bishop. From *Robin Hood* by N.C. Wyeth (1917), p. 140. (*Mary Evans Picture Library*)

As it fell out on a sun-shining day,
When Phebus was in her prime,
Then Robin Hood, that archer good,
In mirth would spend some time.

10   And as he walkd the forrest along,
Some pastime for to spy,
There was he aware of a proud bishop,
And all his company.

'O what shall I do?' said Robin Hood then,
15   'If the Bishop he doth take me;
No mercy he'l show unto me, I know,
But hanged I shall be.'

Then Robin was stout, and turnd him about,
And a little house there he did spy;
20 And to an old wife, for to save his life,
He loud began for to cry.

'Why, who art thou?' said the old woman,
'Come tel it to me for good.'
'I am an out-law, as many do know,
25 My name it is Robin Hood.

'And yonder's the Bishop and all his men,
And if that I taken be,
Then day and night he'l work me spight,
And hanged I shall be.'

30 'If thou be Robin Hood,' said the old wife,
'As thou doth seem to be,
I'le for thee provide, and thee I will hide,
From the Bishop and his company.

'For I well remember, on Saturday night
35 Thou bought me both shoos and hose;
Therefore I'le provide thy person to hide,
And keep thee from thy foes.'

'Then give me soon thy coat of gray,
And take thou my mantle of green;
40 Thy spindle and twine unto me resign,
And take thou my arrows so keen.'

And when that Robin Hood was so araid,
He went straight to his company;
With his spindle and twine, he oft lookt behind
45 For the Bishop and his company.

'O who is yonder,' quoth Little John,
'That now comes over the lee?
An arrow I will at her let flie,
So like an old witch looks she.'

50 'O hold thy hand, hold thy hand,' said Robin then,
'And shoot not thy arrows so keen;
I am Robin Hood, thy master good,
And quickly it shall be seen.'

The Bishop he came to the old womans house,
55   And he called with furious mood,
'Come let me soon see, and bring unto me,
That traitor Robin Hood.'

The old woman he set on a milk-white steed,
Himselfe on a dapple-gray,
60   And for joy he had got Robin Hood,
He went laughing all the way.

But as they were riding the forrest along,
The Bishop he chanc'd for to see
A hundred brave bow-men bold
65   Stand under the green-wood tree.

'O who is yonder,' the Bishop then said,
'That's ranging within yonder wood?'
'Marry,' says the old woman, 'I think it to be
A man calld Robin Hood.'

70   'Why, who art thou,' the Bishop he said,
'Which I have here with me?'
'Why I am an old woman, thou cuckoldly bishop;
Lift up my leg and see.'

'Then woe is me,' the Bishop he said,
75   'That ever I saw this day!'
He turnd him about, but Robin so stout
Calld him and bid him stay.

Then Robin took hold of the Bishops horse,
And ty'd him fast to a tree;
80   Then Little John smil'd his master upon,
For joy of that company.

Robin Hood took his mantle from's back,
And spread it upon the ground,
And out of the Bishops portmantle he
85   Soon told five hundred pound.

'So now let him go,' said Robin Hood;
Said Little John, 'That may not be;
For I vow and protest he shall sing us a mass
Before that he goe from me.'

90   Then Robin Hood took the Bishop by the hand,
      And bound him fast to a tree,
      And made him sing a mass, God wot,
      To him and his yeomandree.

      And then they brought him through the wood,
95   And set him on his dapple-gray,
      And gave the tail within his hand,
      And bade him for Robin Hood pray.

ROBIN HOOD AND THE CURTAL FRIAR

Though this is not one of the earlier ballads in terms of its recording, it appears to have a late medieval origin. It appears in the Percy folio manuscript but more than half has been torn away. It also occurs, in a slightly expanded form, in a number of seventeenth-century versions, the garland of 1663 appearing to be the earliest of these.

      But how many merry moones be in the yeere?
      There are thirteen, I say;
      The midsummer moone is the merryest of all,
      Next to the merry month of May.

Robin and the curtal friar. Illustration in *Robin Hood's Ballads* (1867), p. 175. (*Mary Evans Picture Library*)

5 In summer time, when leaves grow green,
  And flowers are fresh and gay,
  Robin Hood and his merry men
  Were disposed to play.

  Then some would leap, and some would run,
10 And some would use artillery:
  'Which of you can a good bow draw,
  A good archer to be?

  'Which of you can kill a buck?
  Or who can kill a do?
15 Or who can kill a hart of greece,
  Five hundred foot him fro.'

  Will Scadlock he killd a buck
  And Midge he killd a do,
  And Little John killd a hart of greece,
20 Five hundred foot him fro.

  'God's blessing on thy heart,' said Robin Hood,
  'That hath such a shot for me;
  I would ride my horse an hundred miles,
  To finde one could match with thee.'

25 That causd Will Scadlock to laugh,
  He laughed full heartily:
  'There lives a curtal frier in Fountains Abby
  Will beat both him and thee.

  'That curtal frier in Fountains Abby
30 Well can a strong bow draw;
  He will beat you and your yeomen,
  Set them all on a row.'

  Robin Hood took a solemn oath,
  It was by Mary free,
35 That he would neither eat nor drink
  Till the frier he did see.

  Robin Hood put on his harness good,
  And on his head a cap of steel,
  Broad sword and buckler by his side,
40 And they became him weel.

He builded his men in a brake of fearne,
A litle from that nunery;
Sayes, 'If you heare my litle horne blow,
Then looke you come to me.'

45   When Robin came to Fontaines Abey,
Whereas that fryer lay,
He was ware of the fryer where he stood,
And to him thus can he say:

'I am a wet weary man,' said Robin Hood,
50   'Good fellow, as thou may see;
Wilt beare me over this wild water,
For sweete Saint Charity?'

The fryer bethought him of a good deed;
He had done none of long before;
55   He hent up Robin Hood on his backe,
And over he did him beare.

But when he came over that wild water,
A longe sword there he drew:
'Beare me backe againe, bold outlawe,
60   Or of this though shalt have enoughe.'

Then Robin Hood hent the fryar on his back,
And neither sayd good nor ill,
Till he came ore that wild water,
The yeoman he walked still.

65   Then Robin Hood wett his fayre greene hoze
A span above his knee;
Says 'Beare me ore againe, thou cutted fryer
Or it shall breed thy gree.'

The frier took Robin Hood on's back again,
70   And stept up to the knee;
Till he came at the middle stream,
Neither good nor bad spake he.

And coming to the middle stream,
There he threw Robin in:
75   'And chuse thee, chuse thee, fine fellow,
Whether thou wilt sink or swim.'

Robin Hood swam to a bush of broom,
The frier to a wicker wand;
Bold Robin Hood is gone to shore,
80   And took his bow in hand.

One of his best arrows under his belt
To the frier he let flye;
The curtal frier, with his steel buckler,
He put that arrow by.

85   'Shoot on, shoot on, thou fine fellow,
Shoot on as thou hast begun;
If thou shoot here a summers day,
Thy mark I will not shun.'

Robin Hood shot passing well,
90   Till his arrows all were gone;
They took their swords and steel bucklers,
And fought with might and maine,

From ten o'th' clock that day,
Till four i'th' afternoon;
95   Then Robin Hood came to his knees,
Of the frier to beg a boon.

'A boon, a boon, thou curtal frier,
I beg it on my knee;
Give me leave to set my horn to my mouth,
100   And to blow blasts three.'

'That I will do,' said the curtal frier,
'Of thy blasts I have no doubt;
I hope thou'lt blow so passing well
Till both thy eyes fall out.'

105   Robin Hood set his horn to his mouth,
He blew but blasts three;
Half a hundred yeoman, with bows bent,
Came raking over the lee.

'I beshrew thy head,' said the cutted friar,
110   'Thou thinkes I shall be shente;
I thought thou had but a man or two,
And thou hast a whole convent.

'I lett thee have a blast on thy horne,
Now give me leave to whistle another;
115   I cold not bidd thee noe better play
And thou wert my owne borne brother.'

'Now fate on, fute on, thou cutted fryar,
I pray God thou neere be still;
It is not the futing in a fryers fist
120   That can doe me any ill.'

The fryar sett his neave to his mouth,
A lowd blast he did blow;
Then halfe a hundred good bandoggs
Came raking all on a rowe.

125   'Here's for every man a dog,
And I myself for thee.'
'Nay, by my faith,' quoth Robin Hood,
'Frier, that may not be.

'Over God's forbott,' said Robin Hood,
130   'That ever that soe shold bee;
I had rather be mached with three of the tikes
Ere I wold be matched on thee.

'But stay thy tikes, thou fryar,' he said,
'And freindshipp I'le have with thee;
135   But stay thy tikes, thou fryar,' he said,
'And save good yeomanry.'

The fryar he sett his neave to his mouth,
A lowd blast he did blow;
The doggs the coucht downe every one,
140   They couched downe on a rowe.

'What is thy will, thou yeoman?' he said,
'Have done and tell it me.'
'If that thou will goe to merry greenwood,
A noble shall be thy fee.

145   'And every holy day throughout the year,
Changed shall thy garment be,
If thou wilt go to fair Nottingham,
And there remain with me.'

This curtal frier had kept Fountains Dale
150   Seven long years or more;
There was neither knight, lord, nor earl
Could make him yield before.

ROBIN HOOD AND THE GOLDEN ARROW

This is a fairly late ballad that was not recorded until an eighteenth-century garland. It describes the archery contest, a favourite episode in the outlaw tradition that is found as early as the *Gest*. The question must be whether it is a literary reworking of that source, or a long-preserved separate account.

When as the sheriff of Nottingham
Was come with mickle grief,
He talkd no good of Robin Hood,
That strong and sturdy thief.
5   Fal lal dal de.

Robin and the golden arrow. Illustration in *Robin Hood's Ballads* (1867), p. 255. (*Mary Evans Picture Library*)

326

So unto London-road he past,
His losses to unfold
To King Richard, who did regard
The tale that he had told.

10   'Why,' quoth the king, 'what shall I do?
Art thou not sheriff for me?
The law is in force, go take thy course,
Of them that injure thee.

'Go get thee gone, and by thyself
15   Devise some tricking game
For to enthral yon rebels all;
Go take thy course with them.'

So away the sheriff he returnd,
And by the way he thought
20   Of the words of the king, and how the thing
To pass might well be brought.

For within his mind he imagined
That when such matches were,
Those outlaws stout, without doubt,
25   Would be the bowmen there.

So an arrow with a golden head
And shaft of silver white,
Who won the day should bear away,
For his own proper right.

30   Tidings came to brave Robin Hood,
Under the green-wood tree.
'Come prepare you then, my merry men,
We'll go yon sport to see.'

With that stept forth a brave young man,
35   David of Doncaster.
'Master,' he said, 'be ruld by me,
From the green-wood we'll not stir.

'To tell the truth, I'm well informed
Yon match is a wile;
40   The sheriff, I wiss, devises this
Us archers to beguile.'

'O thou smells of a coward,' said Robin Hood,
'Thy words does not please me;
Come on't what will, I'll try my skill
45   At yon brave archery.'

O then bespoke brave Little John:
'Come, let us hither gang,
Come listen to me, how it shall be
That we need not be kend.

50   'Our mantles, all of Lincoln green,
Behind us we will leave;
We'll dress us all so several
They shall not us perceive.

'One shall wear white, another red,
55   One yellow, another blue;
Thus in disguise, to the exercise,
We'll gang, whate'er ensue.'

Forth from the green wood they are gone,
With hearts all firm and stout,
60   Resolving with the sheriffs men
To have a hearty bout.

So themselves they mixed with the rest,
To prevent all suspicion,
For if they should together hold
65   They thought no discretion.

So the sheriff looking round about,
Amongst eight hundred men,
But could not see the sight that he
Had long expected then.

70   Some said, 'If Robin Hood was here,
And all his men to boot,
Sure none of them could pass these men,
So bravely they do shoot.'

'Ay,' quoth the sheriff, and scratchd his head,
75   'I thought he would have been here;
I thought he would, but, tho he's bold,
He durst not now appear.'

O that word grieved Robin Hood to the heart;
He vexed in his blood;
80   'Ere long,' thought he, 'thou shalt well see
That here was Robin Hood.'

Some cried, 'Blue jacket!' Another cried, 'Brown!'
And the third cried, 'Brave Yellow!'
But the fourth man said, 'Yon man in red
85   In this place has no fellow.'

For that was Robin Hood himself,
For he was cloathd in red;
At every shot the prize he got,
For he was both sure and dead.

90   So the arrow with the golden head
And shaft of silver white
Brave Robin Hood won, and bore with him
For his own proper right.

These outlaws there, that very day,
95   To shun all kind of doubt,
By three or four, no less no more,
As they went in, came out.

Until they all assembled were
Under the green wood shade,
100   Where they relate, in pleasant sport,
What brave pastime they made.

Says Robin Hood, 'All my care is,
How that yon sheriff may
Know certainly that it was I
105   That bore his arrow away.'

Says Little John, 'My counsel good
Did take effect before,
So therefore now, if you'll allow,
I will advise once more.'

110   'Speak on, speak on,' said Robin Hood,
'Thy wit's both quick and sound;
I know no man amongst us can
For wit like thee be found.'

'This I advise,' said Little John;
115   'That a letter shall be pend,
And when it is done, to Nottingham
You to the sheriff shall send.'

'That is well advised,' said Robin Hood,
'But how must it be sent?'
120   'Pugh! when you please, it's done with ease,
Master, be you content.

'I'll stick it on my arrow's head,
And shoot it into the town;
The mark shall show where it must go,
125   When ever it lights down.'

The project it was full performd;
The sheriff that letter had;
Which when he read, he scratchd his head,
And rav'd like one that's mad.

130   So we'll leave him chafing in his grease,
Which will do him no good;
Now, my friends, attend, and hear the end
Of honest Robin Hood.

ROBIN HOOD AND THE MONK

This ballad is preserved as Cambridge University manuscript Ff.5.48. The manuscript is damaged by stains and hard to read. It was first printed and given this title by Robert Jamieson in his *Popular Ballads and Songs* of 1806 (II, 54–72). The edition itself was quite heavily edited and erroneous, and a better text appeared in C.H. Hartshorne's *Ancient Metrical Tales* in 1829.

In somer, when the shawes be sheyne,
And leves be large and long,
Hit is full mery in feyre foreste
To here the foulys song,

5   To se the dere draw to the dale,
And leve the hilles hee,
And shadow hem in the leves grene,
Under the grene wode tre.

Hit befel on Whitson
10 Erly in a May mornyng,
The son up feyre can shyne,
And the briddis mery can syng.

'This is a mery mornyng,' seid Litull John,
'Be Hym that dyed on tre;
15 A more mery man then I am one
Lyves not in Cristianté.

'Pluk up thi hert, my dere mayster,'
Litull John can sey,
'And thynk hit is a full fayre tyme
20 In a mornyng of May.'

'Ye, on thyng greves me,' seid Robyn,
'And does my hert mych woo:
That I may not no solem day
To mas nor matyns goo.

25 'Hit is a fourtnet and more,' seid he,
'Syn I my Savyour see;
To day wil I to Notyngham,' seid
    Robyn,
'With the myght of mylde Marye.'

Than spake Moche, the mylner sun,
30 Ever more wel hym betyde!
'Take twelve of thi wyght yemen,
Well weppynd, be thi side.
Such on wolde thi selfe slon,
That twelve dar not abyde.'

35 'Of all my mery men,' seid Robyn,
'Be my feith I wil non have,
But Litull John shall beyre my bow,
Til that me list to drawe.'

'Thou shall beyre thin own,' seid Litull Jon,
40 'Maister, and I wyl beyre myne,
And we well shete a peny,' seid Litull Jon,
Under the grene wode lyne.'

The merry friar sings a goodly song. Illustration from *The Merry Adventures of Robin Hood* by Howard Pyle.

'I wil not shete a peny,' seyd Robyn Hode,
'In feith, Litull John, with the,
45   But ever for on as thou shetis,' seide Robyn,
'In feith I holde the thre.'

Thus shet thei forth, these yemen too,
Bothe at buske and brome,
Til Litull John wan of his maister
50   Five shillings to hose and shone.

A ferly strife fel them betwene,
As they went bi the wey;
Litull John seid he had won five shillings,
And Robyn Hode seid schortly nay.

55   With that Robyn Hode lyed Litul Jon,
And smote hym with his hande;
Litul Jon waxed wroth therwith,
And pulled out his bright bronde.

'Were thou not my maister,' seid Litull John,
60   'Thou shuldis by hit ful sore;
Get the a man wher thou wille,
For thou getis me no more.'

Then Robyn goes to Notyngham,
Hym selfe mornyng allone,
65   And Litull John to mery Scherwode,
The pathes he knew ilkone.

Whan Robyn came to Notyngham,
Sertenly withouten layn,
He prayed to God and myld Mary
70   To bryng hym out save agayn.

He gos in to Seynt Mary chirch,
And knelyd down before the rode;
Alle that ever were the church within
Beheld wel Robyn Hode.

75   Beside hym stod a gret-hedid munke,
I pray to God woo he be!
Ful sone he knew gode Robyn,
As sone as he hym se.

Out at the durre he ran,
80   Ful sone and anon;
Alle the gatis of Notyngham
He made to be sparred everychon.

'Rise up,' he seid, 'thou prowde schereff,
Buske the and make the bowne;
85   I have spyed the kynggis felon,
For sothe he is in this town.

'I have spyed the false felon,
As he stondis at his masse;
Hit is long of the,' seide the munke,
90   'And ever he fro us passe.

'This traytur name is Robyn Hode,
Under the grene wode lynde;
He robbyt me onys of a hundred pound,
Hit shalle never out of my mynde.'

95   Up then rose this prowde schereff,
And radly made hym yare;
Many was the moder son
To the kyrk with hym can fare.

In at the durres thei throly thrast,
100   With staves ful gode wone;
'Alas, alas!' seid Robyn Hode,
'Now mysse I Litull John.'

But Robyn toke out a too-hond sworde,
That hangit down be his kne;
105   Ther as the schereff and his men stode thyckust
Thedurwarde wolde he.

Thryes thorow at them he ran then,
For sothe as I yow sey,
And woundyt mony a moder son,
110   And twelve he slew that day.

His sworde upon the schireff hed
Sertanly he brake in too;
'The smyth that the made,' seid Robyn,
'I pray to God wyrke hym woo!

115 'For now am I weppynlesse,' seid Robyn,
'Alasse! agayn my wyll;
But if I may fle these traytors fro,
I wot thei wil me kyll.'

Robyn in to her churche ran,
120 Thro out hem everilkon,
*   *   *

Sum fel in swonyng as thei were dede,
And lay stil as any stone;
Non of theym were in her mynde
But only Litull Jon.

125 'Let be your rule,' seid Litull Jon,
'For His luf that dyed on tre,
Ye that shulde be dughty men;
Het is gret shame to se.

'Oure maister has bene hard bystode
130 And yet scapyd away;
Pluk up your hertis, and leve this mone,
And harkyn what I shal say.

'He has servyd Oure Lady many a day,
And yet wil, securly;
135 Therfor I trust in hir specialy
No wyckud deth shal he dye.

'Therfor be glad,' seid Litul John,
'And let this mournyng be;
And I shal be the munkis gyde,
140 With the myght of mylde Mary,
And I mete hym,' seid Litul John
'We will go but we too.

'Loke that ye kepe wel owre tristil-tre,
Under the levys smale,
145 And spare non of this venyson,
That gose in thys vale.'

Forthe then went these yemen too,
Litul John and Moche on fere,
And lokid on Moch emys hows;
150   The hye way lay full nere.

Litul John stode at a wyndow in the mornyng,
And lokid forth at a stage;
He was war wher the munke came ridyng,
And with hym a litul page.

155   'Be my feith,' seid Litul John to Moch,
'I can the tel tithyngus gode;
I se wher the munke cumys rydyng,
I know hym be his wyde hode.'

They went in to the way, these yemen bothe,
160   As curtes men and hende;
Thei spyrred tithyngus at the munke,
As they hade bene his frende.

'Fro whens come ye?' seid Litull Jon,
'Tel us tithyngus, I yow pray,
165   Of a false owtlay,
Was takyn yisterday.

'He robbyt me and my felowes bothe
Of twenti marke in serten;
If that false owtlay be takyn,
170   For sothe we wolde be fayn.'

'So did he me,' seid the munke,
Of a hundred pound and more;
I layde furst hande hym apon,
Ye may thonke me therfore.'

175   'I pray God thanke you,' seid Litull John,
'And we wil when we may;
We wil go with you, with your leve,
And bryng yow on your way.

'For Robyn Hode hase many a wilde felow,
180   I tell you in certen;
If thei wist ye rode this way,
In feith ye shulde be slayn.'

As thei went talking be the way,
The munke and Litull John,
185   John toke the munkis horse be the hede,
Ful sone and anon.

Johne toke the munkis horse be the hed,
For sothe as I yow say;
So did Much the litull page,
190   For he shulde not scape away.

Be the golett of the hode
John pulled the munke down;
John was nothyng of hym agast,
He lete hym falle on his crown.

195   Litull John was so agrevyd,
And drew owt his swerde in hye;
The munke saw he shulde be ded,
Lowd mercy can he crye.

'He was my maister,' seid Litull John,
200   'That thou hase browght in bale;
Shalle thou never cum at oure kyng,
For to telle hym tale.'

John smote of the munkis hed,
No longer wolde he dwell;
205   So did Moch the litull page,
For ferd lest he wolde tell.

Ther thei beryed hem bothe,
In nouther mosse nor lyng,
And Litull John and Much in fere
210   Bare the letturs to oure kyng.

Litull John cam in unto the kyng
He knelid down upon his kne:
'God yow save, my lege lorde,
Jhesus yow save and se!

Little John's house. Illustration in *Robin Hood's Ballads* (1867). (*Mary Evans Picture Library*)

215   'God yow save, my lege kyng!'
        To speke John was full bolde;
        He gaf hym the letturs in his hand,
        The kyng did hit unfold.

        The kyng red the letturs anon,
220   And seid, 'So mot I the,
        Ther was never yoman in mery Inglond
        I longut so sore to se.

        'Wher is the munke that these shuld have brought?'
        Oure kyng can say.
225   'Be my trouth,' seid Litull John,
        'He dyed after the way.'

        The kyng gaf Moch and Litul Jon
        Twenti pound in sertan,
        And made theim yemen of the crown,
230   And bade theim go agayn.

He gaf John the seel in hand,
The scheref for to bere,
To bryng Robyn hym to,
And no man do hym dere.

235   John toke his leve at oure kyng,
The sothe as I yow say;
The next way to Notyngham
To take he yede the way.

Whan John came to Notyngham
240   The gatis were sparred ychon;
John callid up the porter,
He answerid sone anon.

'What is the cause,' seid Litul Jon,
'Thou sparris the gates so fast?'
245   'Because of Robyn Hode,' seid porter,
'In depe prison is cast.

'John and Moch and Wyll Scathlok,
For sothe as I yow say,
Thei slew oure men upon oure wallis,
250   And sawten us every day.'

Litull John spyrred after the schereff,
And sone he hym fonde;
He oppyned the kyngus privé seell,
And gaf hym in his honde.

255   Whan the scheref saw the kyngus seell,
He did of his hode anon:
'Wher is the munke that bare the letturs?'
He seid to Litull John.

'He is so fayn of hym,' seid Litul John,
260   'For sothe as I yow say,
He has made hym abot of Westmynster,
A lorde of that abbay.'

The scheref made John gode chere,
And gaf hym wyne of the best;
265   At nyght thei went to her bedde,
And every man to his rest.

When the scheref was on slepe,
Dronken of wyne and ale,
Litul John and Moch for sothe
270   Toke the way unto the gale.

Litul John callid up the jayler,
And bade hym rise anon;
He seyd Robyn Hode had brokyn the prison,
And out of hit was gon.

275   The porter rose anon sertan,
As sone as he herd John calle;
Litul John was redy with a swerd,
And bare hym throw to the walle.

'Now wil I be jayler,' seid Litul John,
280   And toke the keyes in honde;
He toke the way to Robyn Hode,
And sone he hym unbonde.

He gaf hym a gode swerd in his hond,
His hed ther with to kepe,
285   And ther as the wallis were lowyst
Anon down can thei lepe.

Be that the cok began to crow,
The day began to spryng;
The scheref fond the jaylier ded,
290   The comyn bell made he ryng.

He made a crye thoroout al the town,
Wheder he be yoman or knave,
That cowthe bryng hym Robyn Hode,
His warison he shuld have.

295   'For I dar never,' seid the scheref,
'Cum before oure kyng;
For if I do, I wot serten
For sothe he wil me heng.'

The scheref made to seke Notyngham,
300   Bothe be strete and styne,
And Robyn was in mery Scherwode,
As light as lef on lynde.

Then bespake gode Litull John,
To Robyn Hode can he say,
305 'I have done the a gode turne for an ill,
Quit me whan thou may.

'I have done the a gode turne,' seid Litull John,
'For sothe as I the say;
I have brought the under the grene-wode lyne;
310 Fare wel, and have gode day.'

'Nay, be my trouth,' seid Robyn,
'So shall hit never be;
I make the maister,' seid Robyn,
'Of alle my men and me.'

315 'Nay, be my trouth,' seid Litull John,
'So shalle hit never be;
But lat me be a felow,' seid Litull John,
'No noder kepe I be.'

Thus John gate Robyn Hod out of prison,
320 Sertan withoutyn layn;
Whan his men saw hym hol and sounde,
For sothe they were full fayne.

They filled in wyne and made hem glad,
Under the levys smale,
325 And yete pastes of venyson,
That gode was with ale.

Than worde came to oure kyng
How Robyn Hode was gon,
And how the scheref of Notyngham
330 Durst never loke hym upon.

Then bespake oure cumly kyng,
In an angur hye:
'Litull John hase begyled the schereff,
In faith so hase he me.

335 'Litul John has begyled us bothe,
And that full wel I se;
Or ellis the schereff of Notyngham
Hye hongut shulde he be.

'I made hem yemen of the crowne,
340   And gaf hem fee with my hond;
I gaf hem grith,' seid oure kyng,
'Thorowout all mery Inglond.

'I gaf theym grith,' then seid oure kyng;
'I say, so mot I the,
345   For sothe soch a yeman as he is on
In all Inglond ar not thre.

'He is trew to his maister,' seid oure kyng;
'I sey, be swete Seynt John,
He lovys better Robyn Hode
350   Then he dose us ychon.

'Robyn Hode is ever bond to hym,
Bothe in strete and stalle;
Speke no more of this mater,' seid oure kyng,
'But John has begyled us alle.'

355   Thus endys the talkyng of the munke
And Robyn Hode I wysse;
God, that is ever a crowned kyng,
Bryng us alle to His blisse!

ROBIN HOOD AND THE PEDLARS

This ballad may, in part, have been written as early as 1650, but it appears in a nineteenth-century hand, and some such are maintained to be forgeries. *Robin Hood and the Pedlars* is surely one of the forgeries, a work composed most likely in the early nineteenth century by an antiquarian enthusiast who had read plenty of Robin Hood ballads and who had a good measure of off-colour wit.

Will you heare a tale of Robin Hood,
Will Scarlett, and Little John?
Now listen awhile, it will make you smile,
As before it hath many done.

5   They were archers three, of hie degree,
As good as ever drewe bowe;
Their arrowes were long and their armes were strong,
As most had cause to knowe.

But one sommers day, as they toke their way
10   Through the forrest of greene Sherwood,
To kill the kings deare, you shall presently heare
What befell these archers good.

They were ware on the roade of three peddlers with loade,
For each had his packe.
15   Full of all wares for countrie faires,
Trusst up upon his backe.

A good oke staffe, a yard and a halfe,
Each one had in his hande,
And they were all bound to Nottingham towne,
20   As you shall understand.

'Yonder I see bold peddlers three,'
Said Robin to Scarlett and John;
'We'le search their packes upon their backes
Before that they be gone.

25   'Holla, good fellowes!' quod Robin Hood,
'Whither is it ye doe goe?
Now stay and rest, for that is the best,
'Tis well ye should doe soe.'

'Noe rest we neede, on our roade we speede,
30   Till to Nottingham we get.'
'Thou tellst a lewde lye,' said Robin, 'for I
Can see that ye swinke and swet.'

The peddlers three crosst over the lee,
They did not list to fight:
35   'I charge you tarrie,' quod Robin, 'for marry,
This is my owne land by right.

'This is my mannor and this is my parke,
I would have ye for to knowe;
Ye are bolde outlawes, I see by cause
40   Ye are so prest to goe.'

The peddlers three turned round to see
Who it might be they herd;
Then agen went on as they list to be gone,
And never answered word.

Robin carouses with the tinker. Illustration in *Robin Hood's Ballads* (1867), p. 234. (*Mary Evans Picture Library*)

45   Then toke Robin Hood an arrow so good,
          Which he did never lacke,
          And drew his bowe, and the swift arrowe
          Went through the last peddlers packe.

          For him it was well on the packe it fell,
50   Or his life had found an ende;
          And it pierst the skin of his backe within,
          Though the packe did stand his frend.

          Then downe they flung their packes eche one,
          And stayde till Robin came;
55   Quod Robin, 'I saide ye had better stayde;
          Good sooth, ye were to blame.

'And who art thou? by S. Crispin, I
        vowe,
I'le quickly cracke thy head!'
Cried Robin, 'Come on, all three, or
        one;
60   It is not so soone done as said.

'My name, by the Roode, is Robin
        Hood,
And this is Scarlett and John;
It is three to three, ye may plainelie
        see,
Soe now, brave fellowes, laye on.'

65   The first peddlars blowe brake Robins
        bowe
That he had in his hand;
And Scarlett and John, they eche had one
That they unneth could stand.

Illustration from *The Merry Adventures of Robin Hood* by Howard Pyle.

'Now holde your handes,' cride Robin Hood,
70   'For ye have got oken staves;
But tarie till wee can get but three,
And a fig for all your braves.'

Of the peddlers the first, his name Kit o Thirske,
Said, 'We are all content.'
75   So eche tooke a stake for his weapon to make
The peddlers to repent.

Soe to it they fell, and their blowes did ring well
Uppon the others backes,
And gave the peddlers cause to wish
80   They had not cast their packes.

Yet the peddlers three of their blowes were so free
That Robin began for to rue;
And Scarlett and John had such loade laide on
It made the sunne looke blue.

85   At last Kits oke caught Robin a stroke
That made his head to sound;
He staggerd and reelde, till he fell on the fielde,
And the trees with him went round.

Stout Robin hath a narrow escape. Illustration from *The Merry Adventures of Robin Hood* by Howard Pyle.

'Now holde your handes,' cride Little John,
90 And soe said Scarlette eke;
'Our maister is slaine, I telle you plaine,
He never more will speake.'

'Now, heaven forefend he come to that ende,'
Said Kit, 'I love him well;
95 But lett him learne to be wise in turne,
And not with pore peddlers mell.

'In my packe, God wot, I a balsame have got
That soone his hurts will heale';
And into Robin Hoods gaping mouth
100 He presentlie powrde some deale.

'Nowe fare ye well, tis best not to tell
How ye three peddlers met;
Or if ye doe, prithee tell alsoe
How they made ye swinke and swett.'

105   Poore Robin in sound they left on the ground,
And hied them to Nottingham,
While Scarlett and John Robin tended on
Till at length his senses came.

Noe sooner, in haste, did Robin Hood taste
The balsame he had tane,
110   Than he gan to spewe, and up he threwe
The balsame all againe.

And Scarlett and John, who were looking on
Their maister as he did lie,
Had their faces besmeard, both eies and beard,
115   Therwith most piteously.

Thus ended that fray; soe beware alwaye
How ye doe challenge foes;
Looke well aboute they are not to stoute,
Or you may have worst of the blowes.

ROBIN HOOD AND THE POTTER

The ballad survives only in one manuscript, Cambridge E.e.4.35, a collection of popular and moral poems dated around 1500. The text is complete, though at line 271 a line does appear to be missing through scribal error.

FITT 1
In schomer, when the leves spryng,
The bloschoms on every bowe,
So merey doyt the berdys syng
Yn wodys merey now.

5   Herkens, god yemen,
Comley, corteys, and god,
On of the best that yever bare bowe,
Hes name was Roben Hode.

Roben Hood was the yemans name,
10   That was boyt corteys and fre;
For the loffe of owre ladey,
All wemen werschepyd he.

'In schomer when the leves spryng': the opening lines of the only extant copy of *Robin Hood and the Potter, c.* 1500. Cambridge University Library, Ms Ee 4.35, f.14v. *(Reproduced by courtesy of Cambridge University Library)*

Bot as the god yeman stod on a day,
Among hes mery maney,

15   He was ware of a prowd potter,
Cam dryfyng owyr the leye.

'Yonder comet a prod potter,' seyde Roben,
'That long hayt hantyd this wey;
He was never so corteys a man

20   On peney of pawage to pay.'

'Y met hem bot at Wentbreg,' seyde Lytyll John,
'And therefore yeffell mot he the!
Seche thre strokes he me gafe,
Yet by my seydys cleffe they.

25   'Y ley forty shillings,' seyde Lytyll John,
'To pay het thes same day,
Ther ys nat a man among hus all
A wed schall make hem leye.'

'Here ys forty shillings,' seyde Roben,
30   'More, and thow dar say,
That Y schall make that prowde potter,
A wed to me schall he ley.'

There thes money they leyde,
They toke het a yeman to kepe;
35   Roben beffore the potter he breyde,
And bad hem stond stell.

Handys apon hes hors he leyde,
And bad the potter stonde foll stell;
The potter schorteley to hem seyde,
40   'Felow, what ys they well?'

'All thes thre yer, and more, potter,' he seyde,
'Thow hast hantyd thes wey,
Yet were tow never so cortys a man
On peney of pavage to pay.'

45   'What ys they name,' seyde the potter,
'For pavage thow aske of me?'
'Roben Hod ys mey name,
A wed schall thow leffe me.'

'Wed well y non leffe,' seyde the potter,
50   'Nor pavag well Y non pay;
Awey they honde fro mey hors!
Y well the tene eyls, be mey fay.'

The potter to hes cart he went,
He was not to seke;
55   A god to-hande staffe therowt he hent,
Beffore Roben he leppyd.

Roben howt with a swerd bent,
A bokeler en hes honde;
The potter to Roben he went,
60   And seyde, 'Felow, let mey hors go.'

Togeder then went thes to yemen,
Het was a god seyt to se;
Thereof low Robyn hes men,
There they stod onder a tre.

65   Leytell John to hes felow he seyde,
'Yend potter well steffeley stonde':
The potter, with an acward stroke,
Smot the bokeler owt of hes honde.

And ar Roben meyt get het agen
70   Hes bokeler at hes fette,
The potter yn the neke hem toke,
To the gronde sone he yede.

That saw Roben hes men,
As they stod onder a bow;
75   'Let us helpe owre master,' seyde Lytell John,
'Yonder potter,' seyde he, 'els well hem slo.'

Thes wight yemen with a breyde,
To thes master they cam.
Leytell John to hes master seyde,
80   'Ho haet the wager won?

'Schall Y haffe yowre forty shillings,' seyde Lytl John,
'Or ye, master, schall haffe myne?'
'Yeff they were a hundred,' seyde Roben,
'Y feythe, they ben all theyne.'

85   'Het ys fol leytell cortesey,' seyde the potter,
'As I hafe harde weyse men sye,
Yeffe a pore yeman com drywyng over the way,
To let hem of hes gorney.'

'Be mey trowet, thow seys soyt,' seyde Roben,
90   'Thow seys god yemenrey;
And thow dreyffe forthe yevery day,
Thow schalt never be let for me.'

'Y well prey the, god potter,
A felischepe well thow haffe?
95   Geffe me they clothyng, and thow schalt hafe myne;
Y well go to Notynggam.'

'Y grant thereto,' seyde the potter,
'Thow schalt feynde me a felow gode;
Bot thow can sell mey pottys well,
100   Com ayen as thow yede.'

'Nay, be mey trowt,' seyde Roben,
'And then Y bescro mey hede,
Yeffe Y bryng eney pottys ayen,
And eney weyffe well hem chepe.'

105   Than spake Leytell John,
And all hes felowhes heynd,
'Master, be well ware of the screffe of Notynggam,
For he ys leytell howr frende.'

'Thorow the helpe of Howr Ladey,
110   Felowhes, let me alone.
Heyt war howte!' seyde Roben,
'To Notynggam well Y gon.'

Robyn went to Notynggam,
Thes pottys for to sell;
115   The potter abode with Robens men,
There he fered not eylle.

Tho Roben droffe on hes wey,
So merey ower the londe:
Her es more, and affter ys to saye,
120   The best ys beheynde.

FITT 2
When Roben cam to Notynggam,
The soyt yef Y scholde saye,
He set op hes hors anon,
And gaffe hem hotys and haye.

125   Yn the medys of the towne,
There he schowed hes ware;
'Pottys! pottys!' he gan crey foll sone,
'Haffe hansell for the mare!'

Foll effen agenest the screffeys gate
130   Schowed he hes chaffare;
Weyffes and wedowes abowt hem drow,
And chepyd fast of hes ware.

Yet 'Pottys, gret chepe!' creyed Robyn,
'Y loffe yeffell thes to stonde.'
135   And all that say hem sell
Seyde he had be no potter long.

The pottys that were worthe pens feyffe,
He solde tham for pens thre;
Preveley seyde man and weyffe,
140   'Ywnder potter schall never the.'

Thos Roben solde foll fast,
Tell he had pottys bot feyffe;
Op he hem toke of hes car,
And sende hem to the screffeys weyfe.

145   Thereof sche was foll fayne,
'Gereamarsey,' seyde sche, 'sir, than,
When ye com to thes contré ayen,
Y schall bey of the pottys, so mo Y the.'

'Ye schall haffe of the best,' seyde Roben,
150   And sware be the Treneyté";
Foll corteysley sche gan hem call,
'Com deyne with the screfe and me.'

'God amarsey,' seyde Roben,
'Yowre bedyng schall be doyn.'
155   A mayden yn the pottys gan bere,
Roben and the screffe weyffe folowed anon.

Whan Roben yn to the hall cam,
The screffe sone he met;
The potter cowed of corteysey,
160   And sone the screffe he gret.

'Lo, ser, what thes potter hayt geffe yow and me,
Feyffe pottys smalle and grete!'
'He ys foll wellcom,' seyd the screffe,
'Let os was, and to mete.'

165 As they sat at her methe,
With a nobell chere,
To of the screffes men gan speke
Of a gret wager,

Of a schotyng, was god and feyne,
170 Was made the tother daye,
Of forty shillings, the soyt to saye,
Who scholde thes wager gayne.

Styll than sat thes prowde potter,
Thos than thowt he,
175 As Y am a trow Cerstyn man,
Thes schotyng well Y se.

Whan they had fared of the best,
With bred and ale and weyne,
To the bottys the made them prest,
180 With bowes and boltys foll feyne.

The screffes men schot foll fast,
As archares that weren prowe,
There cam non ner ney the marke
Bey halffe a god archares bowe.

185 Stell then stod the prowde potter,
Thos than seyde he;
'And Y had a bow, be the Rode,
On schot scholde yow se.'

'Thow schall haffe a bow,' seyde the screffe,
190 'The best that thow well cheys of thre;
Thou semyst a stalward and a stronge,
Asay schall thow be.'

The screffe commandyd a yeman that stod hem bey
After bowhes to weynde;
195 The best bow that the yeman browthe
Roben set on a stryng.

'Now schall Y wet and thow be god,
And polle het op to they nere.'
'So god me helpe,' seyde the prowde potter,
200 'Thys ys bot ryght weke gere.'

To a quequer Roben went,
A god bolt owthe he toke;
So ney on to the marke he went,
He fayled not a fothe.

205   All they schot a bowthe agen,
The screffes men and he;
Off the marke he welde not fayle,
He cleffed the preke on thre.

The screffes men thowt gret schame
210   The potter the mastry wan;
The screffe lowe and made god game,
And seyde, 'Potter, thow art a man.
Thow art worthey to bere a bowe
Yn what plas that thow goe.'

215   'Yn mey cart Y haffe a bow,
For soyt,' he seyde, 'and that a godde;
Yn mey cart ys the bow
That gaffe me Robyn Hode.'

'Knowest thow Robyn Hode?' seyde the screffe,
220   'Potter, Y prey the tell thow me.'
'A hundred torne Y haffe schot with hem,
Under hes tortyll-tre.'
'Y had lever nar a hundred ponde,' seyde the screffe,
And sware be the Trinity,
225   'That the fals outelawe stod be me.'

'And ye well do afftyr mey red,' seyde the potter,
'And boldeley go with me,
And to morow, or we het bred,
Roben Hode well we se.'

230   'Y well queyt the,' kod the screffe,
'And swere be God of meythe.'
Schetyng thay left, and hom they went,
Her soper was reddy deythe.

FITT 3
Upon the morrow, when het was day,
235   He boskyd hem forthe to reyde;
The potter hes cart forthe gan ray,
And wolde not leffe beheynde.

He toke leffe of the screffys wyffe,
And thankyd her of all thyng:
240   'Dam, for mey loffe and ye well thys were,
Y geffe yow here a golde ryng.'

'Gramarsey,' seyde the weyffe,
'Sir, God eylde het the.'
The screffes hart was never so leythe,
245   The feyre foreyst to se.

And when he cam yn to the foreyst,
Under the leffes grene,
Berdys there sange on bowhes prest,
Het was gret goy to se.

250   'Here het ys merey to be,' seyde Roben,
'For a man that had hawt to spende;
Be mey horne ye schall awet
Yeff Roben Hode be here.'

Roben set hes horne to hes mowthe,
255   And blow a blast that was foll god;
That herde hes men that there stode,
Fer downe yn the wodde.
'I her mey master blow,' seyde Leytell John,
They ran as thay were wode.

260   Whan thay to thar master cam,
Leytell John wold not spare;
'Master, how haffe yow fare yn Notynggam?
How haffe yow solde yowre ware?'

'Ye, be mey trowthe, Leytyll John,
265   Loke thow take no care;
Y haffe browt the screffe of Notynggam,
For all howre chaffare.'

'He ys foll wellcom,' seyde Lytyll John,
'Thes tydyng ys foll godde.'
270   The screffe had lever nar a hundred ponde
He had never seen Roben Hode.

'Had I west that befforen,
At Notynggam when we were,
Thow scholde not com yn feyre forest
275   Of all thes thowsande eyre.'

'That wot Y well,' seyde Roben,
'Y thanke God that ye be here;
Thereffore schall ye leffe yowre hors with hos,
And all yowre hother gere.'

280   'That fend I Godys forbod,' kod the screffe,
'So to lese mey godde.'
'Hether ye cam on hors foll hey,
And hom schall ye go on fote;
And gret well they weyffe at home,
285   The woman ys foll godde.

'Y schall her sende a wheyt palffrey,
Het hambellet as the weynde,
Nere for the loffe of yowre weyffe,
Off more sorow scholde yow seyng.'

290   Thes parted Robyn Hode and the screffe;
To Notynggam he toke the waye;
Hes weyffe feyre welcomed hem hom,
And to hem gan sche saye:

'Seyr, how haffe yow fared yn grene foreyst?
295   Haffe ye browt Roben hom?'
'Dam, the deyell spede hem, bothe bodey and bon;
Y haffe hade a foll gret skorne.

'Of all the god that Y haffe lade to grene wod,
He hayt take het fro me;
300   All bot thes feyre palffrey,
That he hayt sende to the.'

With that sche toke op a lowde lawhyng,
And swhare be Hem that deyed on tre,
'Now haffe yow payed for all the pottys
305   That Roben gaffe to me.

'Now ye be com hom to Notynggam.
Ye schall haffe god ynowe.'
Now speke we of Roben Hode,
And of the pottyr ondyr the grene
    bowhe.

310   'Potter, what was they pottys worthe
To Notynggam that Y ledde with me?'
'They wer worthe to nobellys,'
    seyde he,
'So mot Y treyffe or the;
So cowde Y had for tham,
315   And Y had be there.'

'Thow schalt hafe ten ponde,'
    seyde Roben,
'Of money feyre and fre;
And yever whan thow comest to
    grene wod,
Wellcom, potter, to me.'

Robin wrestles with Will Stuteley. From *Robin Hood* by N.C. Wyeth (1917), p. 53. (*Mary Evans Picture Library*)

320   Thes partyd Robyn, the screffe, and the potter,
Ondernethe the grene wod tre;
God haffe mersey on Roben Hodys solle,
And saffe all god yemanrey!

ROBIN HOOD AND WILL SCARLET
OR
ROBIN HOOD AND THE STRANGER

This ballad is found in seventeenth-century broadsides and early garlands under the title *Robin Hood Newly Revived*. It is called *Robin Hood and Will Scarlet* here as it appears to be dedicated to explaining the arrival in the outlaw band of a well-known figure.

Come listen a while, you gentlemen all,
With a hey down, down, a down down,
That are in this bower within,
For a story of gallant bold Robin Hood
5   I purpose now to begin.

'What time of the day?' quoth Robin Hood then;
Quoth Little John, ''Tis in the prime.'
'Why then we will to the green wood gang,
For we have no vittles to dine.'

10   As Robin Hood walkt the forrest along –
It was in the mid of the day –
There was he met of a deft young man
As ever walkt on the way.

His doublet it was of silk, he said,
15   His stockings like scarlet shone,
And he walkt on along the way,
To Robin Hood then unknown.

A herd of deer was in the bend,
All feeding before his face:
20   'Now the best of ye I'le have to my dinner,
And that in a little space.'

Now the stranger he made no mickle adoe,
But he bends and a right good bow,
And the best buck in the herd he slew,
25   Forty good yards him full froe.

'Well shot, well shot,' quoth Robin Hood then,
'That shot it was shot in time,
And if thou wilt accept of the place
Thou shalt be a bold yeoman of mine.'

30   'Go play the chiven,' the stranger said,
'Make haste and quickly go,
Or with my fist, be sure of this,
I'le give thee buffets store.'

'Thou hadst not best buffet me,' quoth Robin Hood,
35   'For though I seem forlorn,
Yet I can have those that will take my part,
If I but blow my horn.'

'Thou wast not best wind thy horn,' the stranger said,
'Beest thou never so much in hast,
40   For I can draw out a good broad sword,
And quickly cut the blast.'

Then Robin Hood bent a very good bow,
To that shoot, and he wold fain;
The stranger he bent a very good bow,
45   To shoot at bold Robin again.

'O hold thy hand, hold thy hand,' quoth Robin Hood,
'To shoot it would be in vain;
For if we should shoot the one at the other,
The one of us may be slain.

50   'But let's take our swords and our broad bucklers,
And gang under yonder tree.'
'As I hope to be savd,' the stranger he said,
'One foot I will not flee.'

Then Robin Hood lent the stranger a blow,
55   Most scar'd him out of his wit;
'Thou never felt blow,' the stranger he said,
'That shalt be better quit.'

The stranger he drew out a good broad sword,
And hit Robin on the crown,
60   That from every haire of bold Robins head
The blood ran trickling down.

'God a mercy, good fellow!' quoth Robin Hood then,
'And for this that thou hast done,
Tell me, good fellow, what thou art,
65   Tell me where thou doest woon.'

The stranger then answered bold Robin Hood,
'I'le tell thee where I did dwell;
In Maxfield was I bred and born,
My name is Young Gamwell.

70   'For killing of my own fathers steward,
I am forc'd to this English wood,
And for to seek an uncle of mine;
Some call him Robin Hood.'

'But thou art a cousin of Robin Hoods then?
75   The sooner we should have done.'
'As I hope to be sav'd,' the stranger then said,
'I am his own sisters son.'

But Lord! what kissing and courting was there,
When these two cousins did greet!
80   And they went all that summers day,
And Little John did meet.

But when they met with Little John,
He thereunto did say,
'O master, where have you been,
85   You have tarried so long away?'

'I met with a stranger,' quoth Robin Hood then,
'Full sore he hath beaten me.'
'Then I'le have a bout with him,' quoth Little John,
'And try if he can beat me.'

90   'Oh, oh, no,' quoth Robin Hood then,
'Little John, it may be so;
For he's my own dear sisters son,
And cousins I have no mo.

'But he shal be a bold yeoman of mine,
95   My chief man next to thee,
And I Robin Hood and thou Little John,
And Scarlet he shall be,

'And wee'l be three of the bravest outlaws
That is in the North Country.'
100   If you will have any more of bold Robin Hood,
In his second part it will be.

ROBIN HOOD RESCUES THREE YOUNG MEN

This ballad has many slightly different versions, some of which show the influence of other Robin Hood ballads. As a result, the title of this ballad itself is not easy to fix, and it has been given an assortment of titles, including *Robin Hood Rescuing Three Squires*, but only in some versions are the potential victims called squires. In others they are the widow's three sons or three brothers, and sometimes they are Robin's own men. The essence of the ballad remains that Robin disguises himself as the hangman in order to rescue wrongfully condemned men, and a general title, *Robin Hood Rescues Three Young Men*, seems the best.

The ballad is found in a much-damaged form in Percy's folio manuscript, while the earliest surviving complete text is an eighteenth-century garland.

There are twelve months in all the year,
As I hear many men say,
But the merriest month in all the year
Is the merry month of May.

5   Now Robin Hood is to Nottingham
        gone,
      With a link a down and a day,
      And there he met a silly old woman,
      Was weeping on the way.

      'What news? what news, thou silly
        old woman?
10   What news hast thou for me?'
      Said she, 'There's three squires in
        Nottingham town
      To-day is condemned to die.'

      'O have they parishes burnt?' he
        said,
      'Or have they ministers slain?
15   Or have they robbed any virgin,
      Or with other men's wives have lain?'

      'They have no parishes burnt, good
        sir,
      Nor yet have ministers slain,
      Nor have they robbed any virgin,
20   Nor with other men's wives have lain.'

'We find thee bedraggled and downcast.' Illustration from *Bold Robin Hood and his Outlaw Band* by Louis Read.

      'O what have they done?' said bold Robin Hood
      'I pray thee tell to me.'
      'It's for slaying of the king's fallow deer,
      Bearing their long bows with thee.'

25   'Dost thou not mind, old woman,' he said,
      'Since thou made me sup and dine?
      By the truth of my body,' quoth bold Robin Hood,
      'You could not tell it in better time.'

      Now Robin Hood is to Nottingham gone,
30   With a link a down and a day,
      And there he met with a silly old palmer,
      Was walking along the highway.

      'What news? what news, thou silly old man?
      What news, I do thee pray?'
35   Said he, 'Three squires in Nottingham town
      Are condemnd to die this day.'

'Come change thy apparel with me, old man,
Come change thy apparel for mine;
Here is forty shillings in good silver,
40   Go drink it in beer or wine.'

'O thine apparel is good,' he said,
'And mine is ragged and torn;
Wherever you go, wherever you ride,
Laugh neer an old man to scorn.'

45   'Come change thy apparel with me, old churl,
Come change thy apparel with mine;
Here are twenty pieces of good broad gold,
Go feast thy brethren with wine.'

Then he put on the old man's hat,
50   It stood full high on the crown:
'The first bold bargain that I come at,
It shall make thee come down.'

Then he put on the old man's cloak,
Was patchd black, blew, and red;
55   He thought no shame all the day long
To bear the bags of bread.

Then he put on the old man's breeks,
Was patchd from ballup to side:
'By the truth of my body,' bold Robin can say,
60   'This man lovd little pride.'

Then he put on the old man's hose,
Were patchd from knee to waist:
'By the truth of my body,' said bold Robin Hood,
'I'd laugh if I had any list.'

65   Then he put on the old man's shoes,
Were patchd both beneath and aboon,
Then Robin Hood swore a solemn oath,
'It's good habit that makes a man.'

Now Robin Hood is to Nottingham gone,
70   With a link a down and a down,
And there he met with the proud sheriff,
Was walking along the town.

'O save, O save, O sherrif,' he said,
'O save, and you may see!
75   And what will you give to a silly old man
To-day will your hangman be?'

'Some suits, some suits,' the sheriff he said,
'Some suits I'll give to thee;
Some suits, some suits, and pence thirteen
80   To-day's a hangman's fee.'

Then Robin he turns him round about,
And jumps from stock to stone.
'By the truth of my body,' the sheriff he said,
'That's well jumpt, thou nimble old man.'

85   'I was neer a hangman in all my life,
Nor yet intends to trade,
But curst be he,' said bold Robin,
'That first a hangman was made.

'I've a bag for meal, and a bag for malt,
90   And a bag for barley and corn,
A bag for bread, and a bag for beef,
And a bag for my little small horn.

'I have a horn in my pocket,
I got it from Robin Hood,
95   And still when I set it to my mouth,
For thee it blows little good.'

'O wind thy horn, thou proud fellow,
Of thee I have no doubt;
I wish that thou give such a blast,
100   Till both thy eyes fly out.'

The first loud blast that he did blow,
He blew both loud and shrill;
A hundred and fifty of Robin Hood's men
Came riding over the hill.

105   The next loud blast that he did give,
He blew both loud and amain,
And quickly sixty of Robin Hood's men
Came shining over the plain.

'O who are you,' the sheriff he said,
110   'Come tripping over the lee?'
'They're my attendants,' brave Robin did say,
'They'll pay a visit to thee.'

They took the gallows from the slack,
They set it in the glen,
115   They hangd the proud sheriff on that,
Releasd their own three men.

ROBIN HOOD'S BIRTH, BREEDING, VALOUR AND MARRIAGE

This ballad was moderately well known, with three versions surviving from the seventeenth century. It appeared in three eighteenth-century collections, but is not included in the early garlands, which may suggest it was less than fully popular in its distribution. The ballad is obviously a literary confection, and, unlike the author of *Robin Hood and Queen Catherin*, the author of this offering has wandered well outside the Robin Hood tradition for materials. The final reference to the king and the national hope for heirs appears to locate it soon after the Restoration in 1660 when there was a good deal of activity in constructing new forms of the Robin Hood tradition.

Kind gentlemen, will you be patient awhile?
Ay, and then you shall hear anon
A very good ballad of bold Robin Hood,
And of his man, brave Little John.

5   In Locksly town, in Nottinghamshire,
In merry sweet Locksly town,
There bold Robin Hood he was born and was bred,
Bold Robin of famous renown.

The father of Robin a forrester was,
10   And he shot in a lusty long bow,
Two north country miles and an inch at a shot,
As the Pinder of Wakefield does know.

Robin and his mother ride through Sherwood Forest to Nottingham Fair. From *Robin Hood* by N.C. Wyeth (1917), p. 18. (*Mary Evans Picture Library*)

For he brought Adam Bell, and Clim of the Clugh,
And William a Clowdeslé
15   To shoot with our forrester for forty mark,
And the forrester beat them all three.

His mother was neece to the Coventry knight,
Which Warwickshire men call Sir Guy,
For he slew the blue bore that hangs up at the gate,
20   Or mine host of The Bull tells a lye.

Her brother was Gamwel, of Great Gamwel Hall,
And a noble house-keeper was he,
Ay, as ever broke bread in sweet Nottinghamshire,
And a squire of famous degree.

25   The mother of Robin said to her husband,
'My honey, my love, and my dear,
Let Robin and I ride this morning to Gamwel,
To taste of my brothers good cheer.'

And he said, 'I grant thee thy boon, gentle Joan,
30   Take one of my horses, I pray;
The sun is a rising, and therefore make haste,
For tomorrow is Christmas-day.'

Then Robin Hoods fathers grey gelding was brought,
And sadled and bridled was he;
35   God wot, a blew bonnet, his new suit of cloaths,
And a cloak that did reach to his knee.

She got on her holiday kirtle and gown,
They were of a light Lincoln green.
The cloath was homespun, but for colour and make
40   It might a beseemed our queen.

And then Robin got on his basket-hilt sword,
And his dagger on his tother side,
And said, 'My dear mother, let's haste to be gone,
We have forty long miles to ride.'

45   When Robin had mounted his gelding so grey,
His father, without any trouble,
Set her up behind him, and bad her not fear,
For his gelding had oft carried double.

And when she was settled, they rode to their neighbours,
50   And drank and shook hands with them all,
And then Robin gallopt and never gave ore,
Til they lighted at Gamwell Hall.

And now you may think the right worshipful squire
Was joyful his sister to see,
55   For he kist her and kist her, and swore a great oath,
Thou art welcome, kind sister, to me.

To-morrow, when mass had been said in the chapel,
Six tables were coverd in the hall,
And in comes the squire and makes a short speech,
60   It was 'Neighbours, you're welcome all.

'But not a man here shall taste my March beer,
Till a Christmas carrol be sung.'
Then all clapt their hands, and they shouted and sung,
Till the hall and the parlour did ring.

65   Now mustards, braun, roast beef and plumb pies
Were set upon every table,
And noble George Gamwell said, 'Eat and be merry,
And drink, too, as long as you're able.'

When dinner was ended, his chaplain said grace,
70   And 'Be merry, my friends,' said the squire,
'It rains and it blows, but call for more ale,
And lay some more wood on the fire.

'And now call ye Little John hither to me,
For Little John is a fine lad
75   At gambols and juggling and twenty such tricks
As shall make you merry and glad.'

When Little John came, to gambols they went,
Both gentlemen, yeomen and clown;
And what do you think? Why as true as I live
80   Bold Robin Hood put them all down.

And now you may think the right worshipful squire
Was joyful this sight for to see,
For he said, 'Cousin Robin, thou'st go no more home,
But tarry and dwell here with me.

85   'Thou shalt have my land when I dye and till then
       Thou shalt be the staff of my age.'
       'Then grant me my boon, dear uncle,' said Robin,
       'That Little John may be my page.'

       And he said, 'Kind cousin, I grant thee thy boon,
90   With all my heart, so let it be.'
       'Then come hither, Little John,' said Robin Hood
       'Come hither, my page unto me.

       'Go fetch me my bow, my longest long bow,
       And broad arrows, one, two, or three,
95   For when it is fair weather we'll into Sherwood,
       Some merry pastime to see.'

       When Robin Hood came into merry Sherwood
       He winded his bugle so clear,
       And twice five and twenty good yeomen and bold
100   Before Robin Hood did appear.

       'Where are your companions all?' said Robin Hood,
       'For still I want forty and three.'
       Then said a bold yeoman, 'Lo, yonder they stand,
       All under a green wood tree.'

105   As that word was spoke, Clorinda came by,
       The queen of the shepherds was she,
       And her gown was of velvet as green as the grass,
       And her buskin did reach to her knee.

       Her gait it was graceful, her body was straight,
110   And her countenance free from pride;
       A bow in her hand, and quiver and arrows
       Hung dangling by her sweet side.

       Her eye-brows were black, ay and so was her hair,
       And her skin was as smooth as glass;
115   Her visage spoke wisdom, and modesty too:
       Sets with Robin Hood such a lass.

       Said Robin Hood, 'Lady fair, whither away?
       Oh whither, fair lady, away?'
       And she made him answer, 'To kill a fat buck,
120   For tomorrow is Titbury day.'

Said Robin Hood, 'Lady fair, wander with me
A little to yonder green bower;
There sit down to rest you, and you shall be sure
Of a brace or a lease in an hour.'

125   And as we were going towards the green bower
Two hundred good bucks we espy'd;
She chose out the fattest that was in the herd
And she shot him through side and side.

'By the faith of my body,' said bold Robin Hood,
130   'I never saw woman like thee;
And comst thou from east, ay, or comst thou from west,
Thou needst not beg venison of me.

'However, along to my bower you shall go,
And taste of a forresters meat.'
135   And when we come thither, we found as good cheer
As any man needs for to eat.

For there was hot venison and warden pies cold,
Cream-clouted with honey-combs plenty,
And the sarvitors they were, beside Little John,
140   Good yeomen at least four and twenty.

Clorinda said, 'Tell me your name, gentle sir.'
And he said, ''Tis bold Robin Hood;
Squire Gamwel's my uncle, but all my delight
Is to dwell in the merry Sherwood.

145   'For 'tis a fine life, and 'tis void of all strife.'
'So 'tis sir,' Clorinda reply'd.
'But oh,' said bold Robin, 'how sweet would it be,
If Clorinda would be my bride!'

She blusht at the notion, yet after a pause
150   Said, 'Yes, sir, and with all my heart.'
'Then let's send for a priest,' said Robin Hood
'And be married before we do part.'

But she said, 'It may not be so, gentle sir,
For I must be at Titbury feast;
155   And if Robin Hood will go thither with me,
I'll make him the most welcome guest.'

Said Robin Hood, 'Reach me that buck, Little John,
For I'll go along with my dear;
Bid my yeomen kill six brace of bucks,
160   And meet me tomorrow just here.'

Before we had ridden five Staffordshire miles
Eight yeomen, that were too bold,
Bid Robin Hood stand and deliver his buck:
A truer tale never was told.

165   'I will not, faith,' said bold Robin. 'Come, John,
Stand to me and we'll beat 'em all.'
Then both drew their swords, and so cut 'em and slasht 'em,
That five of them did fall.

The three that remaind calld to Robin for quarter,
170   And pitiful John beggd their lives;
When John's boon was granted, he gave them counsel,
And so sent them home to their wives.

This battle was fought near to Titbury town,
When the bagpipes bated the bull;
175   I am king of the fidlers and sware't is a truth,
And I call him that doubts it a gull.

For I saw them fighting, and fidld the while,
And Clorinda sung, 'Hey derry down!
The bumpkins are beaten, put up thy sword, Bob,
180   And now let's dance into the town.'

Before we came to it we heard a strange shouting,
And all that were in it lookd madly,
For some were a bull-back, some dancing a morris,
And some singing Arthur-a-Bradly.

185   And there we see Thomas, our justices clerk,
And Mary, to whom he was kind;
For Tom rode before her and calld Mary 'Madam'
And kist her full sweetly behind.

And so may your worships. But we went to dinner,
190   With Thomas and Mary and Nan;
They all drank a health to Clorinda and told her
Bold Robin Hood was a fine man.

When dinner was ended, Sir Roger, the parson
Of Dubbridge, was sent for in haste;
195   He brought his mass-book and he bade them take hands,
And he joynd them in marriage full fast.

And then, as bold Robin Hood and his sweet bride
Went hand in hand to the green bower,
The birds sung with pleasure in merry Sherwood,
200   And 'twas a most joyful hour.

And when Robin came in the sight of the bower,
'Where are my yeoman?' said he.
And Little John answered 'Lo, yonder they stand,
All under the green wood tree.'

205   Then a garland they brought her, by two and by two,
And plac'd them at the bride's bed;
The music struck up, and we all fell to dance,
Til the bride and the groom were a-bed.

And what they did there must be counsel to me,
210   Because they lay long the next day,
And I had haste home, but I got a good piece
Of the bride-cake, and so came away.

Now out, alas! I had forgotten to tell ye
That marryd they were with a ring;
215   And so will Nan Knight, or be buried a maiden,
And now let us pray for the king:

That he may get children, and they may get more,
To govern and do us some good;
And then I'll make ballads in Robin Hood's bower
220   And sing 'em in merry Sherwood.

ROBIN HOOD'S FISHING

This ballad is found in seventeenth-century broadsides and garlands and was entered in the Stationers' Register in 1631. It does, however, appear to have been cut down to fit onto a broadside sheet.

In sumer time when leaves grow green,
When they do grow both green and long,
Robin Hood that bold outlaw
It is of him I sing my song.

Robin Hood and the tanner fight with quarterstaffs. Woodcut by Thomas Bewick, reproduced in Ritson's *Robin Hood*, p. 189. (*Mary Evans Picture Library*)

5   'The thrassle cock and nightengaal
          Do chaunt and sing with merry good cheer;
          I am weary of the woods,' said hee,
          'And chasing of the fallow deer.

          'The fisher-man more mony hath
10   Then any marchant two or three;
          Therefore I will to Scarburough go
          And there a fisher-man will bee.'

          Hee cald togeather his weight men all,
          To whom he gave or meat or fee,
15   Paid them their wage for halfe a year,
          Well told in gold and good monie.

          'If any of you lack mony to spend
          If your occasions lie to speake with mee,
          If ever you chance to Scarburrough com,
20   Aske for Symon of the Lee.'

Hee tooke his leave there of them all,
It was upon a holy day;
Hee took up his inn at a widdows house,
Which stood nigh to the waters gray.

25   'From whence came thou, thou fine fellow,
A gentleman thou seemist to bee.'
'I'th contrey, dame, where I came from
They call me Symon of the Lee.'

'Gen they call the Symon of the Lee,
30   I wish well may thou brook thy name.'
The outlaw knew his courtisie,
And so replyed 'Gramercy, dame.'

'Symon,' quoth shee, 'wilt bee my man,
I'le give to thee both meat and fee.'
35   'By th'Masse, dame,' bold Robin said,
'I'le sarve yea well for years three.'

'I have a good shipp,' then she said,
'As any goes upon the sea.
Ancors and plancks thou shalt want none
40   Nor masts nor ropes to furnish thee.

'Oars nor sayle thou shalt not want,
Nor hooks faile to thy lines so long.'
'By my truth, dame,' quoth Symon then,
'I weat ther's nothing shall go wrang.'

45   They hoyst up sayle and forth did hale
Merrylie they went to sea
Till they came to th'appoynted place
Where all the fish taken should bee.

Every man bayted his line
50   And in the sea they did him throw;
Symon lobb'd in his lines twaine
But neither gott great nor smaw.

Then bespake the companie,
'Symon's part will bee but small.'
55   'By my troth,' quoth the master man,
'I thinke he will gett none at all.

'What dost thou heer thou long luske,
What the fiend dost thou upon the sea.
Thou hast begger'd the widdow of Scarburrough,
60   I weat for her and her children three.'

Still every day they bayted their lines
And in the sea they did then lay,
But Symon he scrap'd his broad arrows,
I weat he suned them every day.

65   'Were I under Plumpton Parke,' said hee,
'There among my fellows all,
Look so little you sett by mee,
I'd sett by yee twiyce as small.

'Heigh ho,' quoth Symon then,
70   'Farwell to the green leaves on the tree,
Were I in Plumpton Parke againe,
A fisher-man I nare would bee.'

Every man had fish enough,
The shipp was laden to passe home.
75   'Fish as you will,' quoth good Symon,
'I weat for fishes I have none.'

They weyd up ankere, away did sayle,
More of one day then two or three,
But they were awar of a French robber
80   Coming toward them most desperatly.

'Wo is me,' said the master man,
'Alas, that ever I was borne,
For all the fish that wee have tane,
Alas the day, 'tis all forlorne.

85   'For all the gold that I have tane
For the losse of my fish I do not care,
For wee shall prisoners into France,
Not a man of us that they will spare.'

Symon staggerd to the hatches high,
90   Never a foot that he could stand.
'I would gladly give three hundred pounds
For one three hundred foot of land.'

Quoth Symon, 'Then do not them dread,
Neither master do you fear.
95   Give me my bent bow in my hand,
And not a Frenchman I will spare.'

'Hold thy peace thou long lubber,
For thou canst nought but bragg and bost
If I should cast thee over boord,
100   There were nothing but a lubber lost.'

Quoth Symon, 'Ty me to the main mast
That at my marke I may stand fare,
Give me my bent bow in my hand
And not a Frenchman I will spare.'

105   They bound him fast to the main mast tree,
They bound Symon hard and seare,
They gave him a bent bow into his hand,
And not a French man he would spare.

'Whom shall I shoot at, thou master man,
110   For God's love speake the man to mee.'
'Shoot at the steersman of yon shippe,
Thou long luske now let me see.'

Symon he took his noble bow,
An arrow that was both larg and long;
115   The neerest way to the steersmans heart,
The broad arrow it did gang.

He fell from the hatches high
From the hatches he fell downe below,
Another took him by the heels,
120   And into the sea he did him throw.

Then quickly took the helme in hand,
And steerd the shipp most gallantly,
'By my truth,' quod good Symon then,
'The same fate shall follow thee.'

125   Symon he took his noble bow
And arrow which was both streight and long,
The neerest way to the Frenchman's heart
The swallow tayle he gard gang.

He fell from the hatches high
130   From the hatches he fell downe below,
Another took him by the heele
And into the sea did him throw.

The shipp was tossed up and downe
Not one durst venture her to steer,
135   The Scarburough men were very faine
When they saw that robber durst not com near.

'Com up master,' Symon said,
'Two shoots have I shott for thee.
All the rest are for myselfe,
140   This day for Gods love merry be.'

'Gods blessing on thy fingers, Symon,' he said
'For weel I see thou hast good skill;
Gods blessing on thy noble heart,
Who hast employed thy bow so weele.

145   'I vow for fish thou shalt want none,
The best share, Symon, Ile give thee,
And I shall pray thee, good Symon,
Thou do not take thy marke by mee.'

'I had thirty arrows by my side,
150   I thinke I had thirty and three,
Thers not an arrow shall go waste,
But through a French heart it shall flee.

'Lose me from the mast,' he said,
'The pitch ropes they do pinch me sare,
155   Give me a good sword in my hand,
Feind a French man I will spare.'

Together have the two shipps run
The fisher and the waryer free.
Symon borded the noble shipp
160   Found never a man alive but three.

He took a lampe unto his hand
The ship he searched by the light,
He found within that shipp of warr
Twelve hundred pounds in gold so bright.

165   'Com up, master,' Symon said
       'This day for God's love merry bee;
       How shall we share this noble shipp,
       I pray thee master, tell to me.'

       'By my troth,' quoth the masterman,
170   'Symon, good councell Ile give thee:
       Thou won'st the shipp with thine owne hands,
       And master of it thou shalt bee.'

       'One half,' quoth Symon, 'of this shipp,
       Ile deale among my fellows all;
175   The other halfe I freely give
       Unto my dame and her children small.

       'And if it chance to bee my lott,
       That I shall gett but well to land,
       Ile therefore build a chappell good,
180   And it shall stand on Whitby strand.

       'And there Ile keep a preist to sing
       The masse untill the day I dye.
       If Robin Hood com once on shore,
       Hee com no more upon the see.'

ROBIN HOOD'S GOLDEN PRIZE

This mid-seventeenth-century ballad is found in broadsides and garlands, and was recorded in the Stationers' Register in 1656. The story is one found in folklore, the essence being that the outlaw plays a trick on someone – usually a priest – by pretending that a miracle has occurred and money has appeared in return for prayer, when he knew quite well the money was there all the time. This robbery by cunning fits well with the trickster element of Robin Hood and also supports the anti-clerical feeling, so strong a strain in the tradition in this period.

       I have heard talk of bold Robin Hood,
       Derry derry down
       And of brave Little John,
       Of Fryer Tuck, and Will Scarlet,
5   Loxley, and Maid Marion.
       Hey down derry derry down.

       But such a tale as this before
       I think there was never none,
       For Robin Hood disguised himself,
10   And to the wood is gone.

The first encounter between Robin Hood and Little John. Illustration in *Robin Hood's Ballads* (1867), p. 260. (*Mary Evans Picture Library*)

Like to a fryer, bold Robin Hood
Was accoutered in his array;
With hood, gown, beads and crucifix,
He past upon the way.

15   He had not gone miles two or three,
But it was his chance to spy
Two lusty priests, clad all in black,
Come riding gallantly.

        'Benediceté,' then said Robin Hood,
20   'Some pitty on me take;
Cross you my hand with a silver groat,
For Our dear Ladies sake.

        'For I have been wandring all this day,
And nothing could I get;
25   Not so much as one poor cup of drink,
Nor bit of bread to eat.'

'Now, by my holydame,' the priests repli'd,
'We never a peny have;
For we this morning have been robd,
30   And could no mony save.'

'I am much afraid,' said bold Robin Hood,
'That you both do tell a lye,
And now before that you go hence,
I am resolvd to try.'

35   When as the priests heard him say so,
They rode away amain;
But Robin Hood betook him to his heels,
And soon overtook them again.

Then Robin Hood laid hold of them both,
40   And pulld them down from their horse:
'O spare us, fryer!' the priests cry'd out,
'On us have some remorse!'

'You said you had no mony,' quoth he,
'Wherefore, without delay,
45   We three will fall down on our knees,
And for mony we will pray.'

The priests they could not him gainsay,
But down they kneeled with speed.
'Send us, O send us,' then quoth they,
50   'Some mony to serve our need.'

The priests did pray with mournful chear,
Sometimes their hands did wring,
Sometimes they wept and cried aloud,
Whilst Robin did merrily sing.

55   When they had been praying an hours space,
The priests did still lament;
Then quoth bold Robin, 'Now let's see
What mony heaven hath us sent.

'We will be sharers now all alike
60   Of the mony that we have,
And there is never a one of us
That his fellows shall deceive.'

The priests their hands in their pockets put,
But mony would find none.
65   'We'l search our selves,' said Robin Hood,
'Each other, one by one.'

Then Robin Hood took pains to search them both,
And he found good store of gold;
Five hundred peeces presently
70   Upon the grass was told.

'Here is a brave show,' said Robin Hood,
'Such store of gold to see,
And you shall each one have a part,
Cause you prayed so heartily.'

75   He gave them fifty pound a-peece,
And the rest for himself did keep;
The priests durst not speak one word,
But they sighed wondrous deep.

With that the priests rose up from their knees,
80   Thinking to have parted so;
'Nay, stay,' said Robin Hood, 'one thing more
I have to say ere you go.

'You shall be sworn,' said bold Robin Hood,
'Upon this holy grass,
85   That you will never tell lies again,
Which way soever you pass.

'The second oath that you here must take,
All the days of your lives
You never shall tempt maids to sin,
90   Nor lye with other mens wives.

'The last oath you shall take, it is this,
Be charitable to the poor;
Say you have met with a holy fryer,
And I desire no more.'

95   He set them upon their horses again,
And away then they did ride;
And hee returnd to the merry green-wood,
With great joy, mirth, and pride.

ROBIN HOOD'S PROGRESS TO NOTTINGHAM

This ballad appears in several seventeenth-century broadsides and the early garlands. Because of the earlier nature of the story, it should perhaps stand between *The Jolly Pinder of Wakefield* and *Robin Hood and Little John*.

> Robin Hood hee was and a tall young man,
> Derry derry down
> And fifteen winters old,
> And Robin Hood he was a proper young man,
> Of courage stout and bold.
> Hey down derry derry down.
>
> Robin Hood he would and to fair Nottingham,
> With the general for to dine;
> There was he ware of fifteen forresters,
> And a drinking bear, ale, and wine.

5

10

Nottingham at the time of Robin Hood. Illustration by Petherick in *Robin Hood's Ballads* (1867). (*Mary Evans Picture Library*)

'What news? What news?' said bold Robin Hood;
'What news, fain wouldest thou know?
Our king hath provided a shooting-match,
And I'm ready with my bow.'

15   'We ho'd it in scorn,' then said the forresters,
'That ever a boy so young
Should bear a bow before our king,
That's not able to draw one string.'

'I'le hold you twenty marks,' said bold Robin Hood,
20   'By the leave of Our Lady,
That I'le hit a mark a hundred rod,
And I'le cause a hart to dye.'

'We'l hold you twenty mark,' then said the forresters,
'By the leave of Our Lady,
25   Thou hitst not the marke a hundred rod,
Nor causest a hart to dye.'

Robin Hood he bent up a noble bow,
And a broad arrow he let flye,
He hit the mark a hundred rod,
30   And he caused a hart to dy.

Some said hee brake ribs one or two,
And some said hee brake three;
The arrow within the hart would not abide,
But it glanced in two or three.

35   The hart did skip, and the hart did leap,
And the hart lay on the ground.
'The wager is mine,' said bold Robin Hood,
'If't were for a thousand pound.'

'The wager's none of thine,' then said the forresters,
40   'Although thou beest in haste;
Take up thy bow, and get thee hence,
Lest wee thy sides do baste.'

Robin Hood hee took up his noble bow,
And his broad arrows all amain,
45   And Robin Hood he laught, and begun to smile,
As hee went over the plain.

Then Robin Hood hee bent his noble bow,
And his broad arrows he let flye,
Till fourteen of these fifteen forresters
50   Upon the ground did lye.

He that did this quarrel first begin,
Went tripping over the plain,
But Robin Hood he bent his noble bow,
And hee fetcht him back again.

55   'You said I was no archer,' said Robin Hood,
'But say so now again.'
With that he sent another arrow
That split his head in twain.

'You have found mee an archer,' saith Robin Hood,
60   'Which will make your wives for to wring,
And wish that you had never spoke the word,
That I could not draw one string.'

The people that lived in fair Nottingham
Came runing out amain,
65   Supposing to have taken bold Robin Hood,
With the forresters that were slain.

Some lost legs, and some lost arms,
And some did lose their blood,
But Robin Hood hee took up his noble bow,
70   And is gone to the merry green wood.

They carryed these forresters into fair Nottingham,
As many there did know;
They digd them graves in their church-yard,
And they buried them all a row.

ROBYN AND GANDELYN

This poem is preserved only in the Sloane MS 2593, a neatly written repository of lyrics
and carols dated around 1450. However, it does not automatically challenge *Robin Hood
and the Monk* for the status of the earliest extant Robin Hood text, and there remains
serious doubt as to what extent the Robin in this ballad is Robin Hood.

Robynn lyth in grene wode bowndyn.

I herde a carpyng of a clerk,
Al at yone wodes ende,

Of gode Robyn and Gandeleyn;
5   Was ther non other gynge.

Stronge thevys wer tho chylderin non,
But bowmen gode and hende;
He wentyn to wode to getyn hem fleych,
If God wold it hem sende.

10   Al day wentyn tho chylderin too,
And fleych fowndyn he non,
Til it were ageyn evyn;
The chylderin wolde gon hom.

Half an honderid of fat falyf der
15   He comyn ayon,
And alle he wern fayr and fat inow,
But markyd was ther non;
'Be dere God,' seyde gode Robyn,
'Here of we shul have on.'

20   Robyn bent his joly bowe,
Ther in he set a flo;
The fattest der of alle
The herte he clef a to.

He hadde not the der iflawe,
25   Ne half out of the hyde,
There cam a schrewde arwe out of the west,
That felde Robertes pryde.

Gandeleyn lokyd hym est and west,
Be every syde:
30   'Hoo hat myn mayster slayin?
Ho hat don this dede?
Shal I never out of grene wode go
Til I se sydis blede.'

Gandeleyn lokyd hym est and lokyd west,
35   And sowt under the sunne;
He saw a lytil boy
He clepyn Wrennok of Donne.

A good bowe in his hond,
A brod arwe ther ine,
40   And fowre and twenty goode arwys,
Trusyd in a thrumme:
'Be war the, war the, Gandeleyn,
Her of thu shalt han summe.

'Be war the, war the, Gandeleyn,
45   Hir of thu gyst plenté.'
'Ever on for an other,' seyde Gandeleyn;
'Mysaunter have he shal fle.

'Wher-at shal oure marke be?'
Seyde Gandeleyn.
50   'Everyche at otheris herte,'
Seyde Wrennok ageyn.

'Ho shal yeve the ferste schote?'
Seyde Gandeleyn:
'And I shul geve the on be-forn.'
55   Seyd Wrennok ageyn.

Wrennok schette a ful good schote,
And he schet not to hye;
Throw the samclothis of his bryk,
It towchyd neyther thye.

60   'Now hast thou govyn me on beforn,'
Al thus to Wrennok seyde he,
'And throw the myght of our Lady
A bettere I shal yeve the.'

Gandeleyn bent his goode bowe,
65   And set ther in a flo;
He schet throw his grene certyl,
His herte he clef on too.

'Now shalt thu never yelpe, Wrennok,
At ale ne at wyn,
70   That thu hast slawe goode Robyn,
And his knave Gandeleyn.

'Now shalt thu never yelpe, Wrennok,
At wyn ne at ale,
That thu hast slawe goode Robyn,
75   And Gandeleyn his knawe.'

Robyn lyeth in grene wode bowndyn.

THE DEATH OF ROBIN HOOD

This ballad is not recorded until the mid-seventeenth century, while the first full text is from the late eighteenth-century garland *The English Archer* (1786).

When Robin Hood and Little John
Down a down a down a down
Went oer yon bank of broom,
Said Robin Hood bold to Little John,
5   'We have shot for many a pound.
Hey, etc.

'But I am not able to shoot one shot
    more,
My broad arrows will not fly;
But I have a cousin lives down below,
10   Please God, she will bleed me.

'I will never eate nor drinke,'
    Robin Hood said,
'Nor meate will doo me noe good,
Till I have beene att merry
    Churchlees,
My vaines for to let blood.'

15   'That I reade not,' said Will
    Scarllett,
'Master, by the assente of me,
Without halfe a hundred of your
    best bowmen
You take to goe with yee.

'For there a good yeoman doth abide
20   Will be sure to quarrell with thee,
And if thou have need of us, master,
In faith we will not flee.'

Robin Hood fires a last arrow to show Little John where he wishes to be buried. From *Robin Hood* by N.C. Wyeth (1917), p. 361. (*Mary Evans Picture Library*)

'And thou be feard, thou William Scarlett,
Att home I read thee bee.'
25 'And you be wrothe, my deare master,
You shall never heare more of mee.'

'For there shall noe man with me goe,
Nor man with mee ryde,
And Litle John shall be my man,
30 And beare my benbow by my side.'

'You'st beare your bowe, master, your selfe,
And shoote for a peny with mee.'
'To that I doe assent,' Robin Hood sayd,
'And soe, John, lett it bee.'

35 They two bolde children shotten together,
All day theire selfe in ranke,
Until they came to blacke water,
And over it laid a planke.

Upon it there kneeled an old woman,
40 Was banning Robin Hoode;
'Why dost thou bann Robin Hoode?' said Robin,
'Knowst thou of him no good?'

'We women have no benison
To give to Robin Hoode;
45 Wee weepen for his deare body,
That this day must be lett bloode.'

'The dame prior is my aunts daughter,
And nie unto my kinne;
I know shee wold me noe harme this day,
50 For all the world to winne.'

Forth then shotten these children two,
And they did never lin,
Until they came to merry Churchlees,
To merry Churchlees with-in.

55 And when they came to merry Churchlees,
They knoced upon a pin;
Upp then rose dame prioresse,
And lett good Robin in.

Then Robin gave to dame prioresse
60   Twenty pound in gold,
And bad her spend while that wold last,
And shee shold have more when shee wold.

And downe then came dame prioresse,
Downe she came in that ilke,
65   With a pair of blood-irons in her hands,
Were wrapped all in silke.

'Sett a chaffing-dish to the fyer,' said dame prioresse,
'And stripp thou up thy sleeve.'
I hold him but an unwise man
70   That will noe warning leeve.

She laid the blood-irons to Robin Hoods vaine,
Alacke, the more pitye!
And pearct the vaine, and let out the bloode,
That full red was to see.

75   And first it bled, the thicke, thicke bloode,
And afterwards the thinne,
And well then wist good Robin Hoode,
Treason there was within.

He then bethought him of a casement there,
80   Thinking for to get down,
But was so weak he could not leap,
He could not get him down.

He then bethought him of his bugle-horn,
Which hung low down to his knee;
85   He set his horn unto his mouth,
And blew out weak blasts three.

Then Little John, when hearing him,
As he sat under a tree:
'I fear my master is now near dead,
90   He blows so wearily.'

Then Little John to fair Kirkly is gone,
As fast as he can dree;
But when he came to Kirkly-hall,
He broke locks two or three.

95   'What cheere my master?' said Little John;
      'In faith, John, little goode.
      My cousin and Red Roger,
      Between them let my blood.'

      'I have upon a gowne of greene,
100   Is cut short by my knee,
      And in my hand a bright browne brand
      That will well bite for thee.'

      But before then of a shot-windowe
      Good Robin Hood he could glide,
105   Red Roger, with a grounden glave,
      Thrust him through the milke-white side.

      But Robin was light and nimble of foote,
      And thought to abate his pride,
      For betwixt his head and his shoulders
110   He made a wound full wide.

      Says, 'Ly there, ly there, Red Roger,
      The doggs they must thee eate;
      For I may have my houzle,' he said,
      'For I may both goe and speake.'

115   'Now give me mood,' Robin said to Little John,
      'Give me mood with thy hand;
      I trust to God in heaven soe hye
      My houzle will me bestand.'

      'Now give me leave, give me leave, master,' he said,
120   'For Christs love give leave to me,
      To set a fier within this hall,
      And to burne up all Churchlee.'

      'That I reade not,' said Robin Hoode then,
      'Litle John, for it may not be;
125   If I shold doe any widow hurt, at my latter end,
      God,' he said, 'wold blame me.

      'I never hurt fair maid in all my time,
      Nor at mine end shall it be,
      But give me my bent bow in my hand,
130   And a broad arrow I'll let flee;

And where this arrow is taken up,
There shall my grave digged be.

'Lay me a green sod under my head,
And another at my feet;
135   And lay my bent bow by my side,
Which was my music sweet;
And make my grave of gravel and
green,
Which is most right and meet.

'Let me have length and breadth
enough,
140   With a green sod under my head;
That they may say, when I am dead
Here lies bold Robin Hood.'

These words they readily granted
him,
Which did bold Robin please:
145   And there they buried bold Robin
Hood,
Within the fair Kirkleys.

Robin shoots his last shaft. Illustration from *Bold Robin Hood and his Outlaw Band* by Louis Read.

GLOSSARY

As some of the ballads are written in archaic English the following glossary of terms is intended to make the source texts more decipherable and easier to understand. This is not a dictionary of archaic English, but rather a simple description of the terms to be found within the source texts. In many cases it is easy to work out what the author intended as many of the words are simply unusual spellings of words we use today, and if these words are read aloud then their meaning often becomes quite clear. In some cases you will find more than one 'translation'. In these cases it is simply a matter of choice to see which word best fits the situation.

Where letters, or parts of words have been enclosed in brackets; e.g.: anon(e), the spellings *anon* and *anone* might both be found.

a wed schall make hem leye	who can force him to pay
a wed to me schall he ley	a payment he'll make to me
aboon	on top
accorded	agreement
adowne	lower
agast	aghast, afraid
ageyn evyn	toward evening, again evening
allther best	best of all
allther most	most of all
almus	alms
amain	strongly, quickly
and's	and his
ankir	anchorite (religious hermit)
anon(e)	immediately, at once
ar	before
araye	array
archares	archers
arschere	archer
arwe	arrow
as ferre in press	in (as) great danger
asay, assay	try, test
att home I read thee bee	I advise you to stay at home
auncetres	ancestors
avowé	patron
awet	discover
ayen	again
ayre	heir
bale	trouble
ballup	groin
balsame	medicine
bandoggs	fierce dogs
bane	murderer
banis	murderers
banning	lamenting
bare hym throw	run him through (with a sword)
Be Hym	By Christ
be may fay	by my faith
be mey trowet	by my faith
bedesman	religious guide

bedyng	bidding
be-forn	the first (one)
behote	promise(d)
benbow(e)	long bow
benediceté	bless you
benison	blessing
beryed	buried
bescro	beshrew (curse)
beseemed	have suited
besette	beset, besieged
bete	beat
bethought	remembered
beyre	bear, carry
bin	been
blacke monkes	Benedictine monks
blood-irons	surgical knives (for blood-letting)
bloschoms	blossoms
blyve	quickly
bokeler	buckler
boldeley	boldly
bolte	arrow, bolt (for a crossbow)
boltys	arrows
bone	boon, favour
borde	table
borowe	guarantee, security
borrowehode	security (as a pledge)
boskyd	busied
boste	boast
boteler	butler
botes	boots
bottys	targets
boules	bottles
boules of sack	bottles of dry white wine
bower	chamber
bowndyn	bound (in a shroud)
bowne yee	get ready
brace	two, pair
brace or a lease	two or three
braun	boar flesh
breche	breeches
breed thy gree	cause you grief
breeden bale	cause anger, make angry
breeks	breeches
breyde	jumped
bronde	sword
brown swerde	bloodstained sword
brust	burst
bryk	breeches
bryre	branch
buckler	small shield
buffet	cuff, blow
builded	stationed
buske	hasten
buske and brome	bush and shrub

buskin	high boot
busshement	ambush
by the Rode	by the Cross
by thy leve	with your permission
byddynge	pain
bydene	together
bystode	beset
can ken	can tell
capull-hyde	horse-hide
carpyng	singing
carrill	churl, ceorl
castell	castle
Cerstyn	Christian
certen	certain, knew
certyl	kirtle
chaffare	merchandise, wares, business affairs
chafing	cooking
chepe	buy, purchase
chepyd fast	quickly bought
cheys	choose
chiven	chicken
chorle	churl, ceorl
chylderin	children, youths
cleave	split
cleffed	cleft
clipping	embracing
clove	split
clown	yokel
cof(f)er	money chest
coke	cook
cole	cowl (monk's hood worn round the neck)
comet	comes
commaunded	commanded
comyn ayon	came upon
comyn bell	common bell, town bell
contré	county, region
coressed	bodied, built (as in physique)
corteys	courteous
cote of pie	parti-coloured cloak
coucht down	lay down
coursar	courser (a swift horse)
courteysy	manners
cov'nant	contract
cowdest	could
cowthe	could
craftely	skilfully
cream clouted	clotted cream
Cristianté	Christendom
crookt	crooked
curst turne	cursed deed
curtes	courteous, noble
daye is broke	missed the allotted day or appointment
deale	part, portion, measure
dere	harm

derne strete	secret street, secret way
deyell	devil
deyne	dine
deythe	prepared
dight	ready
disgrate	disgraced, deprived of status
donne	brown
dout	fear, doubt
doyn	done
drapar	draper
drawen	drawn, dragged
dree	go, hurry
dreri	sad, dreary
drese	make ready
dreyffe	draw
dreyffe forthe	go forth
droffe	hastened
drow	drew, came close
dryfyng	driving
dughty	doughty
durre	door
durst	dared
dyd of	took off
dydly synne	deadly sin
dyght	done
dyght	clothed
dyghtande	prepared
dynere	dinner
dysheryte	disinherited
effen	even
eftsones	in return
eies	eyes
eke	also
elle	ell (45 inches)
ellys	else
els well hem slo	else he'll kill him
emys	uncle
eney	any
Englonde ryght	England's cause
e're	ever
erle	earl
everichone, everychone	everyone
everilkon	everyone, each one
everyche at otheris herte	each at the other's heart
evyll mote thou cheve	badly may you end (a curse)
ewe	yew (tree)
eylle	well
eyre	ire
fain	gladly
faine	happy, very pleased
falyf der	fallow deer
fare	food, banquet
farley	amazing
fastinge	fasting, without food

fate on	play on
fayled, faylyd	failed, missed
faylyd	faith
fayne	gladly
fe	fee, payment
fee	property
fee	fief
felawe	fellow, companion
felischepe	fellowship
fende me of my fone	defend me from my enemies
ferd	fear(ed)
fere	company, brotherhood
fered	fared, coped
ferly strife	great argument
ferre gone	long ago
fessauntes	pheasants
fet	fetched
fette	feet
fett(e)led	prepared
fettle	prepare
feyre	fair
feythe	faith
finikin	fine
fleych	flesh
fole	fool
foote fluinge	on foot, running
for ay	forever
for sothe	truly
forbott	forbid
forefend	forbid
foriete	forgotten
fostere	forester
foules	birds, fowls
foulys	birds
fourteenyght	fortnight
fourtnet	fortnight
fowndyn	found
frebore blode	freeborn blood
frere	brother
fro the see	from overseas
from's	from his
ful gode wone	plenty of
fute on	whistle on, whistle away
futing	whistling
gadred	gathered
gafe	gave
gale	gaol, jail, prison
gan	did
gan loke	with hatred
ganging	going
gard gang	caused to go
garlande	ring suspended on a stick as a target
gate	got
gatis	gates

gayne	gain, win
geffe	give
gere	gear, equipment
gereamarsey	gramercy
gest	guest
go play the chiven	run away (go play the chicken)
God amarsey	God have mercy, God thank you
God eylde het the	God reward you
god ynowe	goods enough, plenty of goods/property
gode	good
gode(s)	goods, possessions, chattels
gollett	gullett, throat-piece
gorney	journey
gramarcy	thank you
gredy	hungry, greedy
grene wode lyne	linden trees
gret	great
gret chepe	great bargain
gret-hedid	large-headed
gretith	greets
grith	grant pardon
grome	man
ground oak	oak sapling
grounden glave	sharpened sword
gylte	gild
gynge	company, gang, gathering (of people)
had lever	would rather
haffe	have
halfe pounde	ten shillings
halfendell	one half
hambellet	ambles, trots
hansell	present, gift
hantyd	passed
harbengers	messengers
harde	heard
harkyn	harken, listen to
hart	male deer
hawt	anything
haye	hay
hayre	hair
he clepyn	who was called
he gan crey foll sone	he began to shout at once
hed	head
hede	heed, notice
hedys	heads (of an arrow)
hee	high
hem	them
hende	courteous, noble
hent	took
hepe	hip (fruit)
herkens	harken, listen
hertis	hearts
het ys fol leytell cortesey	it is very discourteous
hether	hither

h(e)y(gh) selerer	cellarmaster
heynd	friendly, kind
heyre	heir
heyt war howtw	gee up (command to a horse)
hight	vowed
him fro	from him
ho haet	who has
ho'd	hold
hode	hood
holde	retained by
holden	beholden, obliged
holydame	holy relic, sanctuary
hongut	hanged
hotys	oats
houzle	last rites, confession
howers	hours
howr Ladey	Our Lady (Virgin Mary)
hows	house
howt	pulled out
hoze	hose, stockings
humming	extremely
hundred rod	550 yards
husbonde	small farmer, smallholder
hye	haste
hye	high
hye selerer	chief steward
hyed	hurried
hypped	hopped
idyght	prepared
ier	year(s)
ifedred fre	finely feathered
iflawe	flayed
ilkone	everyone
in bale	into harm
in fay	in truth
in my berde	in my way
inocked	grooved, notched
inow(e)	enough
i-quyte	revenged
isette	seated
iy(e)n	eyes
japis	japes, jokes
jobbing	jabbing, thrusting
kend	known
kepe	keep safe, protect
kill a do	kill a doe
kirtell	tunic
kod	said
kyndnesse	kindness
kyngus privé seell	king's privy seal
kynne	kin
kyrk	church
lap(pe)	wrap
large leve	full permission

launsgay	light lance
lawhyng	laugh
leasynge	lying
lechoure	lecher
lede	carry
lee	area of open ground
le(e)ge	liege
leese	lose
leffe	leave
lege	group (following)
leig	liege
lenyd	leant
leppyd	leapt
lere	learn, face
lese	lose
lesynge	lying
leugh	laughed
leve	permission
lever	rather
lewté, leutye	loyalty
leye	lee, open land
leythe	light
licker	tan (a hide)
lin	stop
list	yearn
loffe	love
long luske	lazy man/fellow
longut	longed
look to	guard
looselye	loosely, inaccurately
lorne	lost
loset	set loose
loth or lefe	liked it or not
loughe	laughed
lowde	loud
lowe	laughed
lubber	person with no sea-legs
lyed	to call someone a liar
lyme	lime (tree)
lyne	trees
lythe and listin	attend
lyveray	livery
lyveray	helping, portion
made the gree	(re)paid my debt
make the bowne	make yourself ready
male	travelling chest, baggage
marchandise	merchandise, but generally used to mean business in general
masars	drinking cups
masteryes	competitions, feats of skill
mastry	mastery, contest
maugré in theyr tethe	in spite of them
maysteer	master
medes	rewards
medys	middle, in the midst

mee froe	from me
mell	tangle
mené	company
mery maney	merry men
messis	masses
met(e)	measured
methe	meal, food
mey hede	myself (my head)
meyné	company, group of men or followers
meyt	might
mickle	much
mickle adoe	great fuss
mijn	mine
moche	much
molde	ground
mone	lament
mood	courage
mote	may, might
mould	ground
mountnaunce of an owre	period of an hour
munkis	monk
mylde Marye	Virgin Mary
mylner sun	miller's son
myne	mine
myrthes	mirth, merriment, amusement
mysaunter	misfortune
myter	mitre (bishop's crown)
naught	nothing
neave	fist
ne(e)r(e)	never
no noder kepe I be	nothing else do I care to be
nobellys	noble
noble	a coin worth 6 shillings and 8 pence
noe cunning a knave to ken	takes no skill to know a knave
none	noon, midday
none of long before	not long before
nother	neither
nought to lere	not (hard) to learn
noumbles, nowmbles	sweetbreads
nouther mosse nor lyng	neither bog nor heath
nye	near
oer	over
of meythe	almighty
okerer	usurer
ondyr	under
on's	on his
on't	of it
ony	any
onys	once
or we het bred	before we eat
ordeyn	organise
ore	over
othe	oath
oures, ouris	hours

owyr	over
palfray, palffrey	palfrey (a saddle horse)
palmer	pilgrim
palmers weed	pilgrim's clothing
passe	escape, travel
pastes	pasties
pavag(e), pawage	road-toll
pearct	pierced
pecis	dishes
pecok	peacock (feather)
pees	peace
pegg	bull's-eye
Phebus	Phoebus (a classical sun-god)
pinder	impounder of stray animals
pinfold	village green, common land
polle het op to they nere	pull it to your ear
portmantle	travelling bag
post to	hurry to
pottle	pot used to serve wine
powdre	poured
preke	peg (used as a target)
prese	crowd
prest	eager
preveley	privately
prick	bull's-eye
pricke foe	centre of the target
pricke-wande	stick that holds up a ring target
prod	proud
prowe	skilful
prude	proud
pryce	prize
pryckynge	hurrying
pryoure	prior (of an abbey)
purveyed	provided
put to wronge	humiliate
pype	cask
quequer	quiver
queyt	reward
quyke	alive
Quyntyne	Quentin
quyte	pay, deliver
radly made hym yare	quickly made himself ready
raking	hurrying
rawstye	rusty
reachles	careless
reddy	ready, already
reden	rode
redly and anone	quickly and at once
reken	reckon, deal with
Renish	Rhine
renne	run, ran
rewe	rue, be sorry
rome	room, space
roode	cross

roote	tip
roundelay	lyrical love song
ruthe	pity
ryall	royal
ryally	royalty
ryght	right
ryvere	river
saf	except, save for
safly	safely, confidently
salued	greeted
samclothis	apron
sare	sore(ly)
sarve	serve
savely	safely, confidently
sawten	assault
Saynt Austyn	Saint Augustine
scapyd	escaped
schall	shall
schall y haffe	shall I have
schame	shame
schert	shirt
schireff	sheriff
schomer	summer
schorteley	shortly, briefly
schortly	shortly, abruptly
schote	shot
schotyng	shooting (match)
schrewde	shrewd, devilish
screffe	sheriff
screffeys	sheriff's
seased	seized
seche	such
seke	hide
seker	steadfast
sele	seal
semblaunce	semblance, appearance
sertenly	certainly
set a flo	set an arrow
sette hym on his kne(e)	kneeled down
sette to wedde	security (as a pledge)
several	differently
seyt	sight
shadow hem	shelter themselves
shawe	thicket
shawes beene sheene	woods are bright
shelynges, shelinges	shillings
shende	destroy
shente	killed, destroyed
shete	shoot
shete a peny	shoot for a penny wager
shining	hurrying
shot-windowe	shuttered window
shrewde hynde	cursed servant
shroggs	shrubs, bushes

shun	hide from
shyt	shut
skorne	harm, scorn
slack	town common
slade	forest glade
slawe	slain
slet	slit, split in two
slist	slit
sliver chest	chased or engraved silver
slo, sloo	slay, kill
slone	slain
smaw	small
smerte	nimble
smerte	smart, hurt
smyt(h)e	smite, strike, cut off
so ever mote I the	so may I always prosper
so mot I the	so may I thrive
solle	soul
som	sum, amount
soon told	immediately counted
soper	supper
sori	sorry, miserable
soriar	sorrier, sadder
sory chere	miserable countenance
sparred	barred
spede	hurry
spight	dislike
sponis	spoons
sporis	spurs
spyrred	asked
spyrred tithyngus	asked for news
stalle	stall, stable
stalworthe	stalwart, strong
stave(s)	crutch(es)
stede	place
steffeley	staunchly
stert	leapt
steven	voice
stint nor lin	stop nor delay
stode	stood
stond stell	stand still
stonde foll stell	stand absolutely still
stroke	conflict
stryfe	strife
stuarde	steward
styne	alleys, passages
styrop	stirrup
sweavens	dreams
swink(e) and swet(t)	labour and sweat
swonyng	swooning
sye	say
symple	simple, humble
symple wedes	clothes
syngynge	singing

take not a grefe	don't be offended
takyll	tackle, equipment, gear
tane	taken
targe	shield
tarrie	rest a while, remain
taryed	delayed
tene	sorrow, trouble, annoyance
teris	tears
the soyt yef y scholde saye	if I were to tell the truth
thedurwarde	thitherward
they height	are named
tho	then
thorow	through
thou'lt	you will
thow	you (thou)
thow seys soyt	tell the truth
thowt	thought
thrassle	thrush (bird)
thre fyngers and mare	by more than three fingers
throly thrast	strenuously pressed
thrumme	bundle
thryfte	luck
thyckust	thickest
thyres	thrice
tidynges	tidings, news
tikes	dogs
tithyngus	tidings, news
to spede	to succeed
to-fore	before, in front of
togyder	together
toke het	took it, gave it
told the gold	counted the gold
tolde	counted
too-hond sworde	two-handed sword
torne	bouts, times, turns
tortyll-tre	trysting tree
towe	two
towe	you
tray	anger
treffye or the	thrive or prosper
Trenyté	Trinity
tristil-tre	trysting or meeting tree
trow	true
trowt	truth
trusty tree	trysting tree
trusyd	tied
trystell-tre	meeting tree (the Major Oak)
tunn	barrel, cask
twinn	twain
twyse	twice
tyde	time
tydynges	tidings, news
tyndes	antlers
unketh	unknown

unneth	hardly, scarcely
unsett steven	unexpected occasion
up-chaunce	by chance
upshott	result
veine	manner
vittles	victuals, food
vylaynesly	vilely, villainously
wan	received
wande	wand, stick (as a target stuck in the ground)
warden pies	pear pies
warison	reward
waryer	warrior
weat	wait
wed, wedde	payment
wed well y non leffe	I will not leave payment
wedowes	widows
weke	weak, feeble
wekys	weeks
wel wight	very strong
wele his mede	his just deserts
welthe	wealth, riches
wend	go, went
wende	go, leave
Wentbreg	Wentbridge
weppynd	weaponed, armed
weppynlesse	weaponless
werschepyd	worshipped
wete	know
weyffe	wife
weyffes	wives, women
weynde	wind
weyne	wine
weyse	wise
wheder	where
whether be ye away?	where are you going?
wheyt	white
whyles	while
wicker wand	willow tree, willow branch
wight	brave, strong, sturdy
wiss	know
wode	crazy, mad
wolde dyne betyme	would dine early
wolwarde	with wool next to the skin
wonnest	dwell
wonynge wane	dwelling place
woo	woe
woodweele	woodwall (golden oriole)
woon	dwell, live
work me spight	do me harm
worthe pens feyffe	worth 5 pence
wott	knows
wrocken	revenged
wroth(e)	angry
wystly	intently

y ley	I wager
y loffe yeffell thes to stonde	I hate to leave these standing
y well the tene eyls	Otherwise I will do thee evil
ychon	each one, each of us
ydyght	fitted
yede	went, fell
yeff	if
yeffell	evil
yeft	gift, prize
yeiwe	yew
yeman	yeoman
yemenrey	yeomanry
yeomandree	yeomanry
yerdes	rods, stakes
yete	ate
yever	ever, whenever
yit	yet
ylke	like, same
Yole	Christmas, Yule
you'st	you must
yowre	your
ys	is
ys beheynde	is yet to come
ywnder	yonder

PART FOUR

Robin shoots with Sir Guy. Illustration from *Bold
Robin Hood and his Outlaw Band* by Louis Read.

The evil Sir Isenbart de Belame and his lords, seated around their table at Wrangby, are startled by the black arrow which Robin and his men fire through the spy hole. Illustration by Walter Crane in *Stories of Robin Hood and His Merry Men* by Henry Gilbert. (*Mary Evans Picture Library/Edwin Wallace*)

Conclusions

Millions of words have been written over several centuries about the life and times of Robin Hood, yet until the start of the twentieth century nobody seemed concerned with the historicity of the characters they wrote about, but instead simply related the various legends in numerous different forms. However, since the early part of the twentieth century writers have become increasingly interested in the historical background to the legends, and have expended many words and volumes on their individual searches for the truth – a truth that would, according to some at least, destroy the very essence of the legends. However, there is historical truth behind most of the legends, if you care to look for it. Once found, this historicity can add tremendously to the legends and, for me at least, it does not harm them in any way.

A legend is by nature a strange beast. It is neither history nor myth, but falls into that grey area between the two. Perhaps we need a new word to describe a legend – *mythtory*. Some elements of the legends are essentially true and based on fact, while others are pure fiction, the elaboration of countless tellers and retellers. In fact, the very essence of a legend is that it is, to some degree, based on fact, or at the very least it started out as a true story.

Searching through the legends to try to determine the historical fact behind them can be a fruitless and thankless task, for more often than not the searcher relies only on relatively late material in which the truth has become so deeply entangled as to be almost unrecognisable. Yet by careful study of early writings, coupled with the efforts of many other commentators, and a variety of other tools (such as etymology, genealogy, and the like), it is possible to weed out the fact from the fiction, or at least a good part of the fact.

Robin Hood was, and should always remain, an enigmatic figure. But did he ever actually live? Whole books have been dedicated to the search for the 'real' Robin Hood, but none has ever arrived at an answer that stands up to close scrutiny. Certainly a great many of the characters and events in the legends of Robin Hood and his Merry Men are historical fact. Many are well known through history lessons at school. We all know of King Richard the Lionheart and his usurping younger brother John, but how many other characters within the framework of the legends stand up to an historical investigation? Perhaps surprisingly, the answer is more than you may at first have thought. Indeed, by looking at the very earliest texts recording the life of Robin Hood it is possible to recognise not only many historical characters, but also several historical events, allowing us to determine with some accuracy just when Robin Hood is alleged to have lived.

Robin Hood hunting birds. Woodcut taken from the *Roxburghe Ballads*, *c.* 1630. (*Mary Evans Picture Library*)

For a considerable period I have been systematically weeding out the fact from the fiction, and my conclusions are that Robin Hood did indeed live, being born around 1160 and dying some eighty-odd years later around 1247. This was a considerable lifespan considering the harsh times those years encompass, and the difficult conditions Robin Hood lived in. However, as I will show you, the real Robin Hood had very little connection with the city of Nottingham, which to this day claims him, and probably never set foot within the city walls.

The legends, which I believe to be quasi-historical accounts, quite clearly state that Robert of Locksley, to give Robin Hood his proper name, was born during the reign of Henry II, and was subsequently outlawed during the last few years of that king's reign, say around 1185, when he would have been about 25 years old. By this time he was lord of the lands that his father, who is never named in the legends, had held for many years previously. It is therefore a simple matter to determine that Robert of Locksley was born sometime between say 1160 and 1165. I prefer the earlier date as this ties him in more closely with the other events mentioned in the legends.

The effigies of Henry II and Eleanor of Aquitaine at Fontevrault Abbey. *(Copyright Douglas Boyd)*

Another important dating clue in the legends concerns the massacre of the Jews at York. History records this event as happening in 1190, while the legends record Robin and his men helping a survivor of the massacre, one Reuben of Stamford. Thus we have another good pointer to the period during which the real Robin Hood lived.

The legends also tell us that Robin Hood was pardoned by Richard I soon after the king had been released from his imprisonment at Hagenau. This would therefore have been in 1194. History gives us that fact. Therefore, we already have a very clear historical picture of the early years of Robin Hood, who spent just nine years, by my reckoning, as an outlaw. At this point there is a distinct gap in the life of the noble outlaw, for the legends next tell of Robert of Locksley witnessing the signing of the Magna Carta at Runnymede on 15 June 1215. (Robin Hood was simply the name he used as an outlaw – Robin being a common version of Robert, and Hood denoting that he was an outlaw, under the hood.) Shortly afterwards King John reneged on his deal with the barons and civil war broke out. It was at about this time that Marian FitzWalter, better known as Maid Marian, was killed, and Robert of Locksley sought revenge. This would have been in 1216, the same year that King John died at Newark Castle; indeed, the more fanciful versions of these events even allude to some involvement by Robin Hood in this nefarious deed.

From 1216 until his death in about 1247 Robin Hood remained in the forests he loved. His death at the hands of his aunt at Kirklees Priory is possibly a fabrication, and he probably died of old age in the forests, though such an end was hardly in keeping with his dramatic life as an outlaw.

Undoubtedly many of the events and characters in the legends are pure fiction. There is no evidence, for example, that Little John, Robin's stalwart second-in-command, ever lived, but I think it is safe to assume that a character similar to him did, and that it is only the name that was invented, an alias for a wanted man (in much the same way that William H. Bonney used the name Billy the Kid). Many commentators have stated quite categorically that Little John was originally called John Little, and while this may indeed be the case, I have found no historical evidence to back up such a claim. And what of Friar Tuck, Alan-a-Dale and the others? Many may have lived, but I do not believe that these were their true names.

The most serious problem facing students of the legends is one of location. For many years the city of Nottingham has claimed Robin Hood as its own, but it seems highly unlikely that Robin Hood ever entered the city (I do not believe the story of the potter of Wentbridge for one minute), so how can that city claim him? The archery contest that Robin is alleged to have won was held outside the city walls, so he would not have had to make his way into the city to take part. Similarly, when Will the Bowman (another alias, I am relatively sure) was about to be hanged, the gallows were erected outside the city. Thus it seems increasingly unlikely that Robin Hood ever entered the city that has so long sought to be associated with him.

Sure enough many of the legends are based in Sherwood Forest, but the naming of that forest as Sherwood reveals that these elements are possibly later, for the forest was originally known as Shirewood, the name under which it still appeared on early

Victorian maps. The Major Oak, the traditional hiding place of Robin and his men, is also a red herring, for this tree only became associated with the outlaw in 1521 upon the publication of John Major's *History of Greater Britain* – hence the naming of the tree. There is absolutely no evidence, either historical or legendary, to connect the outlaw with the tree. In fact, dendrochronology has proved beyond any doubt that the Major Oak would have been little more than a sapling at the time of Robin and his men, and thus hardly capable of hiding a sparrow, let alone Robin and his merry band of outlaws. However, it still remains a potent symbol of the outlaw, and must therefore deserve a place within the legends.

Most of the early legends of Robin Hood are centred on Barnisdale or Barnsdale, an area of South Yorkshire. I personally locate Robin Hood in this area, for several reasons. First, the legends recall that Locksley lies to the south and west of Sheffield, and today there is a Loxley to the west of that city almost on the banks of the River Don. Additionally Robert of Locksley and Maid Marian are said to have played together and fallen in love on Locksley Chase, and today there is a Loxley Chase just to the west of Loxley. However, these two place-names alone are insufficient evidence for my conclusions. For this, one has to study modern and ancient maps, and then connect the places found on those maps to the legends.

Robin Hood was outlawed at Pontefract, which lies at the northern edge of Barnisdale Forest. Surely if Robin Hood had been connected with Sherwood Forest then he would have been outlawed at a town or city lying within or on the edge of that forest, such as Nottingham, Mansfield or Worksop. The legends tell us otherwise, so one up for South Yorkshire.

Just to the north of Wakefield, which also features in the legends and is again in South Yorkshire, there are three places with very interesting names. These are Robin Hood, Stanley and Outwoods (see Map 4 in Appendix One). At first sight these may not be particularly inspiring, but when you consider that many people named their villages after prominent people or events, they begin to take on more significance, especially the last two. Outwoods was the name of Robert of Locksley's manor (according to the legends), while Stane Lea, or Stanley, was the name given by Robin and his men to their camp. There is absolutely no evidence to connect these three villages with the outlaw, but their names do seem to owe something to him, and it may just be that the villagers of long ago were simply trying to remember an historical figure in their naming, and not just some legendary character who had already been claimed by the city of Nottingham and the forest of Sherwood some distance to the south. Perhaps, therefore, we should have more faith in this etymological evidence than we might normally have. I believe that these three villages were indeed named in memory of the historical outlaw, a belief that further enhances my overall conviction that Robin Hood was a Yorkshire man who spent most of his life in the northern reaches of Barnisdale Forest.

Additional evidence for this conviction comes very early on in the legends, for they state that the newly outlawed Robin Hood led his men to Campsall to say mass and make their confessions. Such a journey would have been improbably long if Robin Hood had his camp in Sherwood, but if it was at the Stanley to the east of Pontefract (see Maps 4 and 5) then the trip to Campsall could have been easily and comfortably accomplished within the time-frame alluded to in the legends. One more point in favour of South Yorkshire.

Next look at the location of Kirklees. The latter part of the legends states that Robin Hood travelled on a regular basis to the priory at Kirklees, where his aunt was the abbess, to have his blood let. Again, if Robin had been based in Sherwood the journey would have been improbably long (see Map 4), remembering of course that for the majority of the time Robin would have walked and not ridden. Even by horse the journey would have been wearisome, especially for a man who would have been in his eighties.

All of this points towards Barnisdale in South Yorkshire, rather than Sherwood in Nottinghamshire, and while there are a great many places within the depths of Sherwood Forest, Clumber Forest and Clipstone Forest that have become associated with the outlaw, either through the legends, or from elsewhere, I still believe that Robin Hood, the historical Robin Hood that is, lived in South Yorkshire through the last half of the twelfth century and the first half of the thirteenth. To my mind he is fact, and not simply the creation of wandering minstrels. Like King Arthur, he is the basis for the framework of the legends, though he most likely did not have any part to play in a great many of the stories told about him.

So what about the other outlaws? How do they fit into the picture? I believe that most of the characters spoken of in the legends did in fact live, at around the same time as Robin Hood himself. However, I do not believe that they were ever truly a band of outlaws who moved almost unchallenged from South Yorkshire to Nottinghamshire and back again, a journey that would have taken two or three days at a time, and would have exposed them to attack every time. Rather I believe that it is the legends that have pulled the outlaws together into an organised band that has no actual foundation in history. Each outlaw would have had his own 'patch' in which he operated, and thus it would have appeared, to the casual observer and especially to those who suffered at their hands, that the forests were controlled by the outlaws. Thus word of mouth drew the outlaws together, though if they had actually met they would probably have fought to the death. Robin most likely became known as the leader of the outlaws due to the simple fact that he was the best at what he did!

I believe that most of the characters encountered in the legends about Robin Hood did live, though possibly not all in the time-frame I have asserted for the historical character. Robin Hood lived and operated in South Yorkshire in the northern reaches of Barnisdale Forest, though he was born and originally lived in the south of that forest. The other outlaws occupied their own stretches of forest, and worked their own exclusive patch, both in Barnisdale and in Sherwood, and it is the process of time and countless retellings that has drawn all the individual characters together into one coherent fighting force.

So what of Robin's opponents, the Sheriff of Nottingham, Guy of Gisborne, King John? Well, we already know that John attempted to usurp the throne of England while his brother Richard was absent on the crusade. But how did Robin come to be embroiled in the struggle? Did he truly fight for king and country, or did his actions simply help Richard retain the crown?

Let us deal with Prince John first. While it is safe to assume that the Sheriff of Nottingham sought to ingratiate himself with the man he saw as taking over the crown of England in the absence of the true monarch, there is very little historical evidence to support a close association between prince and sheriff. Many films over many years have shown the prince and the sheriff side-by-side, in close conference about some scheme or other. Yet this is pure fabrication. Prince John did visit Nottingham, that much is fact, and he did meet with the sheriff, but he most certainly did not set up camp there as the films and legends might lead us to believe, and he certainly would not have considered the sheriff as anything more than a menial servant who was furthering his cause.

So what of the Sheriff of Nottingham himself? History tells us that his name was Ralph Murdach, and that he was a rich cordwainer (a shoemaker or worker in leather) who bought his position from the Bishop of Ely. Once installed as the sheriff, he embarked on an extended campaign of high taxation to repay his debt to the grasping bishop, a campaign that made him increasingly unpopular with the people. It should be noted that the Sheriff of Nottingham was also sheriff of the entire county of Nottinghamshire along with neighbouring Derbyshire, so his activities affected large numbers of people. His animosity towards Robin Hood seems to be derived from the fact that the outlaw continually stole the money that was destined to line the sheriff's pockets, as well as those of Prince John and the Bishop of Ely.

Contact between Robin and the sheriff would have been almost non-existent. After all, Robin was a man with a price on his head, so he would not gaily walk into any situation where he might be taken prisoner. The legends say that Robin and the sheriff only came into contact three times: when Robin was disguised as the potter of Wentbridge (a pure fabrication I am sure), at the famous archery contest (which probably did take place), and when Robin was returning to Nottingham with Sir Richard at Lee, this last encounter resulting in the sheriff's death.

Yet this leads to a confusion of fact. The legends quite clearly say that the sheriff died in this third encounter, and yet they also say that the very same man, Ralph Murdach, was forced to surrender Nottingham Castle to Richard after the king had laid siege to the castle and reduced its outer walls to rubble. This confusion is easily answered, for history records two consecutive sheriffs of Nottingham called Ralph Murdach. This may clear up one small fact, but it actually poses more questions in its own right, the most important being which Ralph Murdach was it who was in league with the usurping Prince John, and which Ralph Murdach was it who sought to dispose of Robin Hood? The answer to the latter would almost certainly appear to be the first Ralph Murdach, for it was he who died at the hands of Robin Hood. It would seem very likely that both sheriffs were in league with Prince John, the first simply because the crown demanded taxes from him. The second sheriff, though, may have had a far greater allegiance, as the siege of Nottingham Castle would signify.

The Sheriff of Nottingham is an essential part of the legends of Robin Hood, for, as we all know, every good story has to have its villain! And talking of villains, we should briefly consider Sir Guy of Gisborne.

The historical manor of which Sir Guy was said to have been lord and master was called Birkencar, but that location cannot be accurately determined. However, it seems quite possible that Sir Guy was a Lancastrian, as there is a Gisborne in Lancashire. His association with Robin Hood is somewhat tenuous, though later writings and films have always made him the sidekick and henchman of the scheming Sheriff of Nottingham. The legends tell us that he was a cruel and ruthless master who had for a long time been in league with the monks of St Mary's Abbey as they sought a way to dispossess Robert of Locksley, and it seems quite probable that the outlawing of Robin Hood was engineered by the monks as a way of getting their hands on the lands they so desired.

Yet the legends also tell us that this backfired on Sir Guy as the tenants and villeins of his manor, with the help of the newly outlawed Robin Hood, burnt down his manor. Sir Guy himself only just escaped with his life. This event would have made him no fonder of Robin Hood than he had been before. It was after this that he seems to have become involved with the Sheriff of Nottingham, though he also maintained his connections with the monks of St Mary's Abbey. His only contact with the outlaw comes fairly late in the legends when both he and Robin would have been in their late middle age. In this incident the two battle ferociously, inflicting wounds on each other until, as is always the way when good battles evil, Robin killed the scheming knight.

There are of course many other characters within the legends who stand up to historical scrutiny. Suffice it to say, the more that do stand up to such scrutiny the more probable it becomes that the legends are based on fact and that Robin Hood did indeed once wend his way through the leafy glades of the ancient royal forests of South Yorkshire, and sometimes visited the forests in neighbouring Nottinghamshire.

Nottingham may always remain the city most commonly associated with Robin Hood and his men, but I shall never again be able to consider it the home of the outlaw, for to

Richard I tilting at Saladin, from the *Luttrell Psalter*, Add 42130 f.82. (*British Library, London/Bridgeman Art Library*)

me Pontefract and Sheffield have equal claim to his name, and to association with one of the most enigmatic figures of British folklore, who surely ranks alongside the likes of King Arthur.

The legends that form Part One of this book closely follow the earliest sources, though where those sources are sketchy I have been forced to look further afield for the relevant information. Read the legends with an open mind and an open heart, and you will find in them much that will astound, and much that will confuse. Robin Hood did not fight tyranny and oppression on the side of the common man. He was forced to take to the forests, and only sought to suppress those tyrants he had a quarrel with. He was not the champion of the people. He did not rob from the rich to give to the poor, he robbed from the rich and kept it! He was a man who fought to right the wrongs done to him, and it was only because his actions had a knock-on effect that benefited others that he came to be regarded as the popular champion we today know and love.

Appendices

'Pray more earnestly,' quoth Robin. Illustration from
Bold Robin Hood and his Outlaw Band by Louis Read.

Boy dressed as Robin Hood in an oak tree in Sherwood Forest. (*Getty Images*)

APPENDIX ONE

MAPS

The following maps indicate the location of those places identified within the legends surrounding Robin Hood and his band of followers. These maps are only a guide – precise locations may be found using the Ordnance Survey 1:50,000 Landranger series of maps, coordinates from which are given (where appropriate) in Part Two.

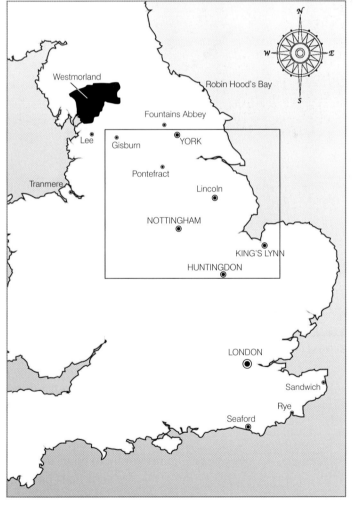

Map 1.

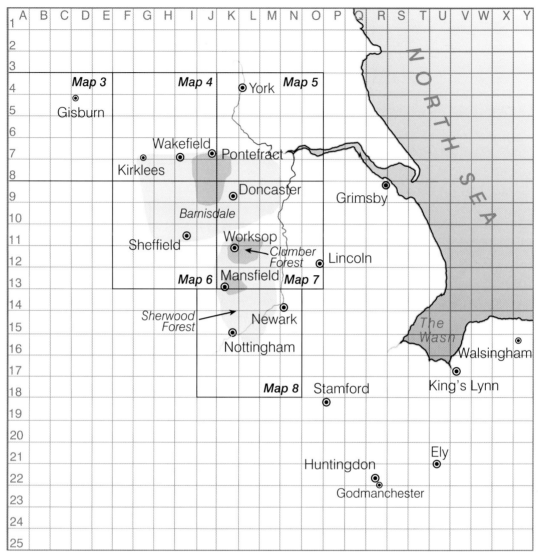

Map 2.

Map 3.

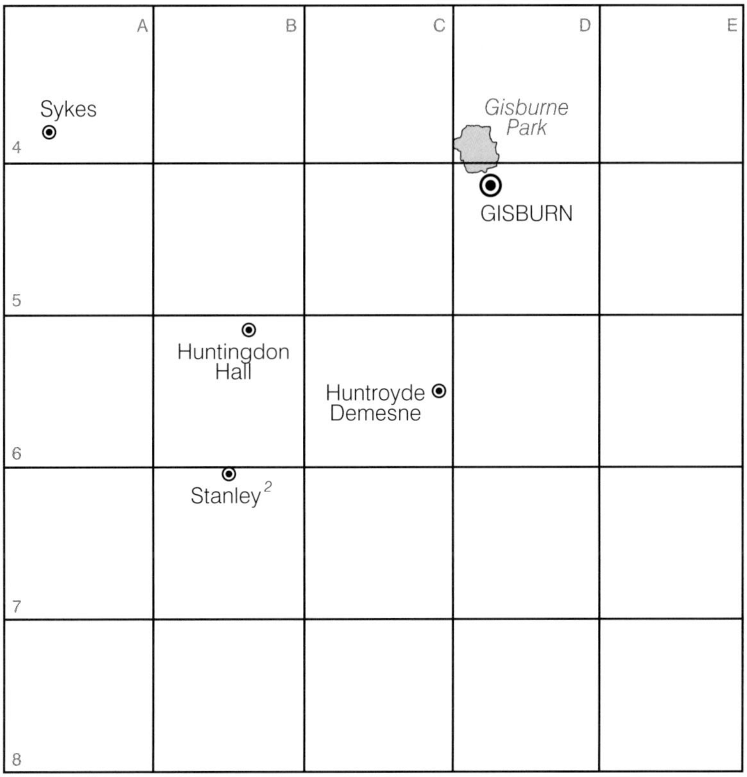

	A	B	C	D	E
4	Sykes ◉			Gisburne Park	
5				◉ GISBURN	
6		◉ Huntingdon Hall	Huntroyde ◉ Demesne		
7		◉ Stanley[2]			
8					

	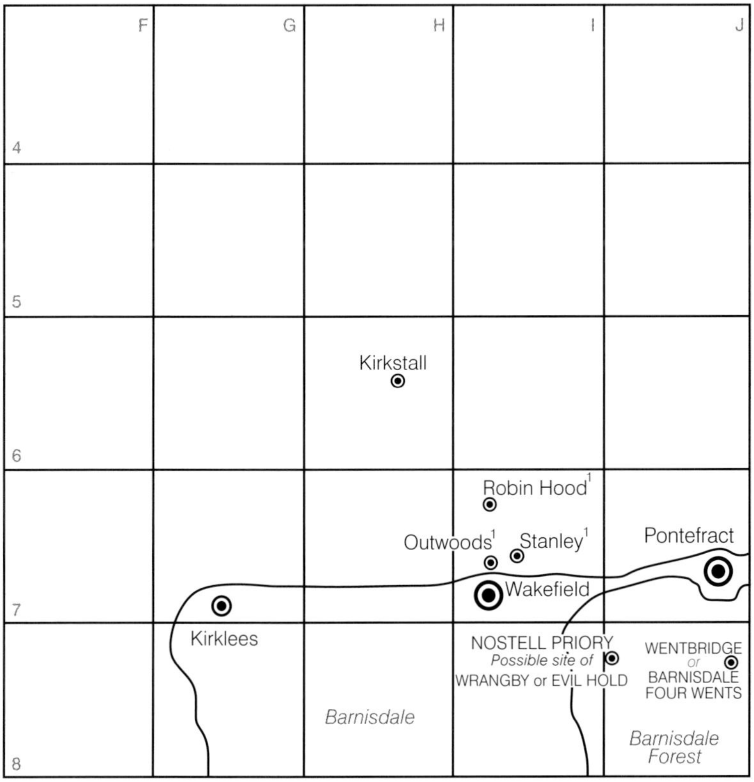 F	G	H	I	J
4					
5					
6			Kirkstall ◉		
7		◉ Kirklees	Robin Hood[1] ◉ Outwoods[1] ◉ ◉ Stanley[1] ◉ Wakefield	Pontefract ◉	
8			Barnisdale	NOSTELL PRIORY Possible site of ◉ WRANGBY or EVIL HOLD	WENTBRIDGE or ◉ BARNISDALE FOUR WENTS Barnisdale Forest

Map 4.

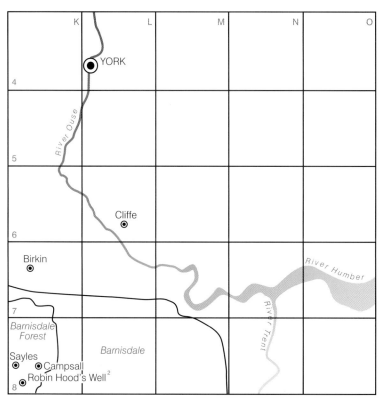

Map 5.

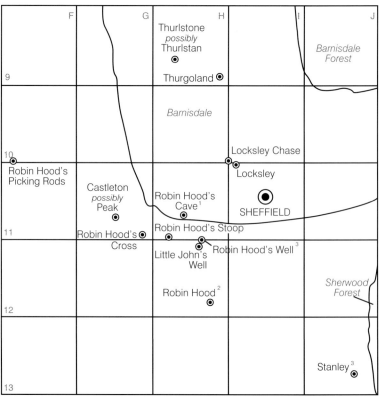

Map 6.

Map 7.

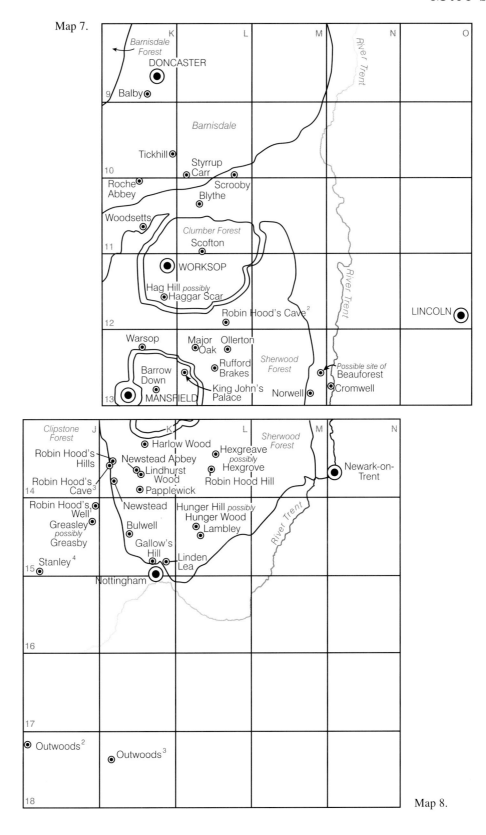

Map 8.

A ROUGH CHRONOLOGY OF THE LIFE AND TIMES OF ROBIN HOOD AND HIS MERRY MEN

1154	Accession of Henry II
c. 1160	Birth of Robert of Locksley
1181	Enactment of the Assize of Arms
c. 1185	Robert of Locksley kills Sir Roger de Longchamp
	Outlawing of Robert of Locksley
	Robert of Locksley kills Sir Hubert of Lynn
	Attempt to burn Sir Guy of Gisborne alive fails

Robin and Little John go their ways in search of adventure. Illustration from *The Merry Adventures of Robin Hood* by Howard Pyle.

Richard I crowned, from *Flores Historiarum* by Matthew Paris, Ms 6712 (A.6.89), f.141r. (*Chetham's Library, Manchester/ Bridgeman Art Library*)

c. 1185	
	Robert of Locksley assumes the name Robin Hood
	Alan de Tranmire kills Sir Ivo le Ravener
	Little John joins the company of outlaws
1186	Robin Hood aids Bennett and Alice of Havelond and kills Thomas of Patherley and Robert of Prestbury
1187	Ralph Murdach becomes Sheriff of Nottingham
	Robin Hood travels to Nottingham disguised as the potter of Wentbridge
	Ralph Murdach is taken prisoner by Robin Hood, but released again
1188	Robin Hood meets Friar Tuck
1189	Sir Ranulf de Greasby, Sir Philip de Scrooby, Sir Bertran le Noir and Sir Ector de Malstane killed at Cromwell by Robin and his men
	Alan-a-Dale is married to Alice de Beauforest
	Death of Henry II and accession of Richard I (5 July)
	William de Longchamp is appointed justiciar
	Richard I leaves on the Third Crusade
	Marriage of Prince John to Avice of Gloucester
1190	Sir Herbrand de Tranmire is lent £400 by Robin Hood to pay Abbot Robert
	Death of Sir Niger le Grym
	Massacre of 150 Jews in York

Robin Hood and Little
John. Illustration from
*Bold Robin Hood and
his Outlaw Band* by
Louis Read.

1190
> Rescue of Reuben of Stamford and his daughter Ruth
> Will the Bowman captured in Nottingham and sentenced to hang
> Will the Bowman is rescued and Richard Malbête taken prisoner
> Richard Malbête hanged by Robin Hood and Sir Laurence of Raby

1191
> William de Longchamp falls from power and is forced to leave the country
> Abbot Robert repays £800, twice the sum owed by Sir Herbrand de Tranmire

1192
> Richard I held to ransom of 150,000 marks in Hagenau
> Abbot Robert dies and Robert de Longchamp is appointed new abbot of St Mary's Abbey
> Archery tournament in Nottingham won by Robin Hood
> Robin Hood forced to take cover in the castle of Sir Richard at Lee
> Death of Sir Richard FitzWalter
> Robin Hood goes to Malaset in search of the Maid Marian
> Sir Richard at Lee and Lady Alice forced to take to the forests

1193	Sir Richard at Lee taken captive by Sheriff of Nottingham
	Sir Richard at Lee rescued by Robin Hood, who kills the Sheriff of Nottingham
	Robin and Marian married by Friar Tuck
1194	Return of Richard I to England along with William de Longchamp
	Royal pardon granted to Robin Hood and his followers
	Robin Hood reverts to Robert of Locksley and lives at Malaset with Marian
	Richard I leaves on his continental campaign
1199	Death of Richard I in France and accession of John (27 May)
1200	Marriage of King John to Isabel of Angoulême
1209	King John excommunicated
1215	Robert of Locksley witnesses the signing of the Magna Carta (15 June)
	Hubert de Burgh appointed justiciar
	The First Barons' War breaks out
	Marian is killed by Sir Isenbart de Belame
1216	Robert of Locksley leads his forces in the siege of the Evil Hold
	Sir Isenbart de Belame and Sir Baldwin the Killer are hanged
	Robert of Locksley returns to the forest and readopts the name Robin Hood
	Death of King John by poison at Newark Castle (19 October) and accession of Henry III (aged 9)
	Magna Carta is reissued
1217	Magna Carta reissued for second time
	Forest Charter is issued
	Royalists defeat the French and the barons at Lincoln and repel the French fleet
	The First Barons' War ends with the treaty of Kingston upon Thames (12 September)
1220	Robin Hood kills Sir Guy of Gisborne
	Will the Bowman killed in battle with Brabant mercenaries
1225	Magna Carta and Forest Charter reissued
1226	Alice of Havelond visits Robin Hood in the forest
	Robin Hood commences his twice yearly visits to Kirklees Priory
1227	Henry III declares himself of age and assumes full power
1232	Hubert de Burgh is dismissed
c. 1247	Death of Robin Hood at Kirklees Priory at the hands of his aunt Dame Ursula
	Burial of Robin Hood in the forest
	Sir Roger of Doncaster flees to France

FILMS ABOUT ROBIN HOOD

The following is a short list of films and television series that have either concentrated on the legendary life of Robin Hood or included his character to some degree. It is as exhaustive a list of films about the legendary outlaw that I have been able to assemble and clearly illustrates just how popular this enigmatic figure has been since the advent of cinematography. I have not, however, included films where Robin Hood may only make a fleeting entrance, such as he does hilariously in the 2001 animation *Shrek*.

Adventures of Robin Hood. Dir. Michael Curtiz. With Errol Flynn, Basil Rathbone and Olivia de Havilland. Warner Bros., 1938

Adventures of Robin Hood. Dir. Bernard Knowles, Lindsay Anderson, Ralph Smart, Terry Bishop. With Richard Greene. CBS, 1955–8 (143 episodes)

Bandits of Sherwood Forest. Dir. George Sherman and Henry Levin. With Cornel Wilde and Anita Louise. Columbia, 1947

A Challenge for Robin Hood. Dir. C.M. Pennington-Richards. With Barrie Ingham and James Hayter. Seven Arts-Hammer, 1967 (British; distributed in USA by Fox)

Ivanhoe. Dir. Herbert Brenon. Independent Moving Pictures, 1913 (British; silent)

Ivanhoe. Dir. Richard Thorpe. Metro-Goldwyn-Mayer, 1952 (British)

Long Live Robin Hood. Dir. George Ferron. With Mark Damon and Louis Davilla. Edde Entertainment, 1993

Men of Sherwood Forest. Dir. Val Guest. With Don Taylor and Eileen Moore. Astor, 1954

The Prince of Thieves. Dir. Philip Ford. With Monte Hall. Republic, 1949

Robin and Marian. Dir. Richard Lester. With Sean Connery and Audrey Hepburn. Columbia Studios, 1976

Robin and the Seven Hoods. Dir. Gordon Douglas. With Frank Sinatra, Dean Martin and Bing Crosby. Warner Bros., 1964

Robin Hood. Dir. Theodore Marston. Mutual Film Corp., 1913 (Silent)

Robin Hood. Dir. Allan Dwan. With Douglas Fairbanks and Wallace Beery. United Artists, 1922

Robin Hood. Dir. Joy Harington. With Patrick Troughton and Josée Richard. BBC, 1953 (6 episodes)

Robin Hood. Dir. Wolfgang Reitherman. Disney, 1973 (Animated)

Robin Hood. Dir. John Irvin. With Patrick Bergin and Uma Thurman. Fox, 1991

Robin Hood and the Pirates. Dir. Giorgio Simoneli. With Lex Barker (Italy, 1961)

Robin Hood Jr. Dir. Frankie Lee. Export & Import Film Co. Inc., 1923 (Silent)

Robin Hood Jr. Dir. Matt McCarthy. With Keith Chegwin and Mandy Tulloch. Brocket, 1975 (British)

Robin Hood of Monterey. Dir. Christy Cabanne. With Gilbert Roland. Monogram Pictures Corp., 1947

Robin Hood: Prince of Thieves. Dir. Kevin Reynolds. With Kevin Costner, Morgan Freeman and Mary-Elizabeth Mastrantonio. Morgan Creek Productions Inc., 1991

Robin Hood and the Sorcerer. Dir. Ian Sharp. Goldcrest Films and Television Productions, 1983

Rogues of Sherwood Forest. Dir. Gordon Douglas. With John Derek and Diana Lynn. Columbia, 1950

Sean Connery as Robin Hood and Audrey Hepburn as Maid Marian in the film *Robin and Marian*, 1976. (© *Bettmann/Corbis, BE063330*)

Errol Flynn as Robin Hood duels with Basil Rathbone as Sir Guy of Gisborne in the film *The Adventures of Robin Hood*, 1938. (*Getty Images*)

Patrick Troughton as Robin Hood in the 1953 BBC television series. (© *BBC/Corbis*)

Douglas Fairbanks as Robin Hood in the film
Robin Hood, 1922. (*Getty Images*)

Son of Robin Hood. Dir. George Sherman. With David Hedison and June Laverick. Argo, 1958 (British)

The Story of Robin Hood. Dir. Richard Todd and Joan Rice. RKO-Disney, 1952 (British title: *The Story of Robin Hood and His Merrie Men*)

Sword of Sherwood Forest. Dir. Terence Fisher. With Richard Greene and Peter Cushing. Hammer Film Productions, 1960 (British; distributed in the US by Columbia)

Tales of Robin Hood. Dir. James Tinling. With Robert Clarke and Mary Hatcher. Lippert Pictures, 1951

Time Bandits. Dir. Terry Gilliam. With John Cleese, Shelley Duvall, Sean Connery and Michael Palin. Handmade Films, 1981

When Things Were Rotten. Written and produced by Mel Brooks. Dir. Jerry Paris and Marty Feldman. ABC, 1975 (13 episodes)

The Zany Adventures of Robin Hood. Dir. Ray Austin. With George Segal, Morgan Fairchild and Roddy McDowall. Bobka Production/Fries Entertainment, 1988

BIBLIOGRAPHY

The following list is, by and large, representative of the books that have been of use during the research for this book.

Alexander, M., *British Folklore, Myths and Legends*, Weidenfeld & Nicholson, 1982

Anderson, W., *Green Man, the Archetype of our Oneness with the Earth*, HarperCollins, 1990

Bailey, H., *Archaic England*, Chapman & Hall, 1919

Barber, R., *Living Legends*, BBC Publications, 1980

Basford, K., *The Green Man*, Boydell & Brewer, 1978

Bellamy, John, *Crime and Public Order in England in the Later Middle Ages*, Routledge, 1973

——, *Robin Hood: An Historical Inquiry*, Croom Helm, 1985

Bernheimer, R., *Wild Men in the Middle Ages*, Cambridge, Mass., 1952

Bord, J. and C., *Earth Rites: Fertility Practices in Pre-Industrial Britain*, Granada, 1974

Briggs, K., *A Dictionary of Fairies*, Allen Lane, 1976

Brodie, A., *The English Mummers and Their Plays*, Routledge, 1970

Burland, C., *Echoes of Magic*, Rowman & Littlefield, 1972

Carpenter, Kevin, *Robin Hood: The Many Faces of that Celebrated English Outlaw*, Bibliotteks-und Enformationssystem der Universität Oldenburg, 1995

Carpenter, R., May, R. and Horowitz, A., *The Complete Adventures of Robin Hood*, Penguin Books, 1991

Chambers, E., *The English Folk Play*, Oxford University Press, 1933

——, *English Literature at the Close of the Middle Ages*, Oxford University Press, 1947

Child, F.J. (ed.), *English and Scottish Popular Ballads*, Houghton Mifflin, Boston, 1888

—— (ed.), *The English and Scottish Popular Ballads*, 5 vols, Dover, New York, 1965

Clawson, W.H., *The Gest of Robin Hood*, University of Toronto Library, 1909

Crosby, R., *Robin Hood's Nottingham*, Heritage Classics, 1989

Dobson, R.B. and Taylor, J., *Rymes of Robin Hood: An Introduction to the English Outlaw*, Alan Sutton Publishing, 1989

Egan, Piers, the Younger, *Robin Hood and Little John, or The Merry Men of Sherwood Forest*, Forster & Hextall, London, 1840

Emery, C., *Tales of Robin Hood*, Baen Books, New York, 1988

Fowler, D.C., *A Literary History of the Popular Ballad*, Duke University Press, Durham, NC, 1968

Fraser, J.G., *The Golden Bough*, Macmillan, 1974

Gilbert, Henry, *Robin Hood and the Men of the Greenwood*, Wordsworth Editions, 1994

Goulstone, J., *The Summer Solstice Games*, private printing, 1985

Green, B., *The Outlaw Robin Hood: His Yorkshire Legend*, Kirklees Cultural Services, 1991

Green, M., *A Harvest of Festivals*, Longman, 1980

Green, R.L., *The Adventures of Robin Hood*, Penguin Books, 1956

Gutch, J.M., *A Lytelle Gest of Robin Hode and other Auncient and Modern Ballads and Songs Relating to the Celebrated Yeoman*, 2 vols, Longman, 1847

Harris, P.V., *The Truth About Robin Hood*, private printing, 1954

Harrison, J., *Ancient Art and Ritual*, Thornton Butterworth, 1918

Hartshorne, C.H. (ed.), *Ancient Metrical Tales*, Pickering, 1829

Hole, C., *English Folk-Heroes*, Batsford, 1948

——, *A Dictionary of British Folk Customs*, Hutchinson, 1976

BIBLIOGRAPHY

Holt, J.C., *Robin Hood*, Thames & Hudson, 1989

Hull, E., *Folklore of the British Isles*, Methuen, 1928

Kaeuper, Richard W., *War, Justice and Public Order*, Clarendon Press, 1988

Keen, M., *The Outlaws of Medieval Legend*, Routledge, 1961

Kenyon, J.P., *Dictionary of British History*, Market House Books Ltd, 1981

Kinsley, J. (ed.), *The Oxford Book of Ballads*, Oxford University Press, 1969

Knight, S., *Robin Hood: A Complete Study of the English Outlaw*, Blackwell, 1994

Lees, Jim, *The Quest for Robin Hood*, Temple Nostalgia Press, 1987

Matthews, John, *Robin Hood: Green Lord of the Wildwood*, Gothic Image Publications, 1993

Poole, Austin Lane, *From Domesday Book to Magna Carta 1087–1216*, Oxford University Press, 1955

Powicke, M., *Military Obligation in Medieval England*, Clarendon Press, 1962

Ritson, J. (ed.), *Robin Hood: A Collection of all the Ancient Poems, Songs and Ballads now extant Relative to the Celebrated English Outlaw*, 2 vols, Egerton & Johnson, 1795

Seawell, Molly Elliot, *Maid Marian and Other Stories*, Appleton, New York, 1891

Serrallier, I., *Robin in the Greenwood*, Oxford University Press, 1967

Sitwell, S., *Primitive Scenes and Festivals*, Faber, 1942

Skeat, W.W. (ed.), *The Tale of Gamelyn*, Clarendon Press, 1884

Spence, L., *Myth and Ritual in Dance, Game and Rhyme*, Watts, 1947

——, *The Fairy Tradition in Britain*, Rider, 1948

——, *The Minor Traditions in British Mythology*, Rider, 1948

——, *British Fairy Origins*, Aquarian Press, 1981

Sutcliff, R., *The Chronicles of Robin Hood*, Oxford University Press, 1950

——, *Heroes and History*, Batsford, 1965

Thomas, W.J., *Early English Prose Romances*, Routledge, 1898

Walker, J.W., *The True History of Robin Hood*, E.P. Publishing, 1973

Wiles, D., *The Early Plays of Robin Hood*, D.S. Brewer, 1981

Wilson, S., *Robin Hood: The Spirit of the Forest*, Neptune, 1993